The Political Economy of
Regionalism in Southern Africa

Margaret C. Lee

**UCT
PRESS**

**University of
Cape Town Press**

LYNNE
RIENNER
PUBLISHERS

BOULDER
LONDON

For Uncle Jake and Georges

The author and publisher are grateful to The BusinessMap Foundation for permission to reproduce several tables in the text.

Whilst every attempt was made to contact copyright holders, the publishers regret that this was not always possible. Any errors or omissions in this regard will be redressed in future editions if brought to the attention of the publishers.

The Political Economy of Regionalism in Southern Africa
© 2003 University of Cape Town Press
PO Box 24309, Lansdowne, 7779

Project management: Fiona Wakelin
Copy editing and proofreading: FPP Productions
Cover design: Pumphaus Design Studio
DTP and design: Charlene Bate

Published in the United States of America in 2003 by
Lynne Rienner Publishers, Inc.
1800 30th Street, Boulder, Colorado 80301
www.rienner.com

and in the United Kingdom by
Lynne Rienner Publishers, Inc.
3 Henrietta Street, Covent Garden, London WC2E 8LU

Library of Congress Cataloging-in-Publication Data
A Cataloging-in-Publication record for this book
is available from the Library of Congress.

ISBN 978-1-58826-224-0 (pbk. : alk. paper)

British Cataloguing in Publication Data
A Cataloguing in Publication record for this book is available
from the British Library.

Printed and bound in the United States of America

The paper used in this publication meets the requirements
of the American National Standard for Permanence of
Paper for Printed Library Materials Z39.48-1992.

Contents

Foreword

This book makes a major contribution to the understanding of the complexity of the process of development in Southern Africa in the last quarter of the twentieth century. It analyses the varied experiences of the independent states of the region in their struggle to strengthen their economies. It also points to the constraints challenging development and integration and argues that it is crucially important to stress the need for dynamic national economies.

The book is an important updated reference tool for decision-makers, academics, and those representing national and international institutions devoted to positive transformations. By bringing together regional and international experiences of integration, it helps a great deal to clarify the challenges to be faced in the process of regional integration. The region needs to pursue its efforts to strengthen ties among SADC member states so as to enable the gradual building up of a community in which different national resources and interests can play a complementing role in achieving the welfare of the people of these states.

Different initiatives have been discussed bilaterally and multilaterally at different levels, with the aim of identifying, designing, and perfecting the mechanisms of regional cooperation and integration. However, as the book recognises, there is still a considerable number of problems to be overcome, many reflecting the long history of colonisation and apartheid in the region.

The book clearly points out that the end of the Cold War influenced important political transformations in the region that led to the end of apartheid and ushered some of our countries into a new era of multiparty democracy. The end of world economic and political bi-polarisation called for the emergence of new strategies of regional cooperation and integration. The resources which each of our countries is endowed with, the levels of economic development, and the geographical settings in the region urge all of us to share the opportunities and face the challenges as we move towards a common future.

In looking at the transport systems and movement of people and goods in the region, the book addresses regional issues that are being seriously debated among SADC member states. Very clearly, coping with the economic legacy of the past and the issues presented by current world trends poses many problems and makes many demands. It is therefore my view that much hard work has to be done before the opportunities are taken and the benefits reaped.

The SADC member states have committed themselves to building a strong platform for peaceful coexistence and true cooperation. The achievement of regional relationships, which will enable balanced development in a geographical and social sense presents us with continuous challenges, the nature of which this book helps us understand.

Professor Margaret Lee has produced a useful piece of research, which in my view is an invitation to researchers, scholars, and all others involved to continue the search for better ways of regional development.

In conclusion, I would like to express my gratitude for having been invited to introduce this book. As one of those who have been in the forefront of the struggle for regional cooperation and integration, I feel honoured to have been given this task. May I urge all those who read this piece of work to draw the attention of others to it? It is my sincere hope that the book will provoke debate and bring others into the struggle for effective regional development.

Joaquim Alberto Chissano
President of the Republic of Mozambique

Preface and Acknowledgments

I began writing this book while living in Harare, Zimbabwe, in 1996–97. Initially I thought of writing a book on the politics of Southern Africa. However, within a year I had abandoned this idea and decided to return to writing on the subject that interests me the most, the Southern African Development Community (SADC). I had written a book on the organisation during the late 1980s and while in Zimbabwe decided that it was time to revisit the conclusions I had drawn about the early years of SADC when it was the Southern African Development Coordination Conference (SADCC).

Of course a great deal had changed in the world and the region since the 1989 publication of my book *SADCC: The Political Economy of Development*. The Cold War era had come to an end and the neo-liberal orthodoxy had become the established economic doctrine throughout the world. In addition, Namibia had gained its independence from the apartheid regime and had become a member of SADC. South Africa's military destabilisation of the Southern Africa region had come to an end and the apartheid regime had seen its demise. The post-apartheid government of South Africa had made the decision to become a member of SADC, to the great disappointment of the members of the Common Market for Eastern and Southern Africa (COMESA), who had hoped that South Africa would become a member of its organisation. SADCC had redefined its goals and objectives and had become SADC, identifying trade integration as a major objective. In addition, the Frontline States, which had been in the forefront of the movement to end white-settler rule in Southern Africa, was dissolved and replaced by the SADC Organ on Politics, Defence, and Security.

With the changing dynamics taking place at both the international and regional levels, I realised that it was impossible during the latter part of the twentieth century to write another book only on SADC. As I struggled with how to approach the topic of regionalism in Southern Africa, it became obvious that while SADC was Southern Africa, Southern Africa was not SADC. With Southern Africa being more than SADC, I was forced, for example, to examine the dynamics of all regional economic organisations, including SADC, COMESA, and the Southern African Customs Union (SACU). At the international level, I realised that it was impossible to understand regionalism in Southern Africa without providing insight into the interaction between the region and the European Union, its most important trading partner, and the United States with the *African Growth and Opportunity Act* (AGOA).

The study of regionalism in any part of the world is a challenging undertaking. I only hope that this book helps to unravel the complexity of the dynamics of regionalism in Southern Africa.

In May 2000, I was invited to give a paper on regionalism in Africa at a conference in Yaoundé, Cameroon on Rethinking African Politics, funded by the Harry Frank Guggenheim Foundation. During my presentation, which included a case study of SADC,

I mentioned that I was in the process of completing a second book on the organisation. After the conference, Karen Colvard, Senior Program Officer at Guggenheim, tempted me with an unbelievable offer. Karen told me that if I completed the manuscript by the end of the year, Guggenheim would sponsor a conference on the manuscript. Experts from anywhere in the world could be invited to critique the manuscript before it was submitted for publication and the venue of the conference could be Zimbabwe or South Africa.

When Karen made this offer, I had been working on the book for three and a half years. Between teaching and travelling to Southern Africa, completing the manuscript had become an arduous task. Karen was a godsend. I accepted her challenge, which required me to make some very difficult professional decisions. Nonetheless, I abandoned teaching and spent the next six months writing. Karen's offer, to my amazement, came with an incredible bonus. As I completed each chapter, she very meticulously read and critiqued each line of the manuscript. Karen's editorial skills and enthusiasm for the subject challenged me to be more rigorous in both my presentation and analysis. Words cannot express my gratitude to Karen for her unwavering support.

The conference on the manuscript was held in Cape Town, South Africa, on 8-10 January 2001. For three days, twelve of us mulled over the manuscript and enjoyed the comfort of the Aphen Hotel in the Cape Town suburb of Constantia. In addition to Karen, I would like to thank the following people for participating in the conference and rigorously critiquing the manuscript: George Agbango, Department of Political Science, Bloomsburg University, Bloomsburg, Pennsylvania; Belmiro Malate, SADC Focal Point for Mozambique, Maputo, Mozambique; Sam Mutanhaurwa, Zimbabwe Ministry of Industry and Trade, Harare, Zimbabwe; Daniel B. Ndlela, Zimconsult, Harare, Zimbabwe; Georges Nzongola-Ntalaja, United Nations Development Programme, Abuja, Nigeria; Roger J. Southall, Department of Political Studies, Rhodes University, Grahamstown, South Africa; Lynne Thomas, Centre for Research into Economics and Finance in Southern Africa, London School of Economics, London, UK; Jeanne Toungara, Department of History, Howard University, Washington, DC; and Yvonne M. Tsikata, World Bank and Economic and Social Research Foundation, Dar es Salaam, Tanzania. Brian Slattery, Karen's assistant at Guggenheim, served as the rapporteur for the conference. A special thanks is extended to Brian, whose copious notes were invaluable as I made revisions to the manuscript following the conference.

I would also like to thank Elliott P. Skinner, Professor Emeritus, Columbia University, Princeton N. Lyman, former United States Ambassador to Nigeria and South Africa, and Professor Ladun Anise, University of Pittsburgh, for their critique of the manuscript. The anonymous reviewers of the manuscript provided invaluable insight and I made major revisions based on their suggestions. While the input from all the reviewers helped me to strengthen, and in some cases reassess my analysis, I assume total responsibility for the content of the book.

My academic home since 1998 has been the African Studies Program at Georgetown University in Washington, DC. The Director of the African Studies Program, Gwendolyn Mikell, has been both a mentor and tremendous source of inspiration. She always encouraged me to complete the book and to this end made available a grant that allowed me to travel to Southern Africa during the spring of 2000. Veronique Dozier, the Administrative Assistant to the African Studies Program, provided encouragement, technical support, and made teaching and writing a much easier enterprise. My excellent research/teaching assistant, Kisha Johnson, was always available to lend a helping hand. I owe a great debt to all three of these individuals.

When I was a Visiting Scholar in the School of International Service at American University during the 1997–98 academic year, Fantu Cheru arranged for me to teach a course on 'Regional Development and Integration in Southern Africa'. Many of my ideas about theories of regionalism in Africa were honed while teaching this course, thanks to lively class discussions. My students at Georgetown also allowed me to indulge in the subject matter of this book. To all my former students, I want to say thanks for the contribution you have made to my intellectual development.

I received a warm welcome at the Centre for Research into Economics and Finance in Southern Africa at the London School of Economics during the summer of 1999. I owe a special thanks to Jonathan L. Leape, the Director of the Centre and Lynne Thomas, Research Officer, for, among other things, giving me access to their forthcoming publications. Wendy Foulds, the Administrative Secretary, ensured that I had access to university resources and that my visit was memorable.

This book would not have been possible without the tremendous assistance of Sam Mutanhaurwa in the Zimbabwe Ministry of Industry and Trade. Between 1997 and 2000, Sam spent hours with me explaining trade relations in the SADC region, including the negotiations for the creation of the SADC FTA. Sam's steadfast commitment to the development of the SADC region, as well as his belief that it is important for the international community to understand the complexity of the political economy of Southern Africa, is commendable.

Hennie Herbst of the South African Department of Foreign Affairs proved to be the perfect host while I was collecting data for the book between 1997 and 2000. He not only scheduled all my appointments in Pretoria, but also arranged for transportation. It was indeed a pleasure working with Hennie and all his colleagues in Foreign Affairs.

In Mozambique, Belmiro Malate, SADC Focal Point and Antonio Matonse, Press Secretary in the President's office, as usual, rolled out the red carpet for me. Both of these individuals were also instrumental in providing support while I was working on my first SADC book published in the late 1980s.

At the SADC Secretariat in Gaborone, Botswana, Esther V. Kanaimba, SADC Public Relations Officer, arranged for me to interview numerous individuals. I owe a special thanks to these individuals as well as others throughout the region that were gracious enough to take the time and energy to give me an interview. Since there are too many to name individually here, I have provided a list of all those interviewed in the appendix.

I also owe a debt of gratitude to the following individuals in Southern Africa: Arjen van Zwieten with the Trade and Industrial Policy Secretariat (TIPS) of South Africa for putting together the SADC trade tables in the appendix; Claude Labbe, Public Relations Officer for the European Commission in Harare, Zimbabwe for arranging for information and interviews; Pat Made, Director of Inter Press Service, Harare, Zimbabwe, for serving as a conduit for information; Daniel B. Ndlela, Zimconsult, Harare, Zimbabwe, for his insights during the earlier stage of the project; Antonio Xavier of Mozambique for providing communications assistance; Esi Honono, Harare, Zimbabwe, for always opening her home to me (many of us lost a true mother friend when Esi made her transition in February 2002); and my South African family, the Mbambelas (Baba Willie, Mama Maria, Nonhlanhla, and Sibusiso) for not only providing me with a place to call home in South Africa, but also for shuttling me back and forth between Katlehong Township and Johannesburg.

For my mother (Carol), brothers (Charles Jr. and William Jacob), and other family members, I want to say thanks for understanding why I was not always available. To all my sister friends – thanks for making this journey easier. And for my mother friends, thanks for being Rocks of Gibraltar.

The book is dedicated to the two men in my life that have had the greatest influence on both my personal and intellectual development – my uncle, Jacob H. Carruthers, Jr. and my husband, Georges Nzongola-Ntalaja. Both of these men are incredible human beings and I feel exceedingly blessed to have them in my life.

Finally, I owe a great debt to my publisher at the University of Cape Town Press, Solani Ngobeni, who pursued this project with such vigour, and my editor, Alex McRae.

Margaret C. Lee
Rockville, MD
March 2003

Acronyms and Abbreviations

ACP	African, Caribbean, and Pacific
ADB	African Development Bank
AEC	African Economic Community
AGOA	*African Growth and Opportunity Act*
AMU	Arab Maghreb Union
ANC	African National Congress
AU	African Union
BLNS countries	Botswana, Lesotho, Namibia, and Swaziland (used in various combinations, e.g. BLS, LNS, etc.)
CAP	Common Agricultural Policy (EU)
CBI	Cross-Border Initiative
CEAO	West African Economic Union
CFM	Mozambique Ports and Railways
CMA	Common Monetary Area
COMESA	Common Market for Eastern and Southern Africa
CONSAS	Constellation of Southern African States
Corridor	Maputo Development Corridor
CSA	Commonwealth Sugar Agreement
CSS	country support strategy
CUSTA	Canada-US Free Trade Agreement
DOT	Department of Trade
DRC	Democratic Republic of the Congo
EAC	East African Community
EC	European Commission
ECA	Economic Commission for Africa
ECCAS	Economic Community of Central African States
ECOWAS	Economic Community of West African States
EDF	European Development Fund
EEC	European Economic Community
EFTA	European Free Trade Association
EIB	European Investment Bank
EPA	economic partnership agreement
EPRD	European Programme for Reconstruction and Development

EU	European Union
Eurostat	Statistical Office of the EU
FAL	Final Act of Lagos
FDI	foreign direct investment
FISCU	Finance and Investment Sector Coordinating Unit
FLS	Frontline States
FRELIMO	Mozambique Liberation Front
FTA	free trade agreement
GATT	General Agreement on Tariffs and Trade
GDP	gross domestic product
GEAR	Growth, Employment, and Redistribution Programme
GSP	Generalised System of Preferences
HCT	High Commission Territory
HLC	high level committee
HS	Harmonised Coding and Description System
ICP	international cooperating partner
IDZP	industrial development zone programme
IDC	Industrial Development Corporation
IFI	international financial institution
IFIAC	International Financial Institution Advisory Commission
IFZ	industrial free zone
IMF	International Monetary Fund
IOC	Indian Ocean Commission
ISI	import-substitution industrialisation
ITC	International Trade Centre (UNCTAD)
LDC	less developed country
LPA	Lagos Plan of Action
M&As	mergers and acquisitions
MCC	Maputo Corridor Company
MDC	more developed country
MDC	Movement for Democratic Change (in the context of Zimbabwe politics: see Chapter 2 only)
MERCOSUR	Southern Cone Common Market
MFN	most favoured nation
MIDP	Motor Industry Development Programme
MISP	Maputo Iron and Steel Project
MMA	Multilateral Monetary Agreement
MMTZ	Malawi, Mozambique, Tanzania, and Zambia
MNC	multinational corporation
MNE	multinational enterprise
MPLA	Movement for the Liberation of Angola
NAFTA	North American Free Trade Agreement

NIP	National Indicative Programme
NTB	non-tariff barrier
OAU	Organisation of African Unity
OECD	Organisation for Economic Cooperation and Development
PAC	Pan Africanist Congress
PDC	previously disadvantaged community
PPP	public-private partnership
Protocol	SADC Protocol on Trade
PTA	Preferential Trade Area for Eastern and Southern Africa
RDP	Reconstruction and Development Programme
RENAMO	Mozambique National Resistance
REPA	regional economic partnership agreement
RIA	regional integration arrangement
RIFF	Regional Integration Facilitation Forum
RIP	Regional Indicative Programme
RMA	Rand Monetary Area
RSA	Republic of South Africa
RTA	regional trade area
SACU	Southern African Customs Union
SADC	Southern African Development Community
SADCC	Southern African Development Coordination Conference
SADF	South African Defence Force
SAF	Structural Adjustment Facility
SAIIA	South African Institute of International Affairs
SAL	structural adjustment loan
SAP	structural adjustment programme
SAPP	Southern African Power Pool
SARB	South African Reserve Bank
SARDC	Southern African Research and Documentation Centre
SATCC	Southern African Transport and Trade Commission
SARS	South African Revenue Service
SCU	Sectoral Coordinating Unit (SADC)
SDI	spatial development initiative
SIP	Strategic Investment Programme
SITCD	SADC Industry and Trade Coordination Division
SMEDP	Small and Medium Enterprise Development Programme
SMME	small, medium, and micro enterprise
SSP	Skills Support Programme
STABEX	An EU programme for the stabilisation of export earnings
SWAPO	South West Africa People's Organisation
SYSMIN	An EU programme for the stabilisation of mineral exports
TDCA	Trade, Development and Cooperation Agreement

The Organ	SADC Organ on Politics, Defence and Security
TIFA	trade and investment framework agreement
TIPS	Trade and Industrial Policy Secretariat
TMA	Trilateral Monetary Agreement
TNF	trade negotiation forum
TNC	transnational corporation
TRAC	Trans African Concessions
TWG	technical working group
UEMOA	West African Economic and Monetary Union
UNCTAD	United Nations Conference on Trade and Development
UNDP	United Nations Development Programme
UNIRIN	United Nations Integrated Regional Information Network
UNITA	National Union for the Total Independence of Angola
UR	Uruguay Round (of GATT)
USAID	United States Agency for International Development
WIDER	World Institute for Development Economics Research
WTO	World Trade Organisation
ZANU-PF	Zimbabwe African National Union – Patriotic Front

Introduction

IN THE FIRST DECADE of the twenty-first century, globalisation and regionalisation processes continue to have a tremendous impact on the transformations occurring within the world economy. Africa, like many other parts of the developing world, tends to be excluded from these processes, becoming more superfluous to both the regionalisation and globalisation of production.

Africa's peripheral status within the world economy has been well documented. Although the continent is a major producer of primary products, sub-Saharan Africa's total income is not much more than Belgium's, and is divided among 48 countries with a median GDP of just over US$2 billion – about the output of a town of 60 000 in a rich country (World Bank, 2000:7).

The average per capita income is lower today than in the late 1960s. In addition, Africa's share of world trade has plummeted since the same period to less than two per cent, costing the continent an estimated US$70 billion annually (World Bank, 2000:5). African financial markets, with perhaps the exception of those in South Africa, are not integrated into global markets, and direct foreign investment into the continent is declining.

Sub-Saharan Africa has the largest number of countries that are considered to be among the poorest in the world, with an estimated 40 per cent of 600 million people living on less than US$1 a day (World Bank, 2000:10). According to the World Bank, the number of poor people in sub-Saharan Africa has grown tremendously, resulting in an increase in its share of the absolute poor in the world from 25 to 30 per cent (World Bank, 2000:10).

Africa's economic marginalisation can be traced back to the many travesties that have befallen the continent, beginning with the early European invasions, the slave trade, and colonial rule. Since gaining their independence from colonial rule, most African countries have been victims of despotic rulers, misguided economic policies, political instability, and abject poverty. The most recent disaster to befall the continent is the HIV/AIDS pandemic. This pandemic is threatening the productivity capacity of the continent, since it is destroying the able-bodied working class. How to prevent Africa from being further marginalised will be one of the greatest challenges of the twenty-first century.

Notwithstanding all this, Africa remains one of the wealthiest regions in the world, and its vast array of natural resources are essential to the globalisation and regionalisation of production. Such resources include gold, diamonds, oil, coltan, copper, cobalt, timber, platinum, and nickel. How to harness these resources, as well as other products produced

1

in Africa, in such a way as to enhance Africa's incorporation into the world economy, has been – and remains – a perennial challenge.

After gaining independence, African governments began creating regional economic organisations with a view to enhancing economic growth and development, and increasing the continent's international economic status. To date, these objectives, as the brief discussion above indicates, have not been achieved. Nonetheless, regionalism, defined as the adoption of a regional project by a formal regional economic organisation designed to enhance the political, economic, social, and cultural integration of member states, continues to be vigorously pursued throughout Africa.

Formal regionalism in Southern Africa has its roots in the creation of the South African apartheid-era relic Customs Union Convention, established in 1889 and transformed into the Southern African Customs Union (SACU) in 1969. The creation of the Southern African Development Coordination Conference (SADCC) in 1980, however, set the stage for regionalism in Southern Africa within the context of the African liberation struggle. In fact, SADCC's major objective in 1980 was to resist further efforts by the apartheid regime, through the expansion of SACU, to increase its regional economic and political hegemony.

With the creation of the Preferential Trade Area for Eastern and Southern Africa (PTA) in 1981, regionalism in Southern Africa took on another dimension. While the SADCC strategy had been designed to decrease regional economic dependency on the apartheid regime and to foster development, the major objective of the PTA was to increase intra-regional trade. Initially these two organisations seemed to complement each other.

During the early 1990s, however, both SADCC and PTA reassessed their goals and objectives in light of the transformation of the world economy and the changing political and economic dynamics taking place in Africa. SADCC was transformed into the Southern African Development Community (SADC) in 1992 and the PTA into the Common Market for Eastern and Southern Africa (COMESA) in 1993. Although for the most part COMESA's objectives remained the same, SADC began to focus on trade integration, which made it even more difficult to make a significant distinction between the two organisations. Since the goals and objectives of SADC and COMESA overlapped, questions were raised about the feasibility of member states participating, in some cases, in all three regional economic organisations (including SACU). Efforts to simplify the regional agenda in Southern Africa through combining SADCC and PTA failed, and so the two organisations finally came to the realisation that co-existence was their only option.

As apartheid came to an end, both SADC and COMESA anticipated that a post-apartheid South Africa would join their organisation. To the dismay of COMESA, South Africa joined SADC in 1994, tremendously enhancing the organisation's legitimacy. Earlier, in 1993, the issue of regionalism in Southern Africa had been made even more complex by the creation of the Cross-Border Initiative (CBI), spearheaded by the World Bank and co-sponsored by the International Monetary Fund (IMF) and the African Development Bank (ADB). Although not a formal regional economic organisation, the major objective of the CBI was to enhance trade integration in Africa. Several members of SADC, COMESA, and SACU are also members of the CBI.

To further complicate the dynamics of regionalism, efforts to revitalise the East Africa Community (EAC) began during the latter part of the 1990s, challenging individual SADC member states' commitment to regionalism in Southern Africa. The overlapping of membership in numerous regional organisations is one of the major challenges to regionalism in Southern Africa. Such overlapping fundamentally undermines regionalism as a result of (1) the inevitable abrogation of rules, regulations, and commitments resulting from the impossible task of simultaneously fulfilling the obligations of more than one organisation with similar goals and objectives; and (2) inefficiency arising from duplication and the overstretching of financial and human resources.

The overlapping membership in regional economic organisations is symptomatic of a larger problem, which is the failure of African leaders and their governments to make a political commitment to regionalism. This is a second major challenge to regionalism in Southern Africa.

Economic and political instability presents a third challenge to regionalism in Southern Africa. In order for regionalism to be successful, stability must exist in both areas. Southern Africa, like the rest of the continent, is beset with macroeconomic instability, largely resulting from economic mismanagement and corruption; marginalisation within the world economy; abject poverty; unacceptable levels of unemployment; poor educational and social service facilities; the HIV/AIDS pandemic; and economic policies imposed by international financial institutions and Western governments.

Political instability at the national level is made most evident by the current (2002–03) crisis in Zimbabwe, which is having serious implications for the entire region. In addition, although the Angolan war has finally ended, political stability remains elusive. Challenges are also posed by the refusal of the monarchy in Swaziland to place the country on a path to democracy, and the current problems in the fledgling democracies of Zambia, Malawi, and Lesotho. Political instability at the regional level is most evident with the conflict in the Democratic Republic of the Congo (DRC), which has created serious political, economic, and military divisions among states within the region.

A fourth challenge to regionalism in Southern Africa rests with the commitment to increase intra-regional trade via the creation of free trade areas. Although the creation of free trade areas, based on the European Union (EU) model of market integration, has been a dismal failure on the African continent, both SADC and COMESA, in 2000, established, respectively, a free trade agreement (FTA) and a free trade area. These new trade regimes must coexist with SACU, which, as a customs union, has a common external tariff against non-member states.

One of the reasons developing countries create FTAs is to secure foreign direct investment (FDI) in order to enhance development. A fifth challenge for the countries in Southern Africa is to make the region more appealing to both domestic and foreign investment.

Finally, the countries in Southern Africa are challenged to find a balance between enhanced openness, both regionally and internationally, and enhanced national development as they pursue their regional agenda. This means, for example, that they must determine if enhancing multilateral liberalisation via the World Trade Organisation (WTO) serves as a conduit for or hindrance to both national and regional development. Related to this is the issue of whether having a national development strategy in place should be a prerequisite to enhanced regional and international openness. Also of importance is the need to determine if the benefits of openness can best be realised by countries in Southern Africa establishing individual trade agreements with the rich countries of the world, or by Southern Africa as a bloc establishing such agreements.

As indicated by the above discussion, the challenges to regionalism in Southern Africa are daunting. This book is about these challenges, which are examined in the context of the political economy of regionalism in Southern Africa. Since SADC is considered the major organisation in Southern Africa facilitating regionalism, a large percentage of the book examines the challenges to regionalism in Southern Africa within the context of SADC.

The first chapter is on Africa and the political economy of regionalism. The objective of the chapter is to outline a theoretical framework for understanding regionalism in Africa. It is also designed to lay the foundation for the recommendations for the way forward for regionalism in Southern Africa as proposed in Chapter 8. In adopting a political economy approach to regionalism, the interaction between the political and economic forces that impact on regionalism both worldwide and in Africa are discussed. The chapter begins by first defining regionalism and regionalisation. Sections that follow are on neo-liberalism, globalisation, theories of regional integration, the new regionalism, and globalisation and regionalisation.

Chapter 2 chronicles the history of SADC. SADC's history as a regional economic organisation is divided into two distinct periods. The first is 1980 to 1992, when the organisation was a coordination conference that refused to allow the apartheid regime of South Africa to become a member. The second is 1992 to the present, when the organisation was transformed into a development community and post-apartheid South Africa was invited to join. While the first period was a very turbulent one for the organisation, the second has proven to be extremely challenging. This section also revisits the very controversial issue of SADC's origin, namely, whether SADC was an initiative created by internal regional forces, or forces external to the region. An examination of SADC's former strategy for regional cooperation and development (the SADC Programme of Action), as well as its institutional structure, follows. Efforts to restructure both of these entities over a two-year period are discussed at length. The restructuring of SADC is crucial if it is to become a more efficient and effective regional entity. The recommended changes are so drastic that, if implemented, they could usher in a new era in the organisation's history.

The last part of the chapter focuses on the current economic and political dynamics of the region within the context of constraints to implementing the SADC regional agenda. South Africa's regional economic hegemony is discussed, as well as the economic status of the SADC member states. Political issues examined include the conflict in the DRC, the Mandela-Mugabe rivalry, and the crisis in Zimbabwe.

The cornerstone of any strategy designed to integrate the economies of a region is increased trade and investment. How to increase trade among the sub-regions in Africa has been at the forefront of the debate on regionalism in Africa. Similarly, the role investment plays in spearheading much needed economic growth and development in order for trade to be increased has also been extensively debated. Most recently, the debate has focused on the need to rely more on domestic rather than foreign investment. This debate has been sparked by the acceptance of the reality that very often the dividends from foreign investments have not contributed to economic growth. In fact, in many cases the result has been the further pillaging of African resources.

The cornerstone of SADC's current strategy is to increase trade among its member states. The movement toward the creation of an FTA was very complex, given the history of trade relations in the region. For example, the region has a long history of unequal trade relations, with the majority of the member states being structurally dependent on South Africa. In addition, as previously mentioned, there exists a myriad of overlapping regional economic organisations.

Chapter 3 begins with a discussion of the issue of overlapping membership in regional economic organisations. This is followed by an analysis of the CBI within the context of the SADC regional agenda. The next part of the chapter examines regional bilateral trade agreements, and this is followed by an overview of the direction of trade in the region, including both formal and informal trade. The latter form of trade, which is often overlooked, is very important for determining how integrated the SADC region really is. The chapter concludes with an assessment of non-tariff barriers (NTBs) to trade.

The long and arduous road to the creation of the SADC FTA is chronicled in Chapter 4. A description and analysis of the SADC Protocol on Trade, which formed the blueprint for the creation of the SADC FTA, is provided in the first section. This is followed by an examination of the modalities of the trade negotiations. The third section provides an in-depth analysis of the negotiations that culminated in the creation of the SADC FTA, and the final section examines issues related to the implementation of the SADC FTA.

For developing countries, market integration is often pursued with a view to attracting both foreign and domestic investment. This is the case because there is deemed to be a positive correlation between investment and enhanced trade and development. Chapter 5 seeks to determine if this is the case in Southern Africa by examining investment trends in the SADC region. The chapter begins with an examination of global investment policy trends. This is followed by a review of the African experience with investment. The next section of the chapter examines the issue of investment in regional transport infrastructure as a catalyst for enhanced regional integration and development. The Maputo Development Corridor is the focus of analysis for this assessment. The remaining two sections of the chapter discuss investment trends in South Africa and the SADC region respectively.

It is impossible to analyse regionalism among the SADC member states without placing the debate within the context of the world economy. The primary question confronting sub-regions in Africa is whether integration at the regional level is a more viable strategy to pursue than integration at the global level. Clearly, both have their advantages and disadvantages. For sub-Saharan African countries, the real concern is the adoption of strategies that will prevent the continent from becoming more marginalised within the world economy.

Chapter 6 begins with a discussion of the WTO and its implications for Southern Africa's economic future. This is followed by an analysis of the *African Growth and Opportunity Act* (AGOA) and its significance for the region's further integration into the world economy. Of special concern is whether AGOA, through its apparel provision, can serve to enhance the regionalisation of production in SADC textile and garment industries.

Chapter 7 examines in depth the relationship between the EU and Southern Africa, since the EU is the most important trading partner of SADC member states. Also, the EU is the largest contributor of economic assistance in the region. This chapter analyses the changing EU-Southern African relationship in light of the post-Cold War era, the successful completion of the Uruguay Round (UR) of the General Agreement on Tariffs and Trade (GATT), and the political and economic changes taking place in Europe. Of particular concern is whether these changes in the geopolitics of the world will diminish the economic status of Southern African countries. This is of special concern, since the EU and South Africa now have in place an FTA. The purpose of this chapter is to assess the implications of EU-Southern African relations for regional development and integration. The first section of the chapter places the EU's relationship with its African, Caribbean, and Pacific (ACP) partners in historical perspective. In the second section, EU-Southern African trade relations are analysed, and in the third section, EU financial and technical assistance to the region is examined. The fourth section looks at EU-South Africa relations, and future EU-Southern Africa trade relations are examined in the final section. Of particular concern is whether EU-Southern African relations serve to advance SADC's regional agenda.

The final chapter contains proposals for the way forward for the SADC member states. It begins with a summary of the major findings of the study. The remainder of the chapter is divided into the following sections: regionalism within the context of SADC realities; the prerequisites for regionalism; further integration into the world economy; and implementation of viable national development strategies.

The study rests on four premises, which are as follows:

▶ Market integration is not a viable strategy for the SADC member states to pursue. Instead, they must adopt a regional strategy that deals with the economic and political realities of the SADC region.

▶ Although market integration is not a viable strategy, many of the prerequisites for market integration must be in place for regionalism to be successful in Southern Africa.

▶ The growing regionalisation of the world economy means that Southern Africa's further integration will likely occur via the triad blocs (North America, Western Europe, and Asia).

▶ Enhanced openness at the regional and international levels will not result in sustained economic development unless national development strategies are in place.

The Political Economy of Regionalism in Southern Africa attempts to unravel the complexity of the SADC region today. It merges the history, economics, and politics of the region in ways that will contribute to both the economic and international relations/international political economy literature on Africa in general and Southern Africa in particular.

ONE

Africa and the Political Economy of Regionalism

A TREMENDOUS RESURGENCE in the literature on regionalism occurred during the 1990s, much of it from the fields of international relations and international political economy. For the most part, this literature, which focused on what has become known as the 'new regionalism', was preoccupied with regionalism in North America, Europe, and Asia, the major trading blocs of the world. Notwithstanding this lack of interest in Africa, regionalism continues to be viewed by many as the only possible way for Africa to arrest its further marginalisation within the world economy, albeit through pursuing a 'new' regional agenda (e.g. Mistry, 2000; Bøås, 2001:27–39). Although there are varying perspectives on exactly what the new regional agenda should consist of, there is a growing consensus that trade/market integration should not be the focus of such regionalism. African regional economic organisations, however, continue to be committed to trade/market integration, although over the decades since independence such integration endeavours have been complemented by other strategies designed to enhance economic and political development.

This chapter builds a theoretical framework that will allow for an understanding of regionalism in Africa. This is achieved by placing regionalism in Africa within the larger context of the literature on regionalism, as well as within the context of the political and economic problems specific to Africa, including policies imposed by external actors. Using the political economy approach, I will examine the interaction between the political and economic forces that impact on regionalism both worldwide and in Africa. Such forces are complex, and consequently must include three levels of analysis: the international, the regional, and the national.

The political economy of regionalism includes an examination of theories of regional integration, the new regionalism, and the globalisation-versus-regionalisation debate. These theories and issues are placed within the context of worldwide regionalism, as well as regionalism in Africa. In addition, with respect to the latter, the impact that neo-liberalism and globalisation have had on African countries will be critiqued. It is important to include neo-liberalism and globalisation in the discussion because they have had serious implications for the African regional agenda. The political economy of regionalism, once placed in historical and theoretical context, will provide the foundation for recommendations for the way forward in dealing with the challenges of regionalism in Southern Africa in the first decade of the twenty-first century (see Chapter 8).

The chapter will begin by defining regionalism and regionalisation. This will be followed by sections on neo-liberalism, globalisation, theories of regional integration, the new regionalism, and globalisation and regionalisation. The implications for regionalism in Africa will be discussed at the end of each section, with the exception of the one on regionalism and regionalisation.

Definitions of Regionalism and Regionalisation

There are many definitions of regionalism, and, as Andrew Hurrell notes, regionalism is an ambiguous term, with no consensus as to what exactly it means (Hurrell, 2000:38). Definitions range from strictly economic perspectives to ones that include any type of activity among actors in a given region. Andrew Wyatt-Walter, from an economic perspective, sees regionalism as a process consisting of a group of countries that implement a set of preferential policies designed to enhance the exchange of goods and/or factors among themselves (Wyatt-Walter, 2000:78). An even more restrictive definition is the notion that economic regionalism as a process is based on the fact that trade and investment in a specific region grows faster than that with the rest of the world (Haggard, 1997:fn. 1).

For some political economy theorists writing on the 'new regionalism', regionalism is all encompassing. For Marianne Marchand, Morten Bøås, and Timothy Shaw, regionalism 'concerns the ideas, identities and ideologies related to a regional project'. As a political project, regionalism can be led either by the state or by non-state actors. Consequently, they say, 'with each regional project (official or not), several complex competing regionalisation "actors" with different regional visions coexist, who sometimes cooperate and who, at other times, are in open conflict with each other' (Marchand *et al.*, 1999:900). Regionalism, as defined by Björn Hettne, is a very complex process that is multidimensional (Hettne, 1999a:17) (see below).

Daniel Bach identities two types of regionalism. The first is formal regionalism, which is represented by 'institutional forms of cooperation or integration' and is defined as 'the aggregation and fusion into broader units of existing territories or fields of intervention'. The second is network regionalism, which is represented by trans-state or informal integration and results in 'the exploitation of dysfunctions and disparities generated by existing boundaries, with debilitating effects on state territorial control' (Bach, 1999a:152).

For the purposes of this study, regionalism is defined as *the adoption of a regional project by a formal regional economic organisation designed to enhance the political, economic, social, cultural, and security integration and/or cooperation of member states.*

Regionalisation, like regionalism, has been variously defined. Perhaps the most generic definition envisages regionalisation as a process that concerns at least two societies within a region, enhancing their social and/or economic integration or interaction (Oman, 1994:34; Hurrell, 2000:39; Hveem, 1999:87). For Helge Hveem, while on the one hand regionalism may cause regionalisation, on the other it may not (Hveem, 1999:87). Bach reinforces the idea that regionalisation can occur with or without the implementation of regionalism and therefore that regionalisation processes may not necessarily be part of or result in the creation of institutional structures (Bach, 2001:2).

For Bach as well as Marchand *et al.*, agents of regionalisation can be led by the state or non-state actors such as transfrontier traders (informal sector), non-governmental actors (e.g. NGOs), and media companies (Bach, 2001:2; Marchand *et al.*, 1999:900). Such agents are not necessarily motivated by a regionalist project (Bach, 2001:2).

For the purposes of this study, regionalisation is defined as *the process by which state and non-state actors seek to enhance their economic, political, cultural, social, and security interaction with societal forces within a region through formal or informal structures.* Such interaction can be either part of a regional project or separate from it. For example, while cross-border informal trade activities can be viewed as both a form of regionalisation and as a means of enhancing the economic integration of a region, the process is not considered a part of regionalism.

Neo-liberalism

Neo-liberalism, the orthodoxy that calls for free markets, has been at the forefront of economic policies in Africa in the guise of IMF/World Bank Structural Adjustment Programmes (SAPs). Policy prescriptions within the context of free markets include limited governmental intervention in the economy; privatisation; the demise of the welfare state; and monetary and fiscal discipline.

The foundation of the neo-liberal orthodoxy is to be found in nineteenth century classical economic liberalism, which believed that people should organise their economic lives around 'the market' (MacEwan, 1999:4). For Adam Smith (1723–90), considered to be the father of modern economics, economic liberalism was the solution to the problem of mercantilism, practised by nation states during the sixteenth, seventeenth, and eighteenth centuries. Mercantilism was an economic system that encouraged wealth accumulation by states as a means of fostering economic and military security. States promoted their exports and shunned imports, because national security was associated with a positive balance of trade. For mercantilists, politics was more important than economics, and therefore market interests were subordinate to the state (Gilpin, 1987:6, 32–3; Gill, 1994:79–80; Gerber, 1999:430).

Advocates of economic liberalism feared what they thought was the heavy hand of the government and abusive state power under mercantilism. Economic liberalism was therefore developed in response to mercantilism and it was to liberate people from abuse by the state. For Adam Smith, such liberation was to take place as a result of the 'individual freedom of the marketplace'. The foundation of economic liberalism is based on the premise that free markets are the most efficient form of economic organisation and that the government should intervene in the economic affairs of the state only when necessary. This idea is best summarised by the notion of *laissez faire* (Gilpin, 1987:27; Balaam & Veseth, 1996:41, 43).

Although there are numerous theoretical variants within the school of economic liberalism,[1] Keynesian economics had a significant impact on economic development from the Great Depression of the 1930s to the late 1970s. Keynesian economic liberalism called for greater state intervention in economic policy. Although an advocate of the free market, Keynes called for governmental intervention to curb inflation, reduce unemployment, and enhance economic development. As a result of the influence of Keynes, liberals searched for the appropriate level of state intervention within the open market system (Balaam & Veseth, 1996:50). It was during the period of the dominance of Keynesian economics that the 'welfare state' came into existence and the state assumed a greater role in controlling both domestic and international economic policy (Yergin, 1998).

Former British Prime Minister Margaret Thatcher and former US President Ronald Reagan are usually given credit for the reincarnation of classical economic liberalism. Both leaders were fundamentally interested in the 'magic of the marketplace' prevailing (Solomon, 1999:13).

Neo-liberals argue that a policy of free trade should be adopted by countries interested in rapid economic growth. Free trade requires the unregulated movement of capital, goods, and services internationally (MacEwan, 1999:31). Theoretically, free trade is at the foundation of the neo-liberal orthodoxy. In reality, however, free trade does not exist (see Dasgupta, 1998:113). According to Arthur MacEwan, 'it is generally recognised within the economic profession that the theoretical case for free trade is not valid' (MacEwan, 1999:30). Further to the point, Robert Gilpin notes that,

> trade protection has never totally disappeared, and indeed, during the past two centuries, restrictions on trade have been a persistent and pervasive feature of the world economy. Historically, protectionism has been more prevalent than has free trade. Although nations want to take advantage of the benefits of free trade, they are frequently unwilling to open their own markets and permit market forces to determine the international distribution of gains from trade. Although the argument favoring free trade remains powerful, the doctrine of trade protection continuously resurfaces in new guises. In fact, there has never really been 'free' trade with either no or few barriers. For this reason, the term 'trade liberalisation' (the movement toward really free trade) is more appropriate than the term 'free trade' (Gilpin, 2000:89).

In spite of its lack of grounding in reality, the neo-liberal orthodoxy became the main prescription for solving the economic crises of the developing world. By the end of the 1980s, it became know as the 'Washington Consensus'.

The term 'Washington Consensus' was coined in 1989 by John Williamson, an economist, who used it to summarise what he determined were the major policy recommendations emanating from the international financial institutions (IFIs), the US Congress, and other Washington-based entities for reforming Latin American economies (Williamson, 1990:7) (see Figure 1.1, opposite). Also known as SAPs,[2] these policies are allegedly designed to restore macroeconomic stability and spearhead structural economic reform. Moisés Naím, the editor of *Foreign Policy*, has noted that with Williamson's ten policy recommendations, '[t]he world was under the impression that a clear and robust consensus existed about what poor countries should do to become more prosperous' (Naím, 2000:87). In fact, there has never been a 'consensus' among economists, including those from the IMF and World Bank, about the Washington Consensus (Naím, 2000:94–5; MacEwan, 1999:8). Further to the point, Naím asks:

> What changes more often, the fashion designs coming from Paris and Milan or the economic policy designs that Washington and Wall Street prescribe to less developed or post-communist countries? Although this comparison may seem frivolous, a review of the ideas that guided thinking and action about economic reforms in the 1990s shows they were as faddish as skirt lengths and tie widths. The difference, of course, is that fashions in economic policy affect how millions of people live and define their children's opportunity for a better future (Naím, 2000:87).

Even though policy prescriptions were constantly changing, along with what was defined as economic success, the notion of a 'Washington Consensus' continued to prevail. In fact, the term became so popular that it took on a life of its own, different from its original intent and content (Naím, 2000:88). The IMF and World Bank joined the bandwagon and announced that consensus-inspired policy reforms would be the basis on which loans would be granted. That there was no consensus was evident by the public debates that occurred among policy experts as to the approach that should be adopted for cementing market reforms (Naím, 2000:94).

FIGURE **1.1**

The Original 1989 'Consensus'

Fiscal discipline
Large and sustained fiscal deficits contribute to inflation and capital flight. Therefore, government should keep them to a minimum.

Public expenditure priorities
Subsidies need to be reduced or eliminated. Government spending should be redirected toward education, health, and infrastructure development.

Tax reform
The tax base 'should be broad' and marginal tax rates 'should be moderate'.

Interest rates
Domestic financial markets should determine a country's interest rates. Positive real interest rates discourage capital flight and increase savings.

Exchange rates
Developing countries must adopt a 'competitive' exchange rate that will bolster exports by making them cheaper abroad.

Trade liberalisation
Tariffs should be minimised and should never be applied on intermediate goods needed to produce exports.

Foreign direct investment
Foreign investment can bring needed capital and skills and, therefore, should be encouraged.

Privatisation
Private industry operates more efficiently because managers either have a 'direct personal stake in the profits of an enterprise or are accountable to those who do'. State-owned enterprises ought to be privatised.

Deregulation
Excessive government regulation can promote corruption and discrimination against smaller enterprises that have minimal access to the higher reaches of the bureaucracy. Governments have to deregulate the economy.

Property rights
Property rights must be enforced. Weak laws and poor judicial systems reduce incentives to save and accumulate wealth.

Source: Naím (2000:89)

To date, there remains no consensus regarding what combination of policy prescriptions are required for reforming economies and fostering prosperity in the developing world. The only point of agreement is that macroeconomic fundamentals must be sound (Naím, 2000:96).

In November 1998, the US Congress established the International Financial Institution Advisory Commission (IFIAC) to ascertain what US policy should be toward seven international institutions, including the IMF and the World Bank. Noted economist Allan H. Meltzer was chair of the commission, which had a total of 11 members.[3] The report of the commission was released in March 2000. In it, major recommendations are made for reforming both the IMF and World Bank. The majority of commission members agreed that the main problems associated with international financial institutions are:

- ▶ overlapping missions and mission creep;
- ▶ lack of transparency and accountability;
- ▶ failure to prevent the increasing depth and severity of international financial and economic crises;
- ▶ ineffectiveness, corruption in developing countries, and waste of resources;
- ▶ commandeering of international resources to meet objectives of the US government or its Treasury Department;
- ▶ failure to develop successful regional and global programs to confront transnational problems in agriculture, transportation, forestry, the environment, and health care;
- ▶ overuse of conditional lending and the imposition of multiple conditions;
- ▶ an inability to enforce commitments on borrowers unwilling to meet them; and
- ▶ reluctance to reduce lending to countries that do not honor their obligations (IFIAC, 2000:17–18).

With respect to the IMF, the Meltzer Commission concluded that '[i]ts system of short-term crisis management is too costly, its responses too slow, its advice often incorrect, and its efforts to influence policy and practice too intrusive' (IFIAC, 2000:4). The report further noted that the conditions imposed on countries that secure loans for long-term economic reform result in job losses and reductions in living standards for the local population (IFIAC, 2000:22). Poorer nations have increased their dependence on the IMF since it was transformed into an avenue for long-term conditional loans. Consequently, the IMF has an unprecedented degree of influence over policymaking for a multilateral institution. The policy of conditionality for loans has not ensured economic progress and in fact it has undermined national sovereignty and at times hindered the development of democratic institutions (IFIAC, 2000:24).

The Meltzer Commission recommends sweeping IMF policy changes. Although noting that the IMF should continue to manage international financial crises, this should be done, according to the Commission, under new rules that encourage member countries to stabilise their financial systems (IFIAC, 2000:4). The report also recommends that the IMF discontinue providing loans for long-term development assistance (e.g. to sub-Saharan Africa) and long-term structural transformation (e.g. to post-communist transitional economies). Finally, the Meltzer Commission recommends that the IMF eliminate its Poverty Reduction and Growth Facility (the successor to the Enhanced Structural Adjustment Facility) (IFIAC, 2000:7).

In April 2001, the IMF released a report on how the organisation intends to refocus its activities. One of the areas for refocusing will be conditionality. Acknowledging that in some cases the IMF had gone beyond its proper areas of involvement and had therefore overstepped its mandate and expertise, the report notes that new policies will include the streamlining of conditionality and the strengthening of ownership of programmes (IMF, 2001:5).

In terms of the World Bank, the Meltzer Commission concluded that with respect to achieving its goal of eradicating poverty throughout the world, the bank is not involved in pursuing activities that would make this goal achievable. Nor is the bank involved in implementing policies that could raise living standards and quality of life, especially for people living in the poorest nations (IFIAC, 2000:7). With respect to Africa, the commission notes that the World Bank has acknowledged a 73 per cent failure rate in its performance (IFIAC, 2000:15). It therefore recommends that instead of concentrating on the volume of lending to the developing world, the bank should focus its resources on reducing poverty and enhancing development (IFIAC, 2000:4–5).

IMF and World Bank officials have also been accused of either prescribing basically the same medicine for all countries and/or proposing policy reforms after only a short visit to countries (Dasgupta, 1998:67; Stiglitz, 1998:4). In addition, once countries undertake a SAP, very few are able to graduate from being under the tutelage of the IMF and World Bank (Dasgupta, 1998:84). With respect to Africa, more resources go to paying off IMF/World Bank loans annually than are actually received by these countries in the form of loans.

The Southeast Asian financial crisis of 1997 finally forced the IMF and World Bank to re-examine the medicine prescribed by the so-called Washington Consensus (see Naím, 2000:100–1; MacEwan, 1999:3; Krugman, 1999; Stiglitz, 1998, 2000; IFIAC, 2000:26–8). This occurred following severe criticism that by forcing countries to adopt the policy prescriptions contained in the so-called Washington Consensus, the crisis was made worse. The Washington Consensus has been further undermined by the ongoing economic instability in Latin America, the continued failures in Africa, and the Russian débâcle (MacEwan, 1999:3; Gilpin, 2000:157–62).

With respect to the Southeast Asian crisis, noted economist Paul Krugman argues that while these countries were indeed more vulnerable to a financial panic in 1997 than they had been previously, this was not because of crony capitalism or bad government policies, but because they had opened their financial markets, with their economies becoming better free market economies. They also were more vulnerable because as a result of their new popularity with international lenders, their debts to the outside world had increased substantially. This debt was in dollars, so when the crisis occurred, Southeast Asian economies were undermined (Krugman, 1999:100–1). Why was China not affected by the crisis? Krugman asked. Because, unlike its neighbours, China had not made its currency convertible, which meant that a government license was needed to convert yuan into dollars (Krugman, 1999:144; Gilpin, 2000:153–5). What is interesting is that, according to the IMF and World Bank, the real test of a country's integration into the world economy is that its currency is fully convertible and all restrictions are removed on the movement of capital (Dasgupta, 1998:101).

The so-called Washington Consensus has not only failed to bring about promised economic reform, it has also failed to stem the growing economic instability caused by financial crises. Nonetheless, the IMF, World Bank, and US government officials remain committed to its implementation (Krugman, 1999:xiii; Naím, 2000:100–1).

With respect to Africa, after two decades of SAPs, there is growing consensus that they have failed, leaving most African countries further marginalised within the world economy (see Mkandawire & Soludo, 1999; Olukoshi, 1998). A large part of the failure, according to former World Bank Chief Economist Joseph Stiglitz, rests with the fact that advocates of the Washington Consensus proposed that a limited set of instruments (e.g. macroeconomic stability, privatisation, and trade liberalisation) be used to achieve the narrow goal of economic growth (Stiglitz, 1998:18). Such policies, he argues, are not only incomplete, but also misguided. In order to correct the inherent problems with the Washington Consensus, Stiglitz advocates the adoption of a post-Washington Consensus that includes policies that will result in increased living standards, sustainable and equitable development, and enhanced democracy (Stiglitz, 1998:1, 18–19).

Although most would agree that it is imperative that African economies structurally adjust, the real issue becomes at what pace and using which policy prescriptions. While the IMF and World Bank policies have been designed to force change at a very rapid pace (shock therapy), a growing body of literature is suggesting that such adjustment must be implemented incrementally (see Mkandawire & Soludo, 1999; Olukoshi, 1998).

Numerous countries in Southern Africa, as in the rest of the continent, have implemented SAPs. They include Lesotho, Malawi, Mauritius, Mozambique, Tanzania, Zambia, and Zimbabwe. In addition, the South Africa government has imposed its own economic stabilisation programme in the guise of its Growth, Employment, and Redistribution (GEAR) strategy. In the wake of such adjustment, these countries have found themselves more vulnerable to the whims of the world economy. In addition, many of the internal conflicts experienced by these countries are the result of the fight for access to limited resources. The implementation of the neo-liberal orthodoxy in the form of SAPs has serious implications for Southern Africa and specifically for the implementation of SADC's regional agenda.

Percy Mistry argues that SAPs have not been region-friendly and consequently they have resulted in 'negative "beggar-thy-neighbor" effects across borders' (Mistry, 2000:566). Consequently, multilateral creditors, wittingly or otherwise, may be contributing to the lack of success of regional integration in Africa (Mistry, 2000:567).

Although SAPs were supposedly designed to reincorporate the informal sector into official structures, they have had the opposite effect in West Africa, according to Kate Meagher. The dramatic expansion of informal cross-border trade as a result of SAPs actually stifled regionalism in West Africa (Meagher, 2001:48).

Criticism of the neo-liberal paradigm (market fundamentalism) ranges from the fact that it has failed to deliver on its promises of economic growth, redistribution, and development for all (Giddens, 2001:2; Stiglitz, 2001:341; Dalziel, 2001:87) to suggestions that the paradigm has been discarded (Giddens, 2001:2).

Stiglitz proposes a new agenda for development in the twenty-first century that transcends the dogma of the 'markets', which suggests markets alone will guarantee desirable outcomes or that the lack of a market or market failure means that the government should assume the responsibility for such activity (Stiglitz, 2001:46). Instead, the new agenda for development expands the objectives of the past and includes a different role for the state. The agenda calls for a partnership to be established between the government and the private sector. This partnership requires the government to assume a catalytic function with respect to both creating and regulating markets. In addition, it is expected that governments will improve their performance, in part through enhanced utilisation of market-like mechanisms that will spearhead competition (Stiglitz, 2001:353).

The neo-liberal orthodoxy in the form of SAPs has served to undermine regionalism in Africa. The so-called Washington Consensus did not result in the anticipated economic reforms, and unilateral liberalisation proved to be counterproductive to enhanced intra-regional trade and served to impede regionalism. In order for SAPs to make a contribution to Africa's regional agenda, Mistry insists that they must become more region-friendly, which means that strands of SAPs that are mutually reinforcing must be woven together with regional initiatives (Mistry, 2000:566–7).

Globalisation

Globalisation has been variously defined, but one of the most constructive definitions is given by Robert Keohane and Joseph Nye, for whom a distinction must be made between globalism and globalisation, with the former being:

> a state of the world involving networks of interdependence at multicontinental distances. The linkages occur through flows and influences of capital and goods, information and ideas, and people and forces, as well as environmentally and biologically relevant substances (such as acid rain or pathogens). Globalisation and deglobalisation refer to the increase or decline of globalism (Keohane & Nye, 2000:105).

The notion that globalism can be increased or decreased is in keeping with the reality that globalisation is not a new phenomenon (see Keohane & Nye, 2000; MacEwan, 1999; Solomon, 1999; UNDP, 2000; Oman, 1994; Gilpin, 2000:294). In fact, when placed in historical context, the world economy has experienced periods of both globalisation and deglobalisation. As Krugman notes, '[i]t is a late-twentieth century conceit that we invented the global economy just yesterday' (cited in Solomon, 1999:193). The current phase of globalisation is part of a continuous process that began about 500 years ago (MacEwan, 1999:26).

There have been three phases of globalisation. The first commenced at the end of the fifteenth century and was characterised by expanded European hegemony over the Western Hemisphere and sea routes becoming global (MacEwan, 1999:28). The second phase commenced during the latter part of the nineteenth century and was characterised by imperialism, and by a tremendous increase in trade and investment during the Industrial Revolution (Keohane & Nye, 2000:107; MacEwan 1999:28). By the beginning of the twentieth century, capital markets were very integrated, some argue more than at the century's end (Keohane & Nye, 2000:109; Gilpin, 2000:47). The third and current phase commenced during the late twentieth century. There is no uniform conceptualisation of how the current phase of globalisation is distinguished from the previous ones (Keohane & Nye, 2000; MacEwan, 1999:26–9; Solomon, 1999:193; UNDP, 2000:30). The United Nations Development Programme (UNDP), in its *Human Development Report 1999* (UNDP, 2000), provides a very useful outline of what is new in the current phase of globalisation (see Figure 1.2, overleaf).

Just as there are advantages to globalisation as identified in Figure 1.2, there are also disadvantages. The advantages of globalisation have not been distributed evenly. In fact, the major beneficiaries have been the core countries of the world economy, along with transnational corporations (TNCs). The countries that have benefitted the least are those on the global periphery. This point is made poignant by statistics compiled by the UNDP. According to the UNDP, by the end of the 1990s, individuals living in the highest income countries and representing one fifth of the world's population had:

▶ 86 per cent of world gross domestic product (GDP) – the bottom fifth just 1 per cent;
▶ 82 per cent of world export markets – the bottom fifth just 1 per cent;

▶ 68 per cent of foreign direct investment – the bottom fifth just 1 per cent; and
▶ 74 per cent of world telephone lines, today's basic means of communication – the bottom fifth just 1.5 per cent (UNDP, 2000:3).

These figures represent an increasing, as opposed to a decreasing, gap between the highest income countries and the lowest (UNDP, 2000:36). In addition, according to the World Bank, 200 million more people were living in absolute poverty (on less than US$1 per day) in 1999 than in 1987 (Mazur, 2000:83).

FIGURE **1.2**

Globalisation: What's Really New?

New markets
▶ Growing global markets in services – banking, insurance, transport
▶ New financial markets – deregulated, globally linked, working around the clock with action at a distance in real time, with new instruments such as derivatives
▶ Deregulation of anti-trust laws and proliferation of mergers and acquisitions
▶ Global consumer markets with global brands.

New actors
▶ Multinational corporations integrating their production and marketing, dominating world production
▶ The WTO – the first multilateral organisation with authority to enforce national governments' compliance with rules
▶ An international criminal court system in the making
▶ A booming international network of NGOs
▶ Regional blocs proliferating and gaining importance – the European Union, the Associate of South-East Asian Nations, Mercosur, the North American Free Trade Association, and SADC, among others
▶ More policy coordination groups – G–7, G–10, G–22, G–77.

New rules and norms
▶ Market economic policies spreading around the world, with greater privatisation and liberalisation than in earlier decades
▶ Widespread adoption of democracy as the choice of political regime
▶ Human rights conventions and instruments building up in both coverage and number of signatories – and growing awareness among people around the world
▶ Consensus goals and action agenda for development
▶ Conventions and agreements on the global environment issues – biodiversity, the depletion of the ozone layer, the disposal of hazardous wastes, desertification, and climate change
▶ Multilateral agreements in trade, taking on such new agendas as environmental and social conditions
▶ New multilateral agreements – dealing with services, intellectual property rights, communication protocols – more binding on national governments than any previous governments
▶ The Multilateral Agreement on Investment under debate.

New (faster and cheaper) tools of communication
▶   Internet and electronic communications linking many people simultaneously
▶   Cellular phones
▶   Fax machines
▶   Faster and cheaper transport by air, rail, and road
▶   Computer-aided design

Source: UNDP (2000:30)

Those who have the greatest opportunities within the global labour force are the highly skilled global elites (e.g. corporate executives, scientists) (UNDP, 2000:3). For many of the unskilled, limited employment opportunities are available, and they are often victims of what Jay Mazur says globalisation looks like to a lot of workers – 'a race to the bottom' (Mazur, 2000:89).

The new international trade regime that developed following the conclusion of the UR of trade negotiations in April 1994 under the GATT was largely developed for TNCs. The international organisation created to oversee the implementation of the new system is the WTO, which came into existence in January 1995. TNCs are able to wield considerable power within the global economy. During a 1990 meeting of the GATT in Brussels, US Trade Representative Carla Hills was accompanied by 400 advisors, which exceeded the total number of trade mission representatives for sub-Saharan Africa and Latin America combined. In addition to the 400 US advisors, representatives from 200 US corporations were present, including IBM, Citibank, and American Express. While Pfizer, Monsanto, and Du Pont were part of an agro-chemical conglomerate dealing with intellectual property rights, the Cargill Coporation was available to deal with grain negotiations. Countries on the periphery of the global economy could not begin to compete with these delegates from the richest country in the world (Dasgupta, 1998:148).

Of major concern to countries on the global periphery is the fact that very often world prices for goods are not determined by the market, but by high income countries who continue to maintain high subsidies on exported goods, especially agricultural products. With such subsidies, it is argued, these countries are able to develop comparative advantages in sectors, such as wheat, where they do not really have a comparative advantage. In addition, fair international competition is further compromised by the reality that world prices for goods are often determined by TNCs where, according to the United Nations Conference on Trade and Development (UNCTAD), an estimated two-thirds of the movement of goods and services occurs as intra-firm and inter-firm transactions (Keet, n.d.a; Gilpin, 2000:169).

The new rules and regulations regarding intellectual property rights are of extreme concern to countries on the global periphery. The real fear, according to the UNDP, is that as a result of the power of TNCs to control research agendas and patents, under trade-related aspects of intellectual property rights as outlined under the Uruguay Round (UR), poor people will likely be marginalised with regard to controlling the world's knowledge (UNDP, 2000:6).

In one sense, sub-Saharan Africa is highly integrated into the world economy, with exports consisting of an estimated 30 per cent of GDP. The problem is that the majority of these exports consist of primary products and thus are subject to price fluctuations on the global market. The prices for many of these commodities are at their lowest in a century and a half, and African countries have not increased their export levels, nor have they been successful in securing significant foreign investment (UNDP, 2000:2, 31).

In essence, African countries find themselves between a rock and a hard place: they stand to become more marginalised within the world economy if they both open their trade regimes to the world economy or keep them closed. This is a perplexing paradox indeed!

With respect to this paradox, G. K. Helleiner cautions African leaders to seriously think about Africa's integration into the global economy given its instability, which increases the vulnerability of countries to external shocks. He therefore argues that 'Africa need not succumb to mindless globalisation via the state's abandonment of its role in the mediation of these links' (Helleiner, 1999:101).

Harvard economist Dani Rodrik argues against relying on openness as a conduit for economic development. According to him, '[o]penness to trade and investment flows is no longer viewed simply as a component of a country's development strategy; it has mutated into the most potent catalyst for economic growth known to humanity' (Rodrik, 2001:55). Rodrik notes that this is problematic, and that unless a viable development strategy is in place, openness will not result in sustained economic growth (Rodrik, 1999:1).

Although the neo-liberal paradigm suggests a correlation exists between trade liberalisation and economic growth, in terms of economic theory, this relationship is either ambiguous or absent (Rodrik, 1999; IMF, 1998:61; Bussolo & Lecomte, 1999:2–3). While there are empirical studies that conclude that a correlation exists between trade liberalisation and economic growth (Sachs & Warner, 1995; Frankel & Romer, 1999), the findings of such studies have been challenged (Rodríguez & Rodrik, 1999). There are studies, however, that do point to a positive correlation between a more open trade regime and higher growth, but such regimes have been underpinned by domestic policy reforms, including macroeconomic stability, human resources development, domestic investment, and good governance (Rodrik, 2001; Bussolo & Lecomte, 1999; Jenkins & Thomas, forthcoming).

With respect to the correlation between a viable development strategy and enhanced integration into the world economy, Rodrik notes that,

> [t]he Asian experience highlights a deeper point. A sound overall development strategy that produces high economic growth is far more effective in achieving integration with the world economy than a purely integrationist strategy that relies on openness to work its magic. *In other words, the globalizers have it exactly backwards. Integration is the result, not the cause, of economic and social development.* A relatively protected economy like Vietnam is integrating with the world economy much more rapidly than an open economy like Haiti because Vietnam unlike Haiti, has a reasonably functional economy and policy (Rodrik, 2001:59; original emphasis).

The advantages of openness make it imperative that African governments maintain open trade regimes. Such advantages include access to new technology and skills, and opportunities for some industries to become more efficient producers with a view to increasing exports. It is important, however, that resources identified for development and building democratic institutions are not diverted to the global regional agenda (Rodrik, 2001:55).

Although in many respects African countries have not benefitted from globalisation, the issue of opening their economies to the world has been an essential component of recommended strategies of development. It has been deemed to be essential in order to arrest the continent's further marginalisation within the world economy. What this discussion on globalisation points to is that African countries must be careful about how and the extent to which they pursue openness.

Finding a balance between openness and development in relation to both international and regional integration can be a challenge. In order for integration into the world economy to be beneficial, a viable national development strategy needs to be in place that includes, as mentioned above, macroeconomic stability, human resources development, domestic investment, and good governance. If such a strategy is not in place, in terms of integration at the international level, such efforts could result in countries being further marginalised within the world economy. At the regional level, it could result in member countries pursuing policies that are counterproductive to their national interests. Therefore, regionalism in Africa must not be seen as a substitute for the need to have in place viable national development strategies.

Although it is the case that the greatest beneficiaries of regionalism are theoretically the regional giant(s), if such countries are not economically and politically stable, the benefits from regionalism will remain elusive. Similarly, the countries that are economically smaller but have viable political and economic structures will be in a better position to withstand the challenges posed by the regional giant(s), especially one that is unstable. In the final analysis, a country with a smaller economy could reap greater benefits from regionalism than one with a larger economy.

Theories of Regional Integration

Regional integration in Africa has been largely pursued within the context of three theories of regional integration. They are market integration, regional cooperation, and development integration. In this section of the chapter, these three theories will be discussed and for the most part will be placed within the context of the SADC experience.

The section begins with a review of market integration, since it is both the strategy that the SADC member states rejected when the organisation was established and the current one being pursued. Regional cooperation, the strategy that guided SADC policy from 1980 to 1992, is next examined, followed by development integration, theoretically adopted by SADC in 1992.

Market Integration

Market integration theory was first referred to as customs union theory. As Tom Østergaard notes, since a customs union represents only one stage in the movement from a free trade area to an economic union, it is theoretically more accurate to refer to the process as market integration (Østergaard, 1993:29).[4] Since market integration and economic integration both refer to the linear progression of degrees of integration, the terms will be used interchangeably.

Economic integration, according to Bela Balassa, is defined as both a process and as a state of affairs. 'Regarded as a process, it encompasses measures designed to abolish discrimination between economic units belonging to different national states; viewed as a state of affairs, it can be represented by the absence of various forms of discrimination between national economies' (Balassa, 1961:1).

Such integration, according to Balassa, can take several forms, representing different degrees of integration: free trade areas, customs unions, common markets, economic unions, and total economic integration. In a *free trade area*, tariffs and quantitative restrictions to trade are removed among member countries, but countries maintain their own tariffs against non-member countries. A *customs union* consists of a free trade area plus the introduction of a common external tariff against non-member countries. With a *common market*, the customs union remains in place and the free flow of the factors of production (capital and labour) is introduced. An *economic union* consists of a common market plus the harmonisation of monetary and fiscal policies; and *total economic integration* consists of the unification of monetary and fiscal policies, along with the creation of a supra-national authority that has the power to enforce decisions (Balassa, 1961:1).

Over the years, the above linear progression of degrees of market integration has been modified to include, for example, a preferential trade area and political union. For some theorists, a *preferential free trade area*, where tariff rates among regional countries are lower than those imposed on external countries, can be the first theoretical type of market integration (Jovanovic, 1992:9), or for others, the pre-integration phase. Also, for some theorists, the last stage of market integration is *political union*, which includes the creation of a supra-national authority. Under these circumstances, the degrees of integration include a free trade area, customs union, common market, complete economic union, and complete political union (see El-Agraa, 1997:2).

The costs and benefits (welfare gains) from integration are based on *trade creation* (a shift from a high-cost external producer to a low-cost regional producer) and *trade diversion* (a shift from a low-cost external producer to a high-cost regional producer) (Gerber, 1999:221–2; Page, 2000:41–4). To the extent that there exists more trade creation than trade diversion, economic integration is deemed to be welfare producing. The possible sources of gain from economic integration, according to Peter Robson, include:

▶ increased production arising from specialisation according to comparative advantage;
▶ increased output arising from the better exploitation of scale economies;
▶ improvements in the terms of trade of the group with the rest of the world;
▶ forced changes in efficiency arising from increased competition within the group; and
▶ integration-induced changes affecting the quantity or quality of factor inputs, such as increased capital inflows and changes in the rate of technological advance (Robson, 1980:3).

Theoretically, it is assumed that in order for these gains to be realised, the following prerequisites need to be in place:

▶ The level of industrial development among member countries must be similar.
▶ National macroeconomic policies must be harmonised.
▶ Regional macroeconomic stability should be in place.
▶ Existing intra-regional trade should be significant.
▶ Member countries should have complementary industrial development.
▶ The prospective benefits from integration should be widely distributed, including opportunities for securing foreign investment.
▶ Factor endowments among member countries should be significantly different.
▶ Member countries must be willing to cede some level of sovereignty to a supra-national body that has enforcement authority.
▶ The region must be politically stable (Mwase & Maasdorp, 1999:200; Collier & Gunning, 1999:94; Onitiri, 1997:414).

In reality, however, market integration has been successfully pursued without all of these prerequisites in place. Nonetheless, successful market integration does require the existence of the majority of them.

That the above conditions for market integration do not exist in Africa has been well established in the literature (see Robson, 1980:151; Ravenhill, 1990:81–5; McCarthy, 1996; Fine & Yeo, 1997). Most countries that are members of regional economic organisations are at different levels of industrial development; national macroeconomic policies are not harmonised, nor is regional macroeconomic stability in place; intra-regional trade represents a small percentage of total foreign trade; member countries have competitive instead of complementary industrial development; the benefits from integration are not widely distributed, resulting in the regional giant(s) benefitting the most; foreign investment is usually polarised around the regional giant(s); most have similar factor endowments; member countries are not willing to cede any level of sovereignty to a supra-national body; and most regions are not politically stable.

To the extent that market integration among developing countries is to be evaluated as desirable, the emphasis should be placed on the dynamic as opposed to the static effects. The static effects are those that impact on trade flows and consumption (Jovanovic, 1992:14), while the dynamic effects include economies of scale, economic growth, investment, efficiency, and technological development (El-Agraa, 1997:45–6; Söderbaum, 1996:11). While static effects are usually realised in the early phase of economic integration, dynamic effects can only be realised over time. Because it is difficult to calculate dynamic gains, often such gains are excluded from the analysis of market integration models (Söderbaum, 1996:11).

One of the most problematic aspects of market integration has to do with the polarisation effects. Specifically, the most developed country or countries in the region experience an overwhelmingly disproportionate amount of the gains. They thus become poles of development, while the less developed member countries become poles of stagnation. Market integration therefore becomes untenable for the latter group. After all, nations choose to participate in these types of regional schemes because of the anticipated economic benefits, including the creation of a wider market for their goods (Østergaard, 1993:28).

Helleiner argues that while African development might be enhanced by efforts to create larger political and economic entities, the real issue to be concerned with is the underutilisation of the potential for greater economic cooperation and not the creation of preferential trade arrangements (Helleiner, 1999:108). In a similar vein, Paul Collier and Jan Gunning argue that, based on the East Asian experience, increased trade is likely to be enhanced following unilateral trade liberalisation as a result of trade reform (Collier & Gunning, 1999:90–1). While in theory this may be the case, in practice, however, in Africa it is often the case that when unilateral liberalisation does take place, tariff barriers are replaced by NTBs, thus inhibiting increased intra-regional trade.

With respect to the potential for increased intra-regional trade among African countries, it has been argued that in many cases such potential has actually been realised. Such arguments are made based on gravity models that indicate that '[i]ntra-African (non-oil) trade is not less' than the predictions of such models, which 'are based on country size (market size and area) and distance between countries, even without intra-Africa trade restrictions' (Helleiner, 1999:108; Jebuni, 1997:362). Only modest gains, therefore, can be expected from efforts to increase such trade. Based on this reality, it has been determined that, in order to increase intra-sub-Saharan trade, the removal of discriminatory distortions and infrastructure biases is only one strategy that must be pursued. The other relates to positive action, which includes putting in place new and effective incentives to intra-regional trade (Jebuni *et al.*, 1999:38).

Regional Cooperation

Regional cooperation consists of collaboration between two or more countries with similar interests, including economic, political, social, and cultural interests (Bourenane, 1997:50–1; Haarlov, 1997:15). Such collaboration, according to Jens Haarlov, can include, for example, the

▶ Execution of joint projects, technical sector cooperation, common running of services and policy harmonisation;
▶ Joint development of common natural resources;
▶ [A] joint stand towards the rest of the world;
▶ Joint promotion of production (Haarlov, 1997:16).

Numerous individuals suggest that regional cooperation is a more realistic approach to be pursued by developing countries than market integration (e.g. McCarthy, 1996:229–30; Zehender, 1983:31–2; Ravenhill, 1985:210, 1986:99; Maasdorp, 1993:246; Leistner, 1997: 122). Regional cooperation allows countries the flexibility to simultaneously develop the region and enhance their economic interaction, without being forced to liberalise their trade regimes at a pace that will be counterproductive to enhanced economic growth and development. As Colin McCarthy notes,

> [f]unction-based cooperation – broadly defined as cooperation between independent countries or agencies on identified projects or schemes – could be a more appropriate means to address Africa's problems .... The advantages of this approach are in its flexibility and pragmatism in circumventing the problems posed by nationalism and equity in the distribution of costs and benefits. It is also better suited to deal with the many fiscal, physical and technical barriers to trade that cannot be addressed by trade policy (McCarthy, 1996:229–30).

If market integration is the ultimate objective, regional cooperation could possibly lay the foundation for it.

In adopting regional cooperation as a strategy in 1980, SADC was attempting to enhance the development of the region in order to bring about regional structural transformation (see Lee, 1989). Of primary concern was altering the economic structures of dependency that existed between the SADC member states and the apartheid regime. Enhanced intra-regional trade through market integration was to be a future goal of the organisation.

The SADC strategy entailed regional coordination to develop sectors (see Chapter 2). SADC referred to its regional cooperation approach of project or sectoral coordination as 'functional cooperation'. According to Rob Davies, functional cooperation

> set out from the premise that cooperation in the formulation and execution of joint projects aimed at overcoming underdevelopment-related deficiencies in the spheres of production and infrastructure should have first priority in programs in Third World regions. Not only was this viewed as essential to remove immediate barriers to regional trade, it has also been seen as means of generating a regional identity and consciousness which would set in train processes of interaction which would lay the ground for a more secure integration than would overly hasteful trade liberalization. The latter, it was agreed would under conditions of underdevelopment tend to benefit stronger partners disproportionately and could thus lead to a polarization ultimately prejudicial to the whole integration effort (Davies, 1997:112).

Of the SADC approach, Emang Motlhabane Maphanyane, a former SADC official, noted that the organisation developed a modest agenda that focused on the rehabilitation of the economic and physical infrastructure of the region (Maphanyane, 1993:175).

Critics of regional cooperation argue that while the scope of cooperation can be wide, usually it is not deep and that changes are not accomplished regarding key issues, including those of policy coordination and harmonisation. While it is argued that policy coordination towards the rest of the world can reach significant levels, it has had limited success with respect to the promotion of production (Haarlov, 1997:58). Others argue that the implicit assumption that project development will result in deeper integration should not be made, although such development may have an impact on eliminating barriers to regional trade and result in the creation of a regional identity among its members. The fact that trade issues are not central to regional cooperation is seen as a problem (Davies, 1997:116).

Supporters of regional cooperation, such as John Ravenhill, suggest that the incremental approach that entails the implementation of limited functional projects appears to avoid many of the problems associated with market integration. Also, a flexible, functionally-specific approach impinges little on the sovereignty of participating states. Thus, in the cooperation approach, regional interaction is a supplement to national development efforts and cannot substitute for these (Haarlov, 1997:60). More specifically, Ravenhill argues that, '[i]f we are serious about overcoming the constraints that impede African cooperation, we should be focusing on the coordination of policies rather than on integration' (Ravenhill, 1990:85). With respect to SADC, Gavin Maasdorp argues that it is more realistic for the organisation to pursue sectoral cooperation as opposed to trade integration, because it is easier to achieve and the benefits can be spread more rapidly (Maasdorp, 1993:246).

In critiquing its regional project coordination approach, SADC noted serious weaknesses in the strategy (SADCC, 1992:27), and therefore approved a new strategy designed to correct the weaknesses (SADCC, 1992:28). As discussed in Chapter 2, these weaknesses are still evident and continue to be a constraint to more efficient cooperation and development. Nonetheless, without adequately addressing these weaknesses, the SADC member states decided, at least in theory, to adopt a new and more difficult strategy to enhance regional integration – development integration.

Development Integration

Development integration, while based on the market integration approach (Haarlov, 1997:30; Østergaard, 1993:33–4[5]), attempts to address the problems created by it. According to Haarlov, the development integration approach

> [i]s born out of the problems and dysfunction of the pure market integration approach ... the market approach's static character, its sole focus on how trade creation and trade diversion will influence welfare, and its tendency to widen economic differences between lesser and more developed areas, when market forces are left to function on their own. The development integration approach's answer to this is to change the agenda in three areas: 1. The objective of the integration process; 2. The timing and level of interstate binding commitments; and 3. The distribution of cost and benefits of cooperation (Haarlov, 1997:30).

With respect to the first area for agenda change, the objective of integration becomes economic and social development (Haarlov, 1997:30). For example, since developing countries have little productive capacity, the 'efficiency maximisation of existing capacity' is not a point of focus. Instead, the development integration model focuses on how to stimulate the creation of productive capacity. With this approach, the theory of integration is linked with the theory of development. Also central to this theory is a much higher degree of state intervention than in market integration. It is through such conscious intervention by regional partners that cooperation and interdependence are promoted (Østergaard, 1993:34).

In terms of the timing and level of interstate binding commitment, a high level of political cooperation is required for implementation (Østergaard, 1993:34). While in the market integration approach political commitment comes at a much later stage, in the development integration approach, political commitment is seen as the backbone of the integration process, since 'co-ordination of policies becomes a simultaneous – or even prior – requisite for trade liberalization ... to prevent, among other problems, unequal inter-country distribution of the benefits deriving from the process' (Haarlov, 1997:31).

The third agenda item concerns the distribution of costs and benefits. This involves an attempt to ensure that the benefits from regional integration are distributed equitably. Since regional integration among developing countries usually results in polarisation and an unequal distribution of gains, redistributive measures that are of a compensatory and corrective nature are implemented. The compensatory measures include financial transfer and tax transfer mechanisms, while corrective measures include planned regional indus-trial development, priority loans, improved conditions for development, the reduction of tariffs at a slower pace, and common fiscal incentives to invest (see Haarlov, 1997:32; Østergaard, 1993:35).

With respect to compensatory measures, a common form of financial transfer mechanism results from customs union revenue. Specifically, the countries that benefit from a larger market provide monetary remuneration to those countries that bear the costs of integration (Haarlov, 1997:32). To date, the 'successful' arrangements of this nature in Africa have been the West African Economic Union[6] and SACU (Østergaard, 1993:35). The latter group includes South Africa and Botswana, Lesotho, Namibia, and Swaziland (the BLNS countries). As the regional economic powerhouse, South Africa enjoys a disproportional share of the gains from the customs union. The BLNS countries are compensated for the resultant polarisation and trade diversion with financial transfers that South Africa calculates by using a very extensive revenue sharing formula (see Maasdorp, 1990; Kumar, 1992; Haarlov, 1997:33). Although over the years the percentage of the customs union revenue transferred to the BLNS states has increased (such revenue accounts for between 17 and 60 per cent of government revenue), the countries argue that they are still not adequately compensated for trade diversion and polarisation. The SACU situation points to the reality that financial transfers do not solve the problem of the unequal distribution of benefits. South Africa continues to be the country of choice for industrial investment (Østergaard, 1993:335–6).

Financial transfers in which the more privileged governments within a regional grouping have made a commitment to provide direct contributions to compensate the less privileged members have proven to be less successful than such arrangements as SACU. Not only are such commitments politically unpopular, but usually the governments have fallen behind in payments. Also, as with the BLNS countries, most recipients do not find the compensation adequate (Ravenhill, 1986:98). This occurs, according to Ravenhill, as a result of the failure of member states 'to address the most fundamental issue in the distribution crisis: the location of industrial production within the region with its spillover effects on employment, technological transfer and learning-by-doing' (Ravenhill, 1985:209).

Compensatory measures also include what is known as a transfer tax. A transfer tax is introduced after a common external tariff agreement has been reached. The transfer tax allows the less developed members of the customs union to impose limited tariffs on goods imported from a member country (Østergaard, 1993:35). An example of a transfer tax system in Africa was that of the earlier East African Community, which was in existence between 1967 and 1977.[7] The EAC included Kenya, Uganda, and Tanzania. The transfer tax system was implemented with a view to rectifying trade asymmetries (Mytelka, 1975:30). Specifically, it was designed to allow Tanzania and Uganda to temporarily protect their industries from competitive industries in Kenya (Hazlewood, 1985:176). According to Østergaard, '[t]heoretically, the transfer tax mechanism ought to lead to the expansion in the less developed member countries of those industries for which the maximum permitted degree of protection would be sufficient to offset the cost advantages in the more developed member states' (Østergaard, 1993:35). The reality of what actually occurs is something different. The EAC tax system has been criticised for not solving the problem of the unequal distribution of gains from regional integration and for possibly encouraging the 'uneconomic duplication of previous investments' (Østergaard, 1993:35).

Measures have been designed to correct the problems created as a result of the unequal distribution of the costs and benefits of regional integration. Corrective measures are said to be one of the most divisive issues of integration, because the more developed countries (MDCs), instead of agreeing to transfer a certain amount of realised gains to the less developed countries (LDCs), must forgo a certain amount of limited resources for development to the LDCs. Without corrective measures, such resources would likely go to the MDCs. Corrective measures, as far as the LDCs are concerned, are extremely important because they actually allow the LDCs to participate in the structural transformation of the region. This is crucial if the LDCs are to alter their regional and international status (Axline, 1977:95).

Planned regional industrial development is not only an essential corrective measure, but it is the most effective, at least in theory (Østergaard, 1993:36). For development-oriented market integration supporters, industrialisation is the key to economic development (McCarthy, 1996:214–15). With planned regional industrial development, industries may be allocated to countries on the basis of comparative advantage. Such industries are then supposed to provide for the needs of the regional market, albeit with some protection conditions in place. Enhanced investment not only has an effect on the balance of payments, but also on employment creation, technology transfer, and infrastructure development (Østergaard, 1993:35–6).

Getting nations to agree on a planned regional industrial development strategy has proved to be extremely difficult. Planners must take into consideration, for example, that often the commitment to regional undertakings is not present at the national level, especially since there are few immediate rewards at this level. National interests consequently prevail over regional interests (Østergaard, 1993:36–7).

In addition, often when agreements are reached regarding the allocation of industries, such plans are not implemented because: (1) politicians, if they do not get what they want when negotiating for industrial planning, will often ignore integration agreements previously signed; (2) often institutions responsible for implementing plans are not geared toward regional goals; (3) although a regional industrial arrangement has been signed, it does not mean that large organisations have the technical capacity to implement it; (4) often national bureaucrats do not understand regional industrial programmes; (5) red tape and inefficiency exist; (6) the question of financing regional plans is not dealt with; and (7) politicians cannot allocate industries at the negotiating table (Østergaard, 1993:37).

Another consideration with respect to planned regional industrial development concerns TNCs. In the majority of cases, TNCs tend to support market integration because it provides them with a larger market for their goods. On the other hand, if there are subsidiaries in member states that produce the same products, then TNCs will likely oppose market integration. Such TNCs are also opposed to industrial planning, because of their ability to monopolise the protected national markets. They therefore prefer to trade with the parent company, because it allows them to reap monopoly profits (Østergaard, 1993:37–8). Planned regional industrial development is also constrained by the need for governments to: (1) harmonise fiscal and monetary policies among themselves; (2) harmonise policies toward foreign investors; and (3) surrender a certain degree of sovereignty (Ravenhill, 1985:209).

A second corrective mechanism consists of the creation of funds and regional development banks. Such banks are designed to provide loans to the LDCs under extremely favourable conditions. Loans can be used for project development designed to increase the productive capacity of these countries (Haarlov, 1997:35). This mechanism, however, has been plagued by lack of resources and clear objectives (see Mytelka, 1975:34–5; Ravenhill, 1985:209; Haarlov, 1997:34; Hazlewood, 1985:176).

The next corrective mechanism consists of improved conditions for development. This includes infrastructural (i.e. roads, railways, telecommunications, energy transmission) and educational (i.e. technical training) development. Ideally, such development should give the LDCs a competitive edge with respect to attracting investors and reducing the costs for such investors when they locate to an LDC (Haarlov, 1997:33–4).

Another corrective mechanism is put in place when the LDCs are allowed to reduce tariffs against regional partners at a slower pace than the MDCs. This mechanism is designed to allow the LDCs a longer time to adjust to the new dynamics of the region (Haarlov, 1997:35). This, however, is not likely to solve the problem of the unequal distribution of costs of and benefits from regional integration (Østergaard, 1993:38).

A fifth corrective mechanism consists of member countries harmonising their investment codes in order to attract investment in the LDCs. Once this is done, the LDCs are given permission to offer more favourable incentives to investors than the MDCs. To date, however, such arrangements have not been successfully implemented in Africa (Haarlov, 1997:35).

Although the development integration model may seem superior to the market integration model, it requires a greater degree of commitment on the part of member states. Consequently, it has proved to be as, if not more, difficult to implement (Haarlov, 1997:35).

According to SADC officials, a development integration approach that includes investment, production, and market or trade integration was considered appropriate for SADC, and therefore member states needed to:

▶ Mobilise and promote greater mobility of investment capital within the region;
▶ Create a single regional market, in which there is increasing and freer movement of goods and services;

▶ Progressively remove barriers to the free movement of people within the sub-continent;

▶ Accord in each country on a reciprocal basis, to all SADCC citizens and SADCC companies, treatment equivalent to that accorded to nationals (SADCC, 1992:28).

In order to realise these goals, the organisation said major constraints needed to be addressed, including:

▶ The various bureaucratic, regulatory and administrative non-tariff barriers to the movement of goods, services and people in the region;

▶ The non-convertibility of currencies and other payment related problems;

▶ The inadequate physical and economic infrastructure in a number of areas;

▶ The low effective demand arising from the underdeveloped nature and lack of compatibility of the economies of countries in the region (SADCC, 1992:28–9).

Although SADC envisages in the future the creation of a single regional market, regional cooperation remains a central part of the organisation's strategy.

In the 1997 *Review and Rationalisation of the SADC Programme of Action*, the consultants concluded that '[t]he development integration approach adopted by SADC is constrained by an inadequate management framework which would clearly articulate goals, policies, strategies and time frames' (SADC, 1997a:3). Clearly, SADC has not outlined a development integration strategy that addresses the theoretical issues identified above. Notwithstanding the fact that economic and social development are high on the agenda, the member states have not made the necessary commitment to political cooperation. In addition, compensatory or corrective measures have not been identified for rectifying prospective problems created by the unequal distribution of costs and benefits arising from integration.

Although in theory SADC has adopted a strategy of development integration, in practice, the organisation appears to be pursuing a combination of regional cooperation and market integration.

Implications for Regionalism in Africa

The implications of theories of regional integration for regionalism in Africa are numerous. The advice by academics and policy makers that African governments need to abandon the EU model of market integration has begun to sound like a stuck record. The attempt by African leaders to mimic Europe needs to be discontinued. That the conditions for the creation of free trade areas, customs unions, etc. do not exist has been reinforced in this section.

The rejection of market integration as a strategy, however, does not mean that the prerequisites for market integration should be rejected. In fact, African countries pursuing regionalism should strive, for example, to increase intra-regional trade, especially in cases where goods are sourced from outside the region (e.g. Western Europe) that are available within the region and are internationally competitive. Similarly, there exists a need for national and regional macroeconomic stability to be in place. Other prerequisites for success include political stability; a political commitment to regionalism; the willingness to cede some level of sovereignty; and efforts to address concerns around the potential unequal benefits stemming from regionalism.

With respect to the question of unequal benefits from regionalism, both development integration theory and regional cooperation theory are instructive with respect to Africa.

Unfortunately, trying to get the regional giant(s) to provide compensatory or corrective measures to problems arising from regional integration is virtually impossible in Africa. Even if, theoretically, the regional giant(s) has such resources, there is not an African country that can realistically afford to give them to a member state, given the dire economic conditions that prevail for the majority of African people.

As a result of the realities in Africa, regional cooperation continues to be viewed as a viable means for developing regions. There is no substitute for regional nations pooling their resources to develop regional infrastructure, transport networks, food security, electricity, etc. All nations benefit from such activities and they tend to result in greater regional unity than does market integration. In fact, the latter, as will be discussed in Chapter 4, has been very divisive in Southern Africa, with countries at odds over protecting their own national interests. There is therefore a growing consensus that regionalism in Africa must transcend the focus on trade integration and move toward, for example, integrating the means of production in the region; the harmonisation of fiscal and monetary policies; helping countries to develop comparative advantages; and sharing regional resources for sustainable development.

New Regionalism

The post-Cold War era spearheaded what is known as the second wave of regionalism or the so-called 'new regionalism'. The first wave took place during the 1960s, while the second wave commenced during the mid-1980s. The latter took off only after the Cold War came to an end in 1989. In fact, it is argued that the new regionalism was made possible by the collapse of the communist system and the decline of US economic hegemony (Hettne, 1999b:xvii).

The 'old' regionalism was sparked by the creation of the European Economic Community (EEC) in 1957, the development of which was largely in response to the perceived need to create a united Europe to serve as a buffer against the Soviet threat. For this reason, the US supported the notion of regionalism in Western Europe (De Melo & Panagariya, 1992:1; Wyatt-Walter, 2000:79–80). In fact, according to Gilpin, although the US had an aversion to trading blocs, in the case of Western Europe, governments were required to lower barriers to intra-regional trade in order to receive American assistance (Gilpin, 2000:58).

Many developing countries, influenced by the EEC, joined the regionalism bandwagon, resulting in regional integration schemes being established in Latin America, Asia, and Africa during the 1960s and the early part of the 1970s. Free trade areas and customs unions were envisaged as avenues for regional development. Import-substitution industrialisation (ISI) at the regional level was the strategy adopted by many of these countries, although ISI at both the national and regional levels was inward-looking. According to Jaime de Melo and Arvind Panagariya, '[i]t was thought that infant industries could first learn to export within a protected regional market – and then face world competition. But for the same reason that import substitution failed in countries, it also failed in the regions' (De Melo & Panagariya, 1992:1–2; see also Oman, 1994:46–8).

With the exception of the EEC (which is today the European Union) and the European Free Trade Area (ETFA), established in 1960, the first wave of regionalism failed. It has been argued that this first wave failed because of lack of US support (De Melo & Panagariya, 1993:5). According to Jagdish Bhagwati, even though the US supported the EEC, the organisation was used as a conduit for US support of multilateralism. In fact, it was under the leadership of the EEC that the multilateral GATT negotiations were facilitated (De Melo & Panagariya, 1993:5).

Björn Hettne argues that the first wave of regionalism failed as a result of the slowdown in integration in Western Europe and the FTAs in the Third World. With respect to the latter, the outcome of regional integration was not development, but the creation of centre-periphery structures at the regional level as well as inter-state conflicts (Hettne, 1994:1).

Although worldwide regionalisation might have been suspended between the mid-1970s and 1989, this was not the case for Africa, since the origins of regionalism in Africa were more political than economic. Specifically, the origins of regionalism in Africa date back to the early efforts by political leaders to liberate the continent from colonial and later neo-colonial rule. The idea of African unity was often placed within the context of regional economic organisations as conduits for post-colonial consolidation, with regional blocs being seen as a means of negotiating more effectively with countries in the developed world who were economically powerful (McCarthy, 1999:15).

As early as 1958, during the All-African People's Conference in Accra, Ghana, regionalism was discussed as a strategy that should be adopted to rectify the problems caused by the smallness of African economies. This idea was reinforced at subsequent continental meetings. When the Organisation of African Unity (OAU) was created in May 1963, regionalism became a central part of its charter (Lyakurwa *et al.*, 1997:159). In 1980, regionalism was reinforced as a necessity on the continent with the adoption by the OAU of the Lagos Plan of Action (LPA), which set a goal of creating a common market for Africa by the year 2000. To this end, sub-Saharan Africa was to be divided into three sub-regions – Western, Central, and Eastern and Southern. According to the LPA, economic integration at the sub-regional level was to be the precursor to economic integration at the continental level. Such integration was to be facilitated in stages by sub-regional economic organisations. They were to begin by establishing FTAs, then common markets, and finally economic unions (Lyakurwa *et al.*, 1997:160). The Economic Community of West African States (ECOWAS) was to facilitate integration in West Africa and the Economic Community of Central African States (ECCAS) in Central Africa. For Eastern and Southern Africa, the LPA created the Preferential Trade Area for Eastern and Southern Africa, which was later transformed into the Common Market for Eastern and Southern Africa.

Although by 1991 it was obvious that the African common market would not be realised by 2000, the heads of state and government of the OAU called for a new regional strategy in the form of the Abuja Treaty. The treaty created the African Economic Community (AEC). It was ratified by the heads of state and government of the OAU in 1994, and the first Ordinary Session of the AEC was finally held in Harare, Zimbabwe at the OAU Summit in 1997. It is anticipated that the AEC will come into existence in 2025.

The LPA model for building the community was adopted for the AEC. This meant that once again sub-regional organisations were to be the building blocs for the community. In fact, the first five years of the AEC were to be devoted to strengthening sub-regional groups (Lyakurwa *et al.*, 1997:159). The sub-regional groups include COMESA, ECCAS, SADC, ECOWAS, and the Arab Maghreb Union (AMU).

A decade after its creation, however, the AEC remains under the control of the Secretary-General of the African Union (AU; formerly the OAU)[8] and it is fundamentally a figment of the imagination of the organisation. Nonetheless, the idea of an AEC continues to receive widespread support on the continent. Why, amidst the failure to date to create viable FTAs, customs unions (with the exception of the apartheid relic, SACU), or common markets,[9] do African leaders continue to support the current regional agenda in Africa? According to Colin McCarthy, it is because 'Pan-Africanism, as an expression of continental identity and coherence distinguishes regional integration in Africa from other regions in the developing world' (McCarthy, 1999:14). In Southern Africa alone, during what was called the interregnum of the 'new' and 'old' regionalism, both SADC and COMESA were established.

Numerous reasons have been given for the resurgence of worldwide regionalism during the post-Cold War era (e.g. see Mistry, 1999:124–7; Wyatt-Walter, 2000:83–97; Fawcett, 2000:17–30; Marchand *et al.*, 1999:897–901; De Melo & Panagariya, 1992, 1993; Gilpin, 2000:11–12, 40–5; Oman, 1994:14). These included the end of the Cold War, which resulted in a multipolar as opposed to a bipolar world; major transformations in the world economy, resulting in enhanced globalisation; the decline of US economic hegemony; and enhanced worldwide democratisation. Another major reason for the resurgence in regionalism was the fact that the US government, for the first time, began to support regionalism over multilateralism. This occurred as the US government became increasingly frustrated by the slow pace of progress toward trade liberalisation with the UR of the GATT. The US government was also concerned about the implications for the US of the creation of a single European Market. With respect to the GATT, US governmental officials felt that more progress could be made toward trade liberalisation through regional as opposed to multilateral negotiations. In 1989, it completed negotiations with Canada for the creation of a Canada-US Free Trade Agreement (CUSTA) and in 1993 with Canada and Mexico for the North American Free Trade Agreement (NAFTA), which came into force on 1 January 1994. As the EU moved toward complete monetary union, the US felt that a countervailing regional bloc to the EU, as well as emerging regional blocs in Asia that were competitive, was necessary (Mistry, 1999:124).

In addition, the resurgent interest in regionalism resulted from the fact that countries in Africa, Latin America, Asia, and Central and Eastern Europe (CEE), as well as the former Soviet Union (FSU), wanted to emulate the EU. For the FSU countries, joining the EU was envisaged as a means to arrest economic decline and to enhance security. The threat of CEE and FSU countries being given preferential access to the EU market resulted in other countries attempting to establish regional integration arrangements (RIAs) with the EU. For those countries in South America and Asia who felt they were disadvantaged by NAFTA and the EU, increased regionalisation was seen as an effective strategy to enhance their bargaining power (Mistry, 1999:124–5; Oman, 1994:20–1).

New regionalism theory in this section of the chapter is divided into four theoretical constructs. The first, known as 'open regionalism', is based on neo-classical and/or neo-liberal economic theory, which emphasises that the markets should drive the integration process. Advocates of open regionalism also posit that the strategy should be outward-looking, high levels of protection should be avoided, and regionalisation should be part of the economic globalisation of the world economy (Söderbaum, 1996:1–2, fn. 4). The second, known as the 'WIDER[10] approach', sees regionalism as a more multidimensional process that will result in greater homogeneity in areas such as culture, politics, economics, security, and diplomacy (Söderbaum, 1996:1–2, fn. 4). The third approach is termed 'new regionalisms – regionalism from below', and suggests that the starting point for formal regional organisation should be informal cross border trade and related activity. The final theoretical approach of the new regionalism is the 'external guarantors model', which advocates that the African regional agenda should be supervised by an external agent in order to guarantee that economic reforms are not reversed and macroeconomic stability is enhanced.

Open Regionalism

Based on trade integration theory, the open regionalism approach envisages regionalism as a conduit for enhanced globalisation/multilateralism,[11] with the latter being defined as the 'multilateral lowering of policy impediments to the movement of goods and services across national and regional boundaries' (Oman, 1994:27). In fact, regionalism is seen as sub-optimal to globalisation.[12] One of the major concerns among those that support multilateralism is that regionalism is a hindrance to multilateralism. The multilateralism-versus-regionalism debate formed a major part of the UR negotiations, with multilaterists expressing concern that regionalism would serve as an impediment to the further liberalisation of the international trade regime.

Supporters of open regionalism posit that the world has been divided into three major trading blocs – North America, Europe, and Asia. Open regionalism (the new regionalism) as conceptualised within the context of neo-classical and/or neo-liberal economics, according to the World Bank, has three distinct features:

▶ The agreements extend beyond conventional arrangements addressing trade in goods. They often also cover the liberalization of trade in services, movements of labour and capital, harmonization of regulatory regimes and co-ordination of domestic policies.

▶ North-South arrangements are based on reciprocity as opposed to one-way, unilaterally defined preferences, as in the Lomé convention. The recent example most commonly referred to is NAFTA.

▶ There is a shift of emphasis in South-South arrangements, whereby free trade areas and customs unions seek to build on national trade liberalization efforts and complement outward-oriented trade strategies (IBRD as quoted in Odén, 1999:159).

Although the central focus for regionalism is on economic factors, the World Bank acknowledges that non-economic motives (e.g. political) may impact on the regional integration process. For the World Bank, this would translate into regional integration arrangements that may not be the optimal economic solution, which, according to it, is global liberalisation (Odén, 1999:159). The World Bank approach to the new regionalism has been appropriately termed 'neoliberal market integration' (Odén, 1999:161).

The neo-liberal paradigm has had a tremendous impact on the regional integration agenda in Africa since the early 1980s. During the 1960s and 70s, attempts at implementing market integration were inward-looking and relied on import substitution industrialisation. Trade regimes were highly protected and high-priced inefficient products manufactured in the regions proved to be no substitute for cheaper, efficient products from the capitalist core. Protectionism, in many cases, prevented countries from importing into their countries inputs needed for enhanced industrialisation. Increased intra-regional trade, the major objective of market integration, was, for the most part, not realised, partially because member countries produced similar products and therefore they did not have comparative advantages. Another problem was the maintenance of tariff barriers and NTBs to trade.

The 1980s witnessed a change that resulted in the development of outward-looking market integration strategies in Africa. This change was largely as a result of the adoption by the West of neo-liberalism as the major doctrine to guide the world economy. As previously noted, neo-liberalism has been at the forefront of economic policies in Africa in the guise of IMF/World Bank SAPs that forced African countries to liberalise their trade regimes and adopt outward-looking trade policies. While unilateral trade liberalisation under SAPs did more to open the economies of Africa than any regional economic organisation has been able to do, such liberalisation has not resulted in increased intra-regional trade among African countries. Instead, trade has been increased with the core states within the capitalist world economy. This increased trade, however, for the most part has been one-way, with the core countries having flooded the African periphery with more efficiently produced and/or cheaper products that, in certain cases, have caused massive industry closings or de-industrialisation.

During this period, the IMF and World Bank explicitly discouraged market integration because it was seen as being counterproductive to the neo-liberal orthodoxy that enhanced the power of the capitalist core to have unlimited ability to export to the African periphery in the name of efficiency and competition. Beginning in the early 1990s, however, these institutions began to support market integration. This reversal in policy was a reflection of the realisation that promoting trade liberalisation at the regional level first was more acceptable to African leaders than unilateral liberalisation at the global level. This was because it was reasoned that the impact of liberalisation would be less harsh at the regional level and give countries the opportunity to prepare to be competitive internationally. In practice, however, this idea was not implemented and African countries were forced to liberalise their trade regimes unilaterally.

In explaining the failure of the member states of ECOWAS to increase intra-regional trade, Otatunde Ojo notes that as a result of the negative impact unilateral liberalisation had on member countries during the 1980s, including de-industrialisation, there was no incentive for ECOWAS states to further liberalise their trade regimes. According to Ojo, 'governments, already losing revenue from the SAP-imposed liberalisation of external trade, have been in no mood to implement free trade further even at the regional level' (Ojo, 1999:122). It is the case that often high tariff barriers have remained in place due to the overwhelming dependence African countries have on customs revenue (see Oyejide, 1999:134–52).

Although there have been other important theoretical contributions to the regionalism debate, the neo-liberal agenda has remained dominant. This is the case despite what James Mittelman calls the 'contradiction between the openness of neo-liberal regionalism and its potential anti-regional thrust. In so far as open regionalism strives for a worldwide market and hooks directly into the global economy, it can skip over regional integration' (Mittelman, 1999:44). In Southern Africa, according to Bertil Odén, open regionalism is the dominant theoretical framework guiding the regional integration process, with globalisation forces influencing countries to open their economies to the world, at both the regional and national levels (Odén, 1999:167–8).

Mittelman proposes an alternative to the neo-liberal regional agenda in what he terms a partial defensive reaction from those that are excluded from the benefits of the globalisation process. Though only in an embryonic phase of development, Mittelman terms the strategy 'transformative regionalism'. Comparing it to the strategy of development integration, transformative regionalism calls for political cooperation at the beginning; equity and balance among member states (e.g. redistribution and regional industrial planning as a conduit for enhanced regional trade); an active state (e.g.

promoting exchange, building infrastructure); and regionalism that begins from the bottom and flows upwards. Such regionalism is to be linked to cultural identities that are new (e.g. environmentalists, women's movements, pro-democracy forces). The strength of transformative regionalism will rest on strong links with civil society. In the final analysis, sustainable growth and democracy will depend on popular support and multiple strata population involvement (Mittelman, 1999:48).

Transformative regionalism combines development integration with 'regionalism from below'. As previously indicated, regional organisations in the developing world have not been successful in implementing development integration (see the section entitled **Theories of Regional Integration**, above), and as will be discussed below, 'regionalism from below' also has never been successfully implemented.

The WIDER Approach

In the early 1990s, the World Institute for Development Economics Research (WIDER) of the UN University in Helsinki initiated a project on the new regionalism. The purpose of the project was to examine the new wave of worldwide regionalisation that went beyond classical integration theory. Emphasis was to be placed on social, political, economic, and cultural issues in the integration process (Hettne, 1999b:xv). The final product of the project was a five-volume edited series (Hettne *et al.*, 1999, 2000a, 2000b, 2000c, 2000d).

Compared to the other theoretical approaches to regionalism discussed in this chapter, the WIDER approach to the new regionalism, as its various authors acknowledge, lacks clear definition (Mistry, 1999:123) and is ambiguous (Odén, 1999:156). Kaisa Lähteenmäki and Jyrki Käkönen maintain that it is not possible to have a meaningful debate about the subject because the points of departure are so far apart (Lähteenmäki and Käkönen, 1999:204). According to Percy Mistry, the new regionalism lacks a rigorous methodology that captures and explains its costs and benefits. The strategy used for the latter tends to be elusive. In addition, the new regionalism 'is often perceived as being based more on emotion than on reason and placing a premium on rhetorical articulation than on analytical incisiveness' (Mistry, 1999:146–7).

Even the pioneer of the WIDER approach, Björn Hettne, admits that 'the new regionalism is a comprehensive process, not easy to grasp' (Hettne, 1999b:xxix). Finally, the new regionalism has been referred to as 'a big tent' that accommodates moderate views as well as extremist rhetoric (Rugman, 2001:15). In the remainder of this section, an attempt will be made to describe and critique several of the major perspectives within the WIDER approach.

Hettne defines the new regionalism as 'a multidimensional process of regional integration which includes economic, political, social and cultural aspects. It is a package rather than a single policy' (Hettne, 1999a:17). The point of departure for Hettne is that globalisation and regionalisation are part of the larger process of structural change taking place at the global level (Hettne, 1999a:2). The new regionalism is a response to globalisation processes, including efforts to initiate a 'counter-process of "deglobalization"' (Hettne, 1999a:6). Regionalisation is therefore 'the political corrective to globalised market-driven disorder and turbulence, not only on the level of the world but also in local systems' (Hettne *et al.*, 1999:xxxi). Hettne sees the development of a regionalised world order as an alternative to a globalised one, which is made possible by multipolarity (Hettne, 1999b:xviii). The model for the new regionalism is the EU, because it is the most advanced regional entity in the world (Hettne, 1994:12).

For Hettne, political issues are more important than economic ones. Instead of regionalism being created 'from above', by the superpowers, for example, the new regionalism is created 'from below' in that constituent states, as well as other actors, are the main entities spearheading regional integration. To this end, the new regionalism is considered to be a world order concept because it not only concerns itself with relations within the single region, but also between single regions. The regionalisation process thus shapes the way the world is configured, which is likely to entail a power structure consisting of core and peripheral regions, with the core divided along centre-periphery dynamics (Hettne, 1999a:7–8). While the core regions are stable politically and dynamic economically in order to facilitate world control, the peripheral regions are more turbulent politically and more stagnant economically. For the latter regions, the only option to arrest their marginalisation is to become more regionalised. Otherwise, they will become further disintegrated, with the most fragile states disappearing and being absorbed by stronger neighbours (Hettne, 1999b:xvii–xviii).

For Lähteenmäki and Käkönen, regionalisation within the new regionalism refers to 'subregional co-operation created from below, not by states or supra-national actors' (Lähteenmäki & Käkönen, 1999:204). As an example of regionalisation created from below, the authors note the 'Four Motors of Europe', based on an agreement between four European cities – Baden-Württemberg in Germany, Rhône Alps in France, Lombardy in Italy, and Catalonia in Spain. The cooperation among these four cities ('Four Motors') has been expanded to Ontario in Canada. Therefore the 'Four Motors' cooperation has gone beyond European borders. This sub-national regionalisation, however, is currently a European phenomenon (Lähteenmäki & Käkönen, 1999:211–12).

The new regionalism has been criticised for being Eurocentric (see Mittelman, 1999:30–3; Marchand *et al.*, 1999:903) and consequently, the end result is a biased under-standing of regionalisation (Marchand *et al.*, 1999:903). It is indeed ironic that the EU is deemed to be the most successful example of the operationlisation of the new regionalism theory, since it seemingly represents the total opposite of what the new regionalism stands for. With the EU, neo-classical economics forms the foundation for unity in the form of market integration theory; regionalism takes place 'from above' rather than 'below', with the state as the major actor; and politics is secondary to economic integration.

For marginalised African states, the new regionalism does not appear to be relevant. Even Hettne argues that African countries should instead rely on the further development of the model of development integration (Hettne, 1994:30), which partially informs Mittelman's strategy of transformative regionalism.

Theorists have attempted to compare the SADC approach to regional integration with that of the new regionalism (Hettne, 1994:31; Mittelman, 1999:30; Odén, 1999:169–70). Notwithstanding the fact that when SADC was created the major objectives of the organisation were more political than economic, it is certainly not the case today. As already discussed, at the centre of the SADC strategy is market integration, which includes efforts to increase intra-regional trade, investments, and capital flows. This, as well as SADC's sectoral development strategy, is being orchestrated at the state level from above as opposed to from below. Although there may be increased private sector involvement in the regionalisation process, for the most part such efforts take place at the request of the state or the SADC Secretariat.

Of primary importance to the SADC regional agenda is South Africa's economic hege-mony. Within the context of the new regionalism, Odén proposes two ways of looking at

SA exploits

South Africa's dominant position within SADC. In the first, the exploitative hegemonic model of regionalisation, the regional hegemon attempts to establish a regime that represents its short-run national interests by exploiting its partners. Tactics used to this end include coercion, authoritarian control, and negative sanctions. In the second, the benevolent hegemonic model of regionalisation, the regional hegemon facilitates relationships that are beneficial to itself and all other member states. To this end, the hegemon takes a long-run perspective on its national interests as well as those of the region (Odén, 1999:173).

For Samir Amin, the new regionalism comprises the creation of large integrated Third World regions (the periphery), especially in Africa and the Arab world, but also in Latin America and Southeast Asia. The creation of such regions represents the most effective response to the growing polarisation as a result of the globalisation process. Regionalisation, therefore, will help facilitate the creation of a global system that is different (Amin, 1999:54). The ultimate objective of the global restructuring would be to reduce further polarisation of the Third World. For Amin, the post-war system is one of 'global disorder' (Amin, 1999:62).

For Third World countries, this configuration of the new regionalism is viewed as a way to increase regional interrelations in order to enhance interdependence and therefore arrest the globalisation process, which results in their economies being linked to the developed countries based on the centre-periphery model (Odén, 1999:157). The approach has been criticised for not identifying the social forces that would facilitate the radical changes suggested (Odén, 1999:164).

New Regionalisms – Regionalism from Below

For the advocates of new regionalisms, regionalisation is on the one hand seen as an integral part of the globalisation process, but on the other it can serve as formal (including state-led) counterforces against this process, in the form, for example, of an economic development strategy. Regionalisation can also be reflective of transborder activities via the second or underground economy (Marchand *et al.*, 1999:900). The advocates contend that just as in social transformation processes that usually occur simultaneously, globalisation and regionalisation result in winners and losers. The latter are further marginalised, and groups of people, entire societies, and regions experience social exclusion (Marchand *et al.*, 1999:900).

For the new regionalisms theorists, the WIDER approach fails to capture the complexity of the dynamics of the regionalisation process. Consequently, there exists a need to challenge the approach with the development of a research agenda that focuses on the fact that a 'multitude of overlapping, disjunct and often contradictory regionalisation processes are currently going on'. Regionalisms in the plural, instead of the singular, should therefore be discussed (Marchand *et al.*, 1999:903).

The major actors in the new regionalisms construct are those in the informal sector. Its advocates note that

> [q]uite often it is here, and not in the formal economy, that we find considerable, albeit not always legal or sustainable, let alone desirable, imagination, innovation and entrepreneurship. The informal second economy covers a whole range of activities, from street vendors and small-scale informal cross-border trade to the warlordism of Sierra Leone and Somalia and the large and intricate cross-border smuggling of gem stones from Angola and Senegal, and drugs from Colombia, Nigeria and Burma to products of child labour in myriad enterprises around parts of the South, including ubiquitous Special Economic Zones (Bøås *et al.*, 1999:1065).

The need to attempt to connect both the formal and informal processes of regionalism is at the heart of the new regionalisms concept. Informal regionalisms (regionalism from below) include the networks and associations connected to the informal politics of small trade and smuggling and crime (Marchand *et al.*, 1999:906).

In terms of the way forward for countries in the South, Bøås *et al.* argue that the first order of business is for these countries to reject the EU model of market integration. The second order of business is to ensure that regional organisations reflect the economic reality of these countries. In many cases, the authors note, regional organisations are out of touch with the reality in Africa. Consequently, they fundamentally ignore the informal economy, which needs to be reattached to the formal economy (Bøås *et al.*, 1999:1065).

They further argue that states in the South should return to a 'Back to Basics' strategy that deals with existing formal and informal trade and cooperation networks. Formal regional organisation should be spearheaded from 'this multitude of informal (and formal) cross-border trade activity' (Bøås *et al.*, 1999:1066; see also Bøås, 2001:36). After all, according to Bøås, in Africa, both the study and practice of regional organisation should transcend the defunct state-centric approach, which should be seen as part of the past (Bøås, 2001:27).

Meagher accuses new regionalist analyses of Africa of showing 'a fascination for informal cross-border trade as a key feature of authentic integrationist initiatives' (Meagher, 2001:41–2). This is evident, for example, with the suggestion by Bøås *et al.* that formal regional organisation strategies in Africa should be spearheaded via informal cross-border trade flows. Christopher Clapham also is criticised for suggesting that the informal trading system in Africa is more effective in terms of economic integration. This is the case because the system is managed by indigenous traders and driven by the needs of the people. Regional integration strategies under the control of national and international bureaucracies are deemed to be ineffectual (Meagher, 2001:42).

For Meagher, the above ideas pose a serious problem because though touted as a new concept, the idea of using the informal economy (regionalism from below) as an avenue to spearhead formal regional integration in Africa is not new and has failed before. In fact, the concept dates back to the late 1980s and early 1990s and has its origins in mainstream neo-liberalists who were anti-regionalist. Such individuals argued that 'regionalism from below could be used to mobilise an internal constituency of neoliberal reform programmes'. This idea of 'integration from below was promoted under the neoliberal banner of trade liberalization as well as under the Francophone West African banner of regional food security' (Meagher, 2001:42). According to Meagher, the strategy of neo-liberal integration from below failed to promote liberalisation, food security, or integration. In addition, its impact was so disastrous, both politically and economically, that its advocates now revile it. The very activities that were supposed to spearhead regional integration became associated with criminal activities (e.g. rent-seeking, corruption, drug trafficking, the plunder of natural resources, and violent conflict). Consequently, informal trade networks have been abandoned by those pursuing a neo-liberal regional agenda (Meagher, 2001:42).

Of the criminal nature of these informal networks or trans-state regionalism, it is argued that such systems serve to undermine the formal regional agenda of countries. This is the case because they fail to promote inter-African trade (as opposed to import-export trade); undermine regional agricultural production and industrial development; have serious negative consequences for populations; challenge the legitimacy of the state, including its territorial control; and further challenge the fiscal capacity of the state (Meagher, 2001:45; Bach, 1999a:153, 161, 163).

In the end, according to Meagher, when placed within the context of liberalisation, informal cross-border trade does not contribute to regional integration and it erodes the prerequisites for such integration as well as potential productive investment (Meagher, 2001:45). Bach agrees with this analysis and argues that trans-state regionalism is limited as an avenue for facilitating formal cooperation endeavours (Bach, 1999a:164).

As a consequence of the above, Meagher suggests that in order to facilitate regional integration in Africa, the state needs to be strengthened. She rejects the notion by many of the new regionalism theorists and neo-liberal advocates that what is needed in Africa is less government. Instead, better government is needed that results in the ability of the state to respond to local, national, and regional interests, which have not been successfully addressed either by liberalisation or informal trade (Meagher, 2001:50).

In the meantime, informal networks or trans-state regionalism activities continue to thrive and in fact are often supported by the state (Bach, 1999a:152, 161; Meagher, 2001:44, 48). The reality is that for a large segment of the population in Africa, it is the only means of economic survival (Bach, 1999a:152, 160–1; Marchand *et al.*, 1999:903–4).

External Guarantors Model

Those advocating that the African regional agenda should be placed under the supervision of an external guarantor argue that mechanisms must be put in place to prevent the reversal of economic reforms and to enhance macroeconomic stability. With respect to the former, it is posited that the IMF, World Bank, and the donor community have not had the power to force African governments to maintain economic reform policies, many of which were implemented under SAPs. Consequently, most policy reforms are reversed, making macroeconomic stability elusive. Such stability, however, might be sustained if policies are anchored in an external guarantor in the form of reciprocal agreements.[13] Such agreements with more powerful governments, according to Helleiner, could possibly serve to 'lock in' reform policies and penalise governments for malfeasance or abrogation of the agreements. Foreign governments would therefore serve as an 'agency of restraint'. In the final analysis, this policy should enhance the credibility of governments, which will be reflected in a greater commitment not to reverse economic reforms. This in turn might improve the investment climate of the countries, since there will be greater assurances of macroeconomic stability, the non-reversal of incentives structures, the enforcement of contracts, and the containment of corruption (Helleiner, 1999:118).

With sustained economic growth as the ultimate rationale for closer regional integration, Jeffrey Fine and Stephen Yeo, in lending support to the external guarantors model, note that

> [w]e depart from traditional approaches to regional integration by suggesting that its virtues lie not in its ability to stimulate new trade, but rather in its ability to provide a framework for locking in sound and stable macroeconomic policies that will in turn induce faster accumulation, and more effective utilization of physical and human capital (Fine & Yeo, 1997:449).

The external guarantor of choice is the EU.

The external guarantor model has it roots in the West African Economic and Monetary Union (UEMOA). The UEMOA was established in 1993 by France and the countries who were members of the West African Economic Union (CEAO) and the West African Monetary Union (UMOA). These countries included Benin, Burkina-Faso, Côte d'Ivoire,

Mali, Mauritania, Niger, Senegal, and Togo. The UEMOA replaced both the CEAO and UMOA. The currency of these countries is linked to the French franc (Fine & Yeo, 1997:449). According to Fine and Yeo, France has deepened its economic commitment to these countries by establishing new multilateral institutions and through the surveillance of macroeconomic policies. The credibility of such policies ultimately rests with France and consequently the county has enhanced its role as a guarantor (Fine & Yeo, 1997:451).

The reality, however, is that France has maintained these economic links with Francophone Africa, established during colonial rule, in order to maintain economic and political control over these countries. The economic development of Francophone African countries is therefore not a priority of France. Consequently, this model for solving the problem of regionalism in Africa is reminiscent of suggestions that Africa needs to be recolonised. The solution to the problem of regionalism in Africa will have to come from within the continent, not from without.

The external guarantors model is said to be a replacement for the failed neo-liberal regional agenda. According to Meagher,

> neoliberal ideologues have created an even newer regionalism, which argues for regional integration as a 'collective agency of restraint' to 'lock in' neoliberal reforms in the interest, not of regional trade but of WTO-style multilateralism and foreign investment. As the key agents of a credible and self-propelling regionalism, forces from below have been dumped in favour of forces from outside, with a particular focus on the European Union (Meagher, 2001:41).

In the final analysis, the new regionalism, with respect to Africa, is criticised for not correcting the problems that resulted in past failures. These problems include unequal levels of economic development; causes of economic and political instability that have an impact on investment and the ability of countries to implement regional integration; the unequal distribution of gains; entities working against the integration project; and poor administrative capacity (Meagher, 2001:40–1).

Implications for Regionalism in Africa

The complex maze of 'new regionalism' theory does not raise any exciting issues for regionalism in Africa. Within the context of the processes of globalisation and regionalisation, the resurgent interest in regionalism in Africa is partially a reaction to globalisation and concerns about Africa being further marginalised within the world economy.

In terms of forces guiding the regional agenda in Africa, 'open regionalism' provides a better insight into how regionalism is being dictated than the 'WIDER approach'. In fact, the latter, for the most part, is obsolete when it comes to homing in on the dynamics of regionalism in Africa. The issues that are of relevance, such as centre-periphery dynamics and the behaviour of regional hegemons, have existed in the international relations and political economy literature for some time.

The open regionalism approach, on the other hand, reinforces the neo-liberal agenda that is being orchestrated from North America and Western Europe. The regionalisation process is being spearheaded in Africa largely vis-à-vis financial resources from the rich countries of the world with conditionalities attached. Notwithstanding the fact that market integration has failed miserably on the continent, there is no shortage, for example, of resources being expended to expedite market integration within SADC and COMESA. Market integration, along with fulfilling WTO obligations, results in greater openness and the creation of larger markets in Africa for North America and the EU. The ultimate *coup d'etat* is the creation of FTAs with African countries, which is foremost on the agenda of both the US and the EU.

Although the concept of 'regionalism from below' is not new, the recent literature on the subject has brought to the forefront the issue of informal cross-border trade networks and regionalism in Africa. On the one hand, such networks serve to economically sustain huge populations marginalised from formal economic structures. On the other, these same networks impede the formal regionalism process. African governments certainly need to find a way to reincorporate informal cross-border trade networks into formal economic structures in order to allow them to contribute positively to the African regional agenda. Contrary to what neo-liberalists argue, the state has an important role to play in African development at both the national and regional levels.

In the final analysis, African leaders must, as has been suggested, develop regional integration strategies that deal with African realities. With regionalism largely being orchestrated externally, this is indeed a daunting task. The real question to ponder is whether African governments have the power, commitment, and fortitude to transcend the practice of implementing 'neo-liberal market integration'.

Globalisation and Regionalisation

All the theorists within the new regionalism school of thought seem to concur that regionalisation and globalisation are simultaneous processes. However, as one critic notes, they do not seem to have clarity regarding whether regionalism serves to complement the processes of globalisation, or contradict such processes (Van Nieuwkerk, 2001:8). The regionalisation-versus-multilateralism/globalisation issue has been highly contested and there exists no shortage of perspectives on whether: (1) regionalisation is a stepping stone or stumbling block to multilateralism/globalisation;[14] (2) regionalisation is a response to globalisation;[15] or (3) the world is becoming more regionalised or globalised.[16] The current debate on regionalisation-versus-multilateralism/globalisation has its roots in the transformation of the world economy beginning in the mid-1980s.

As mentioned previously, until the mid-1980s, the US government was a strong advocate of multilateralism. This changed with the decision by the EU to create a single European market and the prolonged UR negotiations. Furthermore, the end of the Cold War caused the major world powers to reassess their overall commitment to multilateralism. Specifically, the Western allies became more concerned with their own national economic interests, and this was reinforced by the US under the Clinton administration, when a declaration was made 'that economic security had displaced the earlier concern with military security' (Gilpin, 2000:17). The US change was also reflected in increased economic unilateralism, the ratification of NAFTA, and the adoption of a managed trade policy toward Japan (Gilpin, 2000:17; Kegley & Wittkopf, 2001:275–8).

In Western Europe and Japan, as a reflection of the adoption of more nationalistic policies, countries were no longer as willing to follow American leadership. In Europe, Germany became more committed to European integration, and Japan became more committed to a Pacific Asian integrated regional economy. Thus the major powers of the world increased their interest in regional concerns (Gilpin, 2000:17).

As the world has become more regionalised among a select group of nations, it has also become more economically globalised, with, for example, enhanced worldwide foreign direct investment by transnational corporations, resulting in a major transformation of world production; greater interdependence among countries; increased transnational capital flows; and the rapid growth and integration of financial markets. It has even been posited by some that globalisation is creating one integrated global market (see Kegley & Wittkopf, 2001:293; Gray, 1998:1–7). The regionalisation/globalisation phenomenon, however, has proved to be too complex for such simplistic conclusions. In addition to the fact that many of the world powers responded to increased globalisation with increased regionalisation, many nations on the periphery of the world economy have been totally excluded from the globalisation/regionalisation process. As Gilpin notes, 'at the beginning of the new century, the largest segment of the world's population has scarcely been touched by economic globalization. Indeed, Africa and other impoverished regions are more threatened by marginalisation and neglect than by globalization and exploitation' (Gilpin, 2000:302). Others also lament the exclusion of large segments of people from globalisation and/or regionalisation (e.g. Oman, 1994:10; Kegley & Wittkopf, 2001:281; Wyatt-Walker, 2000:76).

Although the regionalisation/globalisation debate is largely centred around the three major issues identified at the beginning of this section, the most important question for the issue of regionalism in Africa is whether Africa is a player in either process.

While numerous scholars argue that regionalisation and globalisation are complementary processes (e.g. Gilpin, 2000:45; Rugman, 2001:15; Oman, 1994:11, 16, 36; Mittelman, 1999:25), there exists a growing body of literature that points to the reality that the three major trading blocs are becoming more regionalised in response to globalisation. In fact, Gilpin warns that '[a]t the opening of the twenty-first century, resolution of the tension between economic globalization and economic regionalization has become critically important to the health of the world economy' (Gilpin, 2000:44). The extent to which the world has become more regionalised around the three major trading blocs – North America, Europe, and Asia – is most evident by the patterns of intra-regional trade and FDI flows.

With respect to the issues of intra-regional trade, statistics indicate that the largest percentage of trade transpires among the member states of the three major trading blocs (Rugman, 2001, chap. 7; Kegley & Wittkopf, 2001:281–3; Gilpin, 2000:21, 169), often referred to as the triad. According to the *Handbook of International Statistics 1999*, almost 70 per cent of imports within Western Europe are accounted for by EU trade; over half of East Asian imports are accounted for by East Asian trade; and two-fifths of imports in North America are internal to the region (Kegley & Wittkopf, 2001:281). Within these regional blocs, protectionist policies are adopted that prevent the expansion of inter-regional trade (Kegley & Wittkopf, 2001:281; Rugman, 2001:10; Gilpin, 2000:295, 337). As Charles Kegley and Eugene Wittkopf note, 'many states remain tempted to enhance their domestic well-being by protectionist means even though, according to commercial liberalism, their relations within their trade partners will be undermined, reducing the benefits free trade would otherwise provide to both' (Kegley & Wittkopf, 2001:284–5).

Rugman argues that the triad blocs could become even more protectionist given the reality that they have in place NTBs to trade as well as investments. Such policies are designed to place limitations on access to their internal markets and/or to provide preferential access to specific partners in exchange for reciprocity. Such regional market access might be good for multinational enterprises (MNEs) based in the triad blocs, but this does not portend well for non-triad-based MNEs, since having access to a triad market is a prerequisite to the development of a global strategy (Rugman, 2001:10).

The protectionists policies implemented by the triad blocs against developing countries have left those countries further marginalised within the world economy. Such protectionism, Rugman predicts, will continue with an anticipated proliferation of regionally-based trade agreements (Rugman, 2001:204).

FDI flows by multinational corporations (MNCs) similarly tend to be concentrated within regions (Rugman, 2001, chap. 7; Kegley & Wittkopf, 2001:232; Oman, 1994:11; Gilpin, 2000:24). This is the case for several reasons. As a counterbalance to globalisation, the regionalisation of production and services has occurred at a rapid pace. For example, since NAFTA was ratified, many American firms have been using Mexico, as opposed to East Asia, for component production and assembly. Similarly, American cars are increasingly being produced in North America, while Japanese firms are importing a large percentage of their manufactured goods from the region and giving sub-contracts to East Asian firms (Gilpin, 2000:181). Fundamentally, the regionalisation of production and services is a reality among the triad blocs (Gilpin, 2000:182; Oman, 1994:17–18).

Another explanation for the regionalisation of production and services by MNCs stems from the reality that they are interested in large or potentially large markets (Gilpin, 2000:24). Protectionist voices in the Organisation for Economic Cooperation and Development (OECD) countries have also had an impact on the regionalisation of trading blocs. Populations in these countries have accused MNCs who have invested in low-wage economies of contributing to high unemployment levels in their home countries (Oman, 1994:18).

Also, it is suggested that with the regionalisation of production, regional economies can be insulated from currency fluctuations and trade wars (Gilpin, 2000:182). Finally, with less emphasis by MNCs on the importance of unskilled labour, natural resources, and factor endowments, the relocation of production to the actual consumers of products has been a growing trend (Gilpin, 2000:168; Oman, 1994:17). For Africa and other developing countries, the regionalisation of productions and services among the triad blocs means the loss of a major comparative advantage within the world economy – low-skilled, labour-intensive production (Oman, 1994:17).

There has been a great deal of debate about how best to arrest Africa's further marginalisation and integrate the continent within the world economy. This section has reinforced the complexity with which the world functions within the context of the two complicated processes of globalisation/multilateralism and regionalisation. What is most disconcerting about both processes is that Africa is seemingly excluded. Enhanced regionalisation in Africa then becomes the only option for arresting the continent's further marginalisation. As the world becomes more regionalised around the triad blocs, it seems that the only viable option for Africa is integration through these blocs. However, this can only be achieved through the regionalisation of production in Africa. Only strong regional markets can strengthen Africa's bargaining leverage in the global economy.

Within the context of strengthening the regionalisation of production, African regional hegemons, such as South Africa and Nigeria, must avoid tactics used by the triad blocs to enhance their access to regional markets by creating special economic relationships with these countries in the form of FTAs. Such agreements undermine the regional agenda and are very divisive. In a similar vein, the triad blocs must be prevented from establishing FTAs with African regional blocs. The removal of trade barriers against the exports of the rich countries of the world will only further undermine the economies of African countries. SAPs have already forced African countries to unilaterally liberalise their trade regimes. The consequences have been devastating to regionalism in Africa, and therefore FTAs will only serve to further challenge regional agendas in Africa.

The regionalisation of production will require African governments to utilise their competitive advantages in ways that will result in raw materials and other resources being developed for export from the region to the triad blocs. A significant portion of revenue generated from such exports should be reinvested in enhancing the productive capacity of regions to enable them to maintain their international competitiveness.

Notes

1 According to Gilpin (1987:27), these include classical, neo-classical, Keynesian, monetarist, Austrian, rational expectations, etc.

2 The World Bank introduced its first SAP in 1980. The policy prescriptions imposed by the IMF are known as stabilisation programmes. In 1986, however, the IMF got involved in structural adjustment with its structural adjustment loans (SALs). Once the IMF got involved in disbursing SALs, the combined programmes of the IMF (stabilisation) and World Bank (structural adjustment) became known as structural adjustment programmes (SAPs).

3 The other members were C. Fred Bergsten, Charles W. Calomiris, Tom Campbell, Edwin J. Feulner, W. Lee Hoskins, Richard L. Huber, Manuel H. Johnson, Jerome I. Levinson, Jeffrey Sachs, and Esteban Edward Tores.

4 While customs unions theory pre-dates Jacob Viner, he is seen as the originator of an approach that challenged the notion of the welfare-gaining properties of customs unions. In his seminal work, *The Customs Union Issue* (New York: Carnegie Endowment for International Peace, 1950), Viner challenged 'the old belief that customs union, representing a step toward free trade, will increase world welfare even if it does not lead to a world welfare maximum'. By introducing the now familiar concepts of trade creation and trade diversion, Viner demonstrated that there can be no general presumption as to the welfare orientation of a customs union. See Aly (1994:36).

5 Østegaard says that he does not know if it is fair to claim that the development integration model represents a separate theory (see p. 33).

6 This organisation is now defunct.

7 For a brief history of the EAC, see Chapter 3.

8 The OAU was officially transformed into the AU in July 2002. The Secretary-General of the OAU will become the President of the Executive Council of the AU.

9 For critiques of regional integration in Africa see, McCarthy (1996, 1999); Lyakurwa *et al.* (1997); Fine and Yeo (1997); Clapham (1998); and Mistry (2000).

10 WIDER stands for the World Institute for Development Economics Research of the United Nations University (Helsinki).

11 The multilaterialism/globalisation issue is a contested area. For example, while Odén suggest that the two terms are used simultaneously, including in World Bank and GATT documents (1999:175), Oman argues that the two terms are not the same (1994:31–2).

12 Odén (1999:157). Most economists adopt this position. See, for example, Wyatt-Walker (2000:80); Oman (1994:9); and Gilpin (2000:44).

13 The idea of an external guarantor has many supporters. See, for example, Helleiner (1999:117–18); McCarthy (1999:41–3); Oyejide (1999:151); Collier and Gunning (1999:91); Fine and Yeo (1997:437–42); Mistry (2000:561).

14 See, for example, Oman (1994:15–16, 36); Mistry (1999:126–7, 149–52); Rugman (2001:15); Hurrell (2000:55–6); Wyatt-Walter (2000:77); Gilpin (2000:45); De Melo and Panagariya (1992:4); Kegley and Wittkopf (2001:284–5).

15   See, for example, Oman (1994:9–10, 16, 36); Hurrell (2000:56); Gilpin (2000:13, 45); Hettne *et al.* (1999:xxxi); Amin (1999); Marchand *et al.* (1999); Bøås *et al.* (1999); Fawcett (2000:19, 26); Hettne (1999); Mistry (2000:157).

16   See, for example, Rugman (2001); Kegley and Wittkopf (2001:281); Oman (1994:11–12, 17–18); Wyatt-Walter (2000:74–5); Gilpin (2000: 24, 42, 168–70, 182).

From Coordination Conference to Development Community

FOR THE FIRST decade of its existence, the major function of SADCC was political, namely, to unite the region against the apartheid regime of South Africa. In this regard, SADCC's major objective was to reduce economic dependence on South Africa. This was to be achieved through regional cooperation and development. Such efforts were primarily funded by Western donors. This, in effect, forced Western governments to become more sensitised to the impact that the apartheid regime was having on the region. In its 1993 document, *Declaration Treaty and Protocol of Southern African Development Community*, the organisation acknowledged the political role it played in the region during its first decade by stating that, '[o]f all the contributions SADCC has made to regional development, the greatest has been in forging a regional identity and a sense of a common destiny among the countries and peoples of Southern Africa' (SADC, 1993:4) In fact, it was not until 1992, when SADCC was transformed into SADC, that the organisation began to focus on trade as a major part of its regional agenda. Notwithstanding this, the issue of regional development, security, and unity remained a central part of SADC's regional agenda.

The purpose of this chapter is to place the history of SADC in perspective. It begins by providing an overview of the SADC region. The second and third sections of the chapter outline SADC's past and present Programme of Action and institutional structures. This is followed by sections that place the SADC region in economic and political perspective.

The SADC Region

The SADC region is one of the wealthiest in the world, with an estimated population of 199 million. The vast resources of the region include oil, gold, diamonds, platinum, silver, coal, uranium, chromium, cobalt, iron ore, manganese, vanadium, copper, lead, nickel, tin, and zinc. In addition, once the hydroelectric potential of the region is developed, SADC member states will have the ability to electrify the entire continent.

The ability of the SADC member states to develop the region to its full potential only became a reality in 1994, when South Africa was transformed from a white-settler apartheid military state into a non-racial democracy. This transformation marked a major watershed in the history of the region because it officially ended white-settler domination. Such domination had its roots in the late fifteenth century, when the Portuguese sailed into the seas surrounding Southern Africa for the first time and later started to colonise Angola and Mozambique. By the end of the nineteenth century, the entire region had been successfully colonised by various European nations in the great scramble for Africa. The majority of

SADC member states[1] were encapsulated into what became known as the white hinterland of Southern Africa. At the helm of this hinterland was South Africa, wielding its economic and political muscle to ensure that all roads led to South Africa. As these nations gained their independence, commencing in the 1960s, the apartheid regime used both the carrot and the stick in an effort to maintain its regional economic and political hegemony. In 1979, on the eve of Zimbabwe's independence, a carrot was placed before the independent countries of the region to join South Africa, along with the four so-called independent states of South Africa – the Transkei, Ciskei, Bophuthatswana, and Venda – in a Constellation of Southern African States (CONSAS). As the regional economic hegemon, South Africa envisaged itself as continuing to maintain this position by enticing the independent nations of the region to join it in enhancing regional cooperation and development.

These nations declined the invitation to join CONSAS, and alternatively, in April 1980, the nine independent nations of Southern Africa (Angola, Botswana, Lesotho, Malawi, Mozambique, Swaziland, Tanzania, Zambia, and Zimbabwe) officially launched the Southern African Development Coordination Conference with the major objectives of decreasing regional economic dependence on South Africa and fostering regional development. Other objectives included the reduction of dependence in general; the forging of links to create a genuine and equitable regional integration; the mobilisation of resources to promote the implementation of national, inter-state, and regional policies; and concerted action to secure international cooperation within the framework of the strategy outlined for economic liberation (SADCC, 1980). The member states at the time agreed to focus on regional cooperation and development instead of market integration,[2] since, they argued, regional cooperation and development had to be the precursor to market integration, which was to be a future goal. The member states were united under a Memorandum of Understanding.

SADCC came into existence during the period of the growing militarisation of the apartheid regime. The history of the organisation, therefore, must be understood within the context of the uniqueness of the geopolitical and economic situation that the member states were confronted with at the time. It was precisely because of the unusual regional circumstances that SADCC developed a strategy that deviated from the EU model of market integration. After all, SADCC was designed to make a greater political statement than an economic one. In refusing to join CONSAS and denying South Africa membership in SADCC, the regional nations became victims of the apartheid regime's intensified regional destabilisation strategy, designed to make SADCC realise that regional development and cooperation were not possible without South Africa's participation.

During the period of regional destabilisation, South Africa was unofficially at war with three regional countries: Angola, Mozambique, and Namibia. South Africa had been involved in waging a war against the government of Angola since 1975, following the Portuguese *coup d'état* of 1974 that resulted in the announcement that both Angola and Mozambique would gain their independence in 1975. Determined that a Marxist government under the leadership of the People's Movement for the Liberation of Angola (MPLA) would not come to power, the apartheid regime supported the US-backed National Union for the Total Independence of Angola (UNITA) in an effort to guarantee its victory. The efforts by the US and South Africa failed, and by early 1976 the MPLA had gained control over the country. This was with the assistance of Cuban troops that had been sent into Angola by President Fidel Castro to prevent an MPLA defeat. With Cuban troops in the country, Angola became embroiled in the East-West conflict. When US President Ronald Reagan assumed office in 1981, Angola was identified as one of the countries where communism had to be 'rolled back' in accordance with the Reagan Doctrine.

South Africa's war against Angola continued throughout the 1970s, but intensified during April and May 1980, following a series of South African Defence Force (SADF) raids on villages. By the beginning of 1981, the SADF had occupied southern Angola, resulting in a permanent state of war in the country. The SADF conceded defeat in Angola by mid-1988, and on 22 December 1988, a cease-fire agreement was signed between Cuba, South Africa, and Angola (Lee, 1996:381–2). Although, in keeping with the cease-fire agreement, both Cuban and South African troops were eventually withdrawn, certain elements of the SADF continued to provide military support to UNITA. Peace remained elusive in Angola until 2002.

In the case of Mozambique, the SADF supported a dissident group, the Mozambique National Resistance (RENAMO), in an effort to destroy the Marxist-oriented government of the Mozambique Liberation Front (FRELIMO). RENAMO was created in 1974 as a 'pseudo-terrorist' organisation by the Rhodesian Intelligence services of the Rhodesian white-settler regime. In 1980, on the eve of Zimbabwe's independence, RENAMO forces were turned over to the SADF, and they began waging a war against the Mozambique government (Lee, 1996:382). A cease-fire agreement was finally reached between the FRELIMO government and RENAMO in 1992, and the first democratic elections were held in 1994.

South Africa's war in Namibia was for the most part against the South West Africa People's Organisation (SWAPO), a liberation movement that was fighting to end South Africa's illegal occupation of the country. The war, which lasted for over 20 years, ended in 1989, and the people of Namibia gained their independence on 21 March 1990.

In addition to the three 'unofficial' wars in Angola, Mozambique, and Namibia, regional destabilisation included the military invasions of capitals, the sabotage of regional infrastructures, killings and abductions, and support of dissident groups. Damage from destabilisation cost the member states US$60.5 billion between 1980 and 1988. There were at least a million deaths and millions were displaced.[3]

South African President P. W. Botha declared in 1989 that South Africa's strategy of regional destabilisation had been a success. The SADCC member states had increased, rather than decreased, their economic dependence on the apartheid regime, and the African National Congress (ANC) no longer had the ability to launch external military attacks against the regime (Lee, 1996:382–3).

In response to regional destabilisation, the SADCC member states rallied to get the international community to isolate the apartheid regime by imposing economic sanctions. There was even an attempt by the Zimbabwean government to impose economic sanctions against South Africa (see Lee, 1988:52–60). The political unrest that took place in South Africa between 1984 and 1986 resulted in the international community finally imposing economic sanctions against the apartheid regime. These sanctions had an impact on the decision made by President F. W. de Klerk, who came to power in September 1989, to end the policy of regional destabilisation and begin the long and arduous transition to a post-apartheid South Africa (Lee, 1997a:237–72).

In 1992, the SADCC member states determined that the time had come to move toward market integration. This decision was sparked by the changes occurring in South Africa and within the world economy. SADCC knew it could no longer have as a major objective decreasing economic dependence on the apartheid regime. Similarly, with enhanced globalisation and the creation of new trading blocs, the SADCC member states felt that market integration was necessary in order to prevent the region from becoming further marginalised within the world economy. This reassessment resulted in the rebirth of the organisation as the Southern African Development Community with the major objective of fostering market integration by implementing a strategy of development integration (see Chapter 1). The overall objectives of SADC are contained in Chapter 3, Article 5, of the 1992 SADC Treaty. They are to:

▶ Achieve development and economic growth, alleviate poverty, enhance the standard and quality of life of the peoples of Southern Africa and support the socially disadvantaged through regional integration;
▶ Evolve common political values, systems and institutions;
▶ Promote and defend peace and security;
▶ Promote self-sustaining development on the basis of collective self-reliance, and the interdependence of Member States;
▶ Achieve complementarity between national and regional strategies and programmes;
▶ Promote and maximise productive employment and utilisation of resources of the Region;
▶ Achieve sustainable utilisation of natural resources and effective protection of the environment;
▶ Strengthen and consolidate the long standing historical and cultural affinities and links among the peoples of the region (SADC, 1993).

In 2000, the SADC member states added to the above list of objectives the combating of HIV/AIDS and poverty eradication. With respect to the latter, Belmiro Malate, former SADC Focal Point for Mozambique, argues that one of the major reasons regional integration is not working among the member states is because of poverty. 'Market integration strategies will only work', according to Malate, 'unless somehow we begin to chip away at poverty and ease the fear of politicians. Regional integration is not working now because nobody is willing to compensate for their neighbours'.[4]

The 1992 SADC Treaty replaced the 1980 SADCC Memorandum of Understanding. By 1997, SADC had 14 member states (the original nine plus Namibia, South Africa, Mauritius, the DRC, and Seychelles).[5]

The 1992 transformation of SADCC into a development community must be placed in context, especially since the organisation was perhaps not ready for the transformation. As previously noted, when SADCC was created, the member states rejected the EU model of market integration, thus becoming the first regional economic organisation in Africa to do so. South Africa's policy of regional destabilisation, however, prevented the member states from actually implementing their unique strategy of regional cooperation and development. Consequently, in 1992, when the organisation was transformed into a development community, the fundamental reasons for the initial rejection of market integration had not changed. The markets of the regional countries remained undiversified and most countries had not developed comparative advantages, a requirement for market integration to be successful. In addition, the infrastructure of the region remained in need of great repair. Thus, without goods to trade and an infrastructure to get the goods to market, the member states were fundamentally no better off than in 1980, even though regional destabilisation had come to an end. Angola and Mozambique were still devastated economically, and other member states were regrouping from the changing geopolitics of the region. Therefore, the decision to move toward market integration seemingly was not realistic. So why did the member states at this juncture in their history resort to a strategy, market integration, that had failed miserably on the continent?

The decision by the SADC[6] member states to make the transformation from regional cooperation to market integration, prior to the foundation being laid for such a transformation, can be traced to SADC's origins, namely, that SADC was an external creation and continues to be largely controlled by Western governments and international financial institutions through their financial support of the organisation. Such support currently represents approximately 86 per cent of the organisation's funding. As an example of the ability of external actors to dictate SADC policy, in July 1998, US Trade Representative Charlene Barshefsky proposed that only those SADC member states that had signed the SADC Protocol on Trade would be eligible for a new US trade benefit designed to increase exports and expedite the formation of the free trade area (Lee, 2000:138). Why did Barshefsky feel that she could make such a statement? Perhaps because of the change in US policy toward SADC that began in 1996. According to Malate,

> [i]n 1996, the US began to have more interest in the region as a whole, but particularly in terms of SADC. In the past we used to have a program of cooperation, where they would give US$50 million for regional cooperation. That was a staple. But, in 1996, they changed. The feeling was they wanted to be more close to the region, not only from the economic point of view, but from the political. The first thing which happened was a memorandum of understanding which was signed between SADC and the American government, designed to promote trade and investment in the region, and the exchange of visits by the business community.[7]

More controversial than the question of external control of SADC is perhaps the issue of SADC's origin. For example, a great deal of the literature about SADC during the 1990s suggests that SADC was created by the Frontline States (FLS)[8] (see Mandaza & Tostensen, 1994, chap. 1; Van Rooyen, 1998:129; Tsikata, 1999; Matsebula, 1998) and in a SADC-commissioned study, the authors go to great lengths, albeit unsuccessfully, to dispel the myth that SADC was created by forces external to the region (see Mandaza & Tostensen, chap. 1). The reality is that SADC was created by external forces. Specifically, according to Daniel Ndlela, the first black consultant to be hired by the organisation, 'the idea of SADC was created in Brussels by a Briton, David Anderson'.[9] Anderson was Managing Director of the Commonwealth Fund for Technical Cooperation (CFTC). He developed the idea of SADC around 1978. As Ndlela notes:

> When Anderson retired from Brussels[10] he sold the idea to Southern African ambassadors in London, particularly the Tanzanian ambassador. The first mission to Africa on the creation of SADC started from London and not from any Southern African capital. Mr Anderson, in the company of an African diplomat, first travelled to Dar es Salaam and conferred with the then influential Tanzanian President Mwalimu Julius Nyerere, who gladly accepted the idea, but with the wise counsel of Julius Nyerere, the mission proceeded to Gaborone to brief the late President of Botswana Sir Seretse Khama. These were the true origins of SADC and the idea fitted in well with the aspirations of the Southern African states who were facing fierce destabilisation from the South African apartheid regime. Thus even after the establishment of SADC, the first Executive Secretary – a Zimbabwean national (Arthur Blummeris) – was retired from Brussels where he was Zimbabwe's ambassador, to come and lead the new organisation. At the SADC Secretariat in Botswana, British officials, including David Anderson, helped to maintain the secretariat.[11]

From the time the SADC Secretariat was established in Gaborone, until 1984, with the exception of the executive secretary (Blummeris) and his personal secretary, the office was staffed by British nationals, who also established SADC's institutional structure.[12] Nonetheless, the FLS bought into the idea of SADC and began to own it. The member states have remained committed to the organisation since its inception in 1980 and therefore SADC developed into a genuine African organisation. However, it was only after Blummeris' death in 1984 that the SADC Secretariat experienced a transformation from being predominantly staffed by British nationals to being staffed by Africans from throughout the region. This was under the leadership of Simba Makoni, who became the second executive secretary in June 1984.[13]

So why the attempt to re-write SADC's history to suggest that it was created by the FLS when it was not? Basically because politically African leaders deem it important that SADC be seen as a homegrown African initiative. As such, SADC garners greater regional and international credibility. It also allows Western governments and IFIs to feel they are supporting a legitimate, indigenous entity. This is extremely important in the wake of ongoing criticism that external actors continue to control the African economic agenda. For African scholars and politicians who know the true origins of SADC, it has been deemed politically incorrect to suggest that SADC was not the idea of the FLS. For Western governmental officials who were either intimately involved or privy to information regarding SADC's creation, it would have been counterproductive to publicly discuss the matter out of fear of the organisation being branded a creation of the 'imperialist' Western powers who just want to continue to have hegemonic control over Southern Africa. The issue of SADC's external creation was not ignored in the SADC literature of the 1980s written by African scholars (Amin *et al.*, 1987:8; Mandaza, 1987:215).

Not only was the organisation an external creation, but, as previously noted, the majority of the funding for SADC was provided by SADC's international cooperating partners, who included Western governments and IFIs. During the 1980s, SADC depended on such funding for over 90 per cent of its budget.

Although SADC was an external creation, it did not receive overwhelming political support from the West during the 1980s. For example, between 1980 and 1986, the West, especially the US government, indicated that it did not envisage the region developing without South Africa's participation. While some Western countries were giving money to fund SADC projects, they continued to support the apartheid regime. Thus, support for SADC seemingly was designed to distract from continued support given to the apartheid regime.[14]

While South Africa had the option of not joining SADC, the SADC member states had always envisaged a post-apartheid South Africa joining the organisation. With this in mind, beginning in 1990, the ANC and the Pan Africanist Congress (PAC) had observer status at the Annual Summit and Annual Consultative Conference. Nonetheless, when South Africa joined SADC, fears abounded that it would dominate the organisation, especially economically.

For the West, South Africa had always been deemed to be the conduit for the development of the region and the gateway to a larger regional market. SADC's decision to become a development community in 1992 with the major objective of fostering market or trade integration must be seen within the context of the geopolitics and economics of the world economy as directed by SADC's major donors. The reality is that if international funding were withdrawn, the organisation would probably not survive. Therefore, it appears that the current movement toward market or trade integration in the SADC region has largely been imposed externally and consequently the member states are being forced to attempt to integrate the region at a much more rapid pace than they have the capacity to.

SADC Programme of Action

As previously noted, at the heart of SADC's strategy when the organisation was created was regional cooperation and development. This was initially to be achieved through a project approach to development, which was later transformed into a strategy of sectoral development. This strategy became known as the SADC Programme of Action and each country was given a regional sector or sub-sector to coordinate. In this way, it was reasoned, each member state would be a direct participant in regional cooperation and development and would benefit from the exercise, albeit not necessarily at the same level.

Having a sector[15] to coordinate meant assuming responsibility for the development and implementation of projects in the sector throughout the region. In the country responsible for the sector, a Sector Coordinating Unit (see below) was established in the relevant ministry (e.g. in the case of Zimbabwe, the Ministry of Agriculture) and contact was established with a designated contact person within all the same ministries throughout the region. At the very foundation of this approach was the assumption that the country given the responsibility for coordinating a sector was the most qualified to do so. Under the best of circumstances, this was an extremely challenging job for any country to undertake. Because of the challenges faced by numerous countries in the coordination process, the idea of sectors being coordinated by countries, as will be discussed below, has been seriously criticised. The sector responsibilities under this structure are outlined below (see Figure 2.1, opposite).

At the February 2000 Annual Consultative Conference held in the valley of Ezulwini in Swaziland, it was reported that the Programme of Action consisted of approximately 378 projects with an estimated value of US$7.7 billion. Funding had been secured for 48 per cent of projects, while an additional eight per cent was under negotiation (SARDC, 2000).

From 1981 to 1996, the major purpose of the Annual Consultative Conferences was for the international cooperating partners (ICPs) to pledge support to specific projects.[16] Such pledges were given directly to member states and not to the SADC Secretariat in Botswana. It was at the Annual Consultative Conference that donor preferences for countries came to light and/or for the development of specific sectors. Prior to the conference, all the sector projects were prepared under the direction of the country responsible for the sector. During the conference, SADC's ICPs reviewed the projects within the sectors and decided which ones they wanted to support. Since all SADC member states presented projects within all the sectors for funding, the outcome of the exercise was perceived to be a win-win situation, because all countries received some level of funding. Although theoretically each country was to present well-developed projects that were of a regional nature, in practice this was not the case. In fact, a large percentage of the projects were more national than regional and therefore should not have been presented for funding. Projects that are considered to be of a regional nature are those that have an impact on at least two countries. An example of a regional project would be the development of a road between Zimbabwe and Mozambique that is used for the transport of goods. In many cases, projects were discussed in advance of the Consultative Conference, so the announcement of pledges became just a formality.

FIGURE 2.1

SADC Sectoral Responsibilities

Angola	Energy
Botswana	Agriculture research Livestock production Animal disease control
Lesotho	Environment and land management Water
Malawi	Inland fisheries Forestry Wildlife
Mauritius	Tourism
Mozambique	Culture, information and sports Transport and communications
Namibia	Marine fisheries and resources Legal sector
South Africa	Finance and investment Health
Swaziland	Human resources development
Tanzania	Industry and trade
Zambia	Employment and labour Mining
Zimbabwe	Crop sector Food, agriculture and natural resources

Although SADC could identify its priorities for sectoral development, this did not mean that the ICPs would support such priorities. A case in point was the 1984 Annual Consultative Conference held in Lusaka, Zambia. While SADC identified as its major priority the development of the regional transport and communications sector, in a position paper the US identified this sector as its third priority. Consequently, limited US funds were pledged for transport and communications. This decision was largely based on the fact that the US Congress had passed legislation that prevented Mozambique from receiving direct development assistance (Lee, 1989:248), as a result of its Marxist-oriented government. Mozambique is responsible for coordinating the SADC transport and communications sector.

During the 1990s, however, the US made a serious commitment to support the transport and communications sector, which continues to be a priority for SADC. SADC has also experienced its greatest success with project implementation in this sector. In fact, the larger majority of projects are in this sector, and during certain periods in SADC's history, they have represented almost half of all SADC projects. The Southern African Transport and Communications Commission (SATCC), located in Mozambique, has been responsible for coordinating the activities of this sector. The projects were divided into seven sub-sectors: roads, railways, ports, civil aviation, telecommunications, postal services, and meteorology.

Although it is impossible in this chapter to provide a summary of all the SADC sectors identified in Figure 2.1, the energy sector has been especially noteworthy. There have been 42 energy projects valued at US$530 million. A total of US$318 million had been secured from SADC's ICPs for project implementation, while an additional US$26 million was under negotiation (SADC, 2000a). The sub-sectors of the energy sector were petroleum, coal, electricity, new and renewable sources of energy, woodfuel, and energy conservation. Located within the electricity sub-sector is the Southern African Power Pool (SAPP). Established in 1995, the major objectives of SAPP are: (1) to enhance the efficient production of electricity and to increase the ability of countries to share electricity resources; (2) to ensure that eventually all SADC member states' electricity systems are interconnected; and (3) to extend electrical grids to rural and underserved communities in order to provide them with access to electricity (see *Business Day*, 22 February 2000; *Namibian*, 7 August 2000; Maasdorp, 1998).

As a result of SAPP, there has been a 15 per cent increase in inter-state electricity trade among SADC member states (*Namibian*, 7 August 2000). The SAPP coordination centre is located in Harare, Zimbabwe within the Zimbabwe Electricity Supply Authority (ZESA). Zimbabwe was chosen as the coordination centre 'because of its central location within the seven-member operating group whose systems are inter-connected' (Alexander's Gas & Oil Connections, 1997). The major objective of the centre is to coordinate the trading of power among SAPP members. Currently, good cooperation and trade exists between Lesotho, the DRC, Malawi, Mozambique, South Africa, Swaziland, Zambia, and Zimbabwe (*Namibian*, 7 August 2000).

There are two categories of SAPP membership – operating and non-operating (see Figure 2.2, below). The former group represents the national utilities of the SADC member states. These seven utility companies are the official members of SAPP, since membership is currently only extended to national utilities of SADC countries. The non-operating members are independent power producers and thus only have observer status (Chimowa, 1998).

FIGURE 2.2

SAPP Members

Operating members	Non-operating members
BPC – Botswana	ENE – Angola
EdM – Mozambique	ESCOM – Malawi
ESKOM – South Africa	LEC – Lesotho
NAMPOWER – Namibia	TANESCO – Tanzania
SNEL – DRC	SEB – Swaziland
ZESCO – Zambia	
ZESA – Zimbabwe	

In 1997, the SADC Secretariat commissioned a report to review the SADC Programme of Action. Among the conclusions of the consultants in the *Review and Rationalisation of the SADC Programme of Action* was that the large number of sectors and sub-sectors could not be sustained (SADC, 1997a:9). To this end, the consultants recommended that SADC should get rid of the sector approach and replace it with 'clusters of inter-locking co-operation arrangements which would be highly flexible and essentially reliant on regional resources'. In addition to the cluster approach resulting in a more fluid programme of action, it was argued that it would not be reliant on donor funds nor based on projects (SADC, 1997a:12).

The overwhelming majority of SADC member states, however, rejected this recommendation and decided to maintain the existing system. Of major concern for many members was that the clusters, which were to total five, would leave them without a sector to coordinate. The system of giving each member state a sector to coordinate has served as a major incentive to keep the smaller members involved in the SADC regional agenda. The end result was that member states tended to feel that they owned their respective sectors. Without this structure and the sense of ownership it fosters, the concern existed that it could have an impact on the degree of participation by some countries. In this respect, the SADC consultants even noted that the notion of ownership is very important and therefore the allocation of sector responsibilities must be maintained (SADC, 1997a:10). This, however, contradicts the above-mentioned recommendation of the consultants that SADC get rid of the sector approach. Notwithstanding this fact, there were ongoing discussions about finding a way to reform the existing system without compromising the unity of the organisation. At the Annual Summit, held in Windhoek, Namibia during August 2000, the member states once again postponed the long-awaited plans to restructure the organisation.

The SADC 1997 consultants' report also noted that approximately 70 per cent of funding for the Programme of Action was given by donors, which 'undermines SADC's ability to create and implement sustainable projects' (SADC, 1997a:25). This dependency on donors for the funding of SADC's Programme of Action had increased to 80 per cent, according to a November 2000 *Report of the SADC Council of Ministers* (SADC, 2000b:28). In order for this dependency on donor funding to be changed, the SADC member states will have to become more committed to financing their regional agenda. It has been suggested that one of the major reasons the organisation has remained united is precisely because each member state benefits from funding provided by SADC's ICPs.

With a view to becoming more self-reliant, the SADC member states plan to establish a regional development fund and develop investment programmes in order to generate additional funds for the SADC Programme of Action. The idea is to ensure sustainability of the Programme of Action. An integral part of the proposed strategy to make SADC more self-reliant entails the involvement of the private sector in helping to implement the SADC agenda (SADC, 2000b:29).

The SADC member states, in the above-mentioned *Report of the SADC Council of Ministers*, once again aimed to evaluate SADC with a view to restructuring it. Unlike previous evaluations, where external consultants had been hired, the SADC member states decided to undertake their own internal evaluation. The Council of Ministers recommended sweeping changes during a meeting in Midrand, South Africa, on 18–24 February 2001, at which time they endorsed a proposal to overhaul SADC's organisational structure (Madakufamba, 2001a). At an extraordinary SADC Summit held in Windhoek, Namibia on 9 March 2001, the heads of state and governments approved the restructuring programme.

With respect to the SADC Programme of Action, the Council of Ministers recommended that the sectoral approach be replaced by the above-mentioned cluster approach. This means that over a two-year period, SADC sectors will be replaced by four core clusters, which are:

▶   trade, finance, industry, and investment;
▶   infrastructure and services;

▶ food, agriculture, and natural resources; and

▶ social and human development.

The four clusters will be called directorates, with each headed by a director who will be recruited from the region. Each director will report to the chief director. The directorates will be under the SADC executive secretary. According to the *Report of the SADC Council of Ministers*, each directorate will have specific functions, as outlined in Figure 2.3. All four directorates will be under the Department of Strategic Planning, Gender and Development and Policy Harmonisation (see Figure 2.5, page 59).

Figure 2.3
SADC Directorates

Trade, finance, industry and investment:
Harmonization of policies, strategies and programmes in the following areas:

(a) Market integration;

(b) Macroeconomic domain;

(c) Investment promotion;

(d) Industrial development, particularly SMEs;

(e) Development of mining and beneficiation of mineral resources;

(f) Sustainable and equitable economic development;

(g) Inter-regional and multilateral economic cooperation;

(h) Functional, efficient and development-oriented financial sector; and

(i) The acquisition, adaptation and application of science and technology to enhance competitiveness.

Infrastructure and services:

(a) Harmonization of transport and communications policies;

(b) Coordination of development, maintenance and administration of transport, water and energy infrastructure;

(c) Promotion of an enabling environment for investment;

(d) Promotion of the development of physical and social infrastructure that contributes to poverty alleviation;

(e) Harmonization of energy policies, strategies and programmes;

(f) Coordinate the development of tourism infrastructure and related services.

Food, agriculture and natural resources:

(a) Ensuring sustainable food security policies and programmes;

(b) Harmonization in phytosanitary, sanitary, crop and animal husbandry policies;

(c) To develop measures to increase agricultural output and the development of agro-based industries;

(d) Harmonization of policies and programmes aimed at effective and sustainable utilization of natural resources such as water, wildlife, fisheries, forestry etc.;

(e) Development and harmonization of sound environmental management policies.

> **Social and human development and special programmes:**
> (a) Harmonization of educational, skills development and training policies, strategies and programmes;
> (b) Harmonization of policies towards social welfare for the vulnerable groups;
> (c) Harmonization of health care policies and standards;
> (d) To harmonize employment policies and labor standards;
> (e) To coordinate the development of policies to effectively combat the HIV/AIDS pandemic and all other communicable diseases;
> (f) To manage special programmes such as combating illicit drugs, small arms trafficking as well as demining;
> (g) To ensure the management of the SADC regional disaster management centre;
> (h) To harmonize and coordinate cultural, information and sports policies and programmes;
> (i) Harmonization of policies at local, national and regional level.

Source: SADC (2000b:21–3)

Although SADC documents indicate that the sectoral approach is being replaced by the directorates, in reality it appears that the sectoral approach is merely being reformed, with activities centralised under the SADC Secretariat. After 21 years, it is unrealistic to expect the member states to abandon overnight an approach that has become institutionalised.

The decision to reform the sectoral approach was influenced by the 1997 *Review and Rationalisation of the SADC Programme of Action* (SADC, 1997a, 1997b) report in which the consultants concluded that 80 per cent of all SADC projects had a strong national character as opposed to a regional character. Consequently, only 20 per cent of projects were priority regional projects (SADC, 2000b:8). This problem was created largely because SADC's decentralised institutional structure meant that there was no mechanism to force member states to be accountable to SADC as a regional economic organisation. The new centralised institutional structure discussed below is designed to remedy this problem. As a former chairperson of the SADC Council of Ministers noted, '[w]e want to centralise our institutions and operations so people know that they are duty-bound to carry out those functions and not just as an extracurricular activity which they do when they feel like doing it' (*Business Day*, 6 March 2001).

SADC's Institutional Structure

When SADC was created, a decentralised institutional structure was put in place. This structure was designed to prevent the problems that had plagued other regional economic organisations in Africa, where huge centralised bureaucratic structures often alienated members from participating in the regional agenda.

The original SADC institutional structure is outlined in Figure 2.4, overleaf. At the helm of SADC is the Summit, which consists of the SADC heads of state and government. The Summit is responsible for policy-making and control of the community. The Summit meets once a year and is headed by a chairperson and vice-chairperson that serve for a designated period of time. The Council of Ministers consists of ministers from each member state responsible for SADC affairs. Their task is to oversee SADC's development, advise the Summit on policy matters, and approve SADC policies, strategies, and programmes. Under the original structure, the council also identified sectors and allocated responsibilities for sectoral development. It meets at least once a year and the chairperson and vice-chairperson of the council represent the countries holding the positions of chairperson and vice-chairperson of the Summit (SADC, 2000a).

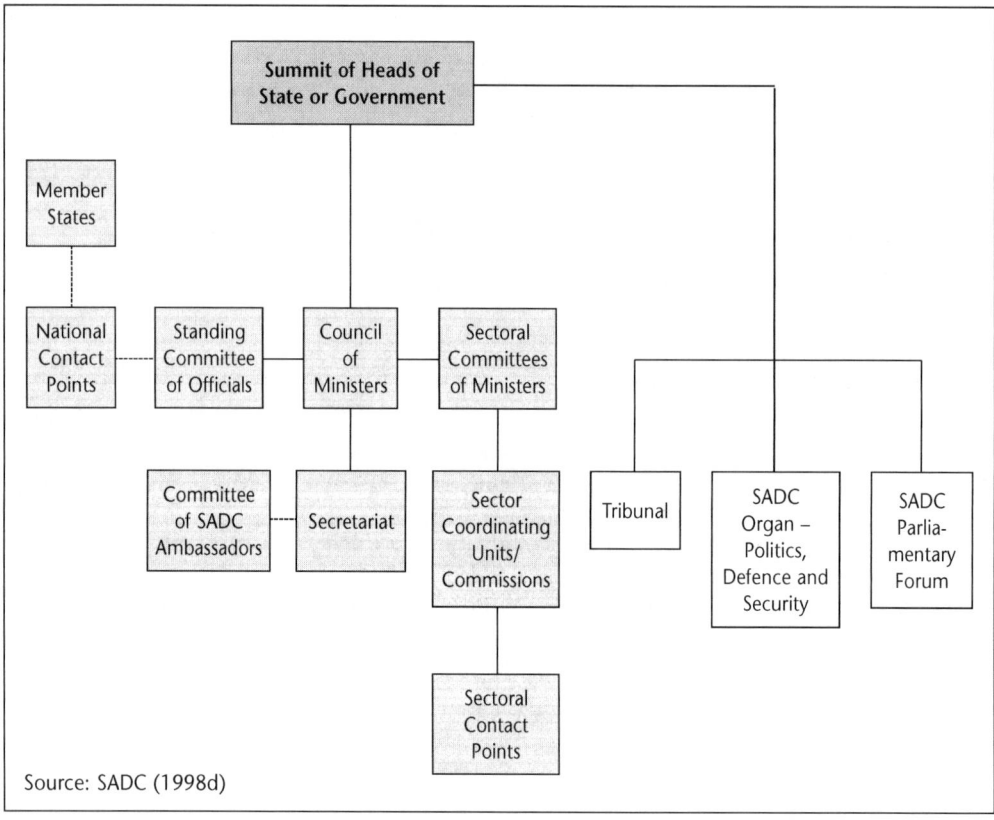

Source: SADC (1998d)

Figure 2.4: SADC's Original Institutional Structure

Each SADC sector had a Sectoral Committee of Ministers, which was chaired by the country responsible for coordinating the sector (SADC, 2000a). The Sectoral Committees of Ministers were responsible for supervising the activities of the Sectoral Coordinating Units (SCUs) and Commissions. The SCUs were responsible for guiding and coordinating regional policies and programmes in designated areas. SCUs were located within the specific ministry of the member state that is responsible for the coordination of a sector. For example, the SCU for the SADC Finance and Investment Sector Coordinating Unit (FISCU) was located within the South African Department of Finance. The sector coordinator for FISCU had to oversee the development of this sector throughout the entire region and therefore liaised with his or her counterparts in all other 13 member states, which were the Sectoral Contact Points. As previously mentioned, this was not an easy task, especially with the primitive communication systems that existed in some countries.

The task was made even more challenging by the fact that the sector coordinator was an employee of his or her country, and not of SADC. This meant that the coordinator had no autonomy and therefore was accountable to his or her employer, and not SADC. Consequently, this system was variously criticised as being, among other things, inefficient. In the *Review and Rationalisation* report, the consultants concluded that '[t]here is a continuing perception that the SCUs serve two masters; SADC and their parent Ministry' (SADC, 1997a:14). Very often it meant that SADC responsibilities were either not fulfilled in a timely manner or not fulfilled at all. Also, usually the parent ministry had to approve all SADC work, although the funding for the work had been paid for by one of SADC's ICPs.

SADC commissions, such as SATCC, are regional institutions. SATCC, as previously noted, is located in Maputo, Mozambique and oversees the implementation of the SADC Programme of Action for the transport and communications sector.

The Standing Committee of Officials consists of permanent secretaries, usually located within the ministries of foreign affairs. The Standing Committee of Officials reports to and advises the council. They meet at least once a year. The members of the committee have also been National Contact Points and thus served as conduits for interaction between government agencies and various SADC entities (SADC, 1997a:14).

At the heart of the decentralised structure of SADC was an inefficient and incompetent SADC Secretariat. In many respects, SADC executive secretaries have not been competent. The third executive secretary, Kaire Mbuende, is a case in point. In fact, he was officially fired by the heads of state and government at the Annual Summit held in Maputo, Mozambique in August 1999. For some time it has been the case that the last place to source information about SADC is from the SADC Secretariat. Prega Ramsamy, former SADC chief economist, replaced Mbuende as acting executive secretary in January 2000. He was selected as permanent SADC executive secretary at the extraordinary SADC Summit held in Windhoek, Namibia on 9 March 2001.

Previously, a SADC member state determined that it was its turn to have a national in charge of the SADC Secretariat, a candidate was nominated, and other member states supported the nomination. Consequently, the selection process was neither competitive nor democratic. This system changed dramatically at the extraordinary Summit in Windhoek. By March 2001, five countries had nominated candidates for executive secretary – Angola, Lesotho, Mauritius, Tanzania, and Swaziland. Although prior to the extraordinary Summit it had been agreed that the executive secretary would be selected at the August 2001 Annual Summit in Malawi, the President of Namibia and SADC Chair, Sam Nujoma, decided that the selection process should not be delayed. While several member states objected to Nujoma's decision, arguing that they needed more time to study the credentials of the candidates, as SADC Chair, Nujoma was able to move the process forward. Nujoma's insistence that the executive secretary be selected at the March Summit stemmed from the fact that he saw an opportunity to advance the candidacy of Albina Assis Africano, Angola's nominee for executive secretary. Concerned that Namibia and Angola wanted to avoid the proper procedure for selecting the executive secretary, the smaller states of SADC (Botswana, Lesotho, and Swaziland) threatened to withdraw from the organisation if the procedure was not followed.

According to newly agreed procedures for selecting the executive secretary, a selection committee is to be formed of neutral SADC countries, which are those that have not nominated candidates. In this case, the committee consisted of ministers from Malawi, Mozambique, Namibia, South Africa, and Zimbabwe (*Business Day*, 12 March 2001, 9

March 2001; *Zimbabwe Independent*, 16 March 2001; SARDC, 2001a). All candidates are interviewed, and the top three are presented for consideration to the Council of Ministers. In turn, the council selects the best candidate and recommends the person to the Summit.

As previously noted, Ramsamy was selected as the new SADC executive secretary. Ramsamy, who is from Mauritius, is considered to be highly competent. Prior to joining SADC, he worked for another regional economic organisation, COMESA. Countries that were opposed to Ramsamy becoming permanent SADC executive secretary raised concerns about what they perceive to be his limited vision for the organisation, namely, that trade takes priority over other regional development areas. Africano, Nujoma's preferred candidate, was deemed by some member states to be a person that would perhaps broaden and transform SADC's leadership. As a former minister of both petroleum and industry in Angola, Africano is also considered to be highly competent. While campaigning for the position of SADC executive secretary, she was Minister in the President's Office. It has been suggested that her candidacy may have been compromised because of gender bias. In addition, it appears that South Africa was ambivalent about the SADC Secretariat being under the leadership of an Angolan national (SARDC, 2001a).

Notwithstanding the criticism that the SADC Secretariat is inefficient and not cost effective, this is partially a result of the fact that, according to the SADC Council of Ministers, when SADC was transformed into a development community in 1992, the institutional structure was not revamped to accommodate the organisation's new agenda. The current difficulties and constraints with the institutional structure include:

▶ Lack of appropriate and effective regional institutions and management systems to spearhead the integration agenda;
▶ The need for mechanisms capable of achieving the high level of political commitment necessary to shape the scope and scale of the process of integration. That implied strengthening the powers and capacity of regional decision-making, coordinating and executing bodies;
▶ Lack of synergy between the objectives and strategies of the Treaty on one hand and the existing SADC Programme of Action (SPA) and the institutional framework on the other;
▶ Limited capacity to mobilise significant levels of the region's own resources for the implementation of its Programme;
▶ The relevance, management limitations and external financial overdependence [*sic*] of the SPA (SADC, 2000b:3–4).

In their *Review and Rationalisation of the SADC Programme of Action*, the SADC consultants severely criticised SADC's dependence on donor funding. With 86 per cent of funding coming from donors, and with SADC lacking a coherent framework for implementing its objectives, the consultants argue that 'the use of these resources is largely determined by donor rather than SADC priorities' (SADC, 1997a:4). They further noted that this phenomenon reinforces the dependency syndrome. Consequently, such funding should be decreased and replaced by regional resources (SADC, 1997a:14, 28).

By 2000, according to the *Report of the SADC Council of Ministers*, SADC's dependence on donor funding for the Programme of Action, as previously noted, was 80 per cent, which represents an increase over the 70 per cent level reported in the 1997 *Review and Rationalisation of the SADC Programme of Action*. This increase is interesting in light of the fact that the member states have not been able to efficiently utilise allocated funds (SADC, 1997b:4).

According to the *Report of the SADC Council of Ministers*, SADC's institutional structure will be changed drastically. Of special note is the planned transformation from a decentralised to a centralised structure. This will shift a significant amount of the responsibility for the operation of SADC from the member states to the SADC Secretariat. The latter, therefore, will be strengthened and given more power in the decision-making process. The new organisational structure is outlined in Figure 2.5 and explained in Figure 2.6.

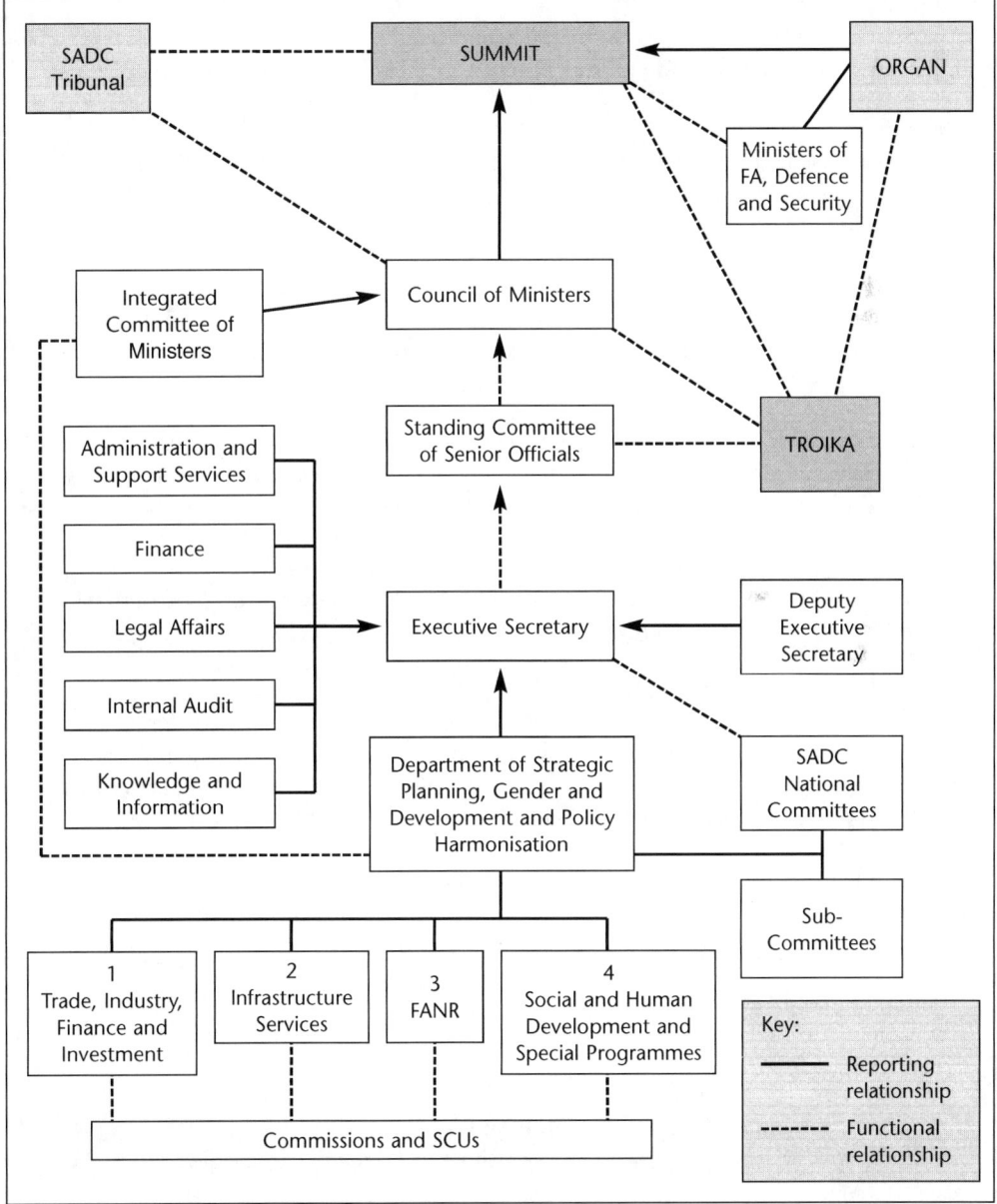

Figure 2.5: SADC's Proposed New Organisational Structure

FIGURE 2.6

Explanation of SADC's Proposed New Organisational Structure

Lines of communications and reporting relationships in above proposed structure will be as follows:

Summit
The Summit shall be the Supreme policy-making body for the Organization to which all other structures will be reporting through the Council of Ministers.

Organ[17]
The Organ shall be responsible for matters related to Politics, Defence and Security in the region. It shall operate on a Troika system and its Chairperson shall report to the Chairperson of the Summit.

The Troika
Shall comprise the Outgoing, Incumbent and Incoming Chairperson. The Troika system shall operate at the levels of Summit, Organ, Council and Standing Committee of Officials.

Council
The Council will oversee the effective implementation of SADC policies and programmes, with the Integrated Committee of Ministers reporting to it. The Council will be composed of Ministers responsible for SADC affairs in Member States and shall report to the Summit.

Tribunal
This is an autonomous legal body that deals with matters referred to it by Summit or Council for adjudication and advice.

The Integrated Committee of Ministers
The Integrated Committee of Ministers will be constituted by the Sectoral Committee of Ministers overseeing each of the core areas of cooperation, (namely Trade, Industry, Finance and Investment; Infrastructure and Services; Food, Agriculture and Natural Resources (FANR); Social and Human Development and Special Programmes) and shall report to Council.

Committee of Ministers of Foreign Affairs, Defence & Security
Shall report to the Organ. In addition, Ministers of Foreign Affairs shall meet as and when required.

Standing Committee of Senior Officials
This Committee shall be a technical advisory Committee to Council as provided for in the Treaty (article 13).

SADC National Committees and Sectoral Committees
These Committees will be working closely with the Secretariat to provide inputs from national levels.

Secretariat
Being the main executing organ of the organization the Secretariat has communication links with all policy organs and functionally reports to Council through the Committee of Senior Officials.

Functional Relationship within the Secretariat

The Executive Secretary
The Executive Secretary shall be the Chief Executive Officer of the Organization responsible for the overall functioning of the Secretariat and shall report to Council as provided for under Article 15 of the Treaty. In the performance of her/his duty, the Deputy Executive Secretary shall assist the Executive Secretary. In this regard, the Executive Secretary shall delegate some of his/her responsibilities to the Deputy.

The key institution within the Secretariat is the Department of Strategic Planning, Gender and Development and Policy Harmonization. The Chief Director shall report to the Executive Secretary and shall be the head this [*sic*] Department which shall comprise four Directorates as reflected in the Organogram. It has direct functional relationship with SADC National Committees and technically advises the Integrated Committees of Ministers.

Commissions and SCUs
While they continue to exist the Commissions and SCUs will technically report to the Executive Secretary through the Strategic Planning Department.

Legal Affairs, Internal Audit, Knowledge and Information, Finance, Administration and Support Services
Units shall report to the Office of the Executive Secretary.

Source: SADC (2000b, Annex 2)

In addition to the planned phase-in of a centralised institutional structure, it is anticipated that SADC commissions and SCUs will be phased out within the two-year period. It is not likely that either type of entity, however, will be phased out. In terms of SADC commissions, the SATCC has been one of the most efficient and successful SADC structures. With respect to the SCUs, they will likely be reformed to accommodate SADC's new institutional structure. It can be anticipated that SCUs will remain important avenues for the SADC Secretariat to liaise with SADC member states.

Of particular note with this new structure is the institutionalisation of the troika system, which will include member states holding the following positions: chair, vice-chair, and outgoing chair. This system will operate at the level of the Summit, the Organ on Politics Defence and Security, the Council of Ministers, and the Standing Committee of Officials (SADC, 2000b:18). This is SADC's way of putting a system of checks and balances in place.

On paper, the proposed restructuring of SADC looks promising. If the planned restructuring is actually implemented, SADC could be transformed into a more efficient and viable regional economic organisation. Raising the needed funds for the restructuring exercise might prove to be a serious challenge for the organisation. It has been estimated that the exercise will cost millions of dollars. This would include the hiring of new staff and the physical expansion of the secretariat to accommodate the staff. Such funding would have to come from member states at a time when the Council of Ministers is considering tightening sanctions against members who default on their membership dues (Madakufamba, 2001b). Notwithstanding this problem, Malate argues that overall there has been an increase in financial contributions made by member states to the organisation.[18]

The Region in Economic Perspective

The most pronounced economic realities in the SADC region are South Africa's economic hegemony and the unequal level of development among and within the member states. Both of these factors pose major challenges to the implementation of market integration and regionalism in general.

South Africa is the most industrialised regional country, and as Figure 2.7, opposite, indicates, it generates 71 per cent of the regional GNP. This figure, however, masks the reality of high South African unemployment and the fact that 53 per cent of the people live in poverty. In fact, poverty is increasing throughout the SADC region, with 73 per cent of the population living in poverty in Zambia, 70 per cent in Mozambique, 66 per cent in Swaziland, 60 per cent in Malawi, 47 per cent in Namibia, and 40 per cent in Botswana (SADC, 2000c:30). An estimated 80 per cent of the population now lives in poverty in Zimbabwe.

According to the UNDP *Human Development Report 2001*, seven SADC countries are classified as least developed. They are Angola, the DRC, Lesotho, Malawi, Mozambique, Tanzania, and Zambia (UNDP, 2001:259). The problem of poverty in the region is further exacerbated by the reality that Southern Africa has the highest HIV/AIDS infection rate in the world among teens and adults: South Africa (20 per cent), Lesotho (24 per cent), Zimbabwe (24 per cent), Swaziland (25 per cent), and Botswana (36 per cent) (UNIRIN, 5 May 2001). This means that the HIV/AIDS pandemic is threatening the productivity capacity of the region, since it is wreaking havoc on the able-bodied working class. The regional productivity capacity is also being challenged by the fact that in 2002, an estimated 13 million people were in need of food assistance as a result of a drought and government mismanagement. The countries affected were Lesotho, Malawi, Mozambique, Swaziland, Zambia, and Zimbabwe.

In the UNDP's 2001 report mentioned above, 162 countries in the world are ranked according to the quality of life afforded the population. The ranking is based on the Human Development Index (HDI), which includes life expectancy, adult literacy, and decent standards of living. The country that provides the best standard of living is Mauritius, which is ranked as 63 in the world. South Africa follows at number 94. The other SADC countries, with the exception of Seychelles, which is not included, are as follows: Namibia (111), Swaziland (113), Botswana (114), Zimbabwe (117), Lesotho (120), Tanzania (140), DRC (142), Zambia (143), Angola (146), Malawi (151), and Mozambique (157) (UNDP, 2001).

According to the UNDP's *Human Development Report 2002*, Seychelles has the highest HDI for all the SADC member states at 47. Since Seychelles was not included in the 2001 report, it is impossible to determine whether this figure represents an increase or decrease in the HDI. For the other SADC member states, the 2002 statistics reveal a decrease in the HDI over 2001. The numbers are as follows: Mauritius (67), South Africa (107), Namibia (122), Swaziland (125), Botswana (126), Zimbabwe (128), Lesotho (132), Tanzania (151),

Zambia (153), DRC (155), Angola (161), Malawi (163), and Mozambique (170) (UNDP, 2002). To put these changed figures into perspective, the 2002 report includes 173 countries, 11 more than the 2001 report. Eight of the new countries have an HDI that is higher than South Africa's HDI of 2001.[19]

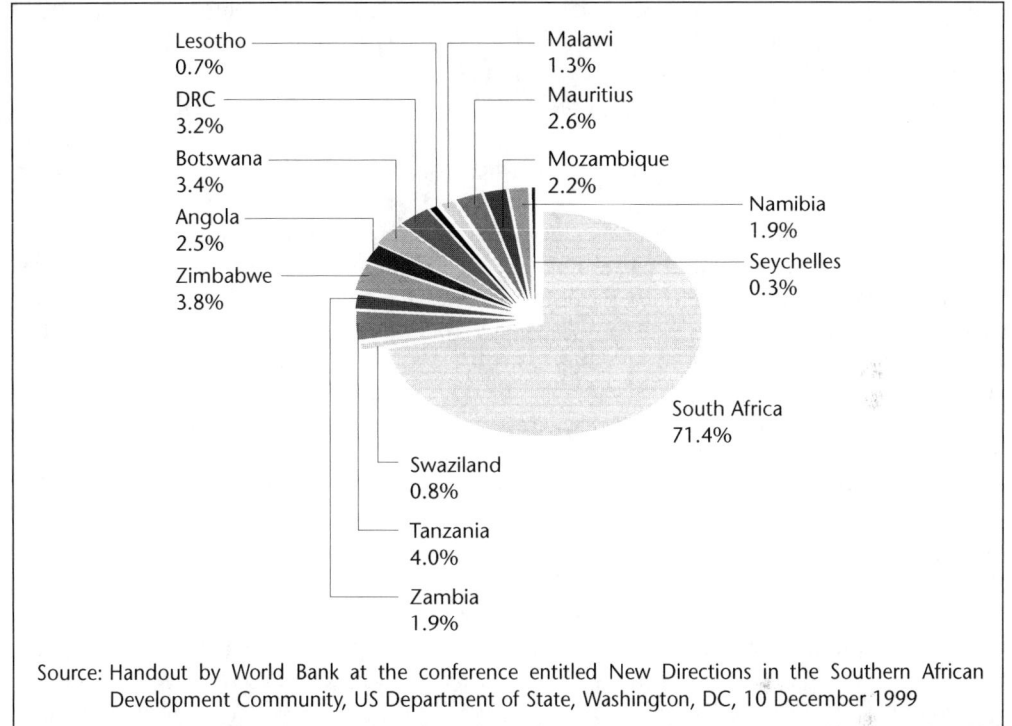

Lesotho 0.7%
DRC 3.2%
Botswana 3.4%
Angola 2.5%
Zimbabwe 3.8%
Malawi 1.3%
Mauritius 2.6%
Mozambique 2.2%
Namibia 1.9%
Seychelles 0.3%
South Africa 71.4%
Swaziland 0.8%
Tanzania 4.0%
Zambia 1.9%

Source: Handout by World Bank at the conference entitled New Directions in the Southern African Development Community, US Department of State, Washington, DC, 10 December 1999

Figure 2.7: South Africa's Regional Economic Hegemony (% of regional GNP)

South Africa's economic dominance is problematic and a source of contention for the other member states. Also problematic is the unequal level of development in the region. As the theoretical literature indicates, it is the regional giants that are the greatest beneficiaries of integration. How to foster some form of equitable regional integration given South Africa's economic dominance and the huge disparity in the level of economic development in the region is a major challenge. South Africa, as this book will show, has wielded its power and influence in a manner that has resulted in some member states being nostalgic about the days when South Africa was prevented from joining SADC. As the regional giant, South Africa is constantly challenged with finding a way to balance its desire to enhance integration with its regional neighbours as well as its international partners. Some perceive that South Africa has a greater commitment to integration at the international as opposed to the regional level. A case in point was the decision by South Africa to negotiate an FTA with the EU. This agreement is perceived as being counter-productive to the SADC regional agenda.

South Africa is not alone in being criticised for implementing economic policies that are counterproductive to this agenda. The country that is having the most devastating impact on the economic situation in the region is Zimbabwe. The political crisis in the country (see below) has resulted in foreign investors deciding that the SADC region is too unstable for investments. As a result, capital is fleeing the region. With respect to the SADC regional agenda, there has been a significant decrease in Zimbabwean exports to and imports from member states. This is having a negative impact on economic integration in the region. In addition, Zimbabwe has increased tariffs on imported goods, going against the new SADC tariff regime. The SADC regional agenda is further being compromised as a result of fuel shortages. Specifically, the National Railways of Zimbabwe (NZR) is having a difficult time maintaining its commitment to transport goods throughout the region. The thousands of refugees that are fleeing Zimbabwe into neighbouring states are also exacerbating the current economic crisis (Rushmere, 2001a, 2001b; Peat, 2001; *Freight & Trading Weekly*, 2001b).

Macroeconomic instability in Zimbabwe has reached a critical point, with inflation reaching 116 per cent during the first half of 2002. Zimbabwe also has high interest rates, serious foreign exchange shortages, increasing government debt, an overvalued and unstable national currency, and high levels of unemployment. In addition, the government has defaulted on its payments to the World Bank and IMF (Coughlin *et al.*, 2001:5).

Zimbabwe is not the only country experiencing macroeconomic instability. Angola and the DRC have triple-digit inflation rates. This is a result of the reality that no fiscal or monetary policy exists in either country as a result of political instability (UN, 2001:95–6). Consequently, there are high levels of unemployment in both countries. Malawi also has high inflation and interest rates, along with an unstable currency. Over the last ten years, the Malawi kwacha has been devalued against the US dollar by 2 220 per cent (Coughlin & Undenge, 2001:5). Malawi also has a high level of unemployment.

Macroeconomic instability in Zambia is characterised by high inflation and interest rates, slow growth, low levels of foreign reserves, and an unstable currency. While in 1992, the exchange rate for the Zambia kwacha was ZK172 to one US dollar, by mid-November 2000, the rate was ZK3 550 to one US dollar (Rubin & Mudenda, 2001:5). Unemployment is also a major problem.

Although Tanzania's macroeconomic environment has begun to stabilise as a result of economic reforms, the country remains extremely poor, continues to experience slow growth, and has large budget deficits (Coughlin & Mworia, 2001:4). Swaziland has high levels of unemployment and slow growth (Rubin, 2001b:3). Although in Mozambique the macroeconomic environment is relatively stable, with fast growth, low to moderate inflation, moderate interest rates, and a high rate of investment (Coughlin, 2001:5), a large percentage of the government's revenue is provided by grants and loans from the international community. Consequently, it is difficult to classify Mozambique as stable economically. In addition, the country has a high rate of unemployment.

Although Namibia is relatively stable economically, the country has a high level of unemployment (Jeetah, 2001:2), and concerns have been raised about the skyrocketing budget deficit (*Namibian*, 25 October 2001). In May 2001, the IMF warned that Lesotho should take measures to curb spending in light of slow growth, high levels of unemployment, and poverty (UNIRIN, 5 May 2001).

Botswana, Mauritius, and South Africa have the strongest economies in the region. Botswana continues to have one of the fastest growing economies in the world and is considered to be the safest place for investments in Africa (Rubin, 2001a:3). As a result of a

GDP growth rate of seven per cent in 2000, Mauritius was classified as one of the best performing developing countries (UN, 2001:93). Nonetheless, Mauritius has a problem with growing unemployment and increasing economic inequalities (Jeetah & Coughlin, 2001:7).

Although over half a million jobs have been lost in the formal economic sector since 1994, and the socio-economic conditions of the majority of people have become worse, the government of South Africa has been successful in stabilising the economy. Inflation is low and the budget deficit has been reduced significantly. The government has not, however, been able to reach its targeted growth rate of six per cent (Jafta & Jeetah, 2001:13). At the end of 2001, the South African rand reached an all-time low against the US dollar. The decline in the value of the rand is said to be partially the result of the crisis in Zimbabwe (BusinessMap, 2001b).

South Africa's economic dominance, the huge economic disparity that exists among member states, macroeconomic instability, the HIV/AIDS pandemic, and growing poverty are not conducive to the implementation of market integration. A priority of SADC must be to remedy these problems, if regionalism in Southern Africa is going to be a success. A successful SADC regional strategy, however, must be dictated by the economic realities of the region.

The Region in Political Perspective

SADC's *raison d'être* as an entity to unify the region politically has been severely challenged in the post-apartheid era. The regional political divisions seemingly initially emanated from personality clashes between former President Nelson Mandela of South Africa and President Robert Mugabe of Zimbabwe. This clash came to a head in 1996 with the creation of the SADC Organ on Politics, Defence and Security. The Organ was created ostensibly to replace the FLS. As we have seen, the FLS had been established in the 1970s with the objective of forcing an end to white minority rule in Southern Africa. Having been successful in this endeavour, it was abolished in 1994, and replaced by the Organ in 1996, to serve as a conduit for peace and security in the region. Mugabe, as the longest serving head of state in the region, became head of the Organ.

The initial clash between Mandela and Mugabe seemingly grew out of the latter's perception that Mandela had usurped his longstanding position as the leader of the SADC member states.[20] Upon being released from prison, not only did Mandela become the heir apparent to this position, but many international organisations left Zimbabwe and headed south. In addition, from 1980, when SADC was created, until 1996, the chairperson of the SADC Summit had always been the president of Botswana, ostensibly since the SADC Secretariat was located in Gaborone, Botswana. This changed, however, in 1996, when Mandela became chair. The clash between Mandela and Mugabe was kept in perspective until June 1996, however, when the SADC Organ was created.

Upon its creation, the Organ became a major point of serious contention between Mandela and Mugabe. Following its establishment, a rift developed between those (led by South Africa) who felt that the Organ should be integrated into SADC and report to the SADC Summit, and the others (led by Zimbabwe) who felt that the Organ should be autonomous and have its own Summit (Matlosa, 2000:15). At the time President Mandela, as Chairperson of SADC, announced that if the Organ were given autonomy, South Africa would relinquish the chairmanship of SADC (Matlosa, 2000:16).

Before this conflict could be resolved, the divisions among the member states were further intensified when, on behalf of the Organ, Zimbabwe, Angola, and Namibia intervened in the conflict in the DRC to prevent the country from being invaded by DRC President Laurent Kabila's enemies, Rwanda and Uganda. Although the SADC member states eventually gave public support to this endeavour, in private, Zimbabwe's intervention (along with that of Angola and Namibia) further divided SADC. This became most evident in April 1999 when Zimbabwe, the DRC, Angola, and Namibia signed their own defence pact, which excluded the other SADC member states. Mugabe, however, was eventually reined in by SADC at the Maputo Summit in August 1999, when he was told that he could not take action in the name of the Organ without first consulting the past chairperson of SADC (President Mbeki, representing South Africa), the current chairperson of SADC (President Joaquim Chissano of Mozambique), and the future chairperson (President Sam Nujoma of Namibia) (*Daily Mail & Guardian Online*, 17 September 1999).

The current division among the member states does not bode well for the implementation of SADC's regional agenda. In fact, a South African scholar has noted that 'SADC is highly personalized', which explains why the current President of South Africa, Thabo Mbeki, has not been focusing on promoting the SADC regional agenda.[21]

The problem of the Organ appeared to be solved during an extraordinary meeting held in Swaziland on 26–27 October 1999, between the Inter-State Security and Defense Committee, a former arm of the FLS that has been integrated into the Organ, and SADC ministers of foreign affairs. The Organ, according to the participants, was in fact part of SADC and consequently it should report to the SADC Summit. An agreement was also reached on the process for refining the draft protocol of the Organ as well as a Defence Pact (Matlosa, 2000:19). The draft protocol was to be presented at the next Annual Summit for ratification by the SADC heads of state and government. Nonetheless, during the next Summit (August 2000) the member states did not resolve the issue of the Organ.

Under the proposed new SADC structure, as indicated above, the Organ will report directly to the Summit (see Figure 2.5, page 59). In addition:

▶ The Organ should be coordinated at the level of Summit on a Troika basis and reporting to [*sic*] the Chairperson of SADC.
▶ The Chairperson and Vice Chairperson of the Organ shall be on a rotation basis for a period of one year.
▶ The Secretariat of the Organ shall be staffed by the Member State holding the Chairpersonship of the Organ (SADC, 2000b:16).

With this structure, Mugabe lost the struggle to have the Organ as an autonomous entity. In August 2001, President Joaquim Chissano of Mozambique became the new Chairperson of the Organ and the President of Tanzania, Benjamin Mkapa, was elected as Deputy Chairperson.

The resolving of the conflict over the Organ, however, will not diminish the deep-rooted animosities and divisions that have erupted in the region since the DRC became a member of SADC. The decision to allow the DRC to join the organisation was undemocratic, led by Mandela. According to the SADC treaty, new members are to be admitted into the organisation based on a unanimous decision by all existing members. This did not occur in the case of the DRC. Mandela, in pushing for the DRC to become a member, reasoned that Kabila could be better controlled inside SADC. According to Christopher Landsberg, Kabila was even offered post-reconstruction aid if he would toe the line (Landsberg,

2000:3). It was not long, however, before the DRC's membership of SADC resulted in the organisation being Balkanised, with Kabila, for example, accusing South Africa of being arrogant and attempting to export South Africa democracy to the DRC, as well as to the continent at large (Landsberg, 2000:3).

In September 1998, South Africa intervened in Lesotho to restore political stability to the country. When South Africa in turn did not intervene in the DRC, Kabila, Mugabe, Nujoma, and President dos Santos of Angola accused South Africa of promoting a double standard in that it had refused to intervene in the DRC on the side of Kabila. These four presidents also accused South Africa of promoting 'regional apartheid' (Landsberg, 2000:3). South Africa was further accused of siding with the forces that were attempting to topple Kabila's government – Uganda, Rwanda, and the Congolese rebels. With respect to the latter, it was felt that the South African government was harbouring them (Landsberg, 2000:3). In the mean time, South Africa was selling arms to Uganda and Rwanda while refusing to sell arms to Kabila, although it was simultaneously selling weapons to Namibia and Zimbabwe (Landsberg, 2000:3).

Notwithstanding South Africa's mistakes in trying to resolve the conflict during Mandela's presidency,[22] President Thabo Mbeki has made resolving the conflict in the Great Lakes Region South Africa's number one foreign policy preoccupation. To this end, he attempted to begin repairing the rift between South Africa and Zimbabwe (the current crisis in Zimbabwe, discussed below, has prevented the countries from resolving their differences). In addition, South Africa took an active role, under the leadership of its foreign minister, Nkosazana Dlamini-Zuma, in attempting to bring about a negotiated settlement to the conflict in the DRC. South Africa was instrumental in laying the foundation for the 1999 Lusaka Peace Accords that resulted in a cease-fire among the warring factions, although it was short-lived. In addition, the Mbeki government played a significant role in convincing the UN to create a peacekeeping force for the DRC – the United Nations Mission for the Congo, established in January 2000. This marked a major shift in policy from the Mandela government, which was interested in a peacemaking, not peacekeeping, role in the DRC. The Mbeki government has allocated R80–100 million for the UN peacekeeping mission and has pledged an additional R1 million for a joint military council (Landsberg, 2000:5–6). Many in the region and throughout the world were hopeful that progress toward resolving the conflict in the DRC would be made following the January 2001 assassination of Kabila, who had refused to implement the Lusaka Accords designed to end the war in the DRC. On 30 July 2002, the governments of the DRC and Rwanda signed a peace pact to end the four-year war. Sceptics of the peace pact, which was brokered by Mbeki and UN Secretary-General Kofi Annan, are concerned that peace and stability in the region will remain elusive.

In addition to the conflict in the DRC, the protracted war in Angola (which ended in 2002) further destabilised the region. In fact, as a result of the wars, neither country was able to participate in the negotiations for the creation of the SADC FTA. There are several other governments that continue to resist the institutionalisation of a culture of democracy, thus increasing the level of political instability in the region. These include Swaziland, Zambia, Malawi, and Zimbabwe. The current political instability in Zimbabwe is having the greatest impact on the ten other countries that are signatories to the SADC FTA.

During the first half of 2000, a wave of violence was unleashed in Zimbabwe that has resulted in the country seemingly spiralling into an abyss. Initially, the major target of this violence was the estimated 4 500 white commercial farmers, who for two decades under majority rule maintained control over 70 per cent of the most fertile agricultural land in the country. Eventually, the victims of violence included anyone who appeared to be opposed to the Zimbabwean government.

The unleashing of government-sanctioned violence followed the rejection by voters in February 2000 of a referendum that would have allowed President Mugabe's government to change the colonially imposed Lancaster House Constitution and replace it with a constitution that had been drafted by the government-created Constitutional Commission. The draft constitution would have allowed Mugabe and the ruling party, the Zimbabwe African National Union – Patriotic Front (ZANU-PF), to further consolidate its power. One of the most controversial aspects of the draft constitution would have given the government authority to expropriate land from white commercial farmers without compensation, thus freeing the land for redistribution to peasants, war veterans, and the urban poor. While the need to redistribute the land in a more equitable manner was not controversial, concerns, however, were raised about the potential economic consequences for the country if the ZANU-PF strategy were adopted. In addition, a large percentage of the population was convinced that the government was not genuinely concerned about land redistribution, but was merely once again politicising the land issue in a desperate attempt to win the forthcoming parliamentary elections (e.g. see Hanekom, 2000; Krieger, 2000; Alexander, 2000; *Daily Mail & Guardian*, 16 May 2000; Matshe, 2000; Cornwell, 2000).

The struggle to defeat the February 2000 referendum was led by the National Constitutional Assembly and the Movement for Democratic Change (MDC). The leader of the MDC is Morgan Tsvangarai, the former leader of the Zimbabwe Congress of Trade Unions (ZCTU). The MDC was established in 1999 by the ZCTU. Over a very short period, many began to view the MDC as a viable option to ZANU-PF, and Tsvangarai as an alternative to Mugabe (Alexander, 2000).

Although initially Mugabe indicated that he would abide by the decision of the electorate with respect to the referendum, by the end of February he announced that the Lancaster House Constitution would be amended to allow the government to expropriate white commercial farms without compensation. To this end he called on war veterans and landless peasants to invade the farms in an effort to undo the injustices that had been inflicted on Zimbabweans since the British stole the land from the indigenous population during colonial rule. On 23 May 2000, the constitution was amended for the sixteenth time, allowing for the seizure of white commercial farmland. The Land Acquisition Act was also amended. With what was termed 'fast track' land resettlement, the government indicated it intended to expropriate five million hectares of white commercial farmland for redistribution to 500 000 families.

The call for land invasions came in the wake of plans for parliamentary elections, which were eventually scheduled for 23 and 24 June 2000. Sensing that the referendum defeat signalled a possible defeat at the polls, Mugabe and ZANU-PF knew that the unresolved land question could once again be used as a tactic to garner the support of Mugabe's loyal followers – the war veterans and the landless peasants. Organised into militia-style groups of 20–30, the war veterans and young men specifically recruited for the purpose opened a campaign of intimidation against white farmers and MDC supporters. The militias received direct and indirect support from ZANU-PF national and local leaders, the Central Intelligence Organisation, the military, and the police, with the latter having been given orders by ZANU-PF not to arrest the farm invaders. In executing their violent attacks, the militias would recruit others to assist, including landless peasants. The actual attackers would number in the hundreds (Zimbabwe Human Rights NGOs Forum, 2000).

The targets of the pre-election violence were MDC supporters (many of whom were white commercial farmers and their farm workers), members of other political parties, and individuals who were apolitical. Although initially the violence was perpetrated against white commercial farmers and their workers, as the June election grew nearer, the militias began indiscriminately attacking other groups and individuals throughout the country. Throughout the pre-election violence, the Mugabe government resisted calls by the judiciary to restore law and order and to remove the farm invaders from lands that were being occupied illegally. Prior to the elections, 841 white commercial farms had been identified for seizure.

The Mugabe government also ignored efforts made by the SADC member states (especially South Africa) and the international community to resolve the conflict peacefully. ZANU-PF was not intimidated by the threat of further suspension of financial aid amidst increased unemployment, foreign currency and fuel shortages, and soaring inflation.

The June parliamentary elections were conducted in a relatively peaceful environment, although at least 35 people were killed during the run-up to elections. For the first time since coming to power in 1980, however, ZANU-PF's political power was seriously challenged. With 60 per cent of eligible voters going to the polls, ZANU-PF only won 62 of the 120 elected seats in parliament, with the opposition MDC winning 57 seats. In the previous election, ZANU-PF had won 117 of the elected seats, with the opposition winning only three seats. However, with Mugabe's ability to make 30 presidential appointments, ZANU-PF retained its parliamentary majority (Krieger, 2000:446; Cornwell, 2000:1–2).

The Zimbabwe presidential election was held on 9–11 March 2002. Mugabe won the election, which was marred by the disenfranchisement of thousands of urban voters, and the abrogation of the rule of law, including political violence, intimidation against the opposition, lack of freedom of the press, and judiciary irregularities. According to John Makumbe,

> [i]nternational observer teams differed in their reports on the presidential election. The Commonwealth Observer Group, along with the Norwegian, Ghana and SADC Parliamentary Forum teams strongly condemned the election arguing that it was held in a climate of fear. They agreed that the conditions under which the election was held were far from peaceful, and not conducive to the holding of free and fair democratic elections. The Nigerian, South African and Namibian teams, however, deemed the election to be free and fair. The Organisation of African Unity team claimed that in general, the election was transparent, credible, free and fair. Some teams went further to indicate that the election results were a true reflection of the wishes of the people of Zimbabwe. Most damaging to the regime was the Commonwealth Observer Mission's report that deemed the election not free and not fair. The result was that Zimbabwe was suspended from the councils of the Commonwealth for a period of twelve months. Practically all Zimbabwean civic observer teams condemned the manner in which the elections were conducted and declared them not free and not fair (Makumbe, forthcoming).

The political violence in Zimbabwe has, and will continue to have, a devastating impact on the country. Socially, the country is faced with a population of victims that will remain psychologically traumatised for some time to come. Once a very peaceful society, the criminal violence that will likely be an outgrowth of the political violence will tear at the very heart of Zimbabwean society for years to come. Similarly, political stability is likely to remain elusive for some time, since the notion of contesting political space at the ballot box has been replaced by contesting political space through violence.

Economically, the country has been devastated by the violence. At least 400 companies had folded by the end of 2001, resulting in the loss of 10 000 jobs. Foreign investment has dropped precipitously (e.g. 61 per cent between January and April 2001). Tourism has fallen by 80 per cent, and at least 12 000 jobs have been lost. By the end of 2001, an estimated 120 000 jobs had been lost in the formal sector. The number of Zimbabweans living below the poverty line has increased from 74 per cent to 80 per cent. Since the violence erupted, unemployment has increased from 50 to an estimated 70 per cent and as mentioned previously, by mid-2002, the level of inflation was 116 per cent. GDP growth was negative 7.7 per cent in 2001 and was projected to be negative 5.7 per cent in 2002 (Ndlela, forthcoming). The country has severe shortages of fuel and electricity, which continue to be provided by South Africa out of fear that Zimbabwe's total economic collapse would have severe economic and political consequences for South Africa and the SADC region (*Business Day*, 20 January 2000, 11 November 2000, 11 April 2001, 1 June 2001; *Insider*, 29 May 2001; *Daily Mail & Guardian*, 17 April 2001; *Zimbabwe Independent*, 20 April 2001).

At the end of June 2001, Mugabe agreed to a Nigerian initiative aimed at resolving the conflict between Zimbabwe and Britain over the land crisis. A meeting of Commonwealth nations was held in Abuja, Nigeria, on 6–7 September 2001, where the Zimbabwe government agreed to bring an end to the illegal land seizures of white-owned land and to restore the rule of law. However, concerns were raised following the Abuja meeting as to whether it would be enforced by the Zimbabwean government.

For the first time in the 18 months of the conflict, the SADC heads of state and government severely criticised Mugabe at the Annual Summit held in Malawi in August. Mbeki admitted that his 'quiet diplomacy' had failed and King Mswati of Swaziland stated that, '[w]e felt that what our colleague is doing was beyond the premises of democracy and he has to be stopped' (*Zimbabwe Standard*, 5 September 2001). The new chairperson of SADC, President Bakili Muluzi, gave a scathing critique of Mugabe at the Summit, which was followed in October by the statement that as SADC chairman he, 'condemned any disregard of the rule of law by any stakeholder in the land conflict in Zimbabwe' (*Financial Gazette*, 4 October 2001).

Following the Abuja meeting, the farm invasions continued along with the violence. By the end of 2001, efforts by the Commonwealth, EU, SADC, and US failed to convince the Mugabe government to restore the rule of law. Both the US and the EU imposed limited sanctions on the Mugabe government, preventing travel by key government officials and freezing financial assets.

Relations between South Africa and Zimbabwe reached an all-time low by the end of 2001. With the Mugabe government having announced that international observers but not monitors would be allowed into the country for the 2002 presidential election, and the refusal to restore the rule of law, Mbeki voiced concern about whether it was possible to have free and fair elections in Zimbabwe. He called on SADC to 'intervene urgently to stop Zimbabwe from descending into chaos with the likely consequence of the crisis spilling into neighbouring countries' (*Business Day*, 4 December 2001). Mugabe responded by accusing Mbeki of providing assistance to those attempting to overthrow his government (*Business Day*, 4 December 2001).

By mid-December 2001, however, the SADC member states decided to adopt a gentler approach to the Zimbabwe government in the hope that the crisis could be resolved

(*Business Day*, 13 December 2001). All the member states, including South Africa, have remained opposed to international or SADC sanctions being imposed against Zimbabwe. With respect to the latter, such sanctions would allegedly be catastrophic, resulting in starvation in Zambia, and in Botswana losing an estimated 40 per cent of its imports (*Insider*, 26 November 2001).

As a result of the crisis in Zimbabwe, the South African government has made a pledge to expedite its land reform programme. Black farmers in South Africa's Mpumalanga province have already announced plans for Zimbabwe-style land invasions (African Eye News Service, 29 May 2001). In Namibia, both black and white farmers have called on the government to expedite land reform in order to prevent Zimbabwe-style land invasions (Reuters, 2 July 2001). And, in September 2001, the SADC ministers of land formed a new regional body to handle land reform in the SADC region. They noted that 'equitable land reform is the platform on which southern Africa can resuscitate its economies, as this should bring peace and political stability to the region' (Madava, 2001).

Notes

1   They included Botswana, Lesotho, Malawi, Mozambique, Namibia, South Africa, Swaziland, Zambia, and Zimbabwe.

2   Market or trade integration consists of the linear progression of degrees of integration – FTA, customs union, common market, etc.

3   For a detailed account of the impact destabilisation had on SADC projects, see Lee (1989:183–240). For excellent overviews of destabilisation in general see Hanlon (1986); Johnson and Martin (1986); Leonard (1983); Cawthra (1986).

4   Statement made by Belmiro Malate, SADC Focal Point for Mozambique, at a seminar sponsored by the Harry Frank Guggenheim Foundation on Regionalism in Southern Africa: The Case of SADC in Cape Town, South Africa, 8–10 January 2001.

5   Namibia became a member in 1990, South Africa in 1994, Mauritius in 1995, and the DRC and Seychelles in 1997.

6   For purposes of clarity, for the remainder of the study, SADC will be used instead of SADCC, unless in a direct quote.

7   Interview with Belmiro Malate, SADC Focal Point for Mozambique, Maputo, Mozambique, 8 June 1998.

8   The FLS was established in the 1970s with the objective of ridding the region of white minority rule. The first members were Tanzania, Angola, Mozambique, and Botswana. Zimbabwe and Namibia became members after independence.

9   Interview with Daniel B. Ndlela, Zimbabwean consultant, Harare, Zimbabwe, 10 August 1999.

10 It has been suggested that Anderson's vision of the creation of SADC partially grew out of his desire to ensure that he had a job after he retired from the EU. He thus created an organisation that would be funded by the EU.

11 Interview with Ndlela (see en. 9).

12 *Ibid.*

13 *Ibid.*

14 For a critique of the Western response to SADC see Lee (1989:241–70); see also Mandaza and Tostensen (1994:81–96).

15 While initially countries were given sectors or sub-sectors to coordinate, they were later just given sectors to coordinate.

16 Even though the policy of using the Annual Consultative Conference for purposes of securing funding for projects was discontinued, SADC's ICPs continue to provide project funding.

17 The full name of the Organ is the SADC Organ on Politics, Defence and Security.

18 Statement by Malate (see en. 4).

19 The new countries are Antigua and Barbuda (52), Cuba (55), Dominica (61), Grenada (83), Saint Kitts and Nevis (44), Saint Lucia (66), Saint Vincent and the Grenadines (91), São Tomé and Príncipe (119), Seychelles (47), Solomon Islands (121), and Vanuatu (131).

20 Chris Landsberg, however, attributes the beginning of the tension between the two leaders to 'South African foot-dragging in renewing the preferential trade agreement between itself and Zimbabwe shortly after the Mandela government assumed power' (Landsberg, 2000:4–5).

21 Comments made by Christopher Landsberg during the question and answer period following a presentation entitled 'Comparing the Mbeki and Obasanjo foreign policies', at a conference sponsored by the Africa Institute of South Africa on A United States of Africa, Pretoria, South Africa, 30 May–2 June 2000.

22 For details see Landsberg (2000).

Overview of Southern African Trade Relations

TRADE RELATIONS IN the SADC region are very complex. Each SADC member, with the exception of Mozambique, is a member of at least one other regional economic organisation (see Figure 3.1, overleaf). They include SACU, COMESA, the EAC, and the Indian Ocean Commission (IOC). All of these organisations, with the exception of the IOC, are committed to market integration. This overlapping membership not only poses a challenge to the likelihood of the SADC regional agenda being implemented, but also raises questions about the political commitment these countries have to regionalism. Trade relations in the region are made even more complex as a result of the externally sponsored CBI, bilateral trade agreements, informal trade, and NTBs.

This chapter will provide an overview of Southern African trade relations. It begins by describing SACU, COMESA, and the EAC and explaining why they pose a challenge to the SADC strategy of market integration. The next section looks at the CBI, which is designed to enhance the region's integration into the world economy. An assessment will be made as to whether this initiative enhances or hinders the implementation of SADC's agenda. Bilateral trade agreements are discussed in the next section, which is followed by a description of the direction of regional trade, including formal and informal trade. The final section examines NTBs to trade. This overview of Southern African trade relations provides background information that will allow for a better understanding of the constraints that exist to implementing market integration among the SADC members.

Overlapping Regional Economic Organisations

While trade integration among the SACU countries already exists in the form of a customs union and the COMESA free trade area, the EAC, and SADC have identified trade integration as a precursor to economic union or total economic integration. The SADC member states are aware of the problems created by this overlapping, which is a further indication that they are not politically committed to regionalism.

As mentioned in the **Introduction**, overlapping membership in more than one regional economic organisation results in (1) the inevitable abrogation of rules, regulations, and commitments due to the impossible task of simultaneously fulfilling the obligations of more than one organisation with similar goals and objectives; and (2) inefficiency arising from duplication and overstretching of financial and human resources. This section of the chapter will provide an in-depth description and analysis of SACU, COMESA, and the EAC. An assessment will be made regarding the potential impact each organisation will have on SADC's objective to implement market integration.

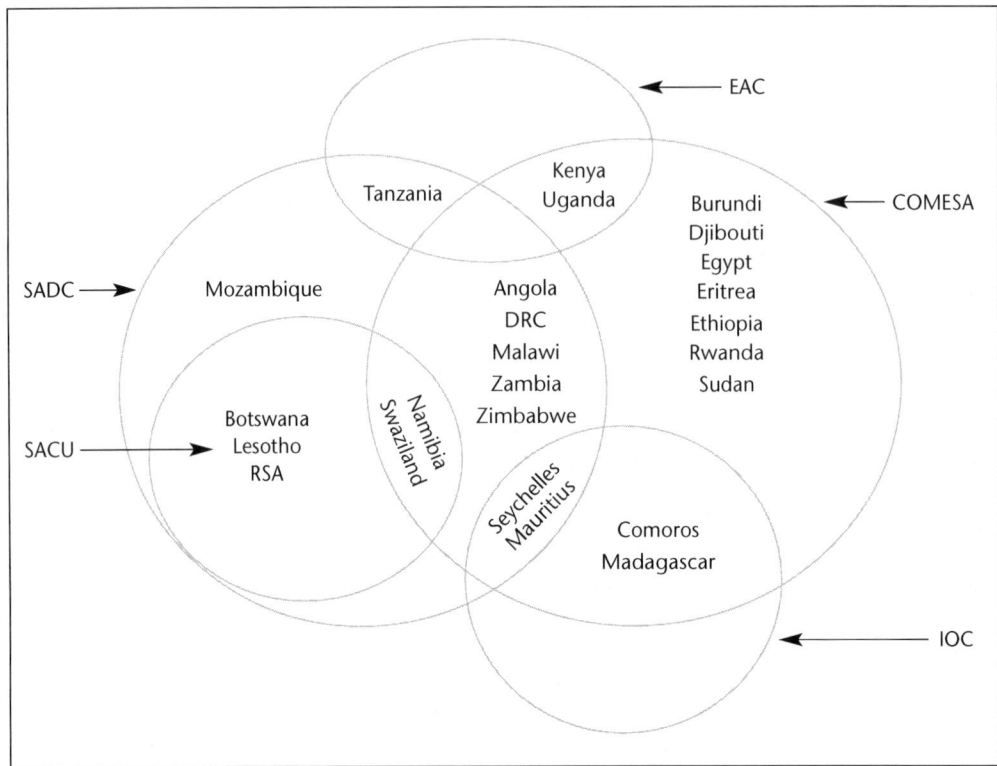

Figure 3.1: Overlapping Membership in Regional Economic Organisations

Southern African Customs Union (SACU)

SACU, the oldest customs union in the world, has its origins in the 1889 Customs Union Convention. The initial members were the Orange Free State (a Boer republic) and the Cape of Good Hope (a British colony). By 1893, British Bechuanaland, Basutoland, and the Bechuanaland Protectorate[1] had been admitted as accessors under the convention. However, they did not have the same rights as the two original members. The 1889 Customs Union Convention was replaced by the 1898 Customs Union Convention, which included as members the Cape, Natal (a British colony), and the Orange Free State. Basutoland and the Bechuanaland Protectorate were excluded. The 1903 Customs Union Convention replaced the short-lived 1898 convention. This new convention included the Cape, Natal, Orange River Colony, Transvaal, and Southern Rhodesia. Basutoland, the Bechuanaland Protectorate, Swaziland, and North-western Rhodesia were accessors to the convention, but, as before, did not share all the rights of the original members. The final convention before the Union of South Africa was created was the 1906 Customs Union Convention. It included all the parties to the 1903 convention (Maasdorp, 1990:10–15).

With the formation of the Union of South Africa in 1910, the 1906 Customs Union Convention was terminated. Since Britain did not allow the High Commission Territories (HCTs) of Basutoland, Bechuanaland, and Swaziland to be incorporated into the union, South Africa, in order to continue to regulate its trade with these territories, established the 1910 Customs Union Agreement. In 1921, South West Africa (later Namibia) was incorporated into the customs union as if it were part of South Africa. As part of the Customs Union Agreement, the HCTs received customs revenue, but only on imports from overseas, not from South Africa. In addition, in order to protect the interests of the white South African farmers, restrictions were placed on the amount of cattle that could be imported from these countries. This policy had a devastating impact on the HCTs. These restrictions remained in place until 1941. Then, in 1963, restrictions were placed on the export of Swaziland timber to South Africa because of the threat it posed to South African pulp mills. On the other hand, the HCTs benefitted from exporting to South Africa wool from Basutoland and sugar from Swaziland. As early as 1925, South Africa adopted a policy of import substitution, which resulted in an attempt to industrialise behind at first high protective barriers and later quantitative restrictions. The tariff barriers imposed by South Africa resulted in trade diversion, which meant that the HCTs were forced to purchase higher-cost, lower-quality South African products. This resulted in a decrease in customs revenue for the HCTs (Maasdorp, 1990:16–20; Sidaway & Gibb, 1998:173).

These early policies implemented by South Africa laid the foundation for both the underdevelopment of the HCTs and their dependence on South Africa. Until the latter part of the 1960s, South Africa had been planning for the eventual incorporation of the HCTs into South Africa. This dream, however, was not realised, and Bechuanaland and Basutoland became independent countries as Botswana and Lesotho in 1966, followed by Swaziland in 1968. A new agreement, the 1969 Southern African Customs Union Agreement, was signed in December 1969. It came into force on 1 March 1970. The new agreement followed earlier complaints by the HCTs that the revenue-sharing arrangement under the 1910 agreement was static, since it was not affected by the levels of imports and exports. Specifically, a fixed share of total customs and excise revenue was allocated to the HCTs and there existed no provisions for the review of their share. This was the case because it was assumed that the proportion of revenue earned by the HCTs would basically remain the same until they were incorporated into South Africa (Maasdorp, 1990:21–2; Sidaway & Gibb, 1998:172). Consequently, until the 1969 agreement, South Africa received 98.6 per cent of the revenue and Botswana, Lesotho, and Swaziland (the BLS countries) only 1.31 per cent (Harvey, 2000a:7).

With the 1969 agreement, a multiplier was added into the revenue-sharing formula to compensate BLS countries for the disadvantages of being in the customs union with South Africa. These disadvantages included trade diversion, polarisation of industrial development, and loss of fiscal sovereignty. The new formula was deemed to be more pro-BLS. In addition, the agreement stipulated that the objectives of SACU include the economic development and diversification of the economies of the least advanced members (Maasdorp, 1990:24). These objectives, however, were never realised.

In terms of economic development, although the agreement pretended to provide for the protection of infant industries and the establishment of new industries, industrial development was seriously impeded by South Africa (see Sidaway & Gibb, 1998:175–6; Maasdorp, 1990:28; Kumar, 1992:9–10; Gibb, 1997:79). In addition, in early 1990, it was revealed that a secret memorandum had been attached to the agreement stipulating that any infant industry in these countries, which, as of 1990, included Namibia as a *de jure* member, that required protection had to have the capacity to supply at least 60 per cent of the SACU demand before protection would be granted. This, of course, proved to be an insurmountable target to achieve (Sidaway & Gibb, 1998:176).

The well-known cases in which South Africa prevented the BLNS countries from industrialising include the attempt by Swaziland to establish a fertiliser factory; breweries proposed in Botswana and Lesotho; a plant for assembling televisions in Lesotho; Namibia's attempt to set up a Citroen motor vehicle assembly plant; a Hyundai vehicle assembly plant in Botswana; and a Peugeot plant in Namibia. In addition, in Namibia, some local businesses were forced to close following the dumping on the market of cheap South African goods (see Adedeji, 1996:21; McGowan & Ahwireng-Obeng, 1998:183; Mwase & Maasdorp, 1999:232–3).

In an interesting development, South Africa, in 1995, cancelled provision 311 of the SACU treaty that allowed the BLNS countries to

> import from outside SACU raw materials for textile production destined for South African markets. According to the president of Botswana's Confederation of Commerce, Industry and Manpower, South African producers of these raw materials cannot meet SACU demand and '[w]here they are able to produce, the materials have tended to be of inferior quality and the South African suppliers have proved incapable of making deliveries on time, thereby adversely affecting the performance of the textile industry in BLNS countries' (McGowan & Ahwireng-Obeng, 1998:182).

The beneficiaries of the cancellation were, of course, South African raw material producers, while the losers were BLNS textile manufacturers (McGowan & Ahwireng-Obeng, 1998:182).

Although the revenue-sharing formula was revised with the 1969 agreement, it remained a source of contention. According to James Sidaway and Richard Gibb,

> [a]t the most basic level, the SACU Agreement provides for the pooling of customs, excise, import surcharges and sales duties among the five member countries. The South African Reserve Bank manages this so-called Common Reserve Pool, and in the first instance, divides the Pool according to annual imports, production and consumption of dutiable goods. A compensation factor is then added to the above which provides for a 42 per cent loading in favor of the BLNS countries. In 1976, the formula was amended so as to provide a 'stabilization factor' in the levels of revenue received by the BLNS .... The stabilization formula guarantees that the BLNS receive between 17 and 23 per cent of the value of their imports of durable goods and duties paid and thereby represents a shift towards readdressing their marginalisation (Sidaway & Gibb, 1998:174).

Under this arrangement, South Africa continued to unilaterally make all policy decisions and control every aspect of economic policy from determining the revenue allocation to its distribution. In reality, the South African Board of Trade, which has no BLNS members, decides on tariffs and duties that are designed to promote the development needs of South Africa, not the BLNS countries (Adedeji, 1996:21–2; Gibb, 1997:79). There continues to be a two-year lag in the distribution of revenue, which, in essence, gives South Africa a two-year interest free loan from these countries.

Notwithstanding the problems for the BLNS countries, including the lack of fiscal autonomy, the SACU arrangement does have its benefits. Foremost is the annual government revenue that the BLNS countries receive from the common revenue pool (see Table 3.1, opposite). For Lesotho, it is 50–60 per cent of government revenue and for Swaziland 50 per cent. The current estimate for Namibia is 28 per cent, although it has been as high as 44 per cent, and for Botswana 17 per cent.[2] Throughout the years, the BLNS countries have complained that they are still not adequately compensated for the disadvantages of belonging to SACU, while South Africa has consistently complained that it cannot afford the burden of the compensatory revenue-sharing payments. In addition, South Africa has repeatedly noted that its residual share of the common revenue pool has been decreasing (Gibb, 1997:80). Table 3.1

does reflect a consistent increase in the allocations to the BLNS countries. While in 1969–70 BLS received only 2.6 per cent of the revenue, by 1991–92, this figure had increased to 32 per cent, partially as a result of Botswana's high growth rates (Sidaway & Gibb, 1998:176). Allegedly, by the end of the 1990s, BLNS were receiving over 50 per cent of the pool (SARB, 2000). Total payments by country for 1999–2000 are outlined in Table 3.2, below.

Other benefits for the BLNS countries include the fact that they do not have to operate their own customs service, have 'free access to supplies from South Africa and access to foreign exchange and a semi-convertible currency ... along with the prospects of accumulation, enrichment and speculation offered by the relatively sophisticated South African financial infrastructure, which in turn is plugged into global circuits' (Sidaway & Gibb, 1998:174–5). Many of these benefits are made possible as a result of the fact that all the countries, except for Botswana, are members of the Common Monetary Area (CMA), which allows for the close coordination of monetary policy (see Kumar, 1992:5; Mayer & Thomas, 1997:12–13).

Table 3.1: BLNS Customs Revenue Payments, 1994–2000

Year	Amount (R millions)
1994	3 089
1995	3 249
1996	3 890
1997	4 363
1998	5 237
1999	5 577
2000	7 197

Source: SARB (1999:S–55)

Table 3.2: BLNS Customs Revenue Payments, 1999–2000

Country	Amount (R)
Botswana	2 551 972
Lesotho	1 183 103
Swaziland	1 221 480
Namibia	2 240 743
Total	**7 197 298**

Source: Customs Union Commission

The CMA has its roots in the informal Rand Area that was established in 1960, when the South African rand replaced the South African pound. The South African rand was the only currency in circulation. In December 1974, the first official monetary agreement was signed between South Africa, Lesotho, and Swaziland. It was known as the Rand Monetary Area (RMA) Agreement. Right before the negotiations ended, Botswana withdrew and announced it would establish its own independent national currency (the pula, which is convertible) along with a central bank. The RMA was replaced in 1986 by the Trilateral Monetary Agreement (TMA), which established the CMA. In 1992, the TMA was replaced by the Multilateral Monetary Agreement (MMA), when Namibia joined the group (Leistner, 1997:117; Maasdorp, 1992:6). The CMA, according to Erich Leistner, works as follows:

▶ The currencies of Lesotho, Namibia and Swaziland are fully backed by the rand.
▶ The South African Reserve Bank acts as central bank for the whole CMA.
▶ The rand circulates freely in all member states, but is legal tender only in South Africa, Lesotho and Namibia.
▶ Lesotho, Swaziland and Namibia manage their gold and foreign exchange reserves themselves.
▶ Swaziland is entitled to change the parity of its currency but up to the present has preferred to maintain parity with the rand. Lesotho and Namibia are obligated to maintain parity with the rand.
▶ Government stock issued by the three smaller countries ranks as prescribed investments up to 1.5 per cent of the prescribed holdings for South African Financial Institutions. This arrangement gives these countries assured access to the South African capital market.
▶ All three countries have access to the South African commercial foreign exchange market, and if the need arises can also obtain foreign exchange from the South African Reserve Bank.
▶ All three apply the system of exchange control laid down by South Africa (Leistner, 1997:117).

Although the South African government complains that SACU is no longer affordable, it benefits tremendously from the SACU arrangement. The greatest benefit is that the BLNS countries are a guaranteed market for South Africa's internationally uncompetitive exports. Approximately 25 per cent of South Africa's manufacturing exports go to the BLNS countries. In addition, approximately 75 per cent of South African trade within the region is accounted for by SACU. Lesotho imports 94 per cent of its goods from South Africa, Swaziland 91 per cent, Botswana 81 per cent, and Namibia 90 per cent (Mwase & Maasdorp, 1999:229–30). In 1997, while South Africa exports to BLNS totalled R21 billion, its imports from these countries were only R5.3 billion. This represented a trade surplus in South Africa's favour of R15.7 billion (see Table 3.3, opposite). An estimated 70 000 manufacturing jobs in South Africa can be attributed to this trade. It also contributes significantly to profits by South African companies (Mwase & Maasdorp, 1999:229).

Another benefit to South Africa stems from the fact that partially as a result of cheap migrant labour, unit price production costs have been low in South Africa, thus ensuring competitive prices for South African products within the customs union. In fact, the BLNS countries face unfair competition from South Africa producers and often 'dumping'. Finally, South Africa benefits from the fact that the BLNS countries pay for a substantial amount of services that flow from South Africa (Mwase & Maasdorp, 1999:229).

In 1999, with a view to eliminating tax evasion on exports that are fictitious and illegal imports, South Africa imposed a value-added tax (VAT) on all goods entering the South African market from the BLNS countries. A tax refund is given for legitimate exports (*The Economist* Intelligence Unit, 1999a:18–19).

Between November 1994 and September 2000, South Africa and the BLNS countries were involved in negotiating a new customs union arrangement. While the negotiations were

Table 3.3: Intra-SACU Trade, 1997, in R million (FOB* less implicit duties)

Country	Imports	Exports
South Africa	5 282.0	21 149.5
Botswana	6 802.1	1 419.9
Lesotho	4 213.5	338.6
Namibia	6 050.3	1 299.9
Swaziland	4 083.5	2 223.6
Total	26 431.4	26 431.4

Source: Industrial Corporation of South Africa   * freight on board

born out of the new political dispensation in South Africa, they had their roots in ongoing complaints by both South Africa and the BLNS countries that the existing agreement was not fair. As mentioned previously, South Africa argued that it could no longer afford the revenue-sharing arrangement and that its share of the common revenue pool was declining. The position of the BLNS countries, according to Ngida Mwase and Gavin Maasdorp, centred around the following points, which were outlined in 1990:

▶ Inadequate compensation for payment delays from the common pool, the loss of fiscal discretion, the price-raising;
▶ The effects of the RSA's protective tariffs and industrial concentration;
▶ Greater protection for BLNS agriculture and infant industries and measures to encourage industrial development;
▶ Arbitrary and unilateral decision-making by the RSA; and
▶ The conversion of the Board of Trade and Industries into a multilateral institution, and establishment of multilateral dispute arbitration procedures (Mwase & Maasdorp, 1999:221).

In 1991, the South African government responded to the BLNS countries by calling for changes in the existing agreement, noting that 'serious attention should be given to the creation of a looser type economic co-operation with broader regional participation' (Mwase & Maasdorp, 1999:222). The timing of this statement was very significant in that by 1991, an end to the apartheid regime was imminent and the BLNS countries were politically dispensable. Specifically, the BLNS countries had been invaluable to the apartheid state. These countries had given the South African government some semblance of much needed legitimacy in that it was able to maintain relationships with legitimate African countries. They were also essential to South Africa's sanctions-busting strategy in that South African companies were able to relocate to these countries and export their products to the rest of the world. Alternatively, they were able to send their products to the BLNS countries for the final production phase before being exported to the world. The impending transformation in South Africa had ended the political needs the apartheid regime had for supporting the economic stability of the BLNS countries. It therefore was to come as no surprise that between 1991 and 1993, Pretoria occasionally made public statements suggesting that the customs union should be dissolved. The director-general of the Department of Trade and Industry, along with the minister of finance and trade, argued for the customs union to be replaced by a newly-created regional cooperation model (Mwase & Maasdorp, 1999:222). According to Mwase and Maasdorp,

> [t]he minister of finance was reportedly on the verge of withdrawing the RSA from SACU, being dissuaded by the department of foreign affairs. In May 1993 it was reported that Pretoria was about to publish a document recommending the dissolution of SACU and the formation of a wider customs union, including Zimbabwe, Zambia, Mozambique and Angola, as well as steps to rationalize this customs union with SADC and the PTA. Such a document was never released. Instead, South Africa suddenly changed its views on SACU (Mwase & Maasdorp, 1999:222).

This reversal likely stemmed from two realities. The first was that South Africa's plans for expanding SACU into a wider customs union that would include the above-mentioned countries would not be accepted by SADC or COMESA (PTA). Therefore, it was in South Africa's best interest to maintain the status quo with BLNS. Although South Africa no longer needed these countries politically, economically they remained indispensable. A second factor for maintaining the status quo stemmed from the fact that the newly installed Transitional Executive Council no doubt made it clear to the Pretoria regime that under the new political dispensation in South Africa, SACU would continue to exist. In 1994, a workshop on SACU was held in Gaborone, Botswana sponsored by the ANC. At this workshop, the ANC indicated its support for making SACU more democratic (Mwase & Maasdorp, 1999:223). In 1995, President Mandela stated that SACU was 'a reflection of the colonial oppressor's mentality', which allowed the apartheid regime to bully and intimidate its small neighbours (McGowan, 1999:4).

Why were some officials of the apartheid regime so anxious to get rid of SACU? In addition to the fact that the BLNS countries had, as previously noted, become politically dispensable, the Pretoria regime knew how costly the customs agreement was to the South African taxpayer. Therefore, it can be reasoned that some apartheid-era government officials were interested in ridding the country of this expense. Although South Africa benefits tremendously from the customs union arrangement, it has always attempted to underestimate such benefits (Mwase & Maasdorp, 1999:228).

In addition to the indispensability of BLNS to South Africa's economy, for the post-apartheid government, maintaining SACU was viewed as necessary in order to maintain political and economic stability in South Africa. Without SACU revenue, the BLNS countries, especially Lesotho and Swaziland, would be economically destabilised. This in turn would likely result in increased illegal immigration to South Africa, thus exacerbating the already overwhelming problem that exists in South Africa due to the huge numbers of both legal and illegal job-seekers. With an increase in both foreign job-seekers and poverty along its borders, political and economic stability in South Africa would be seriously compromised.

Before the April 1994 elections that resulted in an ANC-led government ascending to power, as previously mentioned, the Pretoria regime reversed its position on the need to dissolve SACU and determined that it was an important entity for regional integration. The new vision that the Department of Trade and Industry had for SACU was outlined in a report. The salient features of the report, as outlined by Mwase and Maasdorp, consist of the following:

(1) Economic relations between the various countries should foster mutually beneficial links (a positive-sum game for all); promote economic development in all countries; minimize the economic dominance of any country or countries; promote interdependence; facilitate intra-regional trade and investments flows; and strengthen the competitiveness of individual countries and SACU as a whole in the global economy.

(2) Not all countries benefit equally from membership, but all should be better off inside than outside SACU.

(3) All countries should commit themselves to a policy of good neighbourliness and eschew a position of regional hegemony. South Africa in particular should commit itself to a policy of full co-operation as an equal partner.

(4) A mutually acceptable revision of the revenue-sharing formula holds the key to the renegotiation of the SACU agreement. Since one of the conditions for successful integration is that all members [sic] countries should perceive that they will gain, there will have to be a trade-off to keep the BLNS countries contented if the revenue-sharing formula is amended. The RSA and the BLNS countries have different concerns with regard to the agreement, customs and excise revenue being more important to BLNS than to the RSA. It is accepted that BLNS should be compensated in the agreement, but this need not be through the formula. All other aspects of the agreement should be examined in this regard.

(5) In re-examining the formula, account should be taken of the following:
  ▶ The changed global environment, and in particular the implications of the GATT/WTO agreement for the SACU and for future revenue flows from customs duties;
  ▶ The possibility of a differentiated revenue-sharing formula being applied to each country, since the BLNS economies are not homogeneous, and SACU is of varying importance as a source of revenue;
  ▶ An improved revenue estimation method to overcome the disadvantages to BLNS of the two-year time-lag in cash flows; and
  ▶ A common statistical base for purposes of calculating intra-SACU trade.

(6) In order to assist BLNS countries in their economic development efforts, the following revisions to the remainder of the agreement should be considered:
  ▶ To mitigate the problem of loss of fiscal sovereignty, the RSA Board of Tariffs and Trade would become a SACU Board of Tariffs with representation from each country, and a multilateral authority (or secretariat) independent of any government should be established to administer the agreement;
  ▶ To mitigate the problem of industrial polarization, either RSA subsidies to industries under the regional industrial development programme should be abolished or a common industrial and location policy should be adopted by the entire SACU;
  ▶ Articles relating to infant industry protection in BLNS, and the protection of their agricultural producers should be re-examined, as should the secret memorandum of understanding and its contents, competition policy and operation of non-tariff barriers.

(7) In order to further assist the economic development of BLNS, various ways of increasing co-operation in education, health, and so on, should be investigated, and the role of the Development Bank of Southern Africa as a regional institution should be examined.

(8) The relationship of SACU to the Common Monetary Area (CMA) should be investigated with a view to deepening economic integration to ensure, *inter alia*, free mobility of capital and labour within the SACU area. The concept of 'variable geometry' allows countries to enter into a deeper form of economic integration within the basic customs union arrangement.

(9) Once the agreement has been renegotiated, the relations between SACU and other organizations (for example SADC and COMESA) should be investigated, given the possibility of widening SACU (Mwase & Maasdorp, 1999:224–5).

As Mfundo Nkuhlu, former Chief Director, African Trade Relations, Department of Trade and Industry and current Head of the Africa Economic Programme admits, there is a significant difference between being on the outside and opposed to the SACU policies of the apartheid regime, versus being inside government having to renegotiate with the BLNS countries on behalf of South African interests.[3] Throughout the renegotiations, South Africa allegedly acted as a hegemon, and resisted attempts to make the organisation more democratic. SACU has been referred to as an inconvenience by post-apartheid government officials, and some have indicated that they wish the problem of SACU would disappear. One high-level government official even allegedly stated that South Africa was not in the business of giving financial aid to Southern Africa. Although some may wish for SACU to disappear, having continued access to the markets of the BLNS countries under the customs union is very important for South Africa.

A Customs Union Task Team, consisting of representatives from all countries, was involved in the SACU renegotiations. For the most part, the negotiations were shrouded in secrecy, especially over a new revenue-sharing agreement. Eight negotiating meetings were held between December 1994 and October 1996. The negotiations then reached a stalemate and were not resumed until October 1998, following a meeting in August 1998 of SACU ministers. The issues being negotiated included new institutional structures that would be democratic (Working Group I); a new revenue-sharing formula (Working Group II); and different policy issues (Working Group III).

The first area for SACU negotiations concerned future institutional structures. As previously mentioned, since its inception, the South African government, through its Board of Trade and Tariffs, has unilaterally made all SACU decisions. It has thus, for example, been able to put in place tariff regimes that protect its domestic market. While the South African government wanted to maintain the status quo, this was untenable to the BLNS countries. With the new SACU agreement reached in September 2000, two new institutions will be created. The first is a council of ministers that will have five members, which will serve as SACU's decision-making structure. Decisions are to be taken by consensus. If consensus cannot be reached, a tribunal of experts will be convened to help arbitrate the situation. The second will be a secretariat to be housed either in Swaziland, Lesotho, or Namibia. This institution will establish technical committees to deal with administration issues, including customs, trade and industry, agriculture, and transport (*Business Day*, 13 September 2000, 26 October 2001).

A second area of SACU negotiations concerned policy issues (Working Group III). Agreements have been reached with respect to agricultural, tariff, competition, and industrial policies. In the mean time, sectoral policies are being developed with respect to agriculture (e.g. dairy, wheat, maize, red meat) and industry (e.g. clothing/textiles, motor and component industries, footwear, sugar) (South African DTI, n.d.).

The most contentious issue of the negotiations concerned a new revenue formula (Working Group II), which, as previously mentioned, must be seen within the context of the geopolitics of SACU; namely, that South Africa is committed to not destabilising the economies of the BLNS countries. Aware of this reality, at times it appeared that the BLNS states were negotiating with South Africa from a point of strength. While South Africa was interested in a formula that was 'clean', such a formula might result in the economic destabilisation of Lesotho, Swaziland, and Namibia. A 'clean' formula would be one in which revenue calculations would grow out of verifiable data and tariff duties actually collected. The 'political' formula that was in place was not an economically rational formula in that the calculation of the compensation given to the BLNS countries was not quantifiable. For example, it was impossible to quantify loss of fiscal discretion or polarisation. Since a 'clean' formula would destabilise Lesotho, Namibia, and Swaziland economically, all SACU member states agreed that such a formula was not viable.

On 14 December 1999, to the surprise of his BLNS counterparts, South Africa's Minister of Trade and Industry, Alec Erwin, at a SACU ministerial meeting, presented South Africa's 'new' approach to SACU revenue-sharing. Erwin's BLNS counterparts were surprised because they were under the impression that Working Group II was in the process of finalising a new revenue formula. They therefore considered Erwin's announcement of a new revenue formula to be a major shift in the renegotiation process (SARB, 2000). The new approach combined customs and excise transfers with discretionary budgetary assistance. Contained in a confidential document, according to South African government officials, it would entail the following:

▶ The pool of excise duties should be kept separately and allocated according to the GNP, used as a proxy for consumption, of each member state.
▶ A new discretionary excise subsidy should be allocated to the BLNS countries as compensation for loss of fiscal autonomy in determining excise duties. This subsidy is provisionally set at 100 percent of the calculated share in excise duties.
▶ The customs pool should be distributed according to total intra and extra SACU imports of each member state, i.e. the share of RSA is also now to be calculated. RSA will not receive the residual as before.
▶ A further new discretionary subsidy is proposed for BLNS countries as compensation for cost-raising effects and the loss of involvement in a tariff setting authority. The subsidy is also preliminarily set at 100 percent of the relevant share of BLNS countries in the customs pool (SARB, 2000).

The proposal further stated that:

▶ The total amount to be received by BLNS, that is, calculated payments plus transfers, for purposes of transparency and affordability be limited to 3% of total budget expenditure in RSA from the year 2001–02. For the current year the calculated amounts due in terms of the present formula, amount to 3,3 per cent. This level of 3,3 per cent could still be retained for the year 2000–01.
▶ The total amount allocated the BLNS as indicated ... above, less calculated customs and excise payments and relevant subsidies, is proposed to represent a Budgetary Assistance Fund and distributed to BLNS in accordance with agreed criteria such as population, wealth, education and health. These concepts are still to be defined more fully.
▶ The total amount of explicit subsidies, i.e. Customs and Excise subsidies plus the proposed budgetary assistance, amounts to R5 299 million for 2000–01 compared with total transfers of R7 614 million calculated on the new basis. Subsidies therefore comprise almost 70% of the total transfers in the proposed new scheme.
▶ The present enhancement factor of 42 percent and the stabilisation factor of 17 per cent of total imports by BLNS, will fall away. Revision of historical figures will no longer have an impact on the annual calculations.

▶   The broad principles of the new approach originate from budgetary considerations and have a less complicated structure for calculations. The specific percentages proposed should be subject to change in consultations with BLNS countries (SARB, 2000).

In October 2001, after eight years of negotiations, agreement was reached on a new revenue formula. It appears that the above proposal laid the foundation for the agreement. The agreement (1) allows for the BLNS countries to continue to be subsidised; (2) guarantees that revenue flows to the BLNS countries will be stable and not fall below the current level; (3) ensures that South Africa will not continue to experience a decrease in its share of the revenue pool; (4) has a development component for the poorer countries; and (5) establishes a SACU tariff board that will meet at least quarterly to review applications for tariffs and anti-dumping protection (*Business Day*, 25 & 26 October 2001).

Customs and excise duties are dealt with separately in the new formula. Although South Africa will contribute 80 per cent of the customs pool, it will receive about 50 per cent of the revenue. While 85 per cent of the revenue from the excise pool will be distributed based on the relative GDP of all five countries, the remaining 15 per cent will be distributed as a form of development assistance based on income per capita, with countries that have a lower income per capita receiving more. While South Africa collects approximately R8.5 billion in excise duties, the other countries only collect about R500 million. Although South Africa will contribute 95 per cent of the excise pool it will actually get back approximately 80 per cent (*Business Day*, 26 October 2001).

For the first two years, excise duties will be determined by finance ministers, and the common excise pool will be managed by South Africa. In the mean time, a task force will be created to look into options for a long-term mechanism for management. The new revenue formula will take effect beginning with the 2002 fiscal year (*Business Day*, 25 & 26 October 2001).

Maintaining economic stability in Lesotho is of special concern to South Africa. Since Lesotho is such an economic burden to South Africa, it has been suggested that the country should be incorporated into South Africa as its tenth province. As a province, the people of the country could benefit from all the services accorded South African citizens, and revenue spent on maintaining Lesotho's governmental structure could be redirected to the economic development of the area. Seemingly, both countries would benefit from such an arrangement.

The Lesotho government would likely suggest that such a strategy would be a new form of dominance, while many in South Africa would reject the idea of Lesotho being South Africa's tenth province, arguing that the South African government does not have the resources to assume financial responsibility for another country. Perhaps what such individuals do not know is the extent to which taxpayers' money continues to subsidise Lesotho.

During the SACU negotiations, the long-standing political tensions between South Africa and the BLNS countries surfaced. There continued to be the expectation on the part of some of the BLNS countries that South Africa owes them for their support of the anti-apartheid struggle. On the other hand, there was the perception on the part of South Africa that some members of the BLNS countries did not take the negotiations seriously enough and consequently came to meetings unprepared. One explanation for the lack of preparation was that some representatives from the BLNS countries lacked trade negotiation experience. Consequently, several of the BLNS countries hired consultants from Europe to assist with the negotiations.

The overlapping SACU/SADC membership will be problematic as SADC moves toward the creation of an FTA. Although it has been suggested that one way to solve the problem of overlapping membership in regional economic organisations is for all of SADC to be incorporated into SACU, this would be untenable, because SACU does not function as a real customs union. Instead, it continues to function as an apartheid relic. In order for SADC to be incorporated into SACU, the structure of the organisation would have to change drastically. It could no longer provide huge transfer payments to the BLNS countries. If anything, the more developed members of such an arrangement would have to design a mechanism to compensate all the LDCs for losses as a result of being in the customs union. Is it realistic to imagine South Africa, Zimbabwe, Mauritius, or Botswana contributing to such a pool?

Although SACU is a colonial and later apartheid-era relic, both South Africa and the BLNS countries benefit from the arrangement, and the BLNS countries are committed to remaining in the organisation. As Sidaway and Gibb note, '[f]or the BLSN states, the revenue-sharing formula offers a trade-off between the relative fiscal autonomy and an income to state coffers. In this respect it represents the ascendancy of a *rentier* class in the BLSN states and cements their (sometimes uneasy) relationship to the dominant strata in South Africa' (Sidaway & Gibb, 1998:174).

The SACU reality, coupled with South Africa's decision to make trade agreements (e.g. the EU-SA FTA) that are seemingly counterproductive to regional interests, does not bode well for the creation of a new SADC trade regime. There are inherent contradictions and problems in attempting to create a SADC FTA with a customs union (SACU) in the centre. These contradictions and problems will be exacerbated if SACU moves toward the creation of a common market. The later is envisaged as the next step for SACU, according to Fraizel Ismail, Deputy Director-General of International Trade and Development within the South African Department of Trade and Industry. He also feels that SACU is the model for integration for the rest of Africa (*Business Day*, 26 October 2001).

Regional integration via SACU is clearly the priority for South Africa. Given this reality, a SADC strategy of market integration that includes SACU is doomed to fail. An alternative SADC strategy of regionalism that deals with the reality of SACU's existence therefore needs to be adopted.

South Africa's regional economic dominance has had a significant impact on another regional organisation – COMESA. South Africa refused to join COMESA, whose overall goals and objectives are very similar to SADC's. For some SADC member states, retaining membership in COMESA is designed to make a political statement against South Africa's regional economic hegemony.

Common Market for Eastern and Southern Africa (COMESA)

COMESA began as the Preferential Trade Area for Eastern and Southern Africa (PTA), which was created in 1981. The founding members were the Comoros, Djibouti, Ethiopia, Malawi, Mauritius, Somalia, Uganda, and Zambia. The idea of the PTA dates back to the mid-1960s (see http://www.comesa.int/backgrnd/backhist.htm). The PTA, however, officially grew out of the OAU's Lagos Plan of Action and the Final Act of Lagos (FAL) in 1980, which was supported by the UN Economic Commission for Africa (ECA). Specifically, the LPA and the FAL projected the economic integration of the continent and the eventual creation of an African Economic Community via sub-regional economic organisations. The ECA identified four sub-regions: Eastern and Southern Africa, West Africa, North Africa, and Central Africa. The PTA was one of the three sub-regional economic organisations sponsored by the ECA. The treaty creating the PTA was signed in December 1981, and it came into force in September 1982 (see Aryeetey & Oduro, 1996:20–3; McCarthy, 1996:216–17; http://www.comesa.int/background/backhist.htm).

The major objective of the PTA was to increase intra-regional trade. To this end, the PTA envisaged the linear progression of degrees of integration beginning with a preferential trade area and culminating in the creation of a common market. All tariffs on intra-regional trade were to be removed by 1992. In order to enhance intra-regional trade, numerous institutions were created, including the PTA Trade and Development Bank, the Trade Information Document Centre, the Federation of Chambers of Commerce and Industry, and the PTA Clearing House. The latter, which was located in Harare, Zimbabwe, was created in order to overcome the constraints to intra-regional trade arising from non-convertible currencies and foreign exchange shortages (Leistner, 1997:120). With the opening up of the exchange rates under SAPs and the ability of traders to obtain currency in the marketplace, the need for the PTA Clearing House dwindled and it was closed down.

PTA traveller's cheques were also introduced to help facilitate financial transactions among member states. However, they were eliminated during the latter part of the 1990s. The organisation did not meet its objective of removing all tariffs to intra-regional trade by 1992.

Although increased intra-regional trade was the major objective of the PTA, the organisation had other objectives as outlined in its treaty. They include,

> [t]he promotion of co-operation and development in all fields of economic activity, particularly in trade, customs, industry, transport, communication, agriculture, natural resources and monetary affairs; with the overall aim of raising the standard of living of its people, of fostering closer relations among its member states; to create a common market by the year 2000 which would allow the free movement of goods, capital and labour within the sub-region, and contributing to the progress and development of African countries (Kasekende & Ng'eno, 1999:163).

The PTA was transformed into COMESA in 1993. The member states signed the treaty transforming the PTA in November 1993 and it was ratified in December 1994. The current members of the organisation are Angola, Burundi, Comoros, the DRC, Djibouti, Egypt, Eritrea, Ethiopia, Kenya, Madagascar, Malawi, Mauritius, Namibia, Rwanda, the Seychelles, Sudan, Swaziland, Uganda, Zambia, and Zimbabwe. Of the 14 SADC member states, nine are also members of COMESA.

The transformation of the PTA into COMESA did not alter the major objectives of the organisation. As COMESA, the major areas of cooperation fundamentally remained the same. The organisation determined that a free trade area would be in place by 2000, a customs union by 2004, and monetary union by 2025. On 31 October 2000, a COMESA free trade area did come into force with nine of the 20 COMESA members. They are Egypt, Djibouti, Malawi, Kenya, Mauritius, Madagascar, Sudan, Zambia, and Zimbabwe. These are the only countries that have zero tariffs on intra-COMESA trade, which is a requirement to become a participating member of the free trade area.

By 31 October 2000, Comoros, Eritrea, and Uganda had reduced tariffs by 80 per cent, and Burundi and Rwanda by 60 per cent. Intra-COMESA trade among these countries will be at their respective tariff rates, 80 and 60 per cent. The other members, Angola, the DRC,

Ethiopia, Namibia, the Seychelles, and Swaziland, have not reduced their tariffs at all. Namibia and Swaziland, until 31 October 2000, were given a derogation as members of SACU from reducing their tariffs. In order to participate in the COMESA free trade area, however, they will have to reduce their tariffs by 100 per cent. These two countries might be forced to withdraw from COMESA, because it is not likely that Botswana, Lesotho, and South Africa will agree to COMESA products entering SACU duty-free. Angola and the DRC have been constrained in reducing tariffs by war. The war between Ethiopia and Eritrea (1998–2000) no doubt had an impact on Ethiopia's ability to reduce tariffs. In the case of the Seychelles, allegedly the current trade and tariff structure is being reworked and the government had anticipated that by June 2001 they would have a free trade area (Panafrican News Agency, 23 September 2000).

In preparation for the free trade area, COMESA implemented policies in addition to those related to the removal of tariff barriers to trade. For example, according to COMESA documents, the rules of origin were simplified, with members adopting a local value added criterion of 35 per cent; a single COMESA customs document was adopted; a customs management system was installed in 12 countries (the Automated System of Customs Data – ASYCUDA); and a Trade Information Network (TINET) system was installed in 20 member states. Other successes included a reduction in transport costs, easier movement of goods within the region (largely as a result of the implementation of new transit procedures), and increased intra-regional trade (Panafrican News Agency, 23 September 2000:7). With respect to the latter, though trade has increased among COMESA members, such trade only represents 5–6 per cent of all foreign trade. An ongoing constraint to increased intra-regional trade is the fact that some countries insist on trading in US dollars instead of regional currencies (*Bridges Weekly Trade News Digest*, 2000).

The establishment of a free trade area means that countries extremely dependent on customs revenue will experience losses. COMESA estimates these losses, in most cases, to be minimal and therefore has criticised COMESA members for not joining the FTA because they fear revenue losses. A compensation package has been designed to help countries cope with such losses. This includes transitional compensation funds provided by the co-sponsors of the CBI (see below) to CBI participating countries (COMESA Trade & Customs, 2000).

Although the COMESA free trade area is in force, there exist serious constraints to its successful implementation. They include the fact that most of the member countries export primary products, which account for approximately 90 per cent of exports, the majority of which are exported to non-African markets. In addition, huge disparities exist between Egypt, Kenya, Mauritius, and Zimbabwe, the more developed member countries, and the others (Leistner, 1997:120). Egypt's GDP in 1999, for example, was US$89.2 billion, which was eight times larger than the second strongest economy, Kenya (US$10.6 billion). Comoros has the smallest economy in COMESA, which had a GDP of US$197 million in 1999 (ADB, 2000:215). With respect to this disparity, John Makamure, chief economist of the Zimbabwe National Chamber of Commerce, commented that, although 'COMESA's 300 million people constitute an attractive market ... their dire poverty would mitigate against many benefits derived from the FTA' (*Financial Gazette*, 2 November 2000). Concern has also been raised about the potential the FTA has for regional de-industrialisation (*Bridges Weekly Trade News Digest*, 2000).

As a result of Zimbabwe's economic position in the organisation, some countries have complained that it is not doing much to encourage imports from their countries into Zimbabwe. For example, while in 1998 Zimbabwe's exports to COMESA member states totalled US$436 million, it imported only US$120 million from the members. The greatest import/export disparity, however, exists with Kenya. Kenyan exports to COMESA members in 1998 totalled US$817 million, while its imports were only worth US$77 million. Kenya thus had a trade surplus of US$740 million (Intra-COMESA Imports & Intra-COMESA Exports, n.d.).

Another problem the COMESA member states are confronted with are NTBs to trade. The extent of the problem was revealed in a 1999 COMESA report of the seventh Intergovernmental Committee, which identified the following barriers: 'visa requirements, delays in customs clearance of goods, pre-shipment inspections, cumbersome transit procedures and charges, transport obstacles, high cost of credit and security of transit traffic' (Panafrican News Agency, 21 May 1999).

As previously mentioned, COMESA is also constrained by the various conflicts its members have directly or indirectly been involved in, including Angola, the DRC, Namibia, Rwanda, Uganda, and Zimbabwe. The two-year war (1998–2000) between Ethiopia and Eritrea left these two countries incapable of actively participating in COMESA's regional agenda. In fact, Eritrea has no recorded exports to COMESA member states and very limited imports. Similarly, Angola has no recorded exports to the member states while Rwanda's exports declined from US$11 million in 1991 to US$1 million in 1998 (Intra-COMESA Imports & Intra-COMESA Exports, n.d.).

The COMESA member states are also constrained by the long-standing rivalry that exists between COMESA and SADC. This rivalry has its roots in the 1992 transformation of SADC into a development community with the major objective of fostering trade integration. Prior to this, the two organisations complemented each other: SADC pursued a strategy of regional cooperation via sectoral development and the PTA/COMESA a strategy of trade integration. The overlapping membership in the organisation (nine SADC members were also members of COMESA) was not problematic.

On 31 January 1992, during a COMESA summit, the heads of state and government agreed to a COMESA/SADC merger in order to reduce duplication and enhance the effectiveness of regional cooperation. At the SADC summit held in Windhoek, Namibia, on 17 August 1992, however, the same COMESA/SADC members voted to transform SADC into a development community and not to merge with COMESA. They argued that there was in fact no duplication between SADC and COMESA. Nonetheless, COMESA continued to pursue the merger, which made SADC more determined to resist it. In response to COMESA's aggressiveness, SADC suggested that COMESA should be split geographically into the north and the south, with SADC assuming COMESA's responsibilities in the south. Then, in 1994, at the SADC Annual Summit, the member states passed a resolution calling for SADC members to withdraw from COMESA. This did not happen, however, and in 1996, a joint SADC-COMESA ministerial committee determined that the two organisations should continue to exist as separate entities (see Sidaway & Gibb, 1998:170; Mistry, 1996:170–1; Kasekende & Ng'engo, 1999:187; Mwase & Maasdorp, 1999:198).

Notwithstanding the above, the goals and objectives of the two organisations are very similar and they continue to compete with each other. SADC, however, scored a major victory in 1994 when South Africa joined the organisation and not COMESA. This deprived COMESA of what it had hoped would be a major economic and political boost to its credibility. South Africa's decision not to join COMESA was not necessarily surprising, since it already had the type of access to the COMESA market that it wanted, without having to conform to constraints that would be imposed under a COMESA preferential trade area or a COMESA free trade area. As a non-COMESA country, South Africa is able to freely penetrate the markets of non-SADC COMESA members without reciprocity. In fact, the Kenyan government, for example, has complained about South African goods penetrating its market, while South Africa imposes restraints on Kenyan goods entering its market.

The only three SADC countries that have actually withdrawn from COMESA are Lesotho, Mozambique, and Tanzania. None of these countries made the decision to withdraw as a result of the SADC/COMESA rivalry. The decision by the Tanzanian government to withdraw in September 2000 was in response to the fear that the COMESA free trade area would have a negative impact on its trade regime. While those with manufacturing interests were pleased with this decision, Tanzanian traders were not. The former group were concerned that the free trade area would result in the undermining of industry in the country. Tanzanian traders, on the other hand, feared that their export opportunities with COMESA countries would be seriously compromised, resulting in high import duties and export tariffs.

Since SADC and COMESA are basically implementing the same regional strategy, why have the SADC member states remained in COMESA, or conversely, why have COMESA members remained in SADC? Several reasons account for this continued overlapping of membership. The first is that the member states are not seriously committed to either the SADC or COMESA regional agenda and therefore are not willing to make the necessary sacrifices to relinquish membership in one of the organisations. In the case of SADC members, for example, if they withdraw from the organisation, they would automatically lose out on the project development funding that is provided by SADC's ICPs. This funding is crucial to the unity that continues to exist among the SADC members. It is highly unlikely that the organisation would survive politically or economically without such assistance. In many respects, SADC's ICPs provide the organisation with a built-in compensatory mechanism in that each active member of SADC benefits from being in the organisation via resources allocated for project development. Of the two organisations, then, SADC seems to have the greatest potential for fostering regionalism in Southern Africa. If this is the case, why have the SADC/COMESA members refused to relinquish their COMESA membership?

The answer to this question appears to be more political than economic. Specifically, it relates to South Africa's domination of SADC. Many countries continue to be concerned about the deepening of South Africa's regional economic hegemony, and therefore, maintaining membership in COMESA has become a political safety net for some countries. As the literature on regionalism indicates, many organisations have both economic and political objectives. In fact, often the political objectives are more significant than the economic ones. SADC is a case in point. As mentioned previously, during its first decade, the greatest contribution it made was in uniting the region politically. Similarly, SADC's political objectives have been redefined in light of the changing geopolitics of the region. As the geopolitics of the COMESA region have changed, so too have the political goals and objectives of some member countries. Zimbabwe is a case in point.

The Zimbabwean government did not decide to ratify the COMESA treaty until 1998, although the treaty had been in existence since 1993. The reason for the delay, according to an official from the Zimbabwe Ministry of Industry and Commerce, was because the government was waiting to see whether or not South Africa would be a fair economic player in the region. Convinced that it was not, the Zimbabwe government took steps to deepen its commitment to COMESA by ratifying the treaty. No doubt the political rivalry between Mandela and Mugabe had an impact on this decision. As a member of COMESA, Zimbabwe does not have to compete with its erstwhile South African neighbour for centre stage. In the COMESA forum, Mugabe can assume his role as a 'great statesman' of Africa, and be among friends from the region, including Angola, Namibia, and Zambia, who share his concerns about their powerful neighbour to the south. When threatened by South Africa's hegemony, these countries join Mugabe, on behalf of COMESA, in warning South Africa that the organisation will avenge the injustices the regional giant imposes on them.

A classic case in point was when the EU-SA FTA was completed (see Chapter 7). After the agreement was reached, COMESA announced that it would scrutinise the recent agreement with a view to challenging 'it if it is proved to have negative effects on the region's development' (Panafrican News Agency, 2 June 1999). Then, following the break-down of negotiations for the SADC FTA because of South Africa's insistence on more stringent rules of origin for the clothing and textiles sector, South Africa was warned that COMESA would take action to prevent it from trading in the region, or alternatively, punitive tariffs would be imposed until reforms were made (*Business Day*, 18 June 1999). At the time this warning was made to South Africa in June 1999, the serious rift among the SADC members was in full force and all of South Africa's SADC foes were members of COMESA. Consequently, regional power politics were being played out in the regional economic arena. As will become evident in the next chapter, South Africa managed to dominate the negotiations for the SADC FTA. It is not even feasible for the SADC/COMESA countries to think they can successfully impose any punitive economic sanctions against South Africa. Fundamentally, the SADC/COMESA members are powerless to do anything. They can merely hope their economies will not be adversely affected by the SADC FTA as a result of South Africa's growing regional economic dominance.

As long as the current leaders remain in power in Southern Africa and South Africa continues to flex its economic muscle, COMESA, albeit with insignificant results, will probably continue to be used as a forum for anti-South African rhetoric. Unfortunately, the politics of regionalism in Africa are fundamentally no different than the politics of the state in that both are driven by personalities. Personality politics, at this juncture, are a major hindrance to the implementation of SADC's regional agenda. It is being seriously compromised by the internal SADC rivalry that is playing itself out in COMESA.

A final factor that is often overlooked when analysing the dynamics of SADC and COMESA is that the COMESA Secretariat is located in Zambia, a SADC member state. As long as this is the case, Zambia will have no choice but to remain a member of the organisation. Given this reality, the ties that bind many of the SADC member states as a result of their involvement in the Southern African liberation struggle as FLS will prevent them from abandoning Zambia. The ANC-led South African government, in flexing its political and economic muscle throughout the region, especially when it first came to power, may have underestimated the FLS connection. It was the spirit of the unity of the FLS that was carried over into SADC when it was established in 1980. And it is this same unity that some of the former FLS are now longing for: a unity that was captured in the days before South Africa joined SADC. Today, COMESA is perhaps the closest thing that resembles that unity. Could the unity be once again forsaken for a SADC regional agenda that would allow South Africa to deepen its economic power over the former FLS? If this happened, would there be any integrity for these countries to salvage?

If political unity growing out of FLS bonding partially explains the SADC/COMESA connection, then why did Mozambique and Tanzania, both former members of the FLS, decide to withdraw from COMESA? In both cases it was determined that continued membership in COMESA, including the payment of annual fees to maintain the secretariat, was too costly. Both felt they would be adversely affected by a COMESA FTA. In the case of Mozambique, most of its African trade is with SADC member states, a great deal of which is under preferential trade arrangements. To liberalise its market to non-SADC COMESA countries would likely have negative consequences for Mozambique's weak economy. In addition, the special economic relationship that Mozambique developed with South Africa during the 1990s is too important to be sacrificed for regional personality politics. Mozambique is the largest recipient of South African foreign investment, and the cooperation between the two countries in developing the Maputo Development Corridor (see Chapter 5) has become a model for the region. The corridor links South Africa's business hub, Gauteng Province, with Mozambique's port of Maputo. The endeavour has been so successful for Mozambique that more foreign investment along the corridor is being put on the Mozambique side than the South African side.

With respect to Tanzania's withdrawal from COMESA as a former member of the FLS, two factors must be considered. The first is that Tanzania is in the post-Julius Nyerere era. The current leader of the country does not have the same type of emotional commitment to Southern Africa that existed during the Southern African liberation struggle under the presidency of Nyerere. The second factor is that Tanzania geographically is not located in Southern Africa, although politically it is a member of the region. Now that Kenya, Uganda, and Tanzania have resolved the political and economic divisions that resulted in the collapse of the EAC in 1977, Tanzania has decided to commit its resources to reviving the EAC. It is also removed from SADC regional personality politics.

In order for the politics of the SADC/COMESA rivalry to be resolved, a politics of healing must take place. The first step in the healing process will have to be made by South Africa. Specifically, South Africa will have to genuinely learn how to deal with its SADC neighbours as equal partners and not as subordinates. Given the level of arrogance displayed by South African government and business officials throughout the African continent, this would indeed be a miracle.

Again, the question must be raised about the viability of a SADC strategy of market integration in light of the existence of COMESA. As will be discussed in the next chapter, as a result of the existence of a SADC FTA and a COMESA free trade area, the SADC/COMESA countries can decide to trade in the region based on which agreement offers the greatest advantages. In the mean time, SACU can decide how best to prevent all non-SACU countries from having access to its markets. An alternative strategy to market integration is sorely needed in the region.

East African Community (EAC)

The economic integration of the East African countries of Kenya, Tanzania, and Uganda has its roots in the creation of a common market during the early 1900s. A common market was established between Uganda and Kenya in 1917, and between 1922 and 1927, Tanganyika was gradually integrated into the common market. It was not until 1949, however, that the customs administrations were amalgamated (Hazlewood, 1967:73). With the common market, there existed an extensive degree of integration. The countries had a common currency, free trade, free movement of capital and labour, a common customs and income tax administration, a common university and common research services, and they shared transport and communication services (Hazlewood, 1985:173; Kasekende & Ng'eno, 1999:155–60).

Before these countries gained their independence (Tanzania in 1961, Uganda in 1962, and Kenya in 1963), complaints were being made that the country benefitting the most from integration was Kenya. With a view to preventing the common market from collapsing as a result of the unequal distribution of benefits, the Treaty of East African Cooperation, establishing the East African Community (EAC), consisting of Kenya, Tanzania, and Uganda, was signed in 1967. The objective of the EAC was 'to strengthen and regulate the industrial, commercial and other relations of the partner states to the end that there shall be accelerated, harmonious and balanced development and sustained expansion of economic activities the benefits whereof shall be equitably shared' (Kasekende & Ng'eno, 1999:155).

The EAC experienced its demise in mid-1977. While numerous factors contributed to the death of the EAC, the major factor was the unequal distribution of benefits. As the regional giant, Kenya was the major benefactor, at the expense of Tanzania and Uganda, the least developed countries. Ideological differences also contributed to problems among the members. Although several commissions were established with a view to examining and rectifying the differences, they were not resolved (see Hazlewood, 1985; Aly, 1994; Leistner, 1997:115).

Interest in reviving integration between the three East African countries resulted in the establishment of the Permanent Tripartite Commission in 1996. This was followed in 1997 by the presidents of Kenya, Tanzania, and Uganda signing an agreement in Arusha, Tanzania. The Commission for East African Cooperation (CEAC) Secretariat was established in Arusha. The main objectives of the EAC were outlined in a document prepared by the CEAC entitled *East African Cooperation Development Strategy*. They are:

▶ to promote the spirit of regional cooperation, which is deeply rooted in the history of the region and in the minds of its people, while avoiding the problems of similar endeavours in the past;

▶ to support the existing forces that have a major interest in the strengthening of regional institutions and in the free movement of people, capital, and goods, as well as services and information within the region;

▶ to place immediate emphasis on economic cooperation, with a view to promoting enhanced political cooperation and integration in the long run; and

▶ to reinforce institutional capacities for regional cooperation with the EAC secretariat as a small but effective coordinating body to organise and supervise special activities, studies and research aimed at facilitating decision making in areas relevant to regional integration (World Bank, 1998:291).

The East African Co-operation Treaty establishing the new East African Community was finally ratified by the Tanzanian parliament on 15 June 2000. It had been ratified earlier by Kenya and Uganda. The new EAC was inaugurated by the presidents of Kenya, Tanzania, and Uganda on 15 January 2001, in Arusha, Tanzania. The anticipated EAC customs union is now planned for 2004. Although there are many problems currently associated with economic integration, including poor infrastructure, low investment, rampant corruption (World Bank, 1998:291), and economic disparity, the ultimate objective of the EAC is a single market. If a customs union is created by 2004, the three EAC countries would then presumably impose a common external tariff against the non-EAC COMESA members. Two of the EAC countries (Kenya and Uganda) would represent a customs union (EAC) within a customs union (COMESA). In addition, Tanzania would be a participant in the SADC FTA.

Of the three regional economic organisations discussed in this section, the one that poses the least challenge to the SADC regional agenda is the EAC. Tanzania has limited trade with the SADC region and in fact its membership in SADC is more political than economic. If it is to remain a member of SADC, however, it will have to reconcile the inherent conflicts arising from maintaining membership in both SADC and the EAC.

Cross-Border Initiative

Structural adjustment in Africa took on a new dimension in 1993 with the creation of the Cross-Border Initiative. Spearheaded by the World Bank, the CBI is co-sponsored by the latter, along with the IMF, the African Development Bank, and the EU. The official launching of the CBI was preceded by the 1990 Maastricht Conference on Africa and two years of discussion among the various co-sponsors and prospective participating countries. The CBI 'is a framework of harmonised policies to facilitate a market-driven concept of regional integration in Eastern and Southern Africa and Indian Ocean countries' (Gorjestani, 2000b:1). It is an attempt to integrate strategies of regional integration with SAPs (Haarlov, 1997:37). Although all CBI countries are not under SAPs, they are all required to be involved in macroeconomic reform. To this end, the two major objectives of the CBI, according to Nicolas Gorjestani of the World Bank, are to

▶ Dismantle barriers that have resulted in high cross-border transaction costs by reforming and eliminating intra-regional tariffs, liberalizing exchange and payments systems and through investment deregulation; and
▶ Promote a new integration approach based on competition and efficiency of regional markets with low tariffs vis-à-vis third parties (Gorjestani, 2000b:1).

In order to expedite the pace of regional economic integration, a variable geometry approach was adopted that allows each country to move towards integration at its own pace, with the fastest member, as opposed to the slowest, determining the progress toward integration. In this way, the fastest member states are to encourage the slower members to intensify their economic integration efforts. In fact, a cornerstone of the CBI process is peer pressure, where officials actively involved in implementing the overall strategy are to influence others to get on the bandwagon. Known as 'integration by emergence', in addition to pressuring their peers, countries are expected to take action voluntarily, harmonise policies, and implement regulatory frameworks. Reforms are to be implemented on the basis of reciprocity among the member countries (Gorjestani, 2000b:1; World Bank, 1998:28). The 'integration-by-emergence approach' calls on countries to 'act collectively and in unison within a common framework, but in the absence of formal treaty obligations'. This differs from what is called 'integration by design', in which countries agreed to formal treaty obligations (Gorjestani, 2000b:1). The problem with the latter, which is adopted by most regional economic organisations in Africa, is that the treaty-based approach may have a built-in bias whereby the slowest reformers generally set the pace of integration of the group (Gorjestani, 2000a:1).

Although all members of COMESA, SADC, and the IOC are eligible to join the CBI, participation is on a volunteer basis by a willing sub-set of countries. Currently there are only 14 countries participating: Burundi, Comoros, Kenya, Madagascar, Malawi, Mauritius, Namibia, Rwanda, the Seychelles, Swaziland, Tanzania, Uganda, Zambia, and Zimbabwe. With respect to the above-mentioned sub-regional economic organisations, the CBI is designed to complement them. In fact, according to the World Bank, all three organisations have been actively involved in the CBI discourse. Although supportive of regional integration in Africa, the CBI is designed to help facilitate Africa's integration into the world economy.

Of particular importance to the World Bank is the involvement of the private sector in the CBI. Private sector investment is crucial to the success of the CBI. The idea is to give this sector options for investment beyond the national market. This expansion would also enhance prospects for investment from extra-regional sources (Gorjestani, 2000a:55). In order to help facilitate the CBI agenda, each country has in place a technical working group (TWG) that consists of individuals from both the public and private sectors.

As co-sponsors of the CBI, the World Bank and IMF provide balance of payments budget support to countries under SAPs. To date, hundreds of millions of US dollars have been given to Malawi, Tanzania, Uganda, Zambia, and Madagascar. The ADB has provided resources to Tanzania and Uganda to help them meet their financial requirements. Assistance for human resource and institutional capacity building is also made available by the co-sponsors. Approximately eight institutional development fund grants of an average of just under US$100 000 have been given to support the TWGs. The co-sponsors also provide support to the private sector to assist it with restructuring in order to benefit from the regional as well as the world market (World Bank, 1998:8–9).[4]

The World Bank identifies several major achievements of the CBI, although such achievements must be tempered by the reality that it is impossible to separate CBI achievements from others that are taking place throughout the region. The first CBI achievement is that governmental officials believe that CBI policies are good for their countries. The second achievement has been the integration of the private sector into policy making. For example, ministers and private sector representatives now have dialogues in an open environment about policies. The CBI has created a forum to make such exchanges occur. This is deemed to be the greatest achievement. Consequently, this helped focus the agenda on the kinds of things that matter to the people who actually create employment and invest in the region. The third major achievement is the enhancement of local capacity of policy makers through the creation of the TWGs. This institution-building component of the CBI means that the ownership and design of policies are driven by individuals in each country. In countries where the TWGs are strong, they have been in the forefront of policy making. Consequently, before public policy is made, they are asked to contribute to the debate.[5] Other achievements include greater trade openness, increased private investment, and open regionalism, whereby countries have replaced import substitution trade regimes that are highly protected with ones that have low levels of protection (Gorjestani, 2000b:2).

Notwithstanding these achievements, the CBI has been variously criticised. For example, Marina Mayer and Rosalind Thomas argue that it promotes 'open regionalism' (simultaneous regional and global liberalisation); that it undermines the regional integration strategies of COMESA, SADC, and the IOC; and that

> [t]he CBI is widely viewed as an unwarranted intervention by extra-regional actors in a process which should be driven by the region. Moreover, it is seen as an attempt to create a 'sellers' market' for developed countries rather than a genuine attempt to further the economic interests of the region. In relation to intra-regional trade, this *laissez faire* approach to trade integration is inimical to the region's objective of achieving industrial development through trade integration (Mayer & Thomas, 1997:16).

Haarlov identifies the issue of 'ownership' of the CBI as a prospective problem: namely, whether it is perceived as being a genuine African initiative or one imposed from outside (Haarlov, 1997:154). Others have suggested that some countries joined the CBI because of the prospective monetary benefits. Fudzai Pamacheche and Prega Ramsamy of the SADC Secretariat note that money promised to compensate countries for losses incurred as a result of reductions in tariffs and other requirements has not been forthcoming, except for some resources from the EU.[6] Pamacheche argues that having a 'select group of countries to remove tariff barriers among themselves is counterproductive to regional integration'. Nonetheless, the CBI sponsors feel that this will encourage the other countries that are not a part of the CBI to also move ahead and remove the tariffs 'because they want the market open for the West'.[7] After having written the CBI policy papers for Madagascar, Comoros, and Tanzania, Ramsamy argues that the CBI is just another approach to the SAPs and therefore it is just a question of conditionalities. While working for COMESA, Ramsamy told the co-sponsors of the CBI that they should adopt the agenda of COMESA to 2000. 'Now they have done it, so they have more or less agreed to the agenda of COMESA.'[8]

The CBI co-sponsors have in fact adopted the COMESA agenda. In 1999, a World Bank official noted that 'right now ... COMESA has basically said that the CBI is like hand-in-glove of the COMESA except it represents those countries that are going at a faster pace. So there is no contradiction in terms of policy objectives of COMESA and the CBI, except that the CBI envisages a faster calendar'.[9]

This same official, in response to the criticism that some countries may have joined the CBI because of the prospective financial benefits, admits that this may have been the case in the beginning, but now this has changed. Finally, in response to the criticism that the CBI is not homegrown, the position of the World Bank is that, 'the CBI is not something that was imposed from the outside. It emerged from soul searching, debate and dialogue by country representatives over a two-year period in workshops'. The co-sponsors only facilitated the process.[10] The World Bank official does admit, however, that balance of payments support is withdrawn in cases where countries do not implement IMF/World Bank policies. If IMF/World Bank conditionality remains at the forefront of the CBI, can the CBI really be characterised as a policy created from within? Or is this a classic case of the current Bretton Woods institutions' strategy whereby countries are 'persuaded' into 'owning' IMF/World Bank policy reforms as if they were homegrown?

In order to enhance its relevance, the CBI was transformed into the Regional Integration Facilitation Forum (RIFF) in May 2000 in Mauritius. Through RIFF, the ownership of CBI policies have been placed in the hands of member countries. The COMESA Secretariat has been given the task of facilitating RIFF. In disagreeing with critics who argue that the CBI, and now RIFF, is counterproductive to regional integration in Southern Africa, Daniel Ndlela, a Zimbabwe economic consultant, feels that RIFF programmes are complementary to regional integration:

> The RIFF programme has geared itself to complement the regional integration programmes of COMESA, SADC and the IOC rather than compete or overtake them. I would even argue that in reality the CBI through RIFF has more or less adopted the COMESA agenda. The fact that most of the countries in the region have been implementing structural adjustment programmes and trade liberalisation on their own makes it easier to adhere to both COMESA and SADC FTA programmes, without necessarily impinging on the IMF/World Bank conditionalities. The latter are not necessarily contradictory to the programme of regional economic integration that is pursued by the countries of the sub-region (Ndlela, 2001).

While is may be difficult at this juncture to settle the debate regarding whether or not CBI and RIFF policies are counterproductive to regionalism in Southern Africa, there appears to be a growing consensus that the myriad of overlapping RTAs is counterproductive to regionalism. According to an IMF document, '[t]he excessive number of RTAs which the CBI countries are members may indeed have interfered with the pace of trade liberalization .... These countries are faced with conflicting obligations, different and uncoordinated strategies, inconsistent external liberalization goals, and different and conflicting rules and administrative procedures' (Fajgenbaum *et al.*, 1999:10). The document therefore recommends the rationalisation of the overlapping membership in regional trade agreements in order to enlarge markets, reduce costs, enhance the trade and investment climate, and improve transparency (Fajgenbaum *et al.*, 1999:15).

In April 2001, the EU expressed its concern about the numerous regional economic organisations in Southern Africa by hinting that the EU was examining the possibility of changing its support for such endeavours. As head of the EU unit for Southern Africa, Roger Moore's comments were in reference to SADC, COMESA, and SACU. He noted that 'it was becoming difficult for the EU to fund some of the programmes being undertaken by the three organisations since different protocols and different regimes have been agreed between the same country but under different regional organisations'. He further noted that discussions were taking place to determine how these three organisations intend to rationalise their operations (Panafrican News Agency, April 2001).

The need to rationalise the operations of SADC, SACU, COMESA, and the CBI is clear. This should begin with SADC setting the example by abandoning its strategy of market integration and replacing it with one that would result in less regional competition and more regional development.

Regional Bilateral Trade Agreements

A significant amount of preferential and free trade transpires in the SADC region as a result of bilateral trade agreements. While some of these agreements were established during white-settler and colonial rule in Southern Africa, others are very recent. In fact, it is reported that in March 2001, Zambia and Zimbabwe were on the verge of signing their long-awaited trade agreement. Since both countries joined the COMESA FTA, a trade agreement in 2001 would seemingly be superfluous. Throughout the negotiations for the SADC FTA, Zambia continued to negotiate for a trade deal with SACU, and Mauritius with Zimbabwe and South Africa. These negotiations were taking place simultaneously because, in the final analysis, the SADC Protocol on Trade allows member states to choose to comply with the trade agreement that is most advantageous.

Bilateral trade agreements among the SADC member states play a significant role in enhancing trade between certain countries. These arrangements, however, along with those of SADC, SACU, COMESA, and the CBI, further complicate the trade regime in Southern Africa. Botswana, Malawi, Mozambique, Namibia, South Africa, and Zimbabwe have at least one bilateral trade agreement with another SADC member (see Table 3.4, opposite).

Botswana

Botswana has bilateral agreements with Zimbabwe and Malawi. The former agreement dates back to 1988. It allows for duty-free trade on goods that are manufactured, produced, and grown in the two countries and have at least 25 per cent local value added. Botswana-Zimbabwe trade relations have not always been congenial. A rift developed during trade negotiations in 1988 after the 1956 Open General Import Licensing trade agreement was revoked by Zimbabwe. Zimbabwe then insisted that goods manufactured in Botswana and exported to Zimbabwe had to have at least 25 per cent local content. To guarantee this, a certificate of origin must accompany the goods. The perception was that Zimbabwe wanted to inhibit manufactured goods from Botswana entering its domestic market.

Table 3.4: Bilateral Trade Agreements

Botswana	Malawi	Mozambique
Malawi	South Africa	South Africa
Zimbabwe	Zimbabwe	Malawi
	Botswana	
	Mozambique	
Namibia	**South Africa**	**Zimbabwe**
Zimbabwe	Malawi	South Africa
	Mozambique	Botswana
	Zimbabwe	Malawi
		Namibia

Botswana's agreement with Malawi, which pre-dates that with Zimbabwe, is similar. Botswana and Zambia have held discussions on the possibility of establishing a bilateral agreement similar to that between Botswana and Zimbabwe (Imani Development International, Part II, 1997:15; Ndzinge, 1998:470–1).

Malawi

Malawi has trade agreements with South Africa, Zimbabwe, Botswana, and Mozambique. Malawi and South Africa have a non-reciprocal bilateral trade agreement that dates back to 1990. This agreement was signed before the political transition in South Africa occurred. With the agreement, the South African government wanted to thank Malawi for its unwavering support during the apartheid years. According to the agreement, goods that are grown, manufactured, or produced in Malawi are allowed to enter the South African market duty-free, in most cases, as long as they have 25 per cent local value added content. Import permits are provided for such exports to South Africa by the Director-General of the Department of Agriculture. Allegedly the objective of the agreement is to decrease the huge trade imbalance between Malawi and South Africa. According to the agreement, local industries in both countries can be protected if they are threatened by import volumes. Annual import permits are issued for a minimum of the following Malawian products:

▶ 300 000 kg of unmanufactured tobacco;
▶ 740 metric tons of groundnuts shelled or in the shell;

▶ 100 metric tons of processed ground nuts (Imani Development International, Part II, 1997:38; RSA, 1990):

Other agricultural products exported to South Africa include coffee, tea, and sugar.

Goods that are grown, produced, or manufactured in South Africa enter the Malawian market either under an import permit or based on governmental preferential rates of duty. The rules of origin for South African goods are based on a specified country content (Imani Development International, Part II, 1997:136). Diamonds from South Africa that are rough and uncut and to be used for industrial purposes can enter Malawi duty-free (WTO, 1998:31). Provisions exist in the agreement that allow for the protection of local industries if they are threatened by the agreement (Imani Development International, Part II, 1997:38).

In 1998, clothing and textile companies in South Africa complained that goods from a third country (in Asia) were entering the South African market from Malawi. In addition, the findings of a South African technical mission was that Malawian exports to South Africa exceeded the trade agreement. Consequently, in 1999, the two countries agreed to close the legal loopholes that were undermining the agreement (*Business Day*, 3 May 1999). However, during the same year, protectionist forces in South Africa found a pretext with which to convince the South African government to place an embargo on a large percentage of textile exports from Malawi.

Specifically, in October 1999, the South African Revenue Service (SARS) alleged that some Malawian exporters of clothing were 'smuggling' and participating in other forms of 'customs fraud'. Their goods were seized and officials from South Africa were sent to inspect the factories of suspected Malawian exporters. The report by SARS concluded that given the low wages in Malawi and the fact that most of the raw materials were not sourced from Malawi, it would be difficult for Malawian manufactures to comply with the 25 per cent added value criterion contained in the South Africa/Malawi bilateral trade agreement. Consequently it was recommended that an embargo be placed on Malawian textile exports (Coughlin & Undenge, 2001:2).

Although South Africa was never able to prove the allegations of trans-shipment, the embargo was imposed with the knowledge that the impact would be catastrophic for Malawi's textile industry. In the end, thousands of people lost their jobs and at least nine textile companies were forced to close (Coughlin & Undenge, 2001:2).

In addition to the above, questions have been raised about the highly unorthodox and restrictive value-added definition imposed on both Malawi and Mozambique by SARS. According to a report commissioned by SADC on Malawi's textile and garment industry, the researchers concluded that, '[b]y applying definitions extremely difficult for Malawian garment manufacturers to comply with, the South Africa authorities knew well that, eyes open, they were destroying much of that industry and severely restraining the rest' (Coughlin & Undenge, 2001:2–3).

Malawi and Zimbabwe have a duty-free trade agreement that came into effect on 1 May 1995. All traded commodities are included in the agreement as long as they meet the required 25 per cent local valued-added rules of origin. In addition, the goods must meet national required standards (Imani Development International, Part II, 1997:38).

Although Malawi has had a customs union agreement with Botswana since 1956, it is seldom utilised and most companies do not even know that it exists. The Federations Agreement stipulates that with the exception of 'spirits', 'all goods reared, grown or produced in Botswana are exempt from import duty' (Imani Development International, Part II, 1997:39).

The Malawi-Mozambique arrangement is a Portuguese Trade Agreement that dates back to 1959. In keeping with the agreement, as the following goods are reared in Mozambique, they are exempt from import duty:

▶ live animals (including poultry);
▶ fish (excluding canned fish); and
▶ unmanufactured products of the soil of a vegetable nature (wild or cultivated, including unmanufactured food stuffs) (Imani Development International, Part II, 1997:39).

Mozambique

Mozambique has trade agreements with Malawi (see above) and South Africa. The 1989 preferential trade agreement with South Africa is asymmetric in that Mozambique can export to South Africa a list of specific products (most subject to quotas), without reciprocity. A three per cent tax on imports is placed on these products or 'zero if the MFN rate is at or below 3%' (Imani Development International, Part II, 1997:136; MFN = 'most favoured nation'). Mozambique is applying to introduce new products to the list, which was last agreed upon in 1995 (Imani Development International, Part II, 1997:83). The list is outlined in Table 3.5, below. Rules of origin stipulate that 'at least 35% of the production

Table 3.5: Mozambique Quotas

Fish	2 000 tons
Crayfish	200 tons
Shrimps and prawns	2 500 tons
Crabs, frozen	500 tons
Langoustines	1 000 tons
Squid, octopus	100 tons
Clams	50 tons
Cashew nuts	1 000 tons
Citrus fruit	5 000 tons
Coconut oil	5 000 tons
Cashew nut shell liquid	500 tons
Cotton-seed oil cake	6 000 tons
Cigarettes	US$600 000
New tyres	Quotas determined annually
Inner tubes	Quotas determined annually
Cotton fabrics	US$500 000
Texline/trevira woven fabrics	US$835 000
Clothing	US$790 000
Blankets	US$250 000
Asbestos-cement roofing tiles	US$300 000
Wooden furniture	US$500 000
Handicrafts	US$300 000

Source: South African DTI (1989)

cost is represented by materials and labour performed in the country', and such goods are only for consumption in South Africa and Botswana. Goods re-exported to other SACU members are subjected to full duty payments (Imani Development International, Part II, 1997:83).

Following Mozambique's withdrawal from COMESA in 1997, Zimbabwe continued to grant the country preferential COMESA tariffs with the understanding that the two countries would negotiate a bilateral trade agreement. When this did not happen, Zimbabwe discontinued granting Mozambique COMESA preferential tariff rates, and reimposed regular tariffs on Mozambican exports. This action resulted in Mozambican entrepreneurs urging their government to conclude a trade agreement with Zimbabwe (*The Economist* Intelligence Unit, 1999b:18).

Namibia

Namibia only has a bilateral trade agreement with Zimbabwe. It is a preferential trade agreement, which was ratified on 17 August 1992, and came into force on 30 April 1993. The agreement allows for duty-free access to 'goods grown, produced or manufactured in either country' as long as they have a minimum of 25 per cent local content (Imani Development International, Part II, 1997:108).

Zimbabwe's major exports to Namibia include processed foods, clothing, agriculture, and mineral products. Namibia's major exports to Zimbabwe include agriculture, processed foods, beverages, and base metals products. There has been a significant increase in trade between these two countries since 1993. Zimbabwe maintains a trade surplus with Namibia (Zimbabwe Ministry of Industry and Commerce, 1997).

South Africa

South Africa has bilateral trade agreements with Malawi (see above), Mozambique (see above), and Zimbabwe. The most contentious of all the bilateral relations in the region is that between South Africa and Zimbabwe. The preferential trade agreement between these two countries dates back to 1964. Under this agreement, Zimbabwean clothing and textiles entered the South African market at a customs rate of 20 per cent. For certain areas, there was a rebate of ten per cent, which meant that the customs duty actually paid was ten per cent. Some goods, however, entered the South African market duty-free if they had a local content level of at least 25 per cent. This was especially the case where there were quota allotments.[11]

The rift that developed between South Africa and Zimbabwe dates back to 1992, when the 1964 agreement lapsed. To the dismay of the Zimbabwean government, South African tariffs on many Zimbabwean goods increased, including duties of 85–90 per cent being placed on the country's most competitive manufacturing products – textiles and garments. Three factories in Zimbabwe closed every two weeks and it is estimated that 90 per cent of these closings were the direct result of this increase in tariffs. Twenty thousand people lost their jobs (Dhliwayo, 1997:24; *Business Day*, 23 April 1999). In response, Zimbabwe announced tariff hikes against a large percentage of South African exports.

The two countries reached an agreement on textiles and clothing in August 1996, which came into effect in March 1997. An agreement regarding agricultural products was also finalised in 1997. While the latter agreement was satisfactory to Zimbabwean exporters, the former was not. Specifically, textile and clothing exporters complained that duties were still too high (an average of 30 per cent), quotas were too small and therefore exporters could not export profitably, and the rules of origin were too strict. Consequently, Zimbabwe was not able to fulfil its quota allotment (Chigwedere, 1999). Zimbabwe maintains a huge negative trade balance with South Africa.

With a view to increasing Zimbabwe's access to the South African market, a meeting was held between Nathan Shamuyarira, former Zimbabwe Minister of Industry and Commerce, and Alec Erwin, South African Minster of Trade and Industry, in Bulawayo, Zimbabwe on 15 July 1999. The meeting resulted in an increase in the quotas allocated to Zimbabwe producers in the clothing and textiles sector. These new quota allocations (see Table 3.6, below), according to John Chigwedere of the Ministry of Industry and Commerce, will allow for economies of scale, thus making it more profitable for Zimbabweans to export to South Africa.[12] These allocations were in effect from 1 August 1999 to 31 July 2000.

Table 3.6: New Quota Allocations for Zimbabwe Exports to South Africa

Product description	Old quota	New quota
Yarn	800 000 kg	2 000 000 kg
Blankets	40 000 units	150 000 units
Household linen	145 000 kg	245 000 kg
Protective clothing	R100 000	95 000 units
Industrial gloves	R60 000	1 000 000 pairs
T-shirts & vests	400 000 units	1 000 000 units
Leather	R70 000	6 000 000 sq. dm
Travel goods	R700 000	2 000 000 kg
Trousers & shorts	320 000 units	1 000 000 units
All other classes of clothing	2 407 000 units	1 127 000 units

Source: Zimbabwe Ministry of Industry and Commerce (1999b)

In addition to textiles, clothing, and agriculture, the Zimbabwe government has attempted to open negotiations in areas like manufactured goods not covered by the 1964 agreement. These efforts, however, have not been successful, since the South African government maintains that parliament would have to approve any new agreements. This would entail a cumbersome process that would take at least a year.

The positive outcome of the economic conflict between South Africa and Zimbabwe is a deeper appreciation on the part of the latter regarding accusations made by countries, including Zambia and Malawi, that it had been an unfair trading partner. Zimbabwe continuously exported to these countries far more than it imported from them, always maintaining a huge trade surplus in Zimbabwe's favour. Efforts to get the Zimbabwean government to appreciate how vulnerable Zambia and Malawi felt were of no avail until Zimbabwe developed serious trade problems with South Africa.[13]

Zimbabwe

Zimbabwe has bilateral trade agreements with Botswana, Malawi, Namibia, and South Africa (see above).

Direction of Trade in the SADC Region

Trade in the SADC region can be divided into two classifications: formal and informal. Formal trade is recorded as goods enter the country, while informal trade crosses borders unrecorded. In some cases, the latter is more significant than the former. While informal cross-border trade is an indication of deeper regional integration, it poses serious problems to governments because it undermines the collection of tariff revenues and sector development in certain countries. Therefore it hinders formal regionalism endeavours. This section of the chapter describes both formal and informal trade in the region. The part on formal trade provides a broad overview of the region. For a more comprehensive overview that covers trade by country with detailed tables, see Appendix 1.

Formal Trade

Official trade in the SADC region is characterised by two realities. The first is the huge disparity in trade exported to the SADC member states by SACU (mainly South Africa) versus that which is imported by SACU (mainly South Africa) from the other member states. While in 1997 the trade imbalance was 6:1 in South Africa's favour, by 1998, this had increased to 7:1. According to South African Minister of Trade and Industry Alec Erwin, this figure was 8:1 in 1999. Specifically, Erwin announced in November 2000 that during the previous year South African exports to the rest of SADC were approximately R17 billion, while imports were R2 billion (*Business Day*, 3 November 2000). Although there has been an increase in intra-regional trade since South Africa joined SADC, this is mainly reflective of an increase in South Africa's exports, not an indication of overall enhanced intra-regional trade. In fact, according to one account,

> [t]ens of thousands of workers have reportedly lost their jobs in countries such as Zambia and Zimbabwe because of South African dumping and trade barriers at home. Since South Africa's first democratic elections in 1994, the country has trebled its exports to neighbouring states without increasing its imports to the same degree .... Commerce and industry leaders in Botswana, Malawi, Zambia and Zimbabwe have in the past criticised South Africa for flooding its products into their markets, forcing the closure of local companies and leaving thousands of workers jobless (Chenje, 1998).

Between 1970 and 1993, intra-regional trade was around five per cent (Von Kirchbach & Roelofsen, 1998:6). In terms of increased intra-regional trade since 1994, it was estimated that there was an increase from seven per cent to 17 per cent in 1996 and by 1997 it had increased to 20 per cent (Panafrican News Agency, 18 November 1997; SARDC, 1998b). Table 3.7, opposite, places in perspective overall SADC intra-regional trade for 1995. As indicated by the table, Zimbabwe had the largest percentage of intra-regional trade. It exported to regional countries and imported from them more than any other country. This, however, is no longer the case because of the current crisis in Zimbabwe. For example, in

2000, South Africa's trade with Zimbabwe declined by 6.4 per cent, while Mozambique's trade with South Africa surpassed that of Zimbabwe (*Business Day*, 25 October 2001). Tanzania is ranked last with respect to imports from the region and Angola is last with respect to exports.

Table 3.7: Direction of Trade in SADC Countries, 1995

Country/ Region	Share of SADC imports in total imports (%)	Ranked	Share of SADC exports in total exports (%)	Ranked
Angola	1.49	7	0.1	8
Malawi	20.3	4	12.9	3
Mauritius	8.2	5	0.9	7
Mozambique	22.5	3	3.9	5
SACU/RSA	1.6	6	7.8	4
Tanzania	0.5	8	2.1	6
Zambia	23.1	2	13.1	2
Zimbabwe	30.3	1	39.9	1

Source: COMSEC study, 1997

The second reality about official trade in the SADC region is that only South Africa, Zimbabwe, and Mauritius have significant industrial sectors that allow them to export both industrial as well as primary products. The other member states are exporters of primary products (see Table 3.8, overleaf). South Africa, however, again dominates the region in terms of industrialised products that are exported. It therefore has a competitive advantage over all other member states. In a briefing paper on the negotiations for a SADC FTA, the South African Department of Trade and Industry noted that:

> [o]ur exports to the region are concentrated in high value-added sectors such as minerals and base metals, chemicals, machinery, transport equipment and food and beverages. These sectors generate overall growth and high-wage formal employment in the domestic economy and have grown dramatically – almost tripling between 1992 and 1997 .... Unless our SADC partners are able to expand domestic production and exports to the South African market, they will be unable to absorb a higher volume of exports from us. This rationale – which is underpinned by the view that South Africa cannot be an island of prosperity in a region characterised by poverty – has guided the structure of the tariff offer (South African DTI, 1999:1–2).

The unequal level of industrialisation among member states attempting to integrate their economies by implementing a strategy of market integration can pose a serious problem and result in the unequal distribution of benefits. Implementing a regional industrial strategy that might result in the development of comparative advantages among the less industrialised members of SADC could be one way to remedy this problem and help close the huge trade gap that exists between South Africa and the other member states.

Table 3.8: Major Regional Exports by SADC Member States

Angola	diamonds, mineral products
Botswana	vehicles, road tractors, nickel matte, disodium carbonate, salt and pure sodium chloride, dyed twill, livestock
Lesotho	manufactured products (mainly textiles and leatherwear), crude materials (wool and mohair), food
Malawi	tobacco, tea, coffee, cotton, natural rubber, food
Mauritius	clothing, textiles, tractors, food
Mozambique	food, cotton, oil, wood, tobacco, metals
Namibia	food, copper ores, malt beer
South Africa	machinery, transport equipment, mineral fuels, minerals, chemicals, base metals, food, beverages
Swaziland	food, beverages, refrigerators, wood products
Tanzania	cotton, food, motor vehicles (likely re-exports)
Zambia	copper, electrical and related products
Zimbabwe	food, beverages, crude materials, tobacco, cotton, wooden furniture, textiles, clothing

Source: The majority of information was gathered from Imani Development International (Part II, 1997)

Informal Trade

As a result of tariff and non-tariff barriers to formal trade in Southern Africa and the marginalisation of huge segments of the population from formal economic structures, the informal trade sector is thriving. The Productive Sector Growth and Environment Office of Sustainable Development, Bureau for Africa, of the United States Agency for International Development (USAID) conducted several studies on unrecorded cross-border trade in Eastern and Southern Africa between 1995 and 1996. These studies have begun to fill a gap in the literature on informal trade in these two regions. The countries examined to date in the SADC region are Malawi, Mozambique, and Tanzania. The studies were conducted in order to determine the significance of informal cross-border trade for local, national, and regional food security (Minde & Nakhumwa, 1998:xiii). The findings of the studies are discussed below.

Malawi's Informal Trade with Zambia, Mozambique, and Tanzania

Malawi's informal trade with its neighbours Zambia, Mozambique, and Tanzania in 1995–96, was US$44 million. Malawi exported a total of US$3.3 million to Zambia, US$3.9 million to Mozambique, and US$6.5 million to Tanzania. Malawi's imports from Zambia totalled US$17.2 million, from Mozambique US$6.8 million, and US$6.4 million from Tanzania (see Appendix 2, Table 1). The distribution of the share of informal trade was: Zambia 39 per cent, Malawi 31.1 per cent, Mozambique 15.3 per cent, and Tanzania 14.6 per cent (Minde & Nakhumwa, 1998:xvi).

There exists more informal trade between Malawi and her neighbours than formal trade (see Appendix 2, Table 2). In fact, the only area where formal trade was larger than informal was Malawi's exports to Mozambique. Total formal exports were only 69.3 per cent of informal exports and imports were 30.4 per cent (Minde & Nakhumwa, 1998:39).

The government of Malawi loses a significant amount of revenue as a result of informal trade. While losses from agricultural trade are only estimated as being US$762 000, losses from non-agricultural trade are estimated to be US$12 million, which was about four per cent of Malawi's 1996–97 budget. Since it is estimated that only 60 per cent of informal trade was actually recorded, revenue losses from agricultural goods, for example, could be as high as US$1.3 million (Minde & Nakhumwa, 1998:xvii).

Even though the revenue losses to the government of Malawi are significant, the income generated from informal trade is significant for the traders and their families. In addition, food is made available to communities that may not otherwise have it, and it is made available in smaller quantities, often at affordable prices. The informal agriculture trade sector is consequently very important for enhancing food security. Specifically, 25 per cent of the value of the informal trade, of US$11 million, was income generated. In addition,

> [t]he trade in agricultural commodities provided three types of opportunities: during the period immediately after the harvest, it provided markets for surplus farm produce and income to the local producers; during the long period between harvest and planting, the trade provided the producers with opportunities to invest their capital in other non-agricultural activities; and finally, the imports of grains, pulses and vegetables provided food in low income households in the major towns such as Lilongwe, Blantyre and Zomba (Minde & Nakhumwa, 1998:xvii–xviii).

Mozambique's Informal Trade with Swaziland, Zimbabwe, Malawi, South Africa, Tanzania, and Zambia

Mozambique's informal cross-border trade with her neighbours in 1995–96 was estimated at US$135 million: about US$37 million in exports from Mozambique and US$98 million in imports into Mozambique (Macamo, 1998:42) (see Appendix 2, Table 3). Informal trade between Mozambique and her neighbours represents a significant amount of trade between these countries (see Appendix 2, Table 4). Approximately 89 per cent of Mozambique's trade with Swaziland is informal, 67 per cent of trade with Zambia, and 66 per cent with Tanzania. Revenue losses to the Mozambique government from imports during the 1995–97 period are estimated to be between US$26 million and US$33 million. The benefits of informal trade to the unemployed and poor in Mozambique include enhanced food security, increased employment, and poverty alleviation (Macamo, 1998:46, 50).

Tanzania's Informal Trade with Malawi, Zambia, and Mozambique

Informal cross-border trade between Tanzania and her neighbours Malawi, Zambia, and Mozambique in 1995–96 totalled US$45 million: US$19 million in exports and US$26 million in imports (see Appendix 2, Table 5). The larger percentage of trade was with Zambia (Ackello-Ogutu & Echessah, 1998).

Informal trade between Tanzania and her neighbours is significant in relationship to formal trade. While the overall percentage of informal trade is 48 per cent, 65 per cent of Tanzanian/Malawi trade is informal cross-border (Ackello-Ogutu & Echessah, 1998:23) (see Appendix 2, Table 6). While specific statistics are not available on revenue losses to Tanzania, they no doubt are significant. As in the case of both Malawi and Mozambique, informal cross-border trade makes a significant contribution toward enhanced food security, employment creation, and the alleviation of poverty.

Governments in Southern Africa will need to address the informal cross-border trade sector if market integration is going to be successful. Even with an alternative SADC regionalism strategy, the need exists to incorporate this productive work force back into formal economic structures so that they can contribute to the development of their countries as well as the region. The main purpose in discussing this data on informal cross-border trade in this study, however, is to illustrate that the SADC region is much more economically integrated than statistics indicate. Thus, integration has taken on a form of its own in this sector.

Non-Tariff Barriers to Trade in the SADC Region

Tariff barriers to trade can be important for informal traders, since they are often interested in circumventing them. The same problem does not necessarily exist in the formal trade sector. As a result of SAPs and trade liberalisation in general, tariff barriers to formal trade are not as significant as they once were. In fact, in the region it is estimated that tariff rates on finished goods are 20–25 per cent, intermediate goods 10–20 per cent, and primary products 0–10 per cent (SATCC, 1998:21). Numerous studies point to the fact that NTBs are more of a constraint to intra-regional trade than tariff barriers (see Mistry, 1996:219; Marx & Peters-Berries, 1997:9; Mayer & Thomas 1997:33; interview with Nkuhlu (see en. 3)). Mayer and Thomas argue, for example, that there is a significant difference between official tariff schedules and those that are actually collected, largely as a result of inefficient collection procedures (Mayer & Thomas, 1997:33).

Like tariff barriers to trade, NTBs have also decreased in recent years as a result of trade liberalisation, SAPs, and the removal of most foreign currency and legal restrictions. The major NTBs to trade in the SADC region are therefore a consequence of administrative and bureaucratic problems (Imani Development International, Part II, 1997:81). For example, Fudzai Pamacheche of the SADC Secretariat noted that one of the barriers to trade in the region was 'mistrust among SADC members of each other's capacity to fulfill orders on time and the delays in settling transactions'. He further noted that 'SADC countries tended to earmark low quality goods rejected in foreign markets for sales in the SADC region – another factor that affected confidence in the goods produced in the region'.[14] Lack of currency convertibility and the demand that goods be paid for in foreign exchange (e.g. US dollars) is another constraint to increased intra-regional trade. The NTBs that will be discussed in this section include delays at border posts, customs procedures, transport costs, and import/export licenses.

Delays at Border Posts

Delays at border post throughout the region are a major problem both in terms of hours lost and resultant costs incurred. The worst case of delays is at Beitbridge on the South African/Zimbabwean border. Delays can take up to three days, with a cost of US$75.6 million annually. Delays at five other border posts can take up to an entire day. The total estimated losses as a result of delays at all the border posts in 1995 were US$139.3 million (Mushauri, 1997:7–8).

The delays at border posts are no doubt a reflection of poor management. In his study on transport problems in the region, Joshua Mushauri found, in addition to poor management, that all the various government departments at the border operate independently of each other (Mushauri, 1997:15).

Customs Procedures

At a meeting assessing NTBs to trade sponsored by the Konrad Adenauer Foundation, SADC, and the Advisory Service for Private Business (GTZ), John Indi, Managing Director of Dubi Ltd., who is a cosmetics producer and exporter in Zimbabwe, stated that numerous problems exist in this area, namely,

> [p]roblems with customs officials at border posts, customs forms which are difficult to be completed, the many difficulties and high costs involved to get goods across the border, the changing systems and requirements of customs, the delays at customs, the danger of goods being impounded in case of any suspicions of irregularities, confusing documentation requirements (such as those at the Zimbabwe/Mozambique border), the unreasonable and too high costs of import licenses (2.5% of the value of goods) the physical inspection requirements in case the value exceeded ZWD 25,000, and many more (Konrad Adenauer Foundation *et al.*, 1997:13).

Customs procedures pose a major challenge to increased intra-regional trade. Certainly, the lack of standardised customs documents has been a major constraint to increased intra-regional trade. According to Smak Kaombwe, Planning Coordinator of SATCC, efforts have been made to harmonise customs forms. Border officers even agreed on a form, but they have not implemented the forms. He further argues that there needs to be workshops conducted with personnel at each border post in order to effect the necessary changes.[15]

Transport Costs and Import/Export Licenses and Quotas

Transport costs throughout the region are exceedingly high as a result of both legal and illegal fees. With respect to the former, road user charges are in effect and vary from country to country. A trip on the road from Mutare in Zimbabwe to Beira in Mozambique is estimated to cost US$332 (Mushauri, 1997:16). In addition to high transport fees, corruption is a major problem in the transport process. Although impossible to estimate, some complain that for some routes, the total charge is double the official charge (Mushauri, 1997:16).

Although import/export license requirements and import quotas have decreased tremendously, they still are required in some cases. With respect to import quotas, quantitative restrictions or levies are applied on select agricultural products entering Namibia and Swaziland and quotas are maintained on certain preferential imports entering South Africa from Malawi, Mozambique, and Zimbabwe (Imani Development International, Part I, 1997:82). The SADC member states are divided into three groups with respect to import licenses and two groups with respect to export licenses, according to an Imani Development International study. The import categories are as follows:

▶ Category 1: countries that do not require licenses except for a small category of goods: Malawi, Mauritius, Tanzania, Zambia and Zimbabwe.
▶ Category 2: countries that generally require licenses, but where they are given fairly automatically: Botswana, Lesotho, Namibia, South Africa and Swaziland. (These countries do not require licenses from other SACU members.)
▶ Category 3: countries which require licenses, and where they are not given automatically (Angola, Mozambique).

The export categories are:

▶ Category 1: countries that do not require licenses except for a small category of goods: Botswana, Lesotho, Malawi, Mauritius, Namibia, South Africa, Tanzania, Zambia, and Zimbabwe.

▶ Category 2: countries that generally require licenses: Angola, Mozambique, and Swaziland (Imani Development International, Part I, 1997:82–3).

While the NTBs to trade in the SADC region are significant, ridding the region of the problems does not seem to be insurmountable, but will require the commitment on the part of policy makers to enhance transport efficiency and remove the constraints to increased intra-regional trade. Given the complexity of regional trade relations, it would appear that enhancing the efficiency of customs procedures should be a priority. After all, customs officials will need to be familiar with all the various rules of origin and other regulations guiding the numerous trade agreements, including SACU, SADC, COMESA, the EU-SA FTA, AGOA, and the numerous bilateral trade agreements. Additional workers are clearly needed to handle this complex web that makes up the various trade regimes.

Notes

1   During this period, Bechuanaland, which later became Botswana, was divided into two parts.

2   These figures vary by publication. See, for example, Sidaway and Gibb (1998:174–5); Mwase and Maasdorp (1999:213–14); Sidiropoulos (2000:12); Mayer (1999); Harvey (2000a:8).

3   Interview with Mfundo Nkuhlu, Chief Director, African Trade Relations, South African Department of Trade and Industry, Pretoria, South Africa, June 1998.

4   Interview with World Bank staff, 16 June 1999, World Bank, Washington, DC.

5   *Ibid.*

6   Interview with Fudzai Pamacheche, SADC Principal Economist, and Prega Ramsamy, SADC Acting Executive Secretary, 7 July 1998, Gaborone, Botswana.

7   Interview with Fudzai Pamacheche (see en. 6).

8   Interview with Prega Ramsamy (see en. 6).

9   Interview with World Bank staff (see en. 4).

10 *Ibid.*

11 Interview with John Chigwedere, Ministry of Industry and Commerce, Harare, Zimbabwe, 13 August 1999.

12 *Ibid.*

13 Interview with government official, Ministry of Industry and Commerce, Harare, Zimbabwe, 22 June 1998.

14 Interview with Fudzai Pamacheche (see en. 6).

15 Interview with Smak Kaombwe, Planning Coordinator, SATCC, Maputo, Mozambique, 9 June 1998.

Free Trade Agreement

If Southern African Development Community (SADC) countries were to go to war, it would be over a piece of fabric. Belligerents would consist of South Africa and its Southern African Customs Union (SACU) partners of Botswana, Lesotho, Namibia and Swaziland on the one hand, and the remaining SADC countries of Zimbabwe, Zambia, Mozambique, Malawi, Tanzania, the Democratic Republic of Congo, Mauritius and Seychelles, on the other (*Weekly Mail & Guardian*, 15 June 2000).

THE NEGOTIATIONS FOR the creation of a free trade agreement (as a precursor to a free trade area) in the SADC region were long and arduous. For the most part, the battle lines were drawn between SACU and the non-SACU SADC countries, although at times the BLNS countries broke ranks with South Africa. Was the fight over a piece of cloth or a ton of sugar worth it? In the final analysis, will the SADC region be better or worse off as a result of the decision to create a SADC FTA? Could the resources and time expended have been used to more productive ends in the region?

As Chapter 3 revealed, the region has a long history of unequal trade relations, with the majority of the member states being structurally dependent on South Africa. In fact, as previously mentioned, the trade ratio between South Africa and the other SADC member states was 8:1 in 1999, and may be higher now. While this is clearly untenable, the question is whether a strategy of market integration can spearhead the type of regional structural transformation needed to alter this reality. In other words, can mechanisms be put in place that will allow South Africa's regional economic partners to change their structure of production in a way that will result in increased exports to South Africa and overall enhanced intra-regional trade and development? In the process, can regional production become more complementary as opposed to competitive? Any regional strategy that does not result in a change in the economic patterns leading to a decrease in the economic disparity among the SADC member states will not be positive for the region.

The major purpose of this chapter is to examine the negotiations that resulted in the creation of the SADC FTA, which was launched on 1 September 2000. In order to achieve this objective, the first two sections provide background information. The first examines the SADC Protocol on Trade (Protocol) and the second the modalities of the negotiations. The third section provides a description and analysis of the actual negotiations and the final section of the chapter will examine issues related to the implementation of the SADC FTA.

SADC Protocol on Trade

An integral part of the SADC structure is the creation of protocols that are designed to facilitate the implementation of SADC's regional agenda. This section of the chapter examines the development of the SADC Protocol on Trade, describes the major components of the Protocol, and then critiques it.

Development of the Protocol

The first phase of the effort to lay the foundation for market integration in the SADC region is known as the 'Protocol Development Phase'. Ideally, the development of SADC protocols is a long and arduous process that includes brainstorming workshops with stakeholders, such as NGOs and civil society representatives, and ascertaining the advice of consultants. The protocols are then presented to both the Council of Ministers and the Summit for approval. It appears, however, that in the case of the development of the SADC Protocol on Trade, this procedure was not followed.[1]

The development of the Protocol has its roots in an extraordinary Council of Ministers meeting held in Lusaka, Zambia around December 1995. This special meeting was held specifically to deal with regional trade, following a proposal presented by South Africa, suggesting that a regional working group be formed to handle trade issues. Many of the SADC member states had long been dissatisfied with the performance of the industry and trade sector under the leadership of Tanzania. While South Africa seemed to be a more logical country to oversee the industry and trade sector, taking it from Tanzania and giving it to South Africa, however, was not politically viable.

One of the weaknesses of the SADC Programme of Action up to this point was that it did not have a serious trade component. Most activity in this area consisted of studies, and trade was not considered an important component of cooperation. So it was at this extraordinary meeting of the Council of Ministers that trade was placed on the SADC agenda. The council was directed to make sure that a protocol on trade was developed.

Between January 1996 and the signing of the Protocol at the Annual SADC Summit in Maseru, Lesotho on 24 August 1996, four meetings were held by the Trade Negotiation Forum (TNF) to develop the Protocol. The TNF was the official body established to deal with regional trade issues. TNF 1 to 4 dealt with the Protocol. During the process of preparing for the Protocol, preliminary studies were undertaken, and members of the SADC Secretariat visited the headquarters of the EU, the Southern Cone Common Market (MERCOSUR), and the Association for East Asian Nations (ASEAN) in order to understand their experience with regional integration. Following these visits, the development of the Protocol began in earnest. However, as previously indicated, serious discussion with regional stakeholders did not take place.

The Protocol was signed by 11 of the 12 SADC member states. The only head of state that did not sign the Protocol was José Eduardo Dos Santos, President of the Republic of Angola. Although the other heads of state and government had signed the document, there existed a major period of disagreement over the process by which the Protocol had been developed and the modalities for creating the FTA. In responding to a question regarding the apparent difficulty in getting the member states to agree to the Protocol, Kaire Mbuende, former SADC executive secretary, stated that the negotiations had not been easy because countries had different agendas. Some member states had ideas about liberalisation programmes that were ambitious, while others wanted to liberalise very slowly. Consequently, a lot of hurdles had to be overcome and compromises reached (*SAPEM*, 1996:10).

The Protocol

The signing of the Protocol calls for the elimination of barriers to intra-SADC trade within eight years of its ratification by two-thirds of the member states.

The Protocol consists of 39 articles and five annexes. Articles 1–2 contain definitions and the objectives of the Protocol. Trade in goods is outlined in Articles 3–11. Article 3 calls for the elimination of all barriers to intra-SADC trade and provides a provision for the granting of a grace period for those countries that may be affected negatively by the removal of tariff or NTBs to trade. Article 4 calls for the eventual elimination of all import duties on member states' goods, a process that should accompany the development of an industrialisation strategy that would enhance competition among member states (SADC, 1996:6). Article 5 calls on members not to apply export duties on goods to member states, and Article 6 calls for the elimination of all existing forms of NTBs. Member states are asked in Articles 7 and 8 to phase out quantitative restrictions on imports and exports. Exceptions to Articles 7 and 8 are outlined in Article 9. Article 10 deals with the protection of security interests and Article 11 with the treatment of national goods.

Customs procedures, outlined in Articles 12–15, include rules of origin,[2] cooperation in customs matters, trade facilitation, and transit trade. Trade laws (Articles 16–21) deal with sanitary and phytosanitary measures, standards and technical regulations on trade, anti-dumping and safeguard measures, and protection of infant industries. Article 22 on trade-related investment matters calls for members to create an open cross-border investment regime in order to enhance economic development, diversification, and industrialisation. Other trade-related issues are dealt with in Articles 23–25, including stipulations that SADC member states should adopt policies that allow them to implement their obligations to the WTO in the areas of the General Agreement on Trade in Services (GATS) and the Agreement on Trade-Related Aspects of Intellectual Property Rights. Trade development is contained in Article 26 (SADC, 1996:14–15).

Trade relations among member states and with third countries are outlined in Articles 27–30. Article 27 on preferential trade arrangements allows member countries to maintain existing preferential trade arrangements as well as other trading arrangements, and enter into new ones as long as such arrangements do not conflict with the Protocol. However, SADC member states are challenged to review these existing trade-related arrangements to determine if they are compatible with the objectives of the Protocol. Article 28(1) calls on member states to grant most favoured nation (MFN) treatment to all members and Article 28(2) does not prevent a member state from maintaining preferential trade arrangements with third countries as long as such arrangements are compatible with the Protocol. However, 'any advantage, concession, privilege or power granted to a third country' must also be granted to other member states (SADC, 1996:16). Article 28(3) stipulates that notwithstanding Article 28(2), 'a Member State shall not be obliged to extend preference of another trading bloc of which that Member State was a member at time of entry into force of this Protocol' (SADC, 1996:16–17). Article 29 deals with the coordination of trade policies, while rules regarding cooperation with third countries or groups of third countries are identified in Article 30. Institutional arrangements and dispute settlement procedures are outlined in Articles 31–39.

Critique of the Protocol

The Protocol has been variously criticised. Sheila Page, for example, argues that a limited framework is provided in the Protocol 'for using trade measures for a development strategy' (Page, 1998:2–3). In addition, she posits that the Protocol only covers provisions for business representation and not other economic actors such as labourers, farmers, and commerce. Such actors are represented in other regional organisations (e.g. the EU and MERCOSUR) (Page, 1998:4). Page also criticises the rules of origin as being relatively simple and therefore warns that serious complications will arise when attempts are made to implement these rules of origin, a factor that will be made more complex because of other trade arrangements that some SADC countries have among themselves or with other countries (Page, 1998:5–6).

Heinz-Michael Stahl warns that the provision of the Protocol that allows countries to protect their trade regime with safeguard measures in the event that imports threaten the domestic industry may frustrate SADC's trade liberalisation agenda if used too freely (Stahl, 1997:11). On the other hand, Rashad Cassim and Marina Mayer are most concerned about the fact that there is not a clear linkage in the Protocol between trade and industrial development (Cassim & Mayer, 1997:59). Marina Mayer and Rosalind Thomas argue that as a framework to drive the integration process, the Protocol is deficient (Mayer & Thomas, 1997:31).

The short period of time (seven months) from the development of the Protocol to its signing certainly contributed to many of its weaknesses. Notwithstanding this fact, it does not appear that the SADC member states were under any illusion that the Protocol was designed to go beyond merely laying the foundation for negotiations for the creation of an FTA. Prega Ramsamy, the current SADC executive secretary, reinforced this point by noting that the specifics of the technical details were to be negotiated among the member states (Ramsamy, 1998:3). In fact, the Protocol was amended in August 2000 in order to accommodate new agreements growing out of the FTA negotiations. Although the Protocol was signed by member states in 1996, it was not ratified until January 2000. SADC rules stipulate that protocols must be ratified by a two-thirds majority of member states. All of the countries that were signatories to the 1996 document ratified the Protocol by January 2000, with the exception of Zambia. Zambia finally ratified it in February 2001. The Protocol came into force on 25 January 2000.

Modalities of the Negotiations

The second phase of the effort to lay the foundation for market integration in the SADC region is known as the 'Tariff Schedules Development Phase'. Between August 1996 and August 1997, there was a period of non-activity. During this period, many studies were undertaken, including one by Imani Development International concerning the implications of the implementation of the Protocol and the modalities of a tariff schedule. The actual negotiations for tariff reductions began in April 1997 at the 5th TNF meeting, which was held in Dar es Salaam, Tanzania. The 6th TNF, however, was not held until November 1998. At this meeting, the participants agreed to expedite the negotiation progress until all issues were resolved. When the SADC FTA was launched on 1 September 2000, there had been 19 rounds of negotiations. This section of the chapter will examine the institutional framework and the modalities of the negotiations.

Institutional Framework

The institutional framework included the TNF and the Committee of Senior Officials. The former reported to the latter. In addition, there were two Sub-Committees on Trade Facilitation and Customs, along with a SADC Committee on Sanitary and Phytosanitary Measures and on Technical Barriers to Trade. The objective of the latter two committees was to 'work out Terms of Reference (TORs) and a work programme for the simplification, rationalisation and harmonisation of these para-tariff measures in the phase-in period of the SADC-FTA' (Zimbabwe Ministry of Industry and Commerce, 1999a:15). Other committees were established to handle specific issues that arose during the negotiations. Representatives from all 11 countries participated in the TNF meetings. The meetings were coordinated by the SADC Industry and Trade Coordination Division (SITCD), which is under the leadership of Tanzania. UNCTAD was the official facilitator of the negotiations.

Modalities of Trade Offers

After a great deal of discussion, the member states agreed to adopt a linear approach to tariff reduction, with trade offers being prepared in three categories:

▶ Category A – Products for Immediate Liberalisation upon entry into force of the SADC Trade Protocol;
▶ Category B – Products for Gradual Liberalisation within the 8 year time-frame prescribed by Article 3(b) of the SADC Trade Protocol; and
▶ Category C – Sensitive Products which may not face Tariff Reductions provided this category satisfies the basic principles on substantial liberalization (Zimbabwe Ministry of Industry and Commerce, 1999a:5).   \ol. Later 5-201.

With respect to Category C, it was initially agreed that sensitive products should not be more than ten per cent of regional trade. This was later revised to between five and 20 per cent. The rationale for products to be placed in Category C included social sensitivity, which encompassed levels of employment and staple foods in terms of food security, etc.; revenue sensitivity on the part of government; and business sensitivity with respect to the question of infant industries.

The member states also agreed to incorporate an asymmetrical tariff reduction strategy. For this purpose, the countries were also divided into three categories:

▶ Category 1 – Constitutes all SACU Member States who, as a unit, have offered to liberalize faster than other SADC Member States.
▶ Category II – Constitutes all SADC Member States who are defined as developing countries according to the United Nations criteria, excluding SACU member states (Mauritius and Zimbabwe).
▶ Category III – Constitutes all SADC Member States who are defined as least developed countries according to the United Nations criteria, excluding Category I and Category II (Zimbabwe Ministry of Industry and Commerce, 1999a:3).

The countries in Category III are Malawi, Mozambique, Tanzania, and Zambia.

During the phase-in period, tariff reductions would be implemented at different stages. Specifically, this means that Category I states are scheduled to frontload, Category II states to midload, and Category III states to backload (Zimbabwe Ministry of Industry and Commerce, 1999a:3). Frontloading, midloading, and backloading are defined as follows:

▶ Category I – Frontloading: Commitments to liberalization begin and end in the early part of the agreed-upon phase-in period of the tariff reduction.
▶ Category II – Midloading: Commitments to liberalize start in the middle of the agreed-upon phase-in period of tariff reduction.

▶ Category III – Backloading: Commitments to liberalize start towards the end of the agreed-upon phase-in period of tariff reductions. Member States with a lower level of applied MFN tariff rates would begin implementation at a later date than other Category III Member States (Zimbabwe Ministry of Industry and Commerce, 1999a:3).

Zimbabwe's offer to South Africa as of June 2000 (see Table 4.1, below[3]) illustrates the approach adopted for tariff reductions. According to the offer, 31.9 per cent of trade would be bound at zero tariffs[4] immediately (Category A) upon implementation of the FTA (see the second part of the offer – **Coverage by trade**). This would represent 30.1 per cent of all tariff lines (see the first part of the offer – **Coverage by tariff lines**). In Category B, an additional 46.6 per cent of trade would be bound to zero at the end of the midloading period, 2003–06, representing 78.5 per cent of all trade. This would represent an additional 54.9 per cent of tariff lines, representing 85 per cent of all tariff lines. The number of tariff lines contained in Category C is within the recommended 5–20 per cent for sensitive products. The most controversial issues involving the trade negotiations have been how to deal with sensitive products/sectors and rules of origin (see the section below). This is especially difficult because these are the sectors that are regionally competitive.

Table 4.1: Zimbabwe's Trade Offer to South Africa

General offer – Zimbabwe			
Category:	Coverage by tariff lines	%	Cum. lib.* %
A:	2 137	30.1	30.1
B:	3 895	54.9	85.0
C:	984	13.9	98.8
E:	84	1.2	100.0
Total	7 100	100.0	
Category:	Coverage by trade (US$)	%	Cum. lib. %
A:	342 786 297	31.9	31.9
B:	500 614 956	46.6	78.5
C:	145 039 499	13.5	92.0
E:	85 603 314	8.0	100.0
Total	1 074 044 066	100.0	

Source: 'Record of the 14th Meeting of the SADC Industry and Trade Committee of Ministers' (2000:19)
* Cum. lib. = cumulative liberalisation

With respect to the actual tariff reduction negotiations, they took place section by section, and chapter by chapter. This is the eight-digit Harmonised Coding and Description System (HS).[5] The 21 sections of the HS and their corresponding chapters are outlined in Figure 4.1, opposite.

Prior to the commencement of formal negotiations, the participants agreed that they would be guided by the principle that 'nothing is agreed until everything is agreed'. This principle, which is traditionally the basis for conducting multinational trade negotiations, is designed and adopted to safeguard the legitimate interests of sovereign Governments to withdraw from the trade deal if the negotiations are threatening or perceived to threaten its [sic] vital interests. However, it is also recognized that under this overarching principle a method of work should be adopted to ensure that trade negotiations proceed smoothly and rapidly (7th TNF, January 1999, Annex V).

The negotiators determined that the base date for tariff data would be 1 July 1998. In this regard, they committed themselves to standstill, rollback, and snapback provisions with regard to tariffs that are applicable on this date. Standstill means that whatever tariff agreement was in place when the identified base date for tariff data was agreed to would serve as the foundation for the negotiation for tariff reductions. Rollback means that no member state shall deliberately review its tariff regime to increase it after that date, which is why it is important to agree to the date. Snapback is more a provision for derogation. Member states who snapback are not happy with their present position and therefore want to return to their past position. A case in point might be a country that, as a result of a SAP, has liberalised its tariff regime so that its rates are lower than the rest of the region. In this case, the country may argue that it should not have to make any further reductions and therefore requests that it be allowed to return to its previous tariff regime as a baseline for negotiation.

FIGURE 4.1
Sections of Chapters for Negotiations

Section I	Live animals; animal products (Chapters 1–5)
Section II	Vegetable products (Chapters 6–14)
Section III	Animal/vegetable fats, etc. (Chapter 15)
Section IV	Prepared foodstuffs, spirits, and tobacco (Chapters 16–24)
Section V	Mineral products (Chapters 25–7)
Section VI	Chemicals and allied products (Chapters 28–38)
Section VII	Plastics and rubber (Chapters 39–40)
Section VIII	Raw hides and skins (Chapters 41–3)
Section IX	Wood and articles thereof (Chapters 44–6)
Section X	Pulp and paper products (Chapters 47–9)
Section XI	Textiles and textile articles (Chapters 50–63)
Section XII	Footwear, headgear, etc. (Chapters 64–7)
Section XIII	Articles of stone, plastic, cement, ceramic, glass (Chapters 68–70)
Section XIV	Natural or cultured pearls, precious stones, jewellery, coins (Chapter 71)
Section XV	Base metals and articles (Chapters 72–83)
Section XVI	Machinery, mechanical appliances, electrical equip. (Chapters 84–5)
Section XVII	Vehicles, aircraft, vessels (Chapters 86–9)
Section XVIII	Optical photographic, cinematographic, measuring, etc. (Chapters 90–2)
Section XIX	Arms and ammunition (Chapter 93)
Section XX	Miscellaneous manufactured articles (Chapters 94–6)
Section XXI	Works of art (Chapter 97)
	Reserved for special uses by contracting parties (Chapters 98–9)

It was agreed that the base date for trade data would be 31 December 1996. This, as opposed to a more current date, was decided on because some member states could not produce data for 1997 or 1998. Those who could produce more current data were faced with the prospect that countries who only had 1996 data would not participate in trade negotiations. Since this would defeat the purpose of the negotiation process, all agreed to the date of 31 December 1996. However, during the negotiations, several countries asked to be allowed to use 1997 or 1998 trade data because of problems with 1996 and/or 1997 data. Mozambique was allowed to use 1998 data, while Mauritius and Tanzania used data from 1997. In terms of existing bilateral trade agreements, it was determined that they would remain in place until they become less favourable than the SADC FTA.

In order to facilitate comparisons, all country trade offers were aggregated in US dollars (Zimbabwe Ministry of Industry and Commerce, 1999a:5) and it was also agreed that '[t]rade statistics on share of SADC trade in World trade by country be provided to facilitate a fair assessment of the adequacy or inadequacy of the country offers including coverage of Tariff Lines' (Zimbabwe Ministry of Industry and Commerce, 1999a:3). Other agreements were that technical experts on sanitary and phytosanitary and technical barriers to trade would participate in negotiations for tariff schedules, especially in the sensitive sectors; and that policies that were complementary had to be developed in order to underpin the phase-in period of the FTA (Zimbabwe Ministry of Industry and Commerce, 1999a:10).

The Negotiations

The negotiations for the creation of the SADC FTA were long and arduous. This section will examine the trade offers; handling of sensitive products; rules of origin; non-tariff barriers to trade; and the institutional structure for coordinating the implementation of the Protocol. The last part of the section will identify other areas of negotiation.

Trade Offers

The first country to present its trade offer was South Africa in November 1998. Although South Africa presented the offer, it was made on behalf of all the members of SACU. As a customs union, SACU had to participate in the negotiations as one economic entity. During the discussion of the offer, however, it became apparent that South Africa had not consulted the BLNS countries before presenting it. According to a Zimbabwean governmental official,

> I think SA did its own offer and they tabled it. For the BLNS states there was no consultation to cover their various interests within the offer itself to the extent that they almost wanted to say in one of the TNFs that the SACU offer, we were not agreeable to that. Some of the positions that are being taken up to now, when we discuss sensitive areas like sugar, motor vehicles, we would find more often than not, Botswana and Namibia, they would pull out of the SACU position and they would tell you it's not our position.[6]

The non-SACU SADC representatives at the negotiations initially thought that the BLNS countries went along with the SACU offer because South Africa had promised them something beneficial in return. As negotiations continued, however, it became obvious that South Africa had not made a special offer to the BLNS countries to entice them to approve the SACU offer. As a result, the divisions within SACU continued to surface.

The BLNS countries therefore began to complain that given their status as LDCs, they should be treated differently than South Africa. Mozambique also joined in the debate, arguing that as an LDC it should be treated differently than South Africa.

Out of this debate came the idea of differentiated trade offers, where each non-SACU SADC country would develop two offers – one for South Africa and one for all other SADC countries. Zimbabwe's two offers, for example, are displayed in Tables 4.1 (page 114) and 4.2 (below). With respect to Zimbabwe's offer to all SADC countries with the exception of South Africa (Table 4.2, below), 37.7 per cent of trade would be bound at zero tariffs[7] immediately (Category A) upon implementation of the FTA (see the second part of the offer – **Coverage by trade**). This would represent 30.5 per cent of all tariff lines (see the first part of the offer – **Coverage by tariff lines**). In Category B, an additional 45.1 per cent of trade would be bound to zero at the end of the midloading period, 2003–06, representing 82.8 per cent of all trade. This would represent an additional 62.6 per cent of tariff lines. The amount of tariff lines contained in Category C (5.7 per cent) is within the recommended allocation for sensitive products. In comparing the two offers, while better access is given to Zimbabwe's market under the differentiated offer, overall access under the two offers does not appear to be significantly different.

Table 4.2: Zimbabwe's Differentiated Offer

Differentiated offer – Zimbabwe			
Category:	**Coverage by tariff lines**	**%**	**Cum. lib.* %**
A:	2 166	30.5	30.5
B:	4 447	62.6	93.1
C:	403	5.7	98.8
E:	84	1.2	100.0
Total	**7 100**	**100.0**	
Category:	**Coverage by trade (US$)**	**%**	**Cum. lib. %**
A:	404 562 348	37.7	37.7
B:	484 528 181	45.1	82.8
C:	99 350 223	9.3	92.0
E:	85 603 314	8.0	100.0
Total	**1 074 044 066**	**100.0**	

Source: 'Record of the 14th Meeting of the SADC Industry and Trade Committee of Ministers' (2000:19–20)
* Cum. lib. = cumulative liberalisation

Although the issue of trade offers had been resolved, many felt that South Africa had created the initial problem by unilaterally presenting a trade offer on behalf of all SACU states, even though South Africa knew that it did not reflect the position of the BLNS countries. The non-SACU SADC states resented the fact that they had spent months

Sh gives plan

working on their trade offers, only to realise they needed two separate offers – one for South Africa and one for all other member states.

South Africa's behaviour in this regard reinforced the growing perception that it was only negotiating from the perspective of its own best interest. This was clearly reflected in the South Africa/SACU trade offer. Although according to the offer as of June 2000, 76.5 per cent of SADC exports to South Africa were bound at zero immediately upon implementation of the FTA (see Table 4.3, Category A, below), the majority of SADC exports to South Africa are in Category C, sensitive products, and therefore will not have preferential access to the South African market for some time. The South African Department of Trade and Industry admits this, noting that,

*Short term
and
LT
no real
effect*

> [i]n the short-to-medium term ... the increases in SADC exports is unlikely to have much impact on our economy because current exports are at such low levels that even if they were to increase four-fold the impact would be marginal .... In aggregate, SADC imports account for a mere 2.1% of South Africa's total imports. *In category C (sensitive products) where SADC has the highest level of exports to South Africa relative to the rest of the world, the products that comprise that category will continue to be protected under the special dispensations provided for by the various protocols* (South African DTI, 1999:3–4; emphasis added).

Table 4.3: Summary of South Africa/SACU Trade Offer

Cat.	Coverage lines			Coverage trade		
	Lines	%	Cum. %	Trade (US$ '000)	%	Cum. %
A	4 927	63.13	63.13	484 128	76.54	76.54
B	2 802	35.90	99.04	129 117	20.41	96.95
B1	674	8.64	71.77	28 881	4.57	81.11
B2	364	4.66	76.44	34 902	5.52	86.62
B3	1 405	18.00	94.44	11 039	1.75	88.37
B4	359	4.60	99.04	54 295	8.58	96.95
C	75	0.96	100.00	19 273	3.05	100.00
Total	**7 804**			**632 518**		

Source: 'Record of the 14th Meeting of the SADC Industry and Trade Committee of Ministers' (2000:14–15)

Offers by other countries as of June 2000 are presented in Appendix 3.

Although in January 2000 the member states were still in the process of negotiating final tariff schedules, South Africa published its SADC tariff schedules, which meant that it had become part of South African legislation. This means that South Africa finalised its tariff schedule before the TNF meeting in December 1999, which was in clear defiance of the overarching principle that 'nothing is agreed until everything is agreed'. When queried about this, South African negotiators told the member states that their tariff schedule was a closed chapter. This was the case even though South Africa had received requests from some member states to modify its tariff schedule. Such action reinforced the image that South Africa was not negotiating in good faith. In fact, South Africa was accused by some of taking a devious approach to negotiations.

During the early phase of negotiations, the South African negotiators, who had computers, were perceived as trying to intimidate negotiators from other SADC countries, who did not have them and consequently were negotiating from prepared hard copy documents. The end result of the perceived intimidation was that other SADC governments bought computers for their negotiators.

Throughout the entire negotiations, none of the member states was able to transcend its nationalist perspective to make policy decisions based on the best interests of the region. This problem, namely, the unwillingness of members to concede any sovereignty to a regional entity, has been a major contributing factor to the failure of regionalism in Africa. In the case of the SADC negotiations, the problem may have been complicated by the involvement of external forces in the negotiations in the form of consultants. Zambia was the first country to hire a consultant, a person from Ireland, who was later replaced by a person from France. Malawi also had a consultant, as did Mozambique. Not only did some of the BLNS countries have external consultants, but their consultants often changed the countries they were representing, presumably as a result of better financial offers. In one case, USAID hired a consultant to negotiate for a country. At one meeting, the consultant was the sole representative of that country. It is not clear as to whether the US consultant was hired to represent the interests of the respective country, SADC, or the US government.

During a speech at the World Economic Forum's Southern African Summit in Durban, South Africa in July 1999, US Deputy Secretary of Commerce Obert Mallet was quoted as saying that the region was moving too slowly with trade integration and that,

> [t]he global economy is here, and unlike Europe you don't have 40 years to get your act together .... Unless there is a realisation that the region had to be integrated, unless you decide that within six years we are going to achieve six things, you are not going to make it .... Investors are going to decide Africa is just not ready .... We cannot remain in this posture of standing in the morass saying it is difficult to move because this is Southern Africa (quoted in Ralinala & Saunders, 2000:22).

Allegedly it was after this lashing that the five-year regional development plan was outlined by President Mbeki (Ralinala & Saunders, 2000:22). Is it the SADC region itself that needs to implement market integration, or is it the West that needs the SADC region to implement market integration? What is most unfortunate about Mallet's statement is that it reflects a lack of understanding regarding the complexity of the history of trade relations in the SADC region. It also presupposes that market integration is the most viable strategy to be pursued.

Handling of Sensitive Sectors

The negotiations for the handling of sensitive products/sectors were especially difficult. As previously noted, it was proposed that sensitive products consist of no more than 5–20 per cent of trade (Category C). The most sensitive regional sectors include the automotive industry, footwear and leather, clothing and textiles, and sugar. The major issue regarding these sectors is liberalisation, namely, how much time should be given to allow sensitive products to adjust to market competition before tariffs are removed. The guidelines for handling sensitive products were outlined at the 7th TNF, held in Harare. Member states agreed to adopt the following guidelines:

▶ Terminology – Sensitive products are those products whose liberalisation may start during the agreed upon phase-in period of tariff reductions and could continue beyond the 8 year period.

▶ Product Sensitivity
1. The guidelines for selection of sensitive products should be based on the impact on revenue, employment and domestic industries.
2. Member States must provide reasons to justify their lists of sensitive products.
3. Member States must also indicate steps that they intend to take with regard to the reduction of tariffs on sensitive products.

▶ Coverage
1. The SADC Free Trade Area should cover substantially all trade.
2. The list of sensitive products should be kept as small as possible.

▶ Dynamic Concept
1. Sensitivity of products is likely to change over time. Therefore, Member States are encouraged to review their lists of sensitive products regularly with a view to move such products to either gradual or immediate liberalization lists.
2. Member States agreed to hold a general review meeting on tariff reduction schedules not later than 4 years after entry into force of the Trade Protocol (7th TNF, January 1999:4–5).

Malawi's phase-down tariff schedules for sensitive products and/or products for gradual liberalisation are outlined in Table 4.4, below, to illustrate the process. Although it was agreed that by 2012 all sensitive products would be eliminated and thus would have zero tariffs, some countries have extended their phase-down of sensitive products beyond this time frame ('Record of the 14th Meeting of the SADC Industry and Trade Committee of Ministers', 2000:20). Malawi is a case in point. According to its offer for the phase-down of sensitive products (see Table 4.4, below), by 2012, only those sensitive products with a tariff rate of five per cent will have zero duties. For sensitive products that have a tariff rate of 30 per cent, during the ninth year of the implementation of the FTA, the rate will be reduced to 20 per cent, 15 per cent during year ten, eight per cent during year 11, and four per cent during year 12.

Table 4.4: Malawi's Phase-Down Tariff Offer for Sensitive Products

	Year 9	Year 10	Year 11	Year 12
30%	20%	15%	8%	4%
25%	15%	12%	8%	3%
20%	15%	10%	4%	2%
15%	10%	6%	4%	2%
10%	8%	5%	3%	1%
5%	4%	2%	1%	0%

Source: 'Record of the 8th Special Meeting of the SADC Industry and Trade Committee of Ministers' (2000:19)

Each of the member states has products that are excluded from the phase-down tariff reduction schedule. These products are listed by country in Figure 4.2, below. Notwithstanding the lists, at the TNF held in Dar es Salaam in November 1999, it was agreed that the only permanent exclusions would be arms and ammunition and endangered animals, which fall under Articles 9 and 10 of the Protocol. Consequently, member states were requested to remove from their exclusion lists those products not falling under Articles 9 and 10. Otherwise, they should give a convincing explanation as to why products should remain on the list. All other products should be placed on the schedule for tariff liberalisation ('Record of the 14th Meeting of the SADC Industry and Trade Committee of Ministers', 2000:21–2).

Of major concern to the SADC member states is intra-regional trade in second-hand products. Consequently, a decision was made that intra-regional trade in such goods would not be allowed. It was agreed, however, that each member state could have their own domestic policies for the use of second-hand products ('Record of the 9th Special Meeting of the SADC Industry and Trade Committee of Ministers', 2000:23).

FIGURE 4.2

Exclusion Lists

Malawi
Matches
Sugar
Arms and ammunition

Mozambique
Arms and ammunition
Ivory
Tortoise shells
Sugar

SACU
Second-hand clothing, fuel (HS chap. 27)

Tanzania
Arms and ammunition
Opium
Endangered animals

Zambia
Arms and ammunition
Petroleum

Zimbabwe
Arms and ammunition
Second-hand clothing
Used tyres
Vehicles
Radio-active material

Mauritius
None, except those fulfilling the requirements of the provisions of Articles 9 and 10 of the SADC Protocol on Trade.

Source: 'Record of the 14th Meeting of the SADC Industry and Trade Committee of Ministers' (2000:21)

Of the four sectors identified as sensitive (automotive, footwear and leather, clothing and textiles, and sugar), clothing and textiles and sugar have been extremely contentious. While the former is analysed in the next section on rules of origin, the latter is discussed in this section. The issue of the FTA and the automotive industry is also discussed in this section.

SA = largest amt.
Zimb = most efficient producer

Sugar Industry

Sugar production in the region is among the cheapest in the world, and several countries are major producers, including South Africa, Zimbabwe, Mauritius, Swaziland, and Malawi. Although South Africa produces the largest amount of sugar annually (2.5 million tons during 1999–2000), Zimbabwe is the most efficient producer at US$189 per ton. South Africa's production cost is US$248 per ton, Swaziland's is US$233, Zambia's is US$230, and Malawi's is US$195 (Atkins & Terry, 1998:140). The sector provides job opportunities for many (see Table 4.5, below) and serves as a major source of foreign exchange. Regional production is 4.5 million tons annually, although countries such as Zimbabwe and Mozambique are expected to increase their production in the near future. With respect to the SADC region, the South African Department of Trade and Industry estimates that production will increase to six million tons by 2010 (see Table 4.6, opposite).

Table 4.5: Employment in the SADC Sugar Industries, 1995

Country	Directly employed	Indirectly employed	Total
Angola	n/a	n/a	n/a
Malawi	13 000	15 000	28 000
Mauritius	37 000	20 000	57 000
Mozambique*	n/a	n/a	13 497
South Africa	130 000	12 000	142 000
Swaziland	9 000	20 000	29 000
Tanzania	32 000	20 000	52 000
Zambia	8 000	60 000	68 000
Zimbabwe	19 000	100 000	119 000
SADC total	**248 000**	**247 000**	**508 497**

Source: Atkins and Terry (1998:132)   * Figures for Mozambique as provided in the source

Note: The ACP-derived figures for indirect employment probably relate to the total number of dependents rather than indirect employment.

SACU = sugar quotas

With a view to protecting the SACU market against regional competition, during the trade negotiations, SACU proposed the establishment of a regional sugar protocol that would introduce sugar quotas. Such sugar would enter the SACU market duty-free. The SACU proposal called for

> [t]he sharing of growth in the SACU market, divided amongst all SADC sugar producing countries according to net surpluses exported to the world market. In order to address concerns about the possible adverse effect of a fall in the SACU market growth after the initial 3 year access period, SACU offered to guarantee a minimum annual growth of 45,000 tons ('Record of the 6th Special Meeting of the SADC Industry and Trade Committee of Ministers', 1999:4).

Table 4.6: SADC Sugar Production – Actual and Potential Tonnages (millions of tons)

	1996–97 Actual	Potential (2010)
South Africa	2 275 000	2 700 000
Swaziland	471 000	650 000
Zimbabwe	500 000	800 000
Zambia	150 000	250 000
Malawi	224 000	250 000
Mauritius	570 000	610 000
Tanzania	114 000	220 000
Mozambique	26 000	300 000
Angola	21 000	250 000
Total	**4 351 000**	**6 030 000**

Source: *African Business* (1998)

For the first three years, SACU proposed that SACU's market share of 45 000 tons would be distributed as follows: 40 000 tons to SACU, 3 000 tons to Zambia, and 2 000 tons to Zimbabwe. Malawi, Mauritius, Mozambique, and Tanzania would not receive an allocation. With the offer, South Africa expected the proposed sugar protocol to supercede all other existing sugar agreements. This would mean, for example, that Zimbabwe, which exports 80 000–90 000 tons annually to Botswana and Namibia through bilateral trade agreements, would forfeit these agreements and replace them with one that gives it market access of 2 000 tons annually.[8]

Clearly unhappy with South Africa's offer, the non-SACU SADC countries presented a counterproposal at the 13th TNF in Cape Town during September 1999 that stated the following:

non SACU SADC = unhappy

▶ Market access should be reserved to non-SACU countries on the basis of a 5 per cent share of total SACU consumption. This would represent an annual tonnage of 75 000 tons and would secure a reasonable initial access into the SACU market.
▶ As from year two and the ensuing year, the 75 000 tons would be increased to take into account the actual growth in the SACU market.
▶ The 75 000 tons would be shared among the non-SACU countries who would agree among themselves on the initial quotas.
▶ A reallocation formula would be provided for in the case of shortfalls by individual countries (13th TNF, September 1999:12).

To further illustrate how far apart the SACU and non-SACU countries were on this issue, Zimbabwe indicated that it felt it should have market access of 85 000 tons. And Tanzania 'sought clarification because it did not see logic prevailing when SACU reserves for itself a quota of 40,000 tons' (13th TNF, September 1999:13–14). In response to the non-SACU countries, SACU reinforced its position that free market access on sugar was not possible (13th TNF, September 1999:14).   *different views*

‾, South Africa's protectionist position is based on the fear that free market access to the SACU market would erode its ability to provide for the domestic market, which would result in the country having to export sugar to the world market, where prices are below the cost of production. The South African Sugar Association predicts that if free market access was given to the SACU market without phase-out programmes, some mills would be forced to close and the most vulnerable growers would not be able to survive. Although the larger producers might survive, along with larger millers' estates, they would probably only break even economically. The impact on the industry would consequently result in massive unemployment (Thomas, 2001:81–2).

Protectionist polices adopted by South Africa are no different than those adopted by the richest countries of the world and are designed to prevent the developing countries from having access to their markets due to fear of competition. Ironically, South Africa is using the same strategies against its regional neighbours, while simultaneously calling on the developed countries to open their markets to developing countries. In the case of the sugar industry, if South Africa allowed for unrestricted regional access, consumers in South Africa would benefit from lower sugar prices, resulting in a net economic benefit for the country (Thomas, 2001:82–3).

South Africa's effort to protect its sugar sector may not be succeeding. With respect to protection against non-SACU SADC member states, a Zimbabwean official involved in the trade negotiations noted that

> South Africa is afraid our sugar will penetrate the SACU market, but it is already going there illegally. The Northern Province – how can they be looking for sugar coming from Durban or Cape Town, when just across the valley there is cheaper sugar? It's uneconomic.[9]

SA Sugar is inefficient / not compet.

In addition, South Africa's sugar giants and the DTI are being challenged by industrial sugar users to either decrease the cost of locally produced sugar or face the possibility of them importing sugar. However, as a result of the fact that this is the most protected agriculture sector in the country, huge tariffs are placed on imported sugar. Industrial sugar users argue that as a result of protectionism, South African sugar production is inefficient and non-competitive (*Sunday Times*, 5 March 2000).

At the 8th Special Meeting of the SADC Industry and Trade Committee of Ministers held in Sandton, South Africa during March 2000, another effort was made to resolve this issue. SACU improved its offer, which included the eventual full liberalisation of the SADC sugar sector and an additional quota of 20 000 tons (non-reciprocal, tariff-free) to non-SACU surplus-producing countries. The offer was based on the following principles:

▶ The market access arrangement forming an integral part of a SADC Sugar Cooperation Agreement to be negotiated in the context of TNF.

▶ A committee must be established with representatives from all SADC countries to administer the Sugar Cooperation Agreement. The functions of this committee will be established by the Technical Committee on Sugar on basis [sic] of the terms of reference for cooperation in SADC as already accepted by the meeting of the 15th TNF ('Record of the 8th Special Meeting of the SADC Industry and Trade Committee of Ministers', 2000:13).

The distribution of the allocation of the additional 20 000 tons was to be based on the export exposure of the non-SACU SADC countries. Since the latter countries were still not satisfied with the SACU offer, it was determined that the Committee of Senior Officials needed to continue negotiations in this area.

The problem of access to the SACU sugar market was finally solved with the Sugar Cooperation Agreement. According to the agreement, the SADC sugar industry will be fully liberalised by 2012. Liberalisation will be on a reciprocal basis and will include the removal of NTBs. Such liberalisation, however, would depend on the conditions in the regional sugar industry after five years of the implementation of the SADC FTA. A review will be undertaken in 2006 to determine if conditions prevail in the region for liberalisation. In addition, the agreement stipulates the following for the first five years of the SADC FTA:

▶ Share in growth of the SACU market – the distribution of the growth in SACU market size will be on the basis of relative exposure to the world market. The higher this exposure, the higher will be the share annually ....
▶ Additional access tonnage – an additional 20,000 tons will be made available to non-SACU SADC countries. The 20,000 tons is to be allocated annually on the basis of the relative exposure to the world market for the non-SACU SADC sugar producers.

With respect to the above, the following applies:

▶ Annual growth of the SACU market will be deemed to be 45,000 tons in year 1 increasing to 91,000 tons in year 2 and 138,000 tons in year 3. In years 4 and 5, the growth will be reviewed on the basis of the actual growth of the prior 3 years, subject to tonnage being guaranteed not to fall below 138,000 tons.
▶ In respect of the deemed growth, the denominator will be the total SADC exposure to the world market. In respect of the 20,000 additional tonnage, the denominator will be the total non-SACU SADC exposure to the world market.
▶ The determined allocations are not transferable between countries. In the case of *force majeure*, the quantities not supplied will be re-distributed on the basis of relative exposure to the world market.
▶ Quantities will be measured in metric tons tel quel (MTTQ) in all cases.
▶ Existing bilateral arrangements between SACU and non-SACU SADC member states will not be affected by this arrangement. However, any access by non-SACU SADC countries under the bilaterals will be regarded as preferential access in determining exposure to the world market ('Record of the 14th Meeting of the SADC Industry and Trade Committee of Ministers', 2000:41–2).

The SADC Technical Committee on Sugar was approved as a permanent entity to oversee the Sugar Cooperation Agreement.

South Africa's refusal to allow free access to the SACU sugar market is one of the many ironies of the movement toward market integration in Southern Africa. Theoretically, under market integration, the most efficient and cost-effective producer(s) should dominate the market since they would have a competitive advantage ('the ability to sell a good at the lowest price' (Gerber, 1999:425)) over other producers. In this case, Zimbabwe is the most efficient and cost-effective producer in the region.

Percy Mistry agrees that South Africa should source sugar from the more efficient regional producers. He further notes that in the long term, both South Africa and Mauritius should consider getting out of the sugar industry and diversifying their economies. Zimbabwe might consider this option as well, although it is the most cost-efficient producer in the region. The rationale behind this recommendation is that South Africa, Mauritius, and Zimbabwe have more economic choices than other SADC member states where 'sugar production provides the only viable prospect for trade and economic development and growth' (Mistry, quoted in Thomas, 2001:82).

A great deal is at stake for all the sugar producing SADC member states. It is difficult for countries to be economically rational when faced with the prospect of increased unemployment. Also, the notion of free trade, as discussed in Chapter 1, is applied in reality when it is beneficial to countries.

As the regional giant, South Africa has the ability to wield its power in such a way that it guarantees that its interests are protected. Nonetheless, it appears that the problem over access to the growing SACU sugar market is symptomatic of the larger picture, namely, that implementing market integration in Southern Africa is problematic. There are structural problems in the region if South Africa felt that it had to go to such great lengths to protect its sugar industry. This is especially poignant in that South Africa, as the regional giant, maintains an 8:1 trade ratio in its favour with the other SADC member states. This is not the only sector where South Africa feels it must be protectionist where it does not have a competitive advantage. Unfortunately, as will become evident, South Africa adopted similar protectionist policies throughout the negotiations. Such protectionist positions were taken even if it was projected that sectors in other countries would be undermined. This is not the spirit in which market integration can be successfully implemented. All countries must perceive that there are benefits to be gained, otherwise market integration will result in greater regional polarisation and de-industrialisation. When the prerequisites are in place for market integration, governments that have economies that are diversified, such as South Africa, can make decisions to redirect their resources from a less efficient industry with little value added to one that is more efficient and has more value on the regional market.

Automotive Industry

South Africa overwhelmingly dominates the regional automotive industry (see Table 4.7, opposite). The second largest motor vehicle producer in the region is Zimbabwe, which in 1998 produced 14 000 vehicles, compared to South Africa's 313 000. The 'other' category in Table 4.7 mainly consists of production in Zambia, Botswana, and Mozambique. In Zambia and Botswana, however, production has basically been discontinued. Zambia's small industry was adversely affected by the SAP and economic deterioration, while Botswana was forced to temporarily close its Hyundai plant, where it was assembling vehicles, due to financial difficulties. The Mozambique operation, which is also small, assembles medium and heavy commercial vehicles (Black & Muradzikwa, 2000:7).

Although Zimbabwe has the second largest market for vehicle production in the region, it does not pose a threat to South Africa's market. In fact, as a competitor, Zimbabwe is declining in significance. For example, while Zimbabwe has the capacity to produce 40 000 light vehicles annually (Black & Muradzikwa, 2000:7), only 14 000 were produced in 1998. The declining production is a reflection of the current economic crisis as well as plants that are outmoded, restrictive licensing agreements, and deficient quality. Problems with the export market include, in addition to the above, limited government support, unfair competition from South Africa, and political uncertainty. Of the approximately 30 per cent of vehicles that are imported into Zimbabwe, most are sourced from South Africa, along with original equipment components (Black & Muradzikwa, 2000:8–9). Most of Zimbabwe's automotive exports are to the SACU countries. Such exports have declined significantly since 1993 (Black & Muradzikwa, 2000:9).

Table 4.7: Automotive Production and Sales in SADC ('000 units)

Year	South Africa Production	South Africa Sales	Zimbabwe Production	Zimbabwe Sales	Other SADC Production	Other SADC Sales
1990	343	335	10	9.5	1.4	14
1991	315	308	11.5	8.2	1.4	12
1992	293	284	7	8.2	0.9	13
1993	308	298	7	8.4	0.5	15
1994	313	308	8.5	10	0.4	19
1995	389	387	10	10.8	0.2	22
1996	394	421	15	13	0.2	24
1997	364	399	18	16.5	0.1	27
1998	313	351	14	12.1	10	26

Source: Black and Muradzikwa (2000:7)   *Motor Industry Development Programme*

SACU automotive exports to SADC member states in 1998 totalled R3 billion, which reflects a significant increase over the 1995 figure of R1.7 billion (Black & Muradzikwa, 2000:8). Under the FTA, SACU exports will likely increase tremendously and, in fact, it is speculated that South Africa will be the centre of all automotive activity, with SADC countries having to pay higher prices for vehicles sourced from South Africa (Black & Muradzikwa, 2000:9). Zimbabwe fears that if SACU's recommendations are adopted for the FTA, Zimbabwe would be put out of the motor vehicle business (11th TNF, June 1999:20). With or without an FTA, as explained below, this will probably be the case anyway.

According to Table 4.8, overleaf, for rules of origin in this sector, SACU proposed that South Africa's Motor Industry Development Programme (MIDP) be adopted by all member states. The MIDP, introduced by the South African government in 1995, is designed to liberalise the automotive industry and make it export-oriented. The main provisions of the MIDP, according to Anthony Black, are:

▶ The excise duty based local content system has been changed to a tariff driven programme.
▶ There is no minimum local content requirement.
▶ Tariffs on light vehicles are being phased down to 40% ... and 30% for components by 2002.
▶ Manufacturers of light vehicles are entitled to a duty free allowance (27% of the wholesale value of the vehicle) for the importation of original components.
▶ Import duty on components and vehicles may be offset by import rebate credits derived from the export of vehicles and components.
▶ Provision is made for a Small Vehicle Incentive (SVI) in the form of a higher duty free allowance for low cost vehicles (Black, 1998:6–7).

Table 4.8: Consolidated Negotiating Text, Vehicles, Chapter 87

HS heading no.	Description of products	Comments	Proposed rules by member states
Chapter 87	Vehicles other than railway or tramway rolling-stock, and parts and accessories thereof	*The meeting agreed that SITCD and SADC Secretariat should initiate as soon as possible the convening of a technical committee of the motor industry, which permits attendance by all member States.*	Manufacture in which the c.i.f. value of the material used does not exceed 40% of the ex-factory cost of the product *(SACU Proposal)*
8701	Tractors (other than tractors of heading No. 8709)		MIDP rule to apply *(SACU Proposal)*
8702	Motor vehicles for the transport of ten or more persons		MIDP rule to apply *(SACU Proposal)*
8703	Motor cars		MIDP rule to apply *(SACU Proposal)*
8704	Motor vehicles for the transport of goods		MIDP rule to apply *(SACU Proposal)*
8706	Chassis with engines, for the motor vehicles of headings Nos 8701 and 8705		MIDP rule to apply *(SACU Proposal)*
8707	Bodies for motor vehicles of headings Nos 8701 and 8705		MIDP rule to apply *(SACU Proposal)*
8711, 8712 and 8713	Motorcycles, bicycles and invalid carriages		Manufacture the value added resulting from the process of production account for at least 35 per cent of the ex-factory cost of the product *(Mauritius Proposal)*

Source: 'Record of the 8th Special Meeting of the SADC Industry and Trade Committee of Ministers' (2000:10)

The introduction of the MIDP gave a much-needed boost to the automotive industry. With the financial incentives under the MIDP, the big car manufacturers of the world have been lured to South Africa. The import-export complementation programme, for example, which allows import rebate credits for the export of vehicles and components, means that if foreign car makers export enough, they do not have to pay duties on vehicles imported into the country. The strategy has worked and South Africa has become a profitable export base for cars and, more importantly, for motor industry components (*The Times*, 4 January 2001). While in 1988 automotive exports from South Africa totalled R315 million, by 1999 the figure had grown to an estimated R14 billion. This represents 90 per cent of the total SADC export market. With the automotive industry, South Africa is more integrated at the global level than at the regional (Black & Muradzikwa, 2000:8).

South Africa clearly has a comparative advantage ('opportunity costs of producing a good are lower than those of its trading partner' (Gerber, 1999:425)) over its SADC neighbours in the automobile industry. With the import-export complementation, the industry receives *de facto* export subsidies, which means that Zimbabwe, for example, faces unfair competition from South Africa. As previously indicated, if SACU's proposals are adopted, all SADC countries who produce automobiles would adopt the MIDP. They would therefore be forced to comply with MIDP rules. This would mean that:

▶ A common external tariff is introduced amongst MIDP participating countries aligned to the SACU level of about 50% (light motor vehicles); 24% (for heavy motor vehicles); and 37.5% (for components);
▶ MIDP Rules on Manufacture apply with respect to original equipment component imports (Chapter 98 – SACU);
▶ Import Rebate Credit Certificates (IRCCS) cease to apply to MIDP participating SADC countries; and
▶ No tariff barriers to intra-SADC trade for MIDP participating countries [apply] immediately (Zimbabwe Ministry of Industry and Commerce, 1999a:13).

While South African vehicle assemblers would welcome competition from the SADC region and thus the removal of trade barriers, South African-based vehicle manufacturers are not as positive about an FTA. If an agreement is reached to have a free trade regime for this sector, it would mean that MIDP *de facto* export subsidies would be eliminated. In addition, vehicle manufacturers are concerned about reduced regulatory controls as a result of a large FTA. In cost/benefit analysis terms, the perception is that since they are already heavily entrenched in the regional market, the cost might outweigh the benefits of an automotive free trade regime (Zimbabwe Ministry of Industry and Commerce, 1999a:9).

Rules of Origin

One of the most controversial issues during the negotiations was over the rules of origin. Rules of origin are designed 'to ensure that only products and goods, which are produced and traded among the member states of the FTA, benefit from the agreed preferential market access arrangement' (SADC, 1999a:1). According to the Protocol, there are three rules of origin for classifying products and goods:

(1) Wholly Produced Goods with no import content ... mainly Agricultural produce;
(2) Achievement of Specified Local Content ... 40% local materials or 35% value added. This applies to goods utilizing both imported and local materials;

minimum process occur ⇒ must o

(3) Change of Tariff Heading ... where the Tariff Classification of the inputs is different from that of the resultant product (SADC, 1999b:1).

In addition, a list exists that identifies the minimum process that must occur in order to ensure that a change of tariff heading is the result of significant transformation. According to the Protocol, the exporter identifies the rule that is most appropriate for exported goods. This flexibility is designed to enhance intra-regional trade (SADC, 1999b:1).

Under the Protocol, with respect to originating goods, the SADC region is deemed to be one territory. This means that, '[a]nything sourced within SADC and processed in other SADC countries is deemed to be originating. This should provide a major boost for regional processing and the development of upstream and downstream linkages with a whole range of industries' (SADC, 1999a:5).

The negotiations over rules of origin once again placed South Africa at the centre of controversy. While the non-SACU SADC states were content with the rules of origin as outlined in the Protocol, SACU, under the leadership of South Africa, demanded that SADC adopt new rules of origin that cover all tradeable items in the region, or product-specific rules of origin. This was needed, according to the SACU members, because:

(1) The rules prescribing Local Content is [*sic*] not sufficient for primary and agricultural products and sensitive products such as textiles, clothing, footwear, motor vehicles and motor vehicle components.

(2) The freedom given to exporters to select the rule to apply for a given product should be removed (SADC, 1999b:1).

In essence, SACU wanted 'more meaningful beneficiation of local raw material', and the local content rule replaced by a Change in Tariff Heading rule 'with Product-Specific Processes being the main substantial transformation criteria' (SADC, 1999b:1). With respect to the latter, SACU suggested that there be put in place product-specific rules of origin for textiles, clothing, footwear, and motor vehicles (SADC, 1999a:3). At the 11th TNF, SACU's proposal stipulated the following specific rules of origin:

▶ Application of two-tariff heading changes for textiles and clothing. This means that SADC yarn must be used for the manufacture of SADC originating fabric for intra-SADC trade and SADC fibre must be used for SADC originating clothing for intra-SADC trade.

▶ For footwear, 85% local content is proposed.

▶ For motor vehicles these have to comply with the CKD[10] definition which for light motor vehicles requires that the floor panels, body sides and roof panels may not be attached to each other and that the engine, transmission, axles, radiators, suspension components, steering mechanisms, braking or electrical equipment or instrumentation may not be fitted to the floor panels or chassis frame of the light motor vehicle.

▶ With respect to Replacement Components/parts/accessories, these will be regarded as originating from a SADC country if they meet Rule 2.1(a) or 2.1(b) or 2.1(c) and the value added criterion as set out in Rule 2.1(b)(ii) in Annex 1 of the SADC Protocol on Trade falls away (SADC, 1999a:3).

The non-SACU SADC countries responded by arguing that the rules of origin did not need to be revised prior to the implementation of the Protocol. Furthermore, if SACU's proposals were adopted, the Protocol would have to be amended (SADC, 1999b:2).

The fundamental objection of the non-SACU countries to SACU's proposed rules of origin centred around the perception that SACU was attempting to protect its trade regime against competition from the non-SACU members:

Overall, many delegations felt that the SACU proposal over estimated the industrial capacity of the region and did not take into account the scarce availability of local inputs of the required quality, quantity and the need to produce goods at competitive prices both on the local and on the world markets. They felt that, contrary to the SACU assumption, the product-specific rule proposed by SACU would not lead to increased regional industrialisation nor to foreign direct investment. Rather they considered that product-specific rules as proposed by SACU would imply increased protection of the SACU market. They suggested that in the case of trade deflection or tariff circumvention, alternative trade or administrative instruments such as safeguards or stricter customs procedures should be considered (11th TNF, June 1999:5).

This perception was reinforced following SACU's submission to the TNF in June 1999 regarding its recommendation on product-specific rules of origin. Although SACU had indicated that such rules would apply only to a limited number of sensitive sectors – agriculture, textiles, clothing, leather, footwear, automotive, and chemicals – the proposal actually covered all intra-SADC trade. In addition, the proposed rules of origin were based on those of the Lomé Convention, which was of concern to the non-SACU SADC members (12th TNF, July 1999:4). In the end, however, the member states agreed to develop product-specific rules of origin for all tradeables.

The greatest contention among the SADC member states with respect to rules of origin has been in the textiles and clothing sector (Chapters 50–63). In fact, the failure to agree to rules of origin for this sector contributed significantly to the decision by the member states to reschedule the launching of the SADC FTA from January to September 2000.

The stalemate over textiles and clothing occurred when South Africa insisted that a two-stage transformation process, resulting in a double tariff heading change, was needed in the textile and clothing sector as proof of origin from within the region. A double tariff change results in two changes in the manufacturing process, based on the four-digit HS nomenclature in the manufacturing process (SADC, 1999c:3). A two-stage transformation process would be, for example, the manufacture of fibre into yarn and yarn into cloth. For the non-SACU SADC countries, this proposal would seemingly enhance South Africa's economic domination of the region.

In order to move the negotiations forward, South Africa agreed to a compromise that would allow the non-SACU LDCs to have a derogation on the two-stage transformation process. The issue appeared to be finally settled during the High Level Committee (HLC)[11] meeting held during March 2000, where an agreement was reached between the SACU states and Malawi, Mozambique, Tanzania, and Zambia (see Table 4.9, overleaf). They agreed to two sets of rules of origin:

Option 1: would apply to all SADC Member States with no quotas
Option 2: would apply to the Non-SADC LDCs i.e. Malawi, Mozambique, Tanzania and Zambia (MMTZ) subject to quotas for an initial 5 years [sic] period ('Record of the 8th Special Meeting of the SADC Industry and Trade Committee Ministers', 2000:5).

This would mean that for five years MMTZ could continue to export to regional countries products within the clothing and textile sector that only undergo a one-stage transformation, albeit with quota restrictions. These goods would continue to be considered as having originated from the region. In practice, for example, it would mean that under Option 1 for Chapters 50–60, fabrics must be manufactured from fibres, while under Option 2, fabrics can be manufactured from yarn ('Record of the 8th Special Meeting of the SADC Industry and Trade Committee Ministers', 2000:6). A Textile and Clothing Committee will be established in order to monitor the rules of origin. The agreement, however, would be contingent upon the countries in question giving the BLNS countries greater access to their markets.

Table 4.9: Consolidated Negotiating Text, Rules of Origin, Chapters 50–63

		OPTION 1[12] To all member states: No quota	OPTION 2 To MMTZ: Subject to quota
For fabrics of chapter 50 to 60		▶ Manufacture from fibres	▶ Manufacture from yarn Or ▶ Printing accompanied by at least two preparatory or finishing operations (such as scouring, bleaching, mercerising, heat setting, raising, calendering, shrink resistance processing, permanent finishing, decatizing, impregnating, mending and burling) where the value of the unprinted fabric used does not exceed 47.5% of the ex-works price of the product
For clothing of chapter 61		Obtained by sewing together or otherwise assembling, two or more pieces of knitted or crocheted fabric which have been either cut to form or obtained directly to form: ▶ Manufacture from yarn Other: ▶ Manufacture from fibres	*(Obtained by sewing together or otherwise assembling, two or more pieces of knitted or crocheted fabric which have been either cut to form)* ▶ Laying out and cutting of uncut fabric; assembly of cut components by stitching or other appropriate methods; necessary finishing, including addition of trim and other findings, washing and pressing etc.; and packaging of finished items; Or *(Obtained by sewing together or otherwise assembling, two or more pieces of knitted or crocheted fabric which have been knit directly to form)* ▶ Knitting of shaped components from single yarn; looping and lining of components; necessary finishing, including addition of trim and other findings; washing and pressing etc.; and packaging of finished items

		OPTION 1[12] To all member states: No quota	OPTION 2 To MMTZ: Subject to quota
For clothing of chapter 62		▶ Manufacture from yarn	▶ Laying out and cutting of uncut fabric; assembly of cut components by stitching or other appropriate methods; necessary finishing, including addition of trim and other findings, washing and pressing etc.; and packaging of finished items
Other made up textile articles of chapter 63		▶ Manufacture in which all the materials used are classified within a heading other than that of the product	▶ Laying out and cutting of uncut fabric; assembly of cut components by stitching or other appropriate methods; necessary finishing, including addition of trim and other findings, washing and pressing etc.; and packaging of finished items
Ex 6301 to 6304	Of felt, of non-wovens	Manufacture from: ▶ natural fibres, or ▶ chemical materials or textile pulp	Same rule for all the chapter
	Embroidered	Manufacture from unbleached single yarn or Manufacture from unembroidered fabric (other than knitted or crocheted) provided the value of the unembroidered fabric used does not exceed 40% of the ex-works price of the product	Same rule for all the chapter
	Other	Manufacture from unbleached single yarn	Same rule for all the chapter
Ex 6305		Manufacture from: ▶ natural fibres, ▶ man-made staple fibres not carded or combed or otherwise processed for spinning, or ▶ chemical materials or textile pulp	Same rule for all the chapter

Source: 'Record of the 8th Special Meeting of the SADC Industry and Trade Committee of Ministers' (2000:6)

[handwritten margin note: 5 yrs = not long enough]

During the grace period of five years given to MMTZ, it is anticipated that they will be able to attract the necessary investments that would allow them to conform to the two-stage transformation process. Concern has been raised, however, that five years is too short a period to attract needed investment into the region. In fact, according to a SADC-commissioned study, 'SACU insists that, after the agreement expires ... the rules of origin should revert to double transformation, a condition that the MMTZ countries will not be able to meet without buying nearly all cloth from SACU' (Coughlin, 2001:33). As will be discussed below, sourcing cloth from South Africa will not be cost-efficient. The agreement on Chapters 50–63 (textiles and textile articles) is presented in Table 4.9, above.

[handwritten margin note: SACU vs MMTZ]

The quotas initially proposed by SACU for MMTZ and the counterproposals by MMTZ are outlined in Table 4.10, below. As is evident from the table, there exists a significant difference between the two proposals. On its part, Malawi noted that the SACU quotas allocated by SACU were 'well below their current exports to SACU under the respective tariff lines' ('Record of the 9th Special Meeting of the SADC Industry and Trade Committee of Ministers', 2000:12). Mozambique argued that: (1) quotas cannot be imposed on Mozambican raw cotton that is wholly obtained; (2) the quota proposed for Chapters 61 and 62 was below production capacities; (3) a quota should be given for Chapter 60; (4) quotas should increase annually by 20 per cent; and (5) five years was not long enough to allow for the development of its capacity to meet the requirement for double stage transformation ('Record of the 9th Special Meeting of the SADC Industry and Trade Committee of Ministers', 2000:12).

Table 4.10: Consolidated Table on Quota Proposals by MMTZ and SACU

	Proposed quota limits				
	HS CH 52	HS CH 55	HS CH 60	HS CH 61–2	HS CH 63
	Kg	Kg	Kg	Pieces	Kg
SACU for Malawi	1 200 000	43 000	0	8 565 000	665 000
Malawi	1 400 000	90 000	200 000	12 000 000	800 000
SACU for Mozambique	3 600 000	0	0	3 900 000	170 000
Mozambique	3 600 000	0	300 000	9 000 000	170 000
SACU for Tanzania	1 200 000	0	0	500 000	300 000
Tanzania	1 200 000	0	0	500 000	300 000
SACU for Zambia	1 700 000	390 000	60 000	500 000	300 000
Zambia	4 000 000	1 000 000	60 000	500 000	300 000
Total SACU	7 700 000	433 000	60 000	13 465 000	1 435 000
Total MMTZ	10 200 000	1 090 000	560 000	22 000 000	1 570 000

Source: 'Record of the 9th Special Meeting of the SADC Industry and Trade Committee of Ministers' (2000:11–12)

Zambia complained that SACU's proposed agreement did not allow it to reach its export potential. It therefore not only requested an increase in quota allocations, but also that quota allocations be given for tariff lines that were excluded. They were as follows:

▶ For 54.07 (100% woven polyester fabric): 200,000m^2 subject to rule of origin on man-made fibres/fabrics.

▶ For 58.02 (cotton towelling): 100 metric tonnes.

▶ For 6301.30 and 6301.40 (blankets): 25,000 pieces ('Record of the 9th Special Meeting of the SADC Industry and Trade Committee of Ministers', 2000:12).

Zambia also agreed with Mozambique that quotas should be increased over time.

For Tanzania, the quotas were deemed too low, thus prospectively preventing the country from realising its export potential. Since Tanzania did not attend the 2nd Meeting of the SADC Textiles and Clothing Committee, Table 4.10 does not reflect its request for quota increases. Tanzania requested that SACU review its quota allocation, because the arrangement at present was meaningless. In addition, it noted that '[i]mport intensive segments of the textiles and clothing industry were omitted. These include yarn and fabrics (HS. Code 55.01), knitted and crocheted fabrics (Chapter 60) and Blankets (HS. 63.1)' ('Record of the 9th Special Meeting of the SADC Industry and Trade Committee of Ministers', 2000:14). Given these two realities, Tanzania argued that SACU's offer

amounted to a zero preferential treatment to Tanzania under the LDCs textile and clothing framework. This conclusion was based on the fact that the omitted segments were the ones which precipitated the LDCs SACU dichotomy. Instead SACU [*sic*] offer to Tanzania confined it to its traditional cotton perimeter in a narrow sense. In a narrow sense because under the cotton perimeter Tanzania would have to achieve double transformation anywhere notwithstanding the existence of mills which were not integrated and import intensive but export oriented ('Record of the 9th Special Meeting of the SADC Industry and Trade Committee of Ministers', 2000:14).

While South Africa agreed to consider the increased quota requests of Mozambique, Malawi, and Tanzania, SACU was divided over the issue of tariff treatment for the MMTZ/SACU quota arrangement. South Africa, for example, indicated that an agreement had already been reached to allow goods from MMTZ to enter the SACU market duty-free, while the BLNS countries argued that tariffs should be imposed on these products, since they were given a concession of a single transformation process. In addition, Namibia complained that under the proposed arrangement, it would not benefit substantially. Reminding the participants that the MMTZ/SACU arrangement was contingent upon the BLNS countries having greater access to the markets of MMTZ, Namibia noted that based on their offers, it would not begin to benefit from the FTA until year three or eight, because only then would the products it is interested in exporting under categories B and C experience tariff reductions (18th TNF, August 2000:4). At a meeting held in Johannesburg in February 2001 to iron out remaining tariff issues, Malawi was the only country that accepted SACU's quota offer (African Eyes News Service, 22 February 2001).

As of February 2001, the SACU offer had basically remained the same. Malawi was allocated quotas under Chapter 60, although there was a slight decrease under Chapter 63, and Mozambique received a slight increase in allocation under Chapters 61–2 (Coughlin, 2001:41). The arrangement is for five years commencing 1 August 2001 (Madakufamba, 2001c). For MMTZ, the arrangement means that for five years they can use fabrics imported into the region for making garments exported to the SACU market duty-free, but with quota restrictions. For Malawi, the MMTZ agreement will replace the South Africa-Malawi bilateral trade agreement, which imposed a value-added criterion that has been difficult for Malawi to comply with. Although the new arrangement is generous to the textile industry, the quota restrictions will impose serious constraints on the growth of the country's clothing industry (Coughlin & Undenge, 2001:4). For Zambian manufacturers, the MMTZ arrangement will also remove previous restrictions, such as high SACU duties on human-made fibres that are imported as well as fabric produced from imported yarn and garments made from such fabrics (Musa & Mudenda, 2001:31).

Excluded from the special MMTZ/SACU arrangement, Zimbabwe and Mauritius suggested that those countries that comply with the two-stage transformation should be rewarded with an accelerated tariff reduction schedule, which they were granted (Madakufamba, 2001c). In addition, they requested that the single-stage transformation process be extended to them for Chapters 61–3. This request was made in light of the fact that it will not be possible for their clothing industries to comply with the two-stage transformation, especially for synthetic fabrics. This will therefore mean that under Option 1, the clothing sector of Zimbabwe and Mauritius would be excluded from having duty-free access to the SACU market.

For Zimbabwe, not having duty-free access to the SACU market means that the growth of the textile and garment industries will be hampered. For example, even when South African fabric is used to make garments for export to South Africa, a 13 per cent tariff is imposed on clothes that are covered by the quota and 26 per cent on other clothes under the South Africa-Zimbabwe bilateral trade agreement. In addition, a 22–30 per cent tariff is imposed by SACU on most fabrics of human-made fibres that are imported from outside SADC, even if such fabrics are not available in the region. A 40–60 per cent tariff is then imposed on garments made from the imported fabric (Coughlin et al., 2001:17). In the case of Mauritius, tariffs on some garments exported to SACU are as high as 80 per cent (Jeetah & Coughlin, 2001:25).

In a series of studies commissioned by SADC on the regional textile and garment industries, several recommended that SACU should revisit the double-stage transformation rule imposed on Mauritius and Zimbabwe. In addition to the restrictions imposed on Mauritius and Zimbabwe, the double-stage transformation rules place limitations on Botswana and Swaziland. For Botswana, the tariffs imposed by SACU on Zimbabwean cotton yarn and fabrics increases the cost of garment production for the South African market (Rubin, 2001a:21). A 13 per cent duty is imposed by SACU on yarn imported from non-MMTZ countries and 18 per cent on fabric (Rubin, 2001b:23). Zimbabwean yarns cost, on average, 43 per cent of those in South Africa, while the cost of fabric is approximately 58 per cent of the South African price. Consequently, Zimbabwean yarns and fabrics are more regionally competitive than those of South Africa (Rubin, 2001a:21). Swaziland also needs to be able to import yarn and fabric duty-free from Zimbabwe in order to expand the scope of its South African market and reduce the cost of production so that it can realise economies of scale (Rubin, 2001b:23).

The specific recommendation to revisit the double-stage transformation rule for Zimbabwe and Mauritius is that 'SADC should do all to persuade SACU to allow "single transformation for synthetic fibres and man-made fibre under HS Chapters 61–62 whose inputs are not available in the region" to quality for preferences under SADC' (Jeetah & Coughlin, 2001:27). The explanation SACU gives for its restrictive policies is that if duties are reduced and generous quotas are allowed for garments produced in the region but made from fabric from the Far East, trans-shipment will be encouraged (Coughlin *et al.*, 2001:28). This, however, is only part of the explanation for such restrictions.

The other explanation is that South Africa would like an arrangement in which all fabrics in the region are sourced from SADC member states, thus forbidding any imported fabric entry into the region. In this way, the textiles and clothing sector would develop, enhancing economic development and job creation. South Africa feels that the region should begin diversifying production in this area. For example, according to Mfundo Nkuhlu, former Chief Director, Africa Trade Relations in the South African Department of Trade and Industry, 'we have been pushing our own industry to begin to focus on sophisticated fabrics as a niche that we would like to service in the world market'.[13] For the majority of the other countries, South Africa's idea that all fabric be sourced from the region is considered to be untenable, and it is viewed as yet another ploy to guarantee that South Africa's textile and clothing sector is protected. Currently, South Africa produces a limited variety of human-made fabrics, and *unique fabric*

> [i]nsistence on the use of South African fabrics raises costs, limits variety, and in some cases, could reduce quality. Based on the price date for fabrics, the polyester and poly-cotton bottom weights from South Africa cost (c.i.f. Zimbabwe) about 20% more than comparable fabric from the Far East .... Garment manufacturers also complain about fabric dyeing problems with South African fabric (Coughlin *et al.*, 2001:28).

The non-SACU SADC countries want to be able to source human-made fibres from world-class Far East producers. They include Korea, Indonesia, Hong Kong, China, Taiwan, and Malaysia. The Far East is especially known for the production of light fabrics for women's clothes. The place to source heavy artificial fibres for men's suits is Eastern Europe. Since these are the most efficient and cheapest producers, it would not be cost-effective for SADC countries to try and develop the technology to replicate these fabrics for the sole purpose of increasing intra-regional trade. It is argued that it would take the region more time to attract possible investors to manufacture human-made fibres than it would for the region to open up its trade regime and utilise materials that are coming from world-class producers and continue to trade among themselves. As the SADC study on the textile and garment industries of South Africa notes, given the global access to human-made fibres at low prices, 'the wisdom of diverting scarce resources into additional capacity for human-made fibre production in South Africa should be questioned' (Jafta & Jeetah, 2001:39). Furthermore, in order to prevent these fabrics from entering the region, trade barriers would have to be erected against non-SADC fabric producers.

Clearly, the issue of rules of origin for the SADC textile and clothing sector has not been resolved, although an agreement has been reached that will be in force for five years. Since there is disagreement over the agreement, enforcing the rules of origin for Chapters 50–63 may indeed prove to be a real challenge.

Although this chapter has examined the issue of the rules of origin for the automotive and textile and clothing industries, there are other areas where the rules of origin will be challenging to the SADC regional agenda. These include COMESA and the bilateral trade agreements. In terms of COMESA, the rules of origin are less restrictive than the SADC rules, so the non-SACU SADC/COMESA countries can ignore the SADC rules of origin when trading among themselves. This includes Malawi, Zambia, Zimbabwe, Mauritius, Angola, and the DRC, although the latter two are not yet signatories to the SADC FTA. In addition, Malawi, Zambia, Zimbabwe, and Mauritius, as members of the COMESA free trade area, can totally ignore the SADC FTA and trade among themselves duty-free. With respect to the bilateral trade agreements, since they will remain in force as long as they are more advantageous than the SADC FTA, Zimbabwe, for example, will continue to have greater access to the markets of Namibia and Botswana under their bilateral agreements than under the SADC FTA (Coughlin *et al.*, 2001:27, 29).

Implementation of the SADC FTA

'The most significant thing about the recently introduced SADC free trade agreement is that is has been so insignificant', noted Riaan de Lange, head of the Deloitte & Touche international trade division in South Africa (*Freight & Trading Weekly*, 2000a). Ironically, following the announcement on 1 September 2000 that the SADC FTA was in force, only South Africa and Mauritius had deposited their instruments of implementation and thus were able to accede to the SADC FTA Protocol (BusinessMap, 2000a:20). By January 2001, only three additional countries had deposited their instruments of implementation – Botswana, Lesotho, and Swaziland. This was the case even though the SADC member states were only given six months (September 2000 to February 2001) to deposit the instruments. The deadline for actually implementing the Protocol was 31 August 2001 (*SADC Today*, 2001). By 1 August 2001, all member states had deposited their instruments of implementation (Madakufamba, 2001d). The SADC member states established a Protocol on Trade Implementation Unit (TIU) to oversee the implementation of the SADC Protocol on Trade. It will be housed at the SADC Secretariat in Gaborone, Botswana. The unit will consist of three experts in the areas of trade information, legal affairs, and customs and standards ('Record of the 9th Special Meeting of the SADC Industry and Trade Committee of Ministers', 2000:17).

In order to implement the SADC FTA, the member states must comply with GATT rules regarding free trade areas. According to Article 24 of GATT, a free trade area must substantially cover all trade, and member countries are not supposed to raise their external tariffs. In the case of developing countries, however, there is more leniency, including the fact that, under the enabling clause, they can bypass Article 24. The SADC member states intend to file to the WTO under the enabling clause or Article 24. In any event, the member states have determined that since the 'weighted average of the Member States trade coverage' will go beyond 85 per cent of total SADC trade, WTO requirements for free trade areas like SADC will be met ('Record of the 9th Special Meeting of the SADC Industry and Trade Committee of Ministers', 2000:21). The remainder of this section will examine the impact the implementation of the SADC FTA is likely to have on regional trade relations and the industrial sector.

Regional Trade Relations

Dot Keet reminds us that 'trade negotiations have very little to do with the rhetoric of "partnership" and a lot to do with the ruthless promotion – and, where necessary, protection – of the interests of national and multinational producers, exporters and investors' (Keet, 2000). To this end, she notes that South Africa negotiated with the non-SACU SADC member states in the same way that the EU negotiated with South Africa (see Chapter 7):

[handwritten annotations in top margin: "trade imbalance increase = regional hostility" and "soln = △ production structure"]

> Like the EU, South Africa has been very careful to ensure that most of the products in which the other SADC countries could even remotely offer some competition to South African producers ... have been placed on the list of 'sensitive products' to be dealt with at some future date, or subject to quota limitation (Keet, 2000).

It is precisely such labour-intensive, more efficient products, such as textiles, clothing, and footwear, that would be welfare enhancing for South Africa under a SADC FTA, according to the IMF (IMF, 1998:157).

In light of the reality that non-SACU SADC countries will have limited access to the South African market in sectors where they have competitive advantages, under a SADC FTA, the growing trade imbalance between South Africa and these countries will increase. The increase in this imbalance as a result of a SADC FTA will deepen the regional hostility toward South Africa. Trade diversion, where cheaper and more efficiently produced goods from a non-member country are replaced by more expensive and less efficient products from a member country, is a potential reality in some sectors (e.g. clothing and textiles) as a result of the agreements reached during the TNF. This reality is reinforced by the IMF, which argues that the only way that a SADC FTA could be a welfare-enhancing proposition for the region is if South Africa enhances its efficiency. At the present time, the IMF notes, South Africa is an inefficient supplier in relationship to third countries (IMF, 1998:156).

The only solution to the problem of the worsening trade imbalance between South Africa and the other SADC member states in the long-term is to change the production structures in the region in order to enhance the ability of the non-SACU SADC countries to produce for the South African market. This type of structural transformation has to be planned and can only occur, if possible, over an extended period of time. Planned structural transformation is not possible in an environment of increasing competition growing out of fierce struggles for access to each other's markets.

In the short-term, intra-regional trade can be increased by determining products that are imported into the region by SACU that are produced by non-SACU SADC countries and exported to the developed world. Such products are internationally competitive and therefore should be imported by SACU. Although South Africa talks about how untenable its advantageous 8:1 trade ratio with the region is, it does not seem prepared to seriously try to alter this reality. In this regard, South Africa does not act any differently from other regional hegemons. This behaviour, however, makes it difficult for the non-SACU SADC countries to consider rationalising their membership in other regional economic organisations. The SADC/COMESA countries feel that they are gaining from a more open COMESA trade regime than that offered by SADC. At the same time, they do not want to be excluded from any benefits that might accrue as a result of being a member of SADC. Under conditions of extreme poverty and instability, it is virtually impossible for nations to look beyond their own national interests.

In a study conducted by the World Bank, it was determined that regional FTAs that include South Africa would not be in the best interests of the organisations involved. They recommended that, alternatively, economic cooperation strategies between South Africa and the sub-continent should be pursued (Holden, 1996:v). In a similar vein, Charles Harvey argues that

> a free trade area will not have much chance of surviving, because a significant number of the non-SACU members of SADC do not have the capacity at present to increase their exports to South Africa. They would need, therefore, to attract the investment in new capacity that would make such export growth possible (Harvey, 2000a:11).

Summary

The negotiations for the creation of the SADC FTA revealed the tremendous amount of competition that exists among the SADC member states. This competition exists because, as discussed in Chapter 2, the region is not stable economically. In most of the countries, macroeconomic stability has not been realised and unemployment is a growing problem. Under such conditions, it is very difficult to open vulnerable markets to external competition, which is what trade liberalisation inevitably does. This is even more difficult in a country like Zimbabwe, where there is both economic and political instability. Such instability, as noted in Chapter 2, has resulted in Zimbabwe abrogating its commitments under the new SADC tariff regime and causing economic instability throughout the region.

Specifically, between May and June 2001, Zimbabwe raised import tariffs on a variety of items, including selected clothing, fruit juices, tobacco, clear beer, matches, calendars, trade advertising material, designs, photographs, selected artificial fibres, and blankets. Such increases were in direct contradiction to Zimbabwe's commitment under the new SADC tariff regime. The increases are designed to raise money and decrease the amount of foreign exchange being exported from the country. Also in May, the government imposed a 'carbon tax' (Z$400 or R57) on cross-border carriers for the processing of documents at the border. This tax followed on the heels of increased road user charges imposed in 2000 on foreign carriers and increased toll tariffs at Beitbridge, the border crossing between South Africa and Zimbabwe (*Freight & Trading Weekly*, 2001a; Rushmere, 2001b).

In a further abrogation of SADC rules that stipulate that foreign road hauliers are allowed to pay for services in local currency, the Zimbabwe government announced that all such services (e.g. fuel) must be paid for in foreign currency. In addition, the National Railways of Zimbabwe (NRZ) has been demanding that all exporters must pay in foreign currency, preferably US dollars. This demand comes at a time when the NRZ is having serious problems maintaining its schedule for transporting goods throughout the region. This is the result of both fuel shortages and personnel problems (*Freight & Trading Weekly*, 2001b, 2001c).

As noted in Chapter 1, openness at the international or regional level is not a substitute for viable national development strategies. A strong economy can benefit more from openness than a weak one. It is with good reason that most of the SADC countries are concerned that by giving South Africa greater access to their markets, further economic decline will follow. This is certainly in keeping with the literature on regionalism, which argues that the regional giant gains the most from market integration. If in fact the theoretical literature is correct that only modest gains can be expected from efforts to increase intra-African trade, then it can be anticipated that the SADC FTA will not result in a significant increase in intra-regional trade. To the extent that such trade is increased, it will probably continue to be as a result of increased exports from South Africa to the other SADC member states. This will neither spearhead economic structural transformation, nor strengthen regional economies, nor result in a decrease in the economic disparity in the region.

How to compensate countries for customs revenue losses is an issue that has to be dealt with if market integration is to be successful. In many countries, customs revenue represents a significant part of state revenue. With a SADC FTA, as Table 4.11, opposite, indicates, there will be significant customs revenue losses in Malawi, Mauritius, Zambia, and Zimbabwe. Policies designed to restructure and expand the tax bases of these countries are not likely (Leape, 2000), nor will South Africa have the capacity to compensate them for the losses. In this case, unless compensatory policies are put in place, it appears that Malawi, Mauritius, Zambia, and Zimbabwe stand to lose from a SADC FTA in this regard.

Table 4.11: Estimated Customs Revenue Losses as a Result of a SADC FTA

Country	Percentage
Botswana	3
Lesotho	3
Malawi	23.9
Mauritius	17
Mozambique	5.8
Namibia	3
South Africa	3
Swaziland	3
Tanzania	5.8
Zambia	28.7
Zimbabwe	32.2

Source: Jenkins *et al.* (2000:64)

[handwritten note: bilateral agree above COMESA & SADC tariff schedules]

As mentioned above, concerns have been raised regarding the SADC FTA with respect to the rules of origin. In addition to the challenge with implementing SADC and COMESA rules of origin, the question of rules of origin will be made even more daunting if an effort is made to control EU goods from flooding the regional market as a result of the EU-SA FTA (see Chapter 7). The SADC region could become a haven for non-originating products or trans-shipment. Problems of the forging of 'certificates of origin' have already surfaced (Panafrican News Agency, 6 November 2000). In order to ensure that the rules of origin are enforced, more customs officials will have to be hired.

Perhaps of greater concern are the porous borders in the region. All the SADC member states have reason to be concerned about goods evading customs regulations and penetrating regional markets illegally. This could prove to be a win-win environment for the informal trade sector in that there will likely be more incentives to try and bypass customs regulations. With the level of corruption at border posts, the collection of customs revenue might be further compromised.

With respect to different tariff rates, customs officials once again will have to distinguish between tariff structures for SADC countries versus SADC/COMESA countries. With respect to the latter, it has been agreed that tariff levels that allow for the deepest cuts will be applicable. Then, in 2004, if COMESA's customs union comes into force, these countries will then impose a common external tariff against non-COMESA SADC members. With respect to SADC tariffs, once customs officials determine that SADC tariff schedules are applicable, they will then have to decide which category the goods are in (e.g. frontloading, midloading, or backloading, the particular phase they are in, and whether they are sensitive or not). In the final analysis, however, both SADC and COMESA tariff schedules might be superceded by regional bilateral trade agreements. Added to this seemingly endless maze of complexity will be the negotiations for the possible creation of an EU-SADC FTA (see Chapter 7), which would include yet another set of rules of origin and tariff structure.

[handwritten note: COMPLEX]

Finally, there is the possibility of four other South African free trade areas – one with both Brazil (or MERCOSUR) and India (see Stern & Stevens, 2000), a third with the US growing out of AGOA (see Chapter 6), and a fourth with EFTA (*Business Day*, 2000). Prospects for the first two grow out of South Africa's so-called 'Butterfly Strategy' developed by the South African Department of Foreign Affairs to enhance South Africa's South-South trade relations. According to Francis Kornegay, 'this strategy envisages South Africa and the SADC as the hub of an expanding network of trade relations. Africa is the body of the butterfly, whilst south and east Asia and Latin America are the wings' (Kornegay, n.d.:11–12). The prospective free trade areas with the US and EFTA, no doubt, grow out of South Africa's more important objective of enhanced South-North economic linkages (Kornegay, n.d.:28).

In summary, trade relations in the SADC region by the second decade of the twenty-first century, if all goes as planned, will be very complex. There might be at least seven FTAs – SADC FTA, EU-SA FTA, EU-SADC FTA, SA-Brazil FTA (or SA-MERCOSUR FTA), SA-India FTA, SA-US FTA, and SA-EFTA FTA. Added to this will be SACU and prospectively another customs union (COMESA), and a plethora of bilateral trade agreements. It will indeed be interesting to see which countries survive with viable trade regimes intact under these circumstances.

Regional Industrialisation

As mentioned previously, a perennial problem arising from the creation of free trade areas and customs unions among developing countries is the unequal distribution of benefits. It is the regional giant(s) that benefits the most. In fact, as the ADB notes, '[a] market model of integration could create a further polarisation between a few "haves" and a lot of "have nots" because trade, investments and technology tend to flow to more "developed" countries at the expense of others, in the name of efficient resource allocation' (ADB, 2000:197). As the section above indicates, under a SADC FTA, South Africa, as the regional giant, will be the greatest beneficiary of the new trade regime. In the mean time, many other SADC members stand to lose from the free trade area. With respect to industrialisation, it is also the case that South Africa will likely experience the greatest gains, although this might not be the case with investment (see Chapter 5).

The impact of the SADC FTA on industrialisation in the region could be catastrophic. It is anticipated that there will be losses experienced by the SADC member states as a result of further de-industrialisation resulting from the inability of countries to compete with cheaper South African products that will continue to flood regional markets. Added to this will be the competition from South African businesses that continue their aggressive expansion into the region. Not only is this expansion forcing the closure of local enterprises, but South Africans, instead of using local resources for needed inputs, often source them from South Africa, further contributing to the huge trade imbalance in the region. The sectors most likely to be adversely affected by a SADC FTA are in manufacturing. According to Harvey,

> [e]xposing some non-SACU countries in SADC to free trade with South Africa could have a doubly damaging effect. Firstly, their existing manufacturing sectors would be unable to compete with imports from South Africa, so that much of it would be driven out of business. Secondly, their existing industry would not be able to take immediate advantage of access to the South African market, so that they would gain little or nothing from a SADC free trade area in the short term, and probably not much in the medium term (Harvey, 2000a:5).

The two countries that have previously been able to compete with South Africa in some manufacturing sectors are Mauritius and Zimbabwe. The ability of the latter to be able to continue to compete, however, is being questioned as a result of its current political and economic instability. Economic instability has already increased the level of de-industrialisation in Zimbabwe. In the case of Zambia, trade liberalisation in the name of SAPs revealed the fact that Zambia could not compete with South African manufactured products (Harvey, 2000a:5). With respect to Africa in general, a Tanzanian businessman described South African companies as 'the new colonisers from the south' because they 'are extending their business tentacles almost unimpeded through the rest of Africa'. At the same time, South African corporations, with the support of labour, are ensuring that the South African market is not opened to accept more goods from SADC member states (Sikhakhane, 1998). South Africa's relationship with SACU in this regard can perhaps warn the region about the overwhelming dominant role that South Africa will command in the area of regional industrialisation under a SADC FTA.

In order for regionalism to be successful in Southern Africa, the SADC member states should seriously consider whether or not they want to continue expending financial resources that are badly needed for development and economic transformation on the SADC FTA, which will probably fail to realise its goals and objectives. An environment in which the SADC member states work cooperatively to integrate their economies though the development of regional comparative advantages and the regionalisation of production seemingly has more potential for economic structural transformation than does market integration.

Notes

1   Interview with Zimbabwe government official, Harare, Zimbabwe, 10 August 1999.

2   The details outlining the rules of origin are contained in Annex 1 of the SADC Protocol on Trade.

3   This table does not reflect Zimbabwe's final offer.

4   This includes trade already bound at zero as a result of bilateral trade agreements.

5   The Harmonised Coding and Description System (HS) is the 'product nomenclature for international trade, which is used by the vast majority of countries as a basis for their national tariff nomenclature and trade statistics. The HS consists of 97 chapters (HS 2-digit level), 1 241 headings (HS 4-digit level) and 5 019 subheadings (HS 6-digit level)' (Von Kirchbach & Roelofsen, 1998b:vii).

6   Interview with Zimbabwe government official (see en. 1).

7   This includes trade already bound at zero as a result of bilateral trade agreements.

8   Interview with Zimbabwe government official (see en. 1).

9   *Ibid.*

10   CKD means 'completely knocked-down'.

11   The HLC became the major negotiating forum for outstanding trade issues beginning in 2000.

12   Workings or processes listed at columns 3 or 5 as appropriate of the consolidated negotiating text (CNT) dated 24 March 2000 (19h.00).

13   Interview with Mfundo Nkuhlu, Chief Director, Africa Trade Relations in the South African Department of Trade and Industry, 27 July 1999, Pretoria, South Africa.

Investment

> Also evident is the failure of Africa's regional economic groupings to attract foreign direct investment (FDI). By enlarging markets, improving the proximity to resource inputs, and increasing the potential output size of the firm, integration is expected to play an instrumental role in attracting investment (ADB, 2000:136–8).

ONE OF THE major reasons developing countries have pursued market integration is to enhance the prospects for attracting foreign investment. As the above quotation indicates, African regions have not been successful in attracting FDI as a result of efforts to implement market integration. There are numerous reasons for this failure, including poor infrastructure, political and economic instability, ambiguous investment laws, and a largely unskilled labour force. Nonetheless, attracting FDI remains a cornerstone of the regional agenda of African countries. This occurs often to the neglect of providing incentives to encourage local entrepreneurs to invest in their country or region.

Foreign direct investment (FDI),[1] along with domestic investment, is deemed to be essential for the successful implementation of the SADC regional agenda. This chapter, therefore, examines the issue of investment in the SADC region. It begins by assessing global investment policy trends. This will allow the issue of investment in the region to be placed within the larger global arena. The African experience with FDI is then examined. The next section explores the issue of investment in transport infrastructure as a catalyst for regional integration by looking at the case of the Maputo Development Corridor, which is deemed to be the model for the development of regional transport corridors. A description and analysis of investment in South Africa since 1994 follows. The final section examines investment in the SADC region.

Global Investment Policy Trends

The most significant global investment policy trends identified in UNCTAD's *World Investment Report 2000* are that: (1) FDI is playing a more significant role in the world economy; and (2) global FDI outflows are being driven by mergers and acquisitions (M&As). Given this reality, the report notes that Africa will benefit from FDI when it becomes a more prominent player in world markets. This can only be achieved through integration into the world economy, which includes the networks of the TNCs at the regional or global level (UNCTAD, 2000:40–1). The two trends identified above are discussed in this section of the chapter.

The Role of FDI in the World Economy

According to UNCTAD, there are approximately 63 000 parent firm TNCs that have at least 690 000 foreign affiliates, along with an excess of inter-firm arrangements, making up a network that 'spans virtually all countries and economic activities' (UNCTAD, 2000:xv). These TNCs are responsible for the rapid expansion of international production, which is 'production under the common governance of transnational corporations' (UNCTAD, 2000:3). Such production 'is growing faster than other economic aggregates' (UNCTAD, 2000:3) and is basically being driven by the top 100 (non-financial) TNCs in the world. The expansion of international production has been made possible as a result of changes countries have made in their regulatory environments, including creating more favourable environments for FDI. Bilateral investment treaties have increased, as well as double taxation treaties. Notwithstanding these changes, in 1999, 74 per cent of global FDI flows went to ten countries. Similarly, with respect to the developing world, ten countries received 80 per cent of FDI flows (UNCTAD, 2000:xvi).[2]

The power of the TNCs logically spreads into the trade arena since it is estimated that half of all TNC trade takes place either between the parent firms and their affiliates or among affiliates. Location decisions are therefore largely based on the ability of the TNC to maximise economies of scale. An estimated two-thirds of world trade is under the control of TNCs. Similarly, they account for approximately 75–80 per cent of global research and development (UNCTAD, 2000:17).

Mergers and Acquisitions

The US$1.3 trillion in FDI outflows for 2000[3] is mainly attributable to the increasing growth in cross-border M&As, which peaked at US$1.1 trillion in 2000 (BusinessMap, 2001a). The increase in M&As can be partly attributed to trade liberation and regional integration efforts, since they result in enhanced competition and regional corporate restructuring and consolidation (UNCTAD, 2000:xx).

A cross-border merger, according to UNCTAD, takes place when 'the assets and operations of two firms belonging to two different countries are combined to establish a new legal entity'. A cross-border acquisition, on the other hand, occurs when 'the control of assets and operations is transferred from a local to a foreign company, the former becoming an affiliate of the latter' (UNCTAD, 2000:99). An estimated 97 per cent of M&As are acquisitions. Most M&As are considered as FDIs, with the exception of portfolio and near-portfolio investments. Portfolio investments[4] are acquisitions that have less than ten per cent equity and near-portfolio investments are like portfolio investments, but the sole or primary motivation for such investments is financial, and they are not dependent on the equity share (BusinessMap, 1999a:12; UNCTAD, 2000:xxiii–xxv).

The opposite of M&As are so-called greenfield investments. These are investments in which new businesses are established from scratch. For most developing countries, greenfield investments are preferred over M&As. In the case of the latter, ownership and control is merely transferred from domestic to foreign hands without adding to productivity. In fact, M&As are very often detrimental to the economy, resulting in significant job losses as the new company is restructured with a view to increasing shareholder value (George, 1999). In addition, the acquirer, if a global oligopolist, could end up dominating the local market, thus reducing or eroding competition, and negatively affecting local technological capacity building. When cross-border M&As take place in developing countries, the acquirers are often accused of contributing to the erosion of national sovereignty and to recolonisation (UNCTAD, 2000:xxiii). As the prime minister of Malaysia said in a speech to UNCTAD in February 2000,

> mergers and acquisitions ... are making big corporations even bigger. Now many of these corporations are financially more powerful than medium sized countries. While we welcome their collaboration with our local companies, we fear that if they are allowed into our countries unconditionally they may swallow up all our businesses (UNCTAD, 2000:14).

Foreign investors view cross-border M&As as a means of gaining market power in a new market and of realising synergies. In many cases, however, cross-border M&As have not lived up to expectations (UNCTAD, 2000:xx).

Greenfield investments, on the other hand, do add to the productive capacity of countries. With respect to developing countries, greenfield investments also enhance employment and technological development. These investments, like M&As, however, often do not live up to their expectations and can be problematic as well. In the case of developing countries, greenfield FDI continues to be more significant than M&As (UNCTAD, 2000:xx). In fact, it was only during the latter part of the 1990s that developing countries became significant locations for M&As. With respect to Africa, according to UNCTAD, M&As have been basically concentrated in three countries – Egypt, Morocco, and South Africa. Reasons for this include the fact that privatisation has moved at a slow pace, the limited availability of attractive private sector firms for purchase, and the general atmosphere of the investment climate in Africa (UNCTAD, 2000:xxii).

Foreign Investment in Africa: The Record

The record of FDI in Africa is dubious, and legitimate questions have been raised regarding its contribution to Africa's development. Notwithstanding the well-documented history of the exploitation of Africa by TNCs, commencing with the early European invasions of the continent to the present (e.g. see Rodney, 1974; Nkrumah, 1965; Kwitny, 1986), the current complicity of many African leaders in helping TNCs to further plunder Africa's natural resources (e.g. see Reno, 1998; Global Witness, 1999, 2000; UN, 2000; *Weekly Mail & Guardian*, 1998; Gordon, 1999; Santoro, 1998) makes it impossible to make a blanket indictment against these TNCs alone. Such an indictment should be made against both TNCs and third parties that intervene on their behalf (e.g. governments) and African leaders and entrepreneurs who are involved in plundering Africa's 'blood' natural resources. These resources are so named because the profits from the plunder are used to fuel Africa's wars, which have resulted in millions of deaths, injuries, and displacements and untold misery for millions of Africa's people.

Although Africa currently receives the lowest amount of FDI, this has not always been the case. In fact, in 1970, Africa's FDI per US$1 000 of GDP was greater than that of Asia, Latin America, or the Caribbean. By 1990, however, Africa began to experience a serious decline in FDI. The pattern continued throughout most of the decade (UNCTAD, 1999:3). In 1999, FDI flows to Africa were, according to UNCTAD, US$10 billion, which only represented 1.2 per cent of all FDI. The US$10 billion did, however, reflect a 28 per cent increase over 1998. The current level of FDI to Africa has increased since the early 1990s. It has also stabilised, mainly as a result of the creation of a friendlier environment for investors. The ten top African recipients of FDI inflows in 1999 were Angola, Egypt, Nigeria,

South Africa, Morocco, Mozambique, Sudan, Tunisia, Côte d'Ivoire, and Gabon (UNCTAD, 2000:xviii, 40).

FDI into Africa experienced a decline of more than 13 per cent in 2000, from US$10.5 billion in 1999 to US$9.1 billion in 2000. This puts Africa's share in world FDI at less than one per cent. The decline is attributed to a slowing of FDI into three of Africa's main recipient countries – Angola, Morocco, and South Africa (*Bridges Weekly Trade News Digest*, 2001; BusinessMap, 2001a).

Notwithstanding the above, such figures must be examined with caution. The collection of information regarding capital flows is a very challenging endeavour, and therefore, very often discrepancies in the data exist between collecting agencies. Data collected by UNCTAD and other international organisations may differ from that collected by governments or other entities within the country. According to Nils Bhinda, Stephany Griffith-Jones, and Mathew Martin,

> [a]greement on general trends hides major discrepancies between different data sets. Several international institutions publish data, but these often wildly mistake flows or their composition, though they are supposedly based on a small number of national data sources. Behind these discrepancies lie problems at two levels. First, the international organisations often face major problems in assembling national data on time and interpreting their presentation. Second, African countries also face great problems in constructing consistent, comprehensive or timely databases (Bhinda *et al.*, 1999:5).

In 1999, the US remained the number one investor in Africa, followed by France and the UK. Other countries of note include Germany and the Netherlands (Bhinda *et al.*, 1999:5). US and French FDI is largely concentrated in natural resources, while that of Germany, the Netherlands, and Switzerland is mostly in manufacturing. The UK investments are largely in service industries (Bhinda *et al.*, 1999:41–2). Contrary to popular belief, the returns on investments in Africa are higher than in most other regions in the world (developed as well as developing) (UNCTAD, 1999:17). Nonetheless, Africa has a high remittance rate for the profits of such investments. According to Kennedy Mbekeani, the rate averaged 217 per cent between 1991 and 1995, the only region of the world that had a three-digit rate (Mbekeani, 1997).

The wave of privatisation in Africa has had an impact on FDI, with an estimated 14 per cent of all investment flows between 1990 and 1998 being linked to privatisation (UNCTAD, 1999:42). In a survey undertaken by UNCTAD of 296 top TNCs, investment potential by region in Africa was identified as follows:

▶ North Africa: petroleum, gas and related products, telecommunications and tourism;
▶ West Africa: petroleum, gas and related products, as well as mining, quarrying, agriculture, forestry and telecommunications;
▶ East Africa: tourism, followed at a considerable distance by telecommunications;
▶ Central Africa: a few opportunities in mining and quarrying, and forestry;
▶ Southern Africa: tourism and transport and storage, followed by telecommunications, mining and quarrying, metals and metal products, motor vehicles, food and beverages, pharmaceutical and chemical products and agriculture (UNCTAD, 1999:46–7).

Clearly the greatest amount of investment potential, according to this survey, is perceived to be in Southern Africa. The survey also revealed that TNCs feel that regional integration should be expedited in order to create larger and more attractive markets (UNCTAD, 1999:49).

Various reasons have been cited for Africa's low rate of FDI. They include concerns about policy reversals; the fact that the cost is high for doing business; weak financial, judicial, and legal systems; poor physical and technological infrastructure; and the low productivity of labour (UN, 1999:17). Inadequate human resource capacity is also a constraint to attracting large sums of FDI. In general, there exists a negative image of the continent, largely growing out of its political and economic instability.

African countries have taken numerous measures to enhance the attractiveness of the continent for investment. Perhaps the most important has been IMF/World Bank SAPs. The promised increased investment as a result of SAP reforms, however, has not been forthcoming, once again raising serious questions about their viability. Paul Collier and Jan Gunning argue that the greatest weakness of attempts by Africa to adjust rests with the low levels of private investment. This lack of investment results in a reduction in aggregate growth as well as the ability of the economies to redirect resources into activities for export (Collier & Gunning, 1999:80).

Other measures implemented in an effort to increase FDI include signing both bilateral investment treaties and double taxation treaties, as well as multilateral agreements designed to protect FDIs. Investment promotion centres have also been established in most African countries.

For the developing world in general, FDI has been perceived by many as one of the important avenues for spearheading economic growth and increasing employment. Numerous studies have been undertaken to challenge the correlation between FDI and economic growth and employment in the developing world. Mbekeani, in a study entitled 'Foreign direct investment and economic growth' concludes that in the short run, FDI has no effect on GDP or employment. Consequently, he suggests that greater emphasis by policy makers should be placed on promoting domestic development in order to enhance growth and employment creation (Mbekeani, 1997). According to Panos, although TNCs are responsible for an estimated 80 per cent of all FDI, in 1994, UNCTAD reported that they actually employed only approximately three per cent of the global workforce, with less than half of these jobs (12 million) in the developing world. Panos does note, however, that by 1999 there were indications that this figure had increased (Panos, 1999:12). Susan George argues that there is a negative correlation between TNC investment and employment, especially for the giant firms (George, 1999).

Market integration has long been seen as a means to increase both foreign and domestic investment among developing countries. For the most part, however, market integration has not resulted in increased investment leading to enhanced industrialisation and structural transformation in Africa. This is largely the case because TNCs migrate to areas where high growth rates already exist, or where the potential exists for such growth (Mbekeani, 1997). No region in Africa has been identified as a potential high growth area. Nonetheless, it has been well established that economic growth in general requires increased investment in production structures. It is therefore important for policy makers in the developing world to understand that investment needed for economic growth and employment must come from domestic sources. This is especially important for African policy makers to understand, because, as a recent study of top TNCs revealed, 'a regional initiative has a remote impact on FDI until it convinces investors of the plausibility of economic and political harmony' (A. T. Kearney, 2000:12). Again, a prerequisite for the success of regionalism is economic and political stability.

In the case of Southern Africa, it appears that the growing level of investment in the region is occurring because investors are identifying underutilised potential where profit margins are prospectively significant. It is important to note that a great deal of the investment that will ultimately help facilitate regional development, especially with respect to infrastructure, is being spearheaded from within the region. Such investment will serve to underpin efforts to increase intra-regional trade and economic growth. The need to develop the region is therefore the catalyst for increased domestic, regional, and foreign investment. Such investment does not appear to be the result of the potential for economies of scale growing out of large markets as a result of market integration.

Whether such investment will eventually include the type of FDI that will increase the region's involvement in TNC global and regional production and lead to the further incorporation of Africa into the global economy is a completely different issue. In fact, with the dubious history of TNCs in Africa, the suggestion that Africa become more involved in TNC global and regional production raises questions regarding in whose interests – Africa's or the TNCs'? Again, as noted in Chapter 1, African leaders must be very careful as to how they integrate their economies into the current unstable and volatile global economy. In the final analysis, the experience of Southern Africa might be instructive for understanding the positive correlation between regional investment and economic growth and employment creation.

Investing in Transport Infrastructure: The Case of the Maputo Development Corridor

Touted as the most advanced development corridor in Africa, the Maputo Development Corridor initiative has changed the face of transport infrastructural development in the SADC region. This section of the chapter places in context the importance of transport infrastructural development to both regional integration and development; examines the SADC experience with respect to transport infrastructual development; and then provides an in-depth description and analysis of the Maputo Development Corridor initiative. The final part of the section looks at the implications of the Maputo Development Corridor as a model for transport infrastructure development in the region.

The Role of Transport Infrastructure in Regional Integration

The correlation between efficient and viable infrastructures and development has been well established (e.g. see Driver, 1999; ADB, 2000:183–4; Lipman, 1997). Similarly, a correlation has been established between transport infrastructure and regional cooperation and integration, as well as international competitiveness. With respect to the former, it is argued that '[r]egional co-operation in the transport sector is a prerequisite for regional economic integration' (Lipman, 1997:85). Such cooperation, according to Vivienne Lipman, is vital to regional tourism in that tourists must be able to easily travel to and from the region as well as within it. An efficient transport sector is also essential for developing the infrastructure for other sectors, including telecommunications, energy, agriculture, and water resources (Lipman, 1997:86). In terms of international competitiveness, the ADB posits that without adequate or reliable infrastructure services, the international competitiveness of a country or region is reduced, along with its ability to be involved in international trade. In addition, integration into the world economy is compromised. With respect to regional integration, the ability to attract investment is dependent on a viable transport and communications system (ADB, 2000:183).

Approached from a regional perspective, infrastructural development can result in enhanced reliability and efficiency. This is especially important for land-locked countries (ADB, 2000:183). Key to any regional infrastructure strategy for Africa is reducing high transaction costs, which are usually associated with high transport costs as a result of infrastructural deficiencies, difficulties with contract enforcement, excessive charges for information, and ancillary public services that are of a poor quality (ADB, 2000:183).

When SADC was established in 1980, the member states understood the importance of developing the regional transport network. Therefore, a major priority of the organisation was the development of the regional port transport systems. This remains the case today, and as Amanda Driver notes, without a viable transport infrastructure to facilitate trade, an FTA is not significant (Driver, 1999:18).

The SADC Transport Sector in Historical Perspective

From 1980 onwards, the highest priority was given to the SADC transport and communications sector, because it was understood that regional development was dependent upon a transport and communication system that was reliable and efficient. For example, how could the SADC member states increase intra-regional and international trade without the ability to get their goods to regional and international markets?

To this end, capital investment projects under SADC's surface transport plan were centred on the establishment of viable transportation networks to regional ports. This entailed the combination of various port, railway, and road projects involving five port transport systems: the Maputo, Beira, Nacala, Dar es Salaam, and Lobito port transport systems. Since three of the ports were located in Mozambique, it was designated as the country to assume responsibility for the SADC Transport and Communications sector. The SATCC was established to coordinate the development of this sector.

As previously noted, the major objective of SADC when it was established was to decrease regional economic dependence on the apartheid regime. The development of the port transport systems, also known as the regional corridors, was seen as a viable avenue to achieve this objective by redirecting traffic away from South Africa's transport systems. To prevent the SADC member states from achieving this objective, SADC's port transport systems became a major target of South Africa's regional destabilisation strategy (1980–89). In 1980, approximately 80 per cent of regional goods were transported through South Africa.

Of the three port transport systems in Mozambique (Maputo, Beira, and Nacala), Maputo received the least amount of financial assistance from SADC's ICPs during the 1980s. This was the case because of South Africa's usage of Maputo. During this period, approximately 50 per cent of all goods handled at the port were from South Africa. Consequently, the South African government was investing heavily in the port. Any financial assistance from SADC's ICPs would therefore ultimately be beneficial to South Africa (see Lee, 1989:209; Driver & De Barros, 2000:5). This would have posed a fundamental contradiction in the philosophy of the SADC member states at the time, since they were attempting to isolate the apartheid regime.

In order to understand the current effort to develop the Maputo Corridor, it is important to place in historical context the importance of the port of Maputo for South Africa. The closest port to the Johannesburg area (Gauteng province) is Maputo. Prior to 1975, the port handled 12–14 million tons of goods annually, including 6.2 million tons from South Africa. By 1975, this had decreased to 4.4 million tons. South Africa began to redirect traffic away from Mozambique, when it became clear that FRELIMO was going to ascend to power (Hanlon, 1986:131–2). Maputo traffic was diverted to ports in South Africa (Durban and Richards Bay). Following Mozambique's independence in 1975, there was a further decrease in traffic to Maputo. In addition to traffic being deliberately diverted away from Maputo, the decline in traffic was also a result of the war in Mozambique and South Africa's sabotage of the railway line leading to the port during the 1980s. Nonetheless, as noted above, during the period of regional destabilisation, Maputo continued to be important for South Africa.

While in 1994 Maputo only handled 2.3 million tons, by 1996, this had increased to 3.2 million tons (Arkwright & De Beer, 1998:11). It has remained at approximately three million tons. In August 1995, when the ministers of transport of Mozambique and South Africa met in Mozambique to spearhead the Mozambique Development Corridor initiative, it was with a view to re-establishing the vital transport route between South Africa's industrial centre (Gauteng Province) and Maputo (MCC, 1999:2).

From Port Transport Systems (Transport Corridors) to Development Corridors

The Maputo Development Corridor initiative transformed the concept of SADC port transport systems. Specifically, it introduced two new concepts – public-private partnerships (PPPs) and regional development corridors. With respect to the former, the idea was presented that the development of regional transport corridors should go beyond securing international financial assistance for road, railway, and port projects. Instead, such funding should be secured from governments, along with private investors. The notion of using the private sector to 'finance, develop and operate infrastructure', according to Dave Arkwright and Geoff de Beer, reflects an increasing tendency in which the public sector has been forced to include the private sector in infrastructural development (Arkwright & De Beer, 1998:2). Factors that have contributed to this phenomenon include shortage of governmental revenue and public disenchantment with the delivery of services by publicly owned enterprises. PPPs can serve to rectify some of these problems, while simultaneously allowing the public sector to retain a certain level of control (Arkwright & De Beer, 1998:2–3).

The second concept introduced – regional development corridors – adopts a more comprehensive approach to development. They are designed to develop infrastructure and uplift the living conditions of the communities (SADC, 1997c:9). It was anticipated that investors would find the development corridors more attractive than the SADC port transport systems. This was indeed the case during the Maputo Development Corridor investors' conference held on 6 May 1996. It was at this conference that the Maputo Development Corridor was officially launched.

The Maputo Development Corridor (Corridor)

When the ministers of transport of both Mozambique and South Africa gathered in Mozambique in August 1995 to officially establish the Maputo Development Corridor, the Corridor was not a SADC endeavour. In fact, the SADC member states were at first not pleased with the idea because they were not consulted prior to the creation of the project. An integral part of the culture within SADC dictates that any endeavour that takes place between member states should be placed within the context of regional cooperation or integration. As a new member of SADC and the regional giant, South Africa ignored this culture. Dave Arkwright, former CEO of the Maputo Corridor Company (MCC), notes that as a regional giant, South Africa can act like the US. 'When it is convenient to incorporate the world, go to the UN. When the UN doesn't want to do it, you do it on your own.'[5] While the Mozambican government also ignored this tacit understanding among the member states, it found itself in a more precarious position than South Africa, since it was a long-standing member of SADC. As Arkwright notes, in terms of SADC's guiding principles, Mozambique should have gone to the SADC member states and asked for their approval. Mozambique decided, however, not to consult the other SADC member states, because they felt that with South Africa as a partner they could get away with it. The Mozambique government also believed that the project was too important to worry about the pressure. While South Africa and Mozambique were able to continue with the project as a bilateral arrangement, they decided to forego a multilateral arrangement that would have included Swaziland. With a prospective multilateral arrangement, South Africa and Mozambique would have been forced to conform to SADC rules and regulations. Needless to say, Swaziland was not happy with this decision. Among Swaziland's concerns were the implications of the development of the Corridor, since it had benefitted from the diversion of traffic away from the South African/Mozambican border following its closure in 1975.[6]

To date, the Corridor has basically remained a non-SADC project, even though SADC has adopted the Corridor as the model for developing the regional transport corridors. As Arkwright notes, '[w]hen we started this process, we started it as a bilateral and that raised eyebrows and concerns within SADC. The reason was that we were going to be introducing some policy ideas that ran a little contrary to SADC policies at the time, particularly toll roads'.[7] At the 1996 Maputo Development Corridor investors' conference, while Kaire Mbuende, former SADC executive secretary, congratulated Mozambique and South Africa for the initiative, he noted that 'SADC had not had enough involvement in the discussions'.[8] At the root of the problem is the fact that many SADC countries are jealous of the relationship that Mozambique has with South Africa. The presidents of the two countries meet every six months.[9]

Following the creation of the Corridor project, officials from the other eight provinces of South Africa complained that the government was spending a great deal of money in Mpumalanga and therefore demanded that similar resources be committed to their respective provinces. The government responded to this request by creating the Spatial Development Initiative (SDI), which resulted in the identification of designated areas throughout the country where the possibility for unlocking economic potential exists through enhancing their attractiveness for investment. With increasing private sector investment, it is anticipated that job creation will follow ('Spatial Development Initiatives in Southern Africa', n.d.). Once the concept of SDIs was put in place in 1996, the Corridor was identified as South Africa's first SDI. As the idea of SDIs expanded, the former SADC port transport systems were identified by the South African government as development corridor SDIs or Southern African SDIs (Jourdan, 1998:724). Currently there are at least 20 SDIs, nine of which are development corridors or Southern African SDIs (see Figure 5.1, opposite). The PPP concept is at the heart of all the SDIs.

The Corridor was initiated by the South African Department of Transport, although it is often assumed that it grew out of the efforts of the premier of Mpumalanga province at the time, Matthews Phosa. Actually, however, it was spearheaded by Paul Jourdan and Khetso Gordon. The latter was Director-General for Transportation while the former was Deputy Director-General in the Department of Trade and Industry. The two are known as the

Jourdan-Gordon team. The Corridor, according to Arkwright, 'was very much a top down, Johannesburg-led initiative. It bypassed Mpumalanga'. After all, only the central government could have got the project going from a policy position.[10] Gordon was in charge of the project, since in the beginning it was transport-driven. Numerous entities were brought on board, including the Development Bank of Southern Africa.

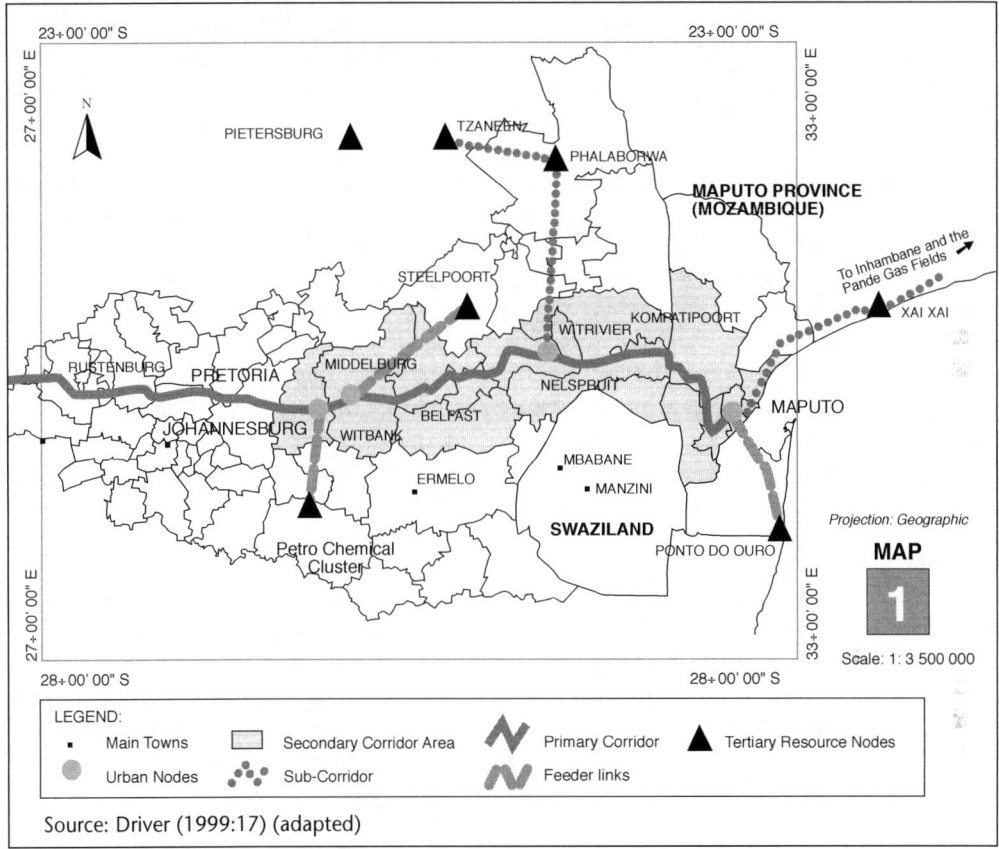

Source: Driver (1999:17) (adapted)

Figure 5.1: Possible Development Corridors and SDI's in the SADC Region

During the early phases of the project, the relationship between the national and provincial governments was a problem, largely because the former did not feel that the latter could contribute anything of significance to the Corridor. This has changed, and the provincial government is responsible for development during the secondary phase of the project (Mitchell, 1998:759). Nonetheless, tensions between certain national government officials and some of those actually involved in facilitating the development of the Corridor still exist. Such tensions largely grow out of different perceptions as to the best strategy for implementing the initiative and who is responsible for failed policies. Also, there exists a difference of opinion, for example, on what types of projects should be encouraged along the Corridor. For the national government, the focus should be on mega projects such as aluminum smelters and steel plants that are government-driven, which is what the SDIs are all about. At the provincial level, however, notwithstanding the importance of mega projects, there exists concern with building capacity in Mpumalanga. This was deemed to be especially important because investors would have certain expectations about Mpumalanga Province. Phosa was removed from being premier of Mpumalanga and sent to the National Assembly, partially because the national government perceived him to be acting out of his self-interest instead of the interests of the national government.

Those in Mpumalanga and Mozambique viewed Phosa and his role in the Corridor differently. The Mozambicans really liked Phosa. In fact, according to Arkwright, over a period of five years, trust was established between Mozambique and Mpumalanga Province as a result of Phosa's actions. This trust was broken with his removal. In fact, Phosa was the preferred conduit for the Corridor because Mozambique really did not like what representatives of the national government were up to. 'The Premier was working on a daily basis on agreements across the border, a much slower process that took into account culture, language, and social issues.'[11] Phosa does remain actively involved in the Corridor initiative.

The conflict between the national government and Mpumalanga Province has its roots in the fact that the ANC-led government feels that it must control everything, hence its promotion of a centralised governmental structure. Although at odds with the national government, the provincial government continued to move forward with its plans to develop the Corridor. This included going beyond the development of mega projects to include environmental management, cultural exchange, and cross-border symmetries.[12]

During the early phase of the development of the Corridor initiative, there was also tension between South Africa and Mozambique. South Africa's initial attitude toward Mozambique was one of arrogance. The South African government felt, for example, that it could just impose its plans for the Corridor on the Mozambicans. This was not the case and, initially, the Mozambicans resisted the efforts by the South Africans. According to Arkwright, 'for South Africa to walk into Mozambique and tell them this is how we're going to do things and it's going to be rapid and we're not going to consult .... They didn't take kindly. So resistance built up in Mozambique to this process among individuals'.[13] At the point at which South Africa proposed incorporating the regional port transport systems into its SDI programme, Mozambique queried as to what South Africa wanted with the Beira or Nacala corridor. They asked, for example, 'is this another form of colonialism creeping in?'[14]

The Mozambicans have been able to flex their muscles because they are in a strong position. At a private sector conference, President Chissano allegedly told participants from the US and Britain, 'the days of you talking about the problems here in Mozambique are over. Don't speak to me about corruption, about crime. Talk to me about investment, because that's what it's about now'.[15] Mozambique has in fact proven itself to be the growth area for the region as well as the investment destination for the future. It therefore holds the key to the Corridor. Investors are interested in Mozambique for several reasons, including the fact that it has a good port, political stability, clarity in its investment policy, and stable domestic institutions. South Africa, on the other hand, is engaged in a conflict between the national and provincial governments and seemingly cannot get itself in order. The Mozambicans have indicated that they are watching South Africa from across the border and questioning whether or not it actually has the ability to deliver.[16] Mozambique is a case in point where political stability provides it with an advantage over the regional hegemon – South Africa.

Although the Corridor was initially transport led, it later became trade-and-industry led. Eventually transport reduced its role and trade and industry increased theirs. This change occurred because the SDIs became synonymous with export-driven processes, with industrial location, processing zones, industrial clusters .... It very quickly moved into a different mode with different players, made more complicated by the fact that the Department of Trade and Industry actually saw the opportunity to branch out in the SDIs into Southern Africa where there is a history of transportation corridors.[17]

With South Africa's regional SDI programme, SADC member states began to ask questions about South Africa's motives. As Arkwright notes, 'the regional SDI programme suddenly became an important issue from the South African perspective because of our attempts to come to grips with tariffs and investment'.[18] Alec Erwin, South African Minister of Trade and Industry, under pressure to resolve the tariff debate, argued that tariff issues on their own do not resolve the debate; that with tariff reductions you need in place programmes that deal with other issues, such as investment, trade, and infrastructure. It is for these strategic reasons that South Africa's government initiated the SADC SDI programme. According to Arkwright, Erwin acknowledges that although efforts have been made to convince other SADC member states that South Africa's interests are regional, there remains a tremendous amount of uncertainty about South African intentions.[19]

Although the focus of the Corridor initiative has been on the area linking the industrial hub of South Africa, Gauteng Province, to the Maputo port, in reality the corridor includes a larger area (see Figure 5.2, overleaf). Specifically,

> [t]he MDC is defined as running from Balmoral, some 20 km west of Witbank, to Maputo harbour. It also comprises two north-south links in Mpumalanga. The Northern Subcorridor runs from Nelspruit to Hazyview and thence into the Northern Province.[20] The Southern Feeder Link integrates the petrochemical complex at Secunda via Bethal with the main corridor at Middelburg. Whilst recognising that any definition of the 'corridor area' will inevitably be arbitrary, Mpumalanga's provincial government has focused attention on the area 50 km either side of the N4 highway, the Northern Subcorridor and the Southern Feeder Link. This area includes about two-thirds of the province (Mitchell, 1998:757).

The major objectives of the Corridor, as outlined in a *Summary Report*, are as follows:

▶ Objective 1 – to rehabilitate the core infrastructure along the corridor with minimum impact to the fiscus (road, rail, port, dredging of port and border post).
▶ Objective 2 – to maximise investment in both the inherent potential of the corridor area and in the added opportunities which the infrastructure rehabilitation will create.
▶ Objective 3 – to ensure that the development impact of this investment is maximised, particularly to disadvantaged communities. Changing the ownership base [*sic*].
▶ Objective 4 – to ensure sustainability by developing policy, strategies and frameworks that encompass a holistic, participatory and integrated approach to development (MCC, 1999).

For both Mozambique and South Africa, the Corridor represented an opportunity to enhance domestic development as well as regional integration and international competitiveness. It has been estimated that with the successful development of the Corridor, the volume of goods handled at Maputo would increase from three to six million tons (Arkwright & De Beer, 1998:11).

On 26 July 1996, the governments of Mozambique and South Africa signed a Framework Agreement for the establishment of the Maputo Development Corridor. The agreement included three ancillary agreements. The first was a protocol for the operation of the

Witbank-Maputo toll road. The second was a statement of intent for upgrading the railway line and the harbour of Maputo, and the third a statement of intent for establishing a Maputo Corridor Company (Driver & De Barros, 2000:7). The latter agreement proved to be extremely problematic, and to date the MCC exists only as a 'virtual' company because the Mozambique government has not bought into the idea. The four major Corridor projects are discussed below.

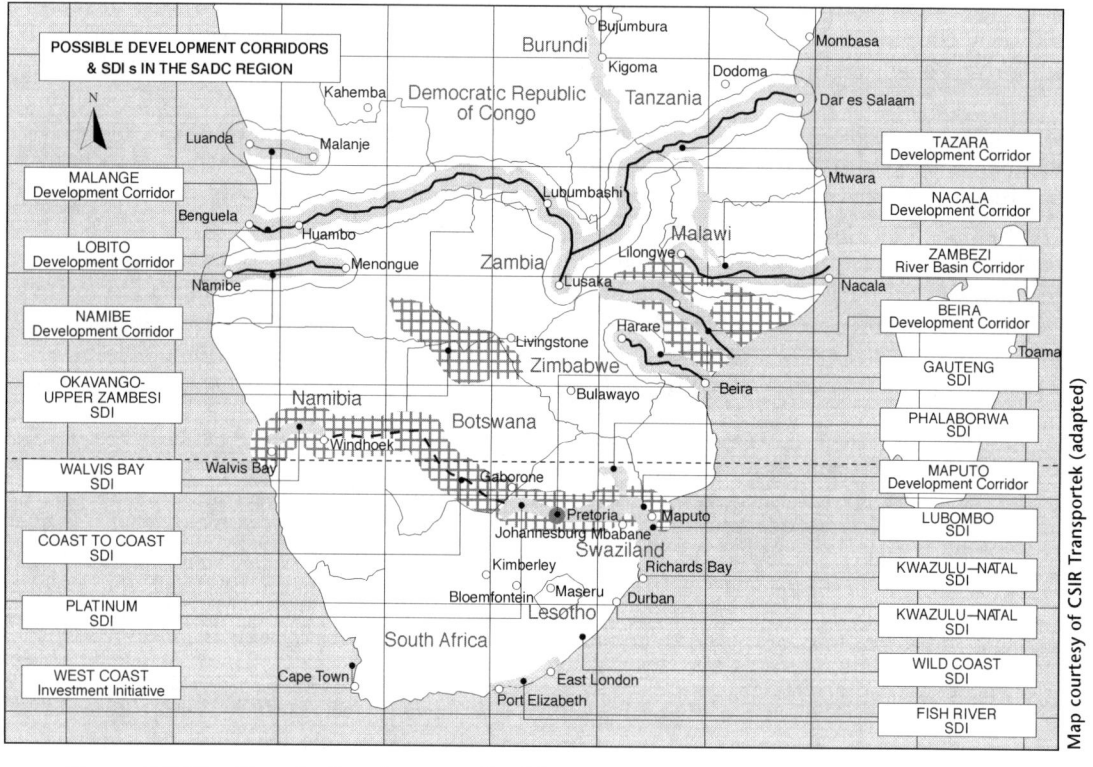

Figure 5.2: The Maputo Development Corridor   Source: *Mpumalanga Report* (1999a:16).

Major Maputo Development Corridor Projects

In order to facilitate development and investment, four major infrastructure projects were identified for the Corridor. They include

- ► the development of a toll road from Witbank to Maputo;
- ► upgrading Maputo harbour;
- ► upgrading three railway lines – Ressano Garcia to Maputo, Goba/Chicualacuala, and Limpopo, and upgrading the interface at the harbour; and
- ► upgrading the Ressano Garcia/Komatipoort border post.

The greatest amount of progress has occurred with respect to the development of the Witbank-to-Maputo toll road. The project is valued at US$400 million and the concession for the toll road was awarded to Trans African Concessions (TRAC) in May 1997. It is a 30-year build-operate-transfer concession. TRAC is a consortium, whose stakeholders are listed in Table 5.1, opposite. The stakeholders who are the principal sponsors of TRAC include three South African firms (Stocks and Stocks, Basil Read, and the South Africa Infrastructure Fund), Bouygues, a French construction group, and the Commonwealth Development Corporation. TRAC's lenders for the project are also outlined in Table 5.1. The project was officially launched on 6 June 1998 by Presidents Chissano of Mozambique and Mandela of South Africa. The event took place at Ressano Garcia in Mozambique and it marked the implementation phase of the Maputo Development Corridor. With respect to awarding the concession, Arkwright notes that, '[t]here was an appreciation that in order to get the first project moving quickly we were going to have to bypass the standard channels of negotiation. The decision to concession the N4 was just taken and it just went. Before everyone knew it, it was enacted, it was law'.[21]

With the concession contract, TRAC was given the responsibility for the 'design, construction, rehabilitation, financing, operation, maintenance and future expansion of a portion of National Route 4 from West of Witbank in South Africa to Maputo in Mozambique as a toll road, together with the construction of toll plazas and other facilities along the route' (TRAC, n.d.). The South African side of the N4, from Witbank to Komatipoort, is 390km. On the Mozambique side, TRAC was responsible for building a new road from Moamba to Maputo, a distance of 50km. The road will be transferred back to the governments of South Africa and Mozambique after 30 years, at which time a decision will have to be made as to whether the road should be concessioned again. During the 30-year period, TRAC will have to pay off the R1.5 billion debt it incurred during the initial construction phase of the project, maintain and patrol the road, operate the toll plazas, and undertake expansions (TRAC, n.d.).

Table 5.1: TRAC Shareholders and Lenders

Shareholders	Lenders
Bouygues	Nedcor Bank
Basil Read	Nedbank Investment Bank
Stocks and Stocks	Future Bank
Commonwealth Development Corporation	Investec
Future Bank Corporation	First National Bank
Investec	Standard Bank
Metropolitan Life	Rand Merchant Bank
Rand Merchant Bank	Mine Officials Pension Fund
Old Mutual	Mine Employees Pension Fund
SA Infrastructure Fund	Commonwealth Development Corporation
SDCM (Mozambique)	Development Bank of Southern Africa
Sanlam	ABSA

Source: TRAC (n.d.)

The project structure of the Corridor toll road is designed so that the governments of Mozambique and South Africa are the concessors and the implementing authority consists of the Chief Directorate of Roads, South African Department of Transport and the Directorate Nacional de Estradas e Pontes de Mozambique. The concessionaire to the project is TRAC. As the concessionaire, TRAC can enter into contracts with independent contractors (Arkwright & De Beer, 1998:7–8).

In accordance with the concession, TRAC was scheduled to build five toll plazas on the N4. As of January 2001, all five toll plazas had opened. The first three, at Middelburg, Machado, and Nkomazi, are on the South African side and were opened between December 1998 and July 1999. Of the other two toll plazas, Moamba was opened in June 2000 and Matola in January 2001. In order to build the Moamba toll road, the Mozambican government had to remove people living in the area. The government maintains that they were adequately compensated for their removal.

The opening of toll roads in South Africa and Mozambique has been controversial since residents, for the first time, have to pay to use the roads. Although residents in the area of the Nkomazi Toll Plaza are eligible for discounts (e.g. taxis would pay R8.50 per trip as opposed to R21), about 500 taxis and 700 community members set up a blockade to prevent the Nkomazi Toll Plaza from opening on schedule. In an open letter to TRAC's CEO, Trevor Jackson, the community committee negotiating with TRAC about the tariffs stated that

> [t]he real issue is whether our community can afford your toll structure. You expect of a generally poor community of 400 000 people with an unemployment rate in excess of 50% to pay R25-million per annum to get to their schools, workplaces, churches, hospitals, shops and recreational facilities (*Lowvelder*, 1999).

In addition, business associations in Mpumalanga warned that with toll fees and the new visa requirements, the drawing power of the province for Mozambican shoppers would be seriously eroded (African Eye News Service, 21 June 2000).

Similar protests and accusations followed the opening of the other four toll roads. In January 2001, residents that live in the area of the Machadodorp and Waterval Boven toll road accused TRAC of splitting the closely knit rural community in half. Since the toll gate separates the two towns, which are 12km apart, residents have to pay fees to shuttle between the two. Although they get a 60 per cent discount, reportedly the toll cost has become so prohibitive for many that some businesses have been forced to close, children have discontinued schooling, and road accidents have increased as a result of residents resorting to alternative roads in order to avoid the toll fees (*Sunday Times*, 14 January 2001). In Mozambique, when the Matola toll road opened, construction workers went on strike and residents threatened to blockade the road if TRAC did not remedy the problem of storm water running off the highway into their houses (African Eye News Service, 17 January 2001).

For the average person using the toll road for the transport of goods, or for other business purposes, toll plaza tariffs are compensated for by the better road and the shorter distance as a result of improvements. This will certainly be the case once the new, more streamlined, border post is in place. Nonetheless, following the opening of the first two toll plazas, there was a significant decrease in the traffic (Driver & De Barros, 2000:19). The decline in the usage of the road almost led to investors withdrawing their equity during the latter part of 1999 because they were not able to recover their expenses. During 2000, however, traffic did improve considerably. One of the main reasons was because it was determined that taking alternative routes was not cost effective (*Traders*, 2000:44).

The second major infrastructure project is the upgrading of the port of Maputo. An especially difficult period in the life of the Corridor ended when, on 17 November 1999, an agreement was signed that would result in the privatisation of Maputo port. The agreement to manage the port for 15 years was given to an international consortium headed by Britain's Mersey Docks and Harbour Company. Other members of the consortium are Skanska of Sweden, Liscont of Portugal, and Moçambique Gestores. A new public/private sector company was formed, Sociedade de Desenvolvimento do Porto de Maputo. The consortium will hold 51 per cent of the shares while CFM (Mozambique Ports and Railways) will hold 49 per cent of the shares. According to the agreement, the only part of the port that will be privatised is the management, with the state maintaining its control over all the physical assets of the port. The agreement also stipulates that CFM will receive an annual fee of US$5 million in addition to a percentage of the pretax earnings of the consortium. For the first five years the percentage will be ten per cent, 12.5 per cent during years six to ten, and 15 per cent during the final five years (*Freight & Trading Weekly*, 2000b). The agreement was scheduled to come into effect by the end of 2000. It is estimated that the consortium will spend US$50–100 million on upgrading the harbour, which will include 'dredging the port channel to increase the depth from 9.5 to 13.5 metres, as well as managing, organising and maintaining port facilities' (Driver & De Barros, 2000:8).

The long-awaited agreement for upgrading the Maputo port was reached after 18 months of political wrangling between CFM and South Africa's Spoornet, which is a division of Transnet (South Africa's transport company). Although Mersey Docks and Harbour Co. were identified as the preferred bidders for the Maputo port in May 1998, they did not accept the bid at the time because of the conflict that developed between CFM and Spoornet. The CMF/Spoornet conflict was related to the third major Corridor infrastructure project, the upgrading of the railway lines that feed into Maputo port.

The problem started during the latter part of 1997, after a Spoornet-led consortium was identified as the preferred bidder for the upgrading of the Komatipoort/Ressano Garcia railway line to South Africa (78km). Consortia 2000, a Portuguese-led consortium, was identified as the preferred bidder for the other two lines: the Goba line to Swaziland (63km) and the Limpopo line to Zimbabwe (521km). Spoornet and CFM were not able to agree on the terms of the concession, which resulted in negotiations being called off in 1998. The dispute was over the amount of money CFM was demanding from Spoornet for the concession. For all three prospective concessionaires, CFM developed a two-part fee structure. The first was based on a certain percentage of revenue collected and the second was an annual fixed fee. After failing to agree on an annual fee structure, CFM ended the negotiations. When this happened, Mersey Docks became reluctant to sign the Maputo port deal out of concern that Spoornet would not be on board to either route traffic to Maputo port, or reroute it, if necessary, to ports in South Africa. Consortia 2000 also began to rethink its involvement in the project. In early 1997, Mersey Docks decided to withdraw from the negotiations, although it was later persuaded to resubmit its bid (*Mpumalanga Report*, 1999b:15; *Lowvelder*, 1999).

At the heart of the CFM/Spoornet wrangling is the distrust that the former has of the latter. In fact, according to Arkwright, 'none of our neighbours trust any of our parastatals – Transnet, Spoornet, Eskom, Telkom. They are regarded as expansionary and colonialist .... So it doesn't surprise me that Rui Fonseca[22] has resisted to get into deals with Spoornet. He was faced with a *fait accompli* when the preferred bidder was announced as Spoornet'.[23] The three railway lines are still up for tender at time of writing.

The last major Corridor infrastructure project is the upgrading of the Ressano Garcia/ Komatipoort border post. At a cost of US$33 million, it is to be a one-stop, 24-hour border post. Currently, the border post requires two stops and it closes at 7 p.m. Travellers reaching the border post after 7 p.m. must wait until the next morning to continue their journey. In order to decrease the time spent at the new border post, pre-clearance facilities will be available in cities or at airports close to the border. Those not able to pre-clear will be able to stop at the border. SARS allocated US$3.3 million for a three-month period to help expedite the project (Driver & De Barros, 2000:8).

During the planning for the Corridor, a shopping list of 180 projects was developed, ostensibly for the purpose of attracting investment along the corridor. Although there have been some investments and pledges (see, for example, Arkwright & De Beer, 1998:5–6; MCC, 1999:4–5), for the most part, the type of investment anticipated along the corridor has not materialised. This is especially the case on the South African side. One of the reasons for this is because, for the most part, investors are attracted to Mpumalanga's untapped natural resources and not its link to Maputo port. Consequently, it has been suggested, a more realistic strategy for attracting investors would be the upgrading of feeder roads (BusinessMap, 1999b). With respect to the issue of marketing Mpumalanga's natural resources, Jenny Briedenhann, CEO of the Mpumalanga Tourism Authority, complained in 1998 that the Corridor was having a negative impact on tourism because its agents were removing advertising signs along the N4 highway. Allegedly, TRAC was paying individuals R50 per sign for removal (WildNet Africa News Archive, 11 May 1998).

Again, as opposed to South Africa, Mozambique is the preferred destination for foreign investors. Although some Corridor proponents often like to claim that investments near Maputo port are secondary Corridor investments, Arkwright, for example, had to admit that in reality, often this is not the case; that, in fact, such investment is not directly or indirectly related to the Corridor. A case in point is the Mozal aluminium smelter, located in Matola, Mozambique and the prospective Pande Gas/Maputo Iron and Steel Project (MISP).

Mozal and Pande Gas/MISP

The US$1.3 billion Mozal Aluminium Smelter project is one of the largest single investments in Mozambique. The investors include South African-rooted offshore company Billiton (47 per cent), Japan's Mitsubishi Group (25 per cent), South Africa's Industrial Development Corporation (IDC) (24 per cent), and the government of Mozambique (four per cent). Backers of the project include Mozfund (established by the IDC), First Rand Bank, Standard Bank, Nedbank, BoE, Rand Merchant Bank, and ABSA (BusinessMap, 2000c).

With modern facilities, it is anticipated that the smelter will have a production capacity of 250 000 tons of aluminium annually. This capacity will double when a second potline is added. On 18 June 2000, the first aluminum was cast at the smelter. This casting occurred 25 months after the project started and six months ahead of schedule, which is perhaps a world record for construction of a greenfield smelter this large. At the peak of its construction, Mozal had 9 000 employees, 70 per cent of whom were Mozambicans. In 2001, it is anticipated that the smelter will generate US$400 million in foreign exchange, which would be more than Mozambique's exports for 1999. Mozal was given industrial free zone (IFZ) status by the Mozambican government during both the construction and operation phases of the project. Mozal will only have to pay one per cent of its turnover in taxes to the Mozambican government for the duration of the project (BusinessMap, 2000c; http://www.mozal.com/news/press/pr58.htm; http://www.ft.com/ftsurvey/country/sc86ea.htm).

Mozal's primary attraction to Mozambique was because of low-priced power from Motraco (Mozambique Transmission Company). Motraco is a joint venture between Eskom (South Africa), Electricidade de Mozambique (Mozambique), and the Swaziland Electricity Board. Two 400kv transmission lines will be built – from Eskom's Arnot power station to Maputo and from Eskom's Camden power station via Swaziland to Maputo (SADC, n.d.). The project's power consumption is 450MW, which is double that of the entire country. Mozal built its own port at Matola, along with roads and bridges. The company also had to rehabilitate telecommunications and water infrastructure. Most of the material for the construction of Mozal was sourced from South Africa. Alumina is being sourced from Western Australia (SADC, n.d.).

Mozal has had its problems. They include employees dying from malaria, worker strikes, difficulties in securing land to house staff, and the resettlement of people moved from the construction site (BusinessMap, 2000c). The latter is always a problem with huge investment projects. Again, it is often the poor who are further marginalised in the name of economic development.

Another big project that is in the making for Mozambique is the Pande Gas/Maputo Iron and Steel Project. A memorandum of understanding was signed between Enron, a US company, and the Maputo provincial government on 17 February 2000, which stipulated that Enron would construct a steel factory at Beluluane, which is 17km west of Maputo, near the Mozal smelter. The steel plant was being jointly sponsored by Enron and the IDC.[24] In addition to the steel plant, a gas field will be developed, along with a gas pipeline. The estimated cost of the project is US$2.4 billion, which will represent the largest single investment in Mozambique. Annual exports are expected to be over US$700 million. This will amount to more than 200 per cent of Mozambique's exports in 1998 (Mozambique News Agency, 2000).

The construction of the plant is scheduled to take place between 2002 and 2004. About 75 per cent of the magnetite (iron) ore for the project is scheduled to be sourced from Phalaborwa in South Africa. This ore is extremely cheap. The remaining 25 per cent of ore, which will be of a higher quality, might be sourced from Brazil. Natural gas for the project will be sourced from Pande in Inhambane Province, Mozambique, 610km north-east of Maputo. A pipeline will transfer the gas to the plant. Until October 2000, gasfields were to be developed by Enron, in partnership with Mozambique's EHN, which is the state-owned National Hydrocarbon Company. During October 2000, however, Enron gave up its rights to the Pande field, which includes the production of the gas and its transport from Pande. Enron is being replaced by a South African company, Sasol (an oil-from-coal company). As part of the new agreement, the Pande gasfield, along with the Temane gasfield, also located in Inhambane, will be treated as a single field (Panafrican News Agency, 26 October 2000). The gas will be used in the iron ore reduction process, which will precede the actual manufacture of steel slabs. It is projected that 3.5 to 4 million steel slabs will be produced annually. An estimated 5 000 people will be employed during the construction phase of the project and 1 000 during the operation of the plant (Mozambique News Agency, 2000:9; *Financial Times*, 18 October 1999).

With a view to attracting further investment, an industrial park has been established at Beluluane, where the Pande Gas/MISP will be located. The park was established as an industrial free zone to encourage downstream activity from Mozal, offering attractive tax incentives, joint-venture programmes with local companies, access to Matola and Maputo harbours and to the N4 Maputo-Witbank highway. Mozal was integrally involved in the Park's establishment to facilitate downstream activity from anchor projects as part of a 'Linkages' programme (BusinessMap, 2000c).

Although one of the poorest countries in the region, Mozambique has attracted more foreign investment than any other country other than South Africa (see the next section on investment in the SADC region). Why has this been the case? Largely because Mozambique's environment is conducive to investment. Labour is cheap, the country offers good tax breaks, has good farmland, and the logistics of the Maputo harbour are appealing (*Business Day*, 21 June 2000).

The Maputo Development Corridor as a Model for Transport Infrastructure in the SADC Region?

Any assessment of the significance of the Maputo Development Corridor must be placed within the context of its impact on the region as well as the two countries directly involved – South Africa and Mozambique. In terms of the region, attempts are being made to replicate the Corridor model. The notion of PPPs to enhance transport infrastructure development has begun to transform this sector, which is most evident by examining other SADC development corridors (e.g. see Saunders, 1999; Heese 1999a:41; *Mail & Guardian*, 1 October 2000; BusinessMap, 1999d; SARDC, 1998a; *South Africa: Journal of Trade, Industry & Investment*, 2000). The question to be raised, however, is whether or not the Corridor model should be replicated throughout the region. Perhaps the most significant outcome of the Corridor is that the SADC member states understand that there is an alternative to the organisation's previous reliance on donor assistance for transport infrastructure development. PPPs have consequently been established with a view to upgrading the infrastructure of several SADC transport corridors. Notwithstanding the need for SADC member states to decrease their reliance on their ICPs for infrastructural development, it would behove most countries to be somewhat conservative in their expectations in securing public-private investment agreements.

The Corridor experience points to the reality that investors are interested in investing in areas where the profit margins are high. For any number of the SADC development corridors, the environment is not conducive for attracting investment. In these cases, the initial SADC port transport system that merely focused on the establishment of viable transport networks to regional ports might be the best strategy to pursue. After all, communities should not have to forego transport infrastructual development simply because investors do not find their communities profitable. However, to the extent that a corridor has underutilised potential that is attractive to investors, it is important that a comprehensive development strategy be adopted.

If the true potential of PPPs in the transport infrastructure sector is to be realised, BusinessMap SA, a consultancy firm that provides investment advice to investors and tracks FDI in South Africa as well as the SADC region, warns that SADC countries must put in place the necessary reforms to attract large sums of private investment. This includes national legislative and regulatory regime reforms as well as economic stability (BusinessMap, 1999c). What has not been determined in the case of SDIs (including development corridors) is whether the SDIs themselves spark investment, or whether the

SDIs are developed around existing or potential investment. In fact, it has been difficult to identify investment projects that have occurred as a result of the Corridor, since several projects were being developed prior to its launch (Mitchell, 1998:783).

Although both South Africa and Mozambique have benefitted from the Corridor, the originators of the idea may have been overly ambitious. With respect to the impact of the toll road on the local population, for example, Arkwright admits that the level of hostility from the community was not anticipated.[25] Also not anticipated was the limited employment and business opportunities for previously disadvantaged communities (PDCs). In terms of employment opportunities, it had been projected that 35 000 permanent new jobs would be created (MCC, 1998). But, as Jonathan Mitchell notes, at most the toll road project would create 2 000 jobs in the province for about 42 months (Mitchell, 1998:764). In the final analysis, he thinks the Corridor will create about 7 000 permanent jobs in Mpumalanga. This is based on the fact that since most investment tends to be capital intensive, for each US$200 000 of capital investment, only one job is created. With capital investment projected at US$1.5 billion, 7 000 permanent jobs would be created (Mitchell, 1998:764). Arkwright, however, noted that by 1999, approximately 15 000 jobs had been created.[26] A distinction, however, was not made between permanent and temporary jobs.

In addition to jobs, high expectations have been raised with respect to business opportunities that would be available to the PDCs. One local company that has benefitted from the Corridor is the Soshanguve Bakgoni Women's Group, an SMME. In September 1998, they won a contract worth R400 000 for numerous projects along the Witbank and Maputo toll road. The contract was awarded by SBB, which is responsible for upgrading the N4 toll road. SBB, together with TRAC, have awarded 220 SMME contracts worth over R40 million (*Lowvelder*, 1999:36). How many of these have been actually given to PDCs is not known.

Although the disadvantaged communities may not have benefitted to the degree expected, clearly there have been significant benefits to select individuals or groups with respect to jobs created. Again, however, it is difficult to determine which jobs are a direct result of the Corridor and which are not.

In the final analysis, questions have been raised regarding the ultimate viability of the Corridor in the context of ports in South Africa. The first question to be raised is its cost effectiveness, namely, will the investment in the Corridor result in increased usage of the Maputo port? The port is in direct competition with Durban port. Although the distance from Gauteng Province to Durban is longer than from Gauteng to Maputo, when delays at the Ressano Garcia/Komatipoort border post are factored in, the trip to Maputo is longer. In addition, the toll road tariffs to Durban port are much smaller than those to Maputo, since the former are subsidised by the government. This means that currently it is more cost effective to travel on the Johannesburg-to-Durban route (Driver & De Barros, 2000:20).

The Durban advantage is likely to change over the next few years due to the fact that the toll road to Durban, the N3, was concessioned for upgrading in May 1999 by a company called N3TC. With the upgrading, toll road tariffs will increase. At this point, the Maputo and Durban ports may be similarly competitive (Driver & De Barros, 2000:20).

Also of importance is the fact that although the Durban port is congested, it is better connected to the global shipping world. Consequently, more shipping lines call at Durban than at Maputo. With respect to Maputo port, Driver and De Barros note that, '[u]nless more cargo comes to the Maputo port, shipping lines will be reluctant to call there; unless more shipping lines call, cargo owners will be reluctant to send their cargo there' (Driver & De Barros, 2000:20).

Notwithstanding the great potential that exists for infrastructure development by adopting the PPP approach, the major downside of this approach is that areas that may be in the most need of development could be side-lined simply because the profit margins for huge investments are not significant. In such cases, it is important for governments to ensure that infrastructure development still occurs. It is usually the case that big investments mean the further marginalisation of the PDCs. This is certainly evident with respect to the Corridor and will likely be the case with other SDIs. The human factor must therefore be seriously considered when planning for huge investment projects.

Although the Corridor has had its share of growing pains, the initiative, along with greenfield operations, represents the tremendous potential that exists for intra-regional investment, economic growth, and employment creation. This is the potential key to the successful implementation of regionalism in Southern Africa. Not only is regional infrastructural development a gateway to long-term economic development, but, as the ADB notes,

> regional collaboration of this sort tends to be less threatening than the trade-focused market integration variety. This is because it often provides clear gains for all concerned, imposes little or no loss of national sovereignty, and typically calls for no special compensation arrangements (ADB, 2000:183).

Investment in South Africa

Although market integration in Africa has failed to attract FDI, the expectation exists that increased FDI will follow the creation of the SADC FTA. If the findings of a study conducted by A. T. Kearney (a noted consultancy firm that is highly respected for its annual FDI rankings) are true, these expectations must be seriously tempered. A significant finding of the study was that the more corporate executives know about South Africa, the less they have expectations that investment opportunities will increase as a result of SADC. They also indicated, when asked how SADC affects South Africa's investment climate, that although usually it is the case that regional initiatives result in greater investment opportunities, they anticipate that it will take years for such opportunities to develop. The problem with investors visualising enhanced opportunities in the SADC region rests with the perception that the business structure is underdeveloped, political and economic structures are not stable, and there is market asymmetry in relationship to South Africa. This asymmetry is evident by the small market size of the other SADC member states and what potential investors deem to be their non-existent consumer market. The respondents to the study, which was undertaken by A. T. Kearney's Global Business Policy Council, were selected senior executives from Global 1 000 companies (the largest firms in the world) (A. T. Kearney, 2000:2, 12–13).

The influential weekly South African magazine, *Financial Mail*, in an editorial, responded to the A. T. Kearney report by saying that,

> SA is unique in that it, unlike, say Portugal or Argentina, is not blessed with dynamic neighbours with which to form dynamic trading partnerships. It thus needs its own unique strategy and whatever our spiritual or emotional commitments to the African renaissance may be, we must be sure, always, to put our own interests first (*Financial Mail*, 2000).

Does this mean white South African corporate interests, or the interests of the people of South Africa?

Notwithstanding the arrogance of the response by the *Financial Mail*, the A. T. Kearney findings, if accurate, are a real blow to the SADC regional agenda, as well as the expectation that the SADC FTA will serve to boost South Africa's fledgling economic growth. As the regional giant, it was anticipated that South Africa would serve to spearhead regional economic growth via increased FDI flows vying for access to a larger regional market. Such investment would also serve as a catalyst to enhance employment opportunities in South Africa. With the loss of over half a million jobs in the formal sector since 1994, the government of South Africa is desperately attempting to attract foreign investment in the country in hopes of reversing this trend.

At the heart of the government's strategy for economic growth is its Growth, Employment, and Redistribution programme. Launched in 1996, according to the government to underpin the existing Reconstruction and Development Programme (RDP), GEAR is an investment-led strategy that focuses on macroeconomic stability. Instead of attempting to correct the injustices of the apartheid era through a top-down strategy that would require governmental intervention to begin to redistribute the wealth of the country and spearhead economic growth, GEAR maintains that apartheid era injustices can be corrected through the market. Specifically, this means that with increased foreign investment, the economy will grow, and jobs will be created. With access to capital, the poor and marginalised masses will acquire the economic resources to invest in their own social upliftment.[27] This miracle is to transpire in a country that is deemed to have the second largest economic disparity in the world. (The largest is that of Brazil.) Unfortunately for South Africa, income disparities have increased since 1994 (Reuters, 27 February 2000).

Among the fallacies of the GEAR strategy was the premise that FDI would spearhead growth. As Yash Tandon notes, it is FDIs that are attracted to growth and not FDIs that bring growth (Tandon, 2000:3). Nonetheless, proclamations that the dearth of FDI is the Achilles heel of economic recovery in South Africa are still being made (e.g. see *Daily Mail & Guardian*, 2000a), along with the acceptance that GEAR has not resulted in the levels of FDI that were predicted (*Daily Mail & Guardian*, 2000b). In addition to FDI following growth, it also follows domestic investment. If national entrepreneurs do not feel South Africa is worth investing in, why should foreign investors? Jeremy Cronin, deputy general secretary of the South African Communist Party, perhaps has a greater sense of reality when he notes that, 'much more emphasis needs to be placed now on the government playing a leading role in getting the real economy going. It must mobilise domestic investment, both public and private. It is then that foreign investors will say, "You are investing in your own economy. So we will, too"' (*Daily Mail & Guardian*, 2000b).

The remainder of this section examines South African governmental strategies to attract both domestic and foreign investment. This will be followed by a description and analysis of investment trends in South Africa.

The Struggle to Increase Investment in South Africa

In a further attempt to separate itself from its 'beleaguered' neighbours, in a three-page special advertising supplement to the *New York Times* of 18 September 2000, the article actually introducing South Africa to prospective investors states that, '[i]n its endeavor to catch up with the most highly developed countries, South Africa sets out with a big head-start over its neighbors' (*New York Times*, 2000). Reinforcing this mindset, Howard Barrell, writing in the *Daily Mail and Guardian*, noted that in terms of foreign investment, South

Africa is suffering because clear distinctions are not made between South Africa and the rest of Africa. This is important because South Africa is different (*Daily Mail & Guardian*, 2000b).

Is it that TNCs do not have the capacity to see South Africa for the real potential that it has or do some South Africans have delusions of grandeur? In any event, this 'out of Africa' syndrome is very problematic for the SADC regional agenda.

'Beleaguered' itself when it comes to economic growth and attracting FDI, on 6 September 2000, the South African DTI announced a new strategy aimed at increasing the prospects of domestic investment in the country. It appears that this new strategy accepts the argument previously made that if the South African economy is to reverse its present economic decline, it will have to come from policies implemented from within. The strategy consists of four major programmes: the Small and Medium Enterprise Development Programme (SMEDP); the Skills Support Programme (SSP); the Industrial Development Zone Programme (IDZP); and the Strategic Investment Programme (SIP). The overall objective of the programme is to enhance South Africa's international competitiveness.

The SMEDP is designed to provide cash incentives for new industries and the expansion of existing ones. The actual investment value of these enterprises must be less than R100 million. Cash grants can be given for the following sectors: manufacturing, tourism, information technology, agro-processing, recycling, biotechnology, aqua-culture, and culture (Theobald, 2000). Under a previous programme, grants were only made available in the manufacturing sector with investment ventures of only R3 million. The actual monetary amounts of the cash grants are calculated based on '10% of qualifying investment cost, which would be paid over two or three years, if a labour usage criterion is met. The grant is tax-free' (*Business Day*, 20 October 2000). According to Trade and Industry Minister Erwin, R200 to R300 million will be allocated for the programme, with actual grants ranging in value from R3 to R50 million. The objectives of the programme include enhancing the international competitiveness of South African companies, job and wealth creation, enhancing entrepreneurship and empowerment, and utilising South African raw materials. The focus on small and medium enterprises is based on the reality that they create more jobs per rand investment than larger enterprises (*Business Day*, 7 & 11 September 2000).

The objective of the SSP is to provide resources for businesses to increase their spending on skill development. A cash grant is provided for up to 50 per cent of new staff training as a result of new projects or the expansion of existing ones. The grant stipulates that an approved training programme must be in place and pay-outs are for up to three years based on performance (*Business Day*, 20 October 2000).

With the IDZP, purpose-built, state-of-the-art industrial estates will be created with links to an international airport or port. The major objective of the programme is to make South Africa's manufacturing sector internationally competitive. Customs procedures will be streamlined and goods imported into the country for export production will enter South Africa duty-free (Theobald, 2000; *Business Day*, 20 October 2000).

The final programme, the SIP, is designed to provide incentives for investments that are over R100 million. The programme, which was initially put on hold following a decision by Finance Minister Trevor Manuel that it would be too costly, was later approved. It has been projected that the cost of the overall economic incentive programme will exceed R1 billion after a few years (*Business Day*, 11 September, 10 November 2000).

SDIs and macroeconomic stability are at the forefront of the government's strategy to attract FDI. Investment promotion incentives include the restructuring of state assets and the development of a National Industrial Participation Programme. To help facilitate the investment process, provincial investment agencies have been established as well as a national agency – Investment South Africa. On the books is a plan by President Mbeki to establish an international investment council (Heese, 1999b:12–13).

The A. T. Kearney study recommends that the South African government should focus on attracting investment in service industries, where it has a comparative advantage as a result of its English-speaking population, good infrastructure, and Western business tradition. In arguing that FDI from the service sector would be logical, given the reality of South Africa's investment environment, the A. T. Kearney study posits that it would help solve the unemployment problem, since labour-intensive jobs would be created. Attracting service industry FDI is a growing trend in emerging markets (Heese, 1999b:18–19).

Iraj Abedian, Chief Economist at Standard Bank, and one of the architects of GEAR, posits that instead of the South African government making appeals for any type of FDI, a strategy should be adopted that focuses on luring potential investors to particular industries and sectors that may be attractive investment destinations. Abedian also stresses that the government should increase the pace of privatisation and provide other incentives for foreign investors, including tax holidays (*Daily Mail & Guardian*, 2000b).

Because it is viewed as a high risk destination, numerous constraints to FDI flows exist in South Africa. They include violence and high crime rates; the perception that the labour market is inflexible (e.g. it is difficult to lay off workers and to comply with employment equity legislation); there is a shortage of skilled labour; and the labour force is expensive and not necessarily productive when placed within the global context. The smallness of South Africa's market size is another constraint to FDI flows, along with the fact that the economy is not experiencing high growth rates. The rising rate of HIV/AIDS and the fact that labour unions are not afraid to strike further discourage FDI flows (A. T. Kearney, 2000:13, 15–16, 20; *Washington Post*, 17 October 1999).

Investment Trends in South Africa

Determining the correct data for FDI flows into South Africa is a difficult task. According to UNCTAD, FDI into South Africa between 1994 and 1999 has oscillated between US$300 million and US$1.7 billion (A. T. Kearney, 2000:6). On the other hand, according to BusinessMap, FDI flows during this period have oscillated between US$1.7 billion and US$3.2 billion (Heese, 1999b:13). BusinessMap makes it very clear that it only records South African FDI that exceeds R10 million or investments that are expected to exceed this amount. In addition, FDI figures reflect 'firm intentions, new investments, investments (into significant shares of corporate assets), expansions in productive capacity, mergers and acquisitions, as well as failed investments' (Heese, 1999b:12).

The top three investors in South Africa in 1999 were the US, Malaysia, and the UK.[28] US investments consist of new and reinvestments, with the latter accounting for a large percentage. Currently, 386 US companies are actively involved in South Africa in the following sectors: transport and transport equipment; telecommunications and information technology; professional services; pharmaceutical and medical products; manufacturing; motor and components; media, print, and publishing; machinery; food beverages and tobacco; financial services; chemicals, plastics, and rubber (BusinessMap, 2002:14–16).

As the second largest investor in South Africa in 1999, Malaysian investment declined following the Asian financial crisis of 1998. Malaysia's major investments have been in the telecommunications/IT and energy and oil sectors. Investments from the UK, the third largest investor in 1999, have been diverse and include the following sectors: financial services; motor and components; hotels, leisure, and gaming; water services; construction; media and print; property; and manufacturing (BusinessMap, 2002:17). The top ten investment deals in South Africa between 1994 and 1999 are displayed in Table 5.2.

Table 5.2: Top Investments in South Africa, 1994–99

Investment	Investor	Country	Sector	Rm	Year
Telkom	SBC Communication	US/Malaysia	Telecom and IT	5 630	1997
Engen	Petronas	Malaysia	Energy and oil	4 000	1998
Sentrachem	Dow chemicals	US	Chemicals, plastics and rubber products	2 320	1997
Engen	Petronas	Malaysia	Energy and oil	1 900	1996
Blue Circle Cement	Lafarge – France	France	Construction, building materials and engineering	1 530	1998
SA Bottling Co.	Coca-Cola	US	Food, beverages and tobacco	1 400	1995
Western Areas Ltd	Placer Dome Inc.	Canada	Mining and quarrying	1 410	1998
SAA	Swissair	Switzerland	Transport and transport equipment	1 400	1999
Tavistock Colleries	Lonrho Plc	UK	Mining and quarrying	1 400	1998
Safmarine	A P Moller	Denmark	Transport and transport equipment	1 222	1999

Source: Heese (1999b:20)

Table 5.3 (opposite) provides a break-down of investments by sectors from all FDI flows between 1994 and 1999.

The majority of FDI flows into South Africa between 1994 and 1999 were concentrated in mergers and acquisitions instead of greenfield operations, which Karen Heese argues is reason for alarm, because it means that investors are not comfortable with getting involved in new or expansive ventures. The only way that FDI can have an impact on the South African economy is if it expands productive capacity. Greenfield operations, however, will not be established by firms unless there is significant growth in the domestic market or improved locational benefits (BusinessMap, 2002:19).

Table 5.3: FDI in South Africa, Sector Profile, 1994–99

Sector	Rm
Telecom and IT	8 768.0
Energy and oil	8 517.0
Food, beverages and tobacco	5 642.0
Motor and components	5 536.4
Transport and transport equipment	4 539.0
Mining and quarrying	3 958.5
Chemicals, plastics and rubber products	3 497.5
Hotel, leisure and gaming	2 936.0
Metal products and mineral beneficiation	2 704.0
Other manufacturing	2 608.0

Source: Heese (1999b:19)

In addition to FDI flows continuing to decline and the dearth of flows going into green-field operations, there continues to be an increase in the outward flow of investment from South Africa. According to a recent KPMG Corporate Finance survey, outward investment exceeds inward investment by a ratio of 24:1. The South African government is seriously challenged by these figures, which raises questions as to how to curtail increasing outflows of investment without discouraging inward flows (BusinessMap, 2000d:2–3). It is important to note that inward investment into South Africa has increased ten-fold since 1994.

There are numerous reasons for the huge outward flow of investment. Outward investment flows can be largely accounted for by the desire for companies to have access to both international and regional markets, and to become internationally competitive. The expansion into the SADC market is partially a reflection of the South African domestic market being saturated and of high production costs. For some South African firms, the profit margins of their subsidiaries in the SADC region are four times higher than in South Africa (BusinessMap, 1998b:2).

During the 1970s until 1988, according to Rafiq Bagus, a South African CEO, outward flows of foreign investment were a reflection of the capital flight that occurred because of political instability in the country. The capital flight that took place in the early and mid-1990s was a result of the uncertainty investors felt about the future of the country (*Business Day*, 30 September 2000). Related to this was the decision by some corporations to split up their assets largely to prevent them from being disturbed in case the ANC-led government decided to nationalise certain economic entities in an effort to begin to redistribute the wealth in the country. This was considered as a possible option in order to begin to remedy the injustices of apartheid (Heese, 2000:397).

The expectation that market integration will result in increased FDI and lead to economic growth and development is not likely to happen in South Africa. The greatest hope for economic growth and employment creation rests with increased domestic investment. If economic growth is spearheaded from within, larger FDI flows might follow. However, even if this occurs, there is no guarantee that it will enhance South Africa's productive capacity. Enhanced economic growth and employment creation from domestic investment could certainly have an overall positive impact on regional economic growth.

Investment in the SADC Region

FDI flows into the SADC region increased during the 1990s. This reflects a general improvement in the regional environment for attracting investors. Countries have gone to great lengths to provide incentives for both domestic and foreign investors. Such incentives include reforms that decrease the restrictions on foreign ownership, increase the ability to repatriate capital, and provide investment guarantees. In addition, financial and fiscal incentives have been put in place, including export processing zones (Saunders 1999:55).[29]

Nonetheless, constraints to FDI remain serious in the SADC region. The most problematic constraints relate to political and economic instability in Angola, the DRC, and Zimbabwe. With respect to the latter, not only has foreign investment declined significantly, but disinvestment has occurred as a result of the crisis in that country. In the case of Angola, while FDI flows continue to be significant for the country's oil sector, most of the profits received by the government went into financing the recently ended war, leaving the masses in the country in abject poverty and unimaginable misery. Both the DRC and Angola continue to be plundered of their wealth by both TNCs and government leaders and entrepreneurs. The destruction of the infrastructure in both countries made greenfield investments impossible, and both conflicts had implications for FDI flows into other SADC countries. Namibia and Zambia have had to deal with the wars crossing into their borders, further destroying already dilapidated infrastructure. These countries became the homes of many refugees fleeing the conflicts.

In addition to political instability and its resultant economic instability, other factors serve as constraints to investment in the SADC region. These include inadequate physical infrastructure, corruption, complex tax systems, red tape, lack of skilled labour, and HIV/AIDS (e.g. see Mbekeani, 1999; Heese, 2000).

The remainder of this section is divided into two parts. The first part looks at FDI in the SADC region and the second focuses on South African FDI. The latter is the number one investment destination in Southern Africa.

International Investment

According to BusinessMap, the three largest investors in Southern Africa are South Africa, the US, and the UK. The largest percentage of FDI goes to Mozambique (BusinessMap, 2000b). The majority of investments into the region are concentrated in areas related to natural resources, including medal products and mineral beneficiation, mining, energy and oil, food, beverages, and tobacco (see Table 5.4, opposite).

Unlike FDI flows to South Africa, the larger percentage of FDI in the SADC region excluding South Africa is in new investments and not mergers and acquisitions (Saunders, 1999:58). A significant percentage of this is accounted for as a result of investment in the mining sector and the Mozal plant (Saunders, 1999:58).

Table 5.4: FDI in SADC, 1996–99 (Rm)

| Sector | January – June | | | | |
	1996	1997	1998	1999	Total
Metal products and mineral beneficiation	0.00	2 823.99	2 753.20	1.30	5 578.49
Mining	234.03	1 306.13	1 356.25	329.20	3 225.61
Energy and oil	909.55	21.71	18.50	0.00	949.79
Food, beverages and tobacco	77.12	419.82	118.99	0.00	615.93
Agriculture, forestry and fishing	56.12	57.80	100.62	0.00	214.54
Telecom and IT	0.00	5.29	105.23	95.00	205.52
Hotel, leisure and gambling	10.04	11.69	174.08	0.00	195.81
All other combined	28.68	204.36	256.91	1 600.00	2 089.95
Total	**1 315.54**	**4 850.82**	**4 883.78**	**2 025.50**	**13 075.64**
Amounts include intentions and actual investments					

Source: Saunders (1999:58)

South African Investment

Any attempt to track FDI flows from South Africa into the SADC region is formidable. BusinessMap estimates that between 1994 and 2000, South African FDI flows into the region totalled US$5 billion (BusinessMap, 2000b:2). With respect to this data, it is important to note that BusinessMap only records investments and intended investments that are worth at least US$1 million. In recognition of the importance of investing in the region, South African companies are allowed to invest larger sums in the SADC member states than in other parts of the world (Mowatt & Zulu, n.d.:1). The amount allocated per investment has been increased from R250 million to R750 million.

South African investment by individual country between 1996 and 1998 is outlined in Table 5.5 (overleaf). The largest recipient was Mozambique, followed by Zimbabwe.

Most of the FDI flows are in the following sectors: metal products and mineral benefication; mining and quarrying; food, beverages and tobacco; agriculture; and forestry and fishing. Most of these investments have added limited productive value to regional economies. According to BusinessMap, growing FDI into the SADC region reflects opportunities as a result of privatisation and the discovery of new bodies of ore (BusinessMap, 2000b:2).

The verdict is still out as to whether or not South African FDI flows into the region will enhance economic growth and development. This is partially the case because of the negative impact that some South African FDI flows are having. Also, as previously mentioned, questions have been raised as to how serious South African investors are committed to the SADC region beyond the need to have access to a larger market in order to enhance profit margins.

Table 5.5: South African FDI in SADC, 1996–98 (US$m)

Target country	1996	1997	1998	Total
Angola		0.78	103.00	103.78
Botswana	8.35	9.99	57.25	75.59
Lesotho		2.43		2.43
Malawi	1.62		41.30	42.92
Mauritius			7.30	7.30
Mozambique	126.03	1 380.893	393.21	1 900.13
Namibia	5.81	15.39	124.45	145.65
Swaziland		32.61	48.77	81.38
Tanzania	0.83	26.30	443.29	470.42
Zambia	4.50	186.24	212.39	403.13
Zimbabwe		586.52	340.24	926.76
Total	**147.14**	**2 241.15**	**1 771.19**	**4 159.49**
Note: Figures include actual deals and firm intentions				

Source: Saunders (1999:61)

As BusinessMap notes, South African FDI

> has not always benefited host countries, nor has it always been well received – small retailers, for instance, have found themselves unable to compete with the bulk of supplies and more competitive prices brought in by South African competitors. In addition, some South African retailers have failed to source locally, increasing resentment and the perception that South Africans are arrogant, self-serving and aggressive (BusinessMap, 2000b:2).

Other factors that have had negative repercussions for South African investors include transactions that are dishonest or unscrupulous and the unwillingness to tolerate local etiquette (BusinessMap, 2000b:2–3).

Unlike other countries that might buffer their investments through aid projects, this is not the case with South African investors. In addition, some South African investors maintain practices of bribery, and retrenchments often follow such investments. To make matters worse, according to BusinessMap, 'some South African policy makers have exacerbated the situation by implying that it's their prerogative as the regional power to dictate the conditions of regional infrastructure programmes, laying the ground rules of a "new wave of imperialism"' (BusinessMap, 2000b:3). Needless to say, many in the SADC region are ambivalent at best about the contribution that South African FDI flows can really make to enhancing SADC economic growth and development.

If regionalism in Southern Africa is to be a success, South Africa and its regional neighbours need to somehow reconcile the ambivalent feelings about South African FDI flows. This is necessary because, as has been argued, it is only through regional and domestic investment that needed growth and employment creation will be realised. The previous history of TNCs in Africa should be a sobering reminder that the SADC member states collectively must spearhead economic growth. Therefore, any expectation that market integration will result in increased FDI flows should be tempered by the reality that TNCs are not in the business of rescuing countries or regions from economic crises.

Notes

1   UNCTAD defines FDI as 'an investment involving a long-term relationship and reflecting a lasting interest and control of a resident entity in one economy (foreign direct investor or parent enterprise) in an enterprise resident in an economy other than that of the foreign direct investor (FDI) enterprise or affiliate enterprise or foreign affiliate' (UNCTAD, 2000:267).

2   The ten largest recipients among the developed countries were the US (US$275 533m), UK (US$82 182m), Sweden (US$59 968m), France (US$39 101m), Netherlands (US$33 785m), Germany (US$26 833m), Canada (US$25 061m), Ireland (US$18 322m), Belgium and Luxembourg (US$15 862m), and Japan (US$12 741m). The ten largest recipients among the developing countries were China (US$40 400m), Brazil (US$31 397m), Argentina (US$23 153m), Hong Kong (US$23 068m), Mexico (US$11 233m), Republic of Korea (US$10 340m), Chile (US$9 221m), Poland (US$7 500m), Singapore (US$6 984m), and Thailand (US$6 078m). For more details see UNCTAD (2000, Annex, Table B.1, p. 283).

3   Scathing critiques have been written of the methodology used by UNCTAD to collect and analyse FDI data. These studies also critique the assumptions made and the conclusions drawn by UNCTAD. See, for example, Tandon (2000); Nadal (2000).

4   Portfolio investments include bonds, equities, and money market instruments. Such instruments are traded (or tradeable) and are often commitments made for a short period (BusinessMap, 1999a:12).

5   Interview with Dave Arkwright, Nelspruit, South Africa, 25 July 1999.

6   *Ibid.*

7   *Ibid.*

8   *Ibid.*

9   Based on discussions at a seminar on SADC sponsored by the Harry Frank Guggenheim Foundation, Cape Town, South Africa, 8–10 January 2001.

10 Interview with Dave Arkwright (see en. 5).

11 *Ibid.*

12 *Ibid.*

13 *Ibid.*

14 *Ibid.*

15 *Ibid.*

16 *Ibid.*

17 *Ibid.*

18 *Ibid.*

19 *Ibid.*

20 Now called Limpopo Province.

21 Interview with Dave Arkwright (see en. 5).

22 Fonseca is the president of CFM.

23   Interview with Dave Arkwright (see en. 5).

24   The possibility exists that Enron has withdrawn from this project due to its financial and legal problems.

25   Interview with Dave Arkwright (see en. 5).

26   *Ibid.*

27   For analyses of South Africa's GEAR policy, see Lee (1997b); Bell (1998); Marais (1998:146–76).

28   In 2001, the three top investors in South Africa were Saudi Arabia, Germany, and the US (BusinessMap, 2002).

29   For more detail about SADC investment incentives see Hill (2000); *South Africa: Journal of Trade, Industry & Investment* (1999); Harvey (2000b).

Further Marginalisation or Integration?

THERE EXISTS AN ongoing debate as to how best Africa can be integrated into the world economy and decrease its marginalisation. One school of thought, supported by Rubens Ricupero, Secretary-General of UNCTAD, is that regional and sub-regional integration in Africa is crucial in order to help Africa prepare for being integrated into the world economy (*THISDAY*, 23 September 2001). Similarly, others suggest that Africa has no alternative but to integrate at the regional level in order to arrest being further marginalised within the world economy (e.g. see Mistry, 2000:570–1; Amin, 1999:54; Hettne, 1999:xviii). Those adopting this position see increased regionalism as a necessary response to increased globalisation. The other school of thought challenges in various ways the viability of pursuing regional integration strategies. In these cases, integration into the world economy at the international level seemingly is the only viable strategy for African countries to pursue (e.g. see Herbst, 1998:33; De Melo & Panagriya, 1992:20; Mwase & Maasdorp, 1999:201; Fine & Yeo 1997:429; Collier & Gunning, 1999:95).

African countries are challenged by the realities of globalisation to pursue integration into the world economy at both the regional and international levels. With respect to the international level, the question for Africa is whether such integration is best pursued through multilateralism or via the triad blocs. In the case of multilateralism, the best option for integration would be through the WTO, while integration via the triad blocs would take place through increased trade with and investment from North America, the EU, or Asia.

Two options available for prospectively enhancing Africa's further integration into the world economy will be examined in this chapter. The first is the WTO, which has the task of overseeing an international trade regime that is ostensibly fair and representative of the best interests of all its member countries. The second is the US-sponsored *African Growth and Opportunity Act*. This initiative is designed to increase Africa's access to the US market and subsequent integration into the world economy. At the same time, AGOA is theoretically designed to enhance regional integration throughout the continent. While the discussion on the WTO will primarily focus on the entire African continent, the discussion on AGOA will focus on both the continent and the SADC region. The question to be raised in this chapter is whether the WTO and AGOA are viable options for arresting African/Southern African marginalisation.

World Trade Organisation

The General Agreement on Tariffs and Trade was created in 1947 as an international agreement that was later transformed into a *de facto* international organisation. This was the case because the US Congress refused to approve the creation of the International Trade Organisation when the IMF and World Bank were established. The major objective of GATT was to oversee the reduction of tariff and NTBs to trade. The creation of a 'freer', as opposed to a 'free', international trade regime was to take place through a series of trade negotiation rounds. To date there have been eight rounds.[1]

The eighth round, known as the Uruguay Round, took place between 1986 and 1993. The final Uruguay agreements were ratified in 1994. The agreements resulted in sweeping changes for the international trade regime. The most significant was the creation in 1995 of the WTO. The WTO is a rules-based multilateral entity that is responsible for overseeing the implementation of trade policies growing out of GATT negotiations as well as subsequent agreements. With the WTO, GATT is therefore preserved. The WTO consists of 'twenty-nine separate legal texts, plus more than twenty-five declarations, memoranda of understanding, and joint statements' (Gerber, 1999:22).

In addition to creating a new institution, the UR resulted in (1) new trade rules, including those related to subsidies; (2) new issues, such as the General Agreement on Trade in Services, the Agreement on Trade Related Aspects of Intellectual Property Rights, and Agreement on Trade Related Investment Measures; and (3) trade barrier reductions. The latter includes across-the-board tariff cuts of 40 per cent for most industrial products; reductions in agricultural export subsidies as well as some domestic production subsidies; the conversion of non-tariff barriers into tariffs; and the phasing out of textile quotas over a ten-year period and the implementation of tariff cuts (Gerber, 1999:113).

The World Bank, in a publication on Africa entitled *Can Africa Claim the 21st Century?*, argues on the one hand that the WTO offers an opportunity for Africa to take advantage of a multilateral forum with a rules-based system for trade and development. On the other hand, the World Bank acknowledges that for some LDCs to implement WTO obligations, the cost would be the equivalent of an entire year's development budget. In addition, as a result of increased global liberalisation, African countries will continue to experience an erosion in preferences (World Bank, 2000:231). With such prohibitive fees and other constraints, the African Development Bank argues that of all the international organisations, the African voice is least heard in the WTO (ADB, 2000:192).

It has been estimated that as a result of the new trade regime growing out of the UR, African losses will total US$3 billion annually. These losses will occur in spite of efforts taken by most African countries to liberalise their trade regimes as a result of SAPs. Africa's share of world exports has declined even with trade liberalisation. For example, while in 1980 Africa's share of world exports was 5.8 per cent (Fleshman, 1999:32), currently it is less than two per cent. Why has this been the case? Partially because of poor economic policies, but also because developed countries have not opened their markets to developing countries. Perhaps this is because it has been estimated that if developing countries 'increased their share of world exports by just five percent, this would generate US$350bn – several times as much as they receive in aid' (Oxfam, 2002:6). According to *Africa Recovery*, a publication of the United Nations Department of Public Information, tariffs on manufactured products entering developed countries from developing countries on average are four times higher than tariffs imposed on exports from other developed countries. These high tariffs are usually placed on products in which developing countries are competitive, including processed agricultural products, textiles, leather goods, and shoes (Oxfam, 2002:6). *The Economist* predicts that if rich countries remove their subsidies, thus giving developing countries fairer access to their markets, financial benefits to poor countries would be three times the amount of money they receive annually in overseas development assistance (*The Economist*, 2001:70).

With respect to the unfair trade regime that is stacked in favour of the rich countries in the world, UN Secretary-General Kofi Annan noted that the livelihoods of millions of farmers in the developing world are being threatened because they cannot compete with subsidised imports (Fleshman, 1999:33). In an international forum held in London on 26 February 2001, the President of the World Bank, James Wolfensohn, called on the rich countries of the world to open their markets to poor countries by reducing their agricultural subsidies. The countries of the Organisation for Economic Cooperation and Development (OECD), Wolfensohn noted, spend more than $US300 billion annually on agriculture subsidies, which is approximately the equivalent of the GDP of sub-Saharan Africa (World Bank, 2001).

Joseph Stiglitz asks the question, 'How can the advanced economies preach the gospel of competition and free markets, yet turn to managed trade and restricted markets when their own interests are in jeopardy?' (Stiglitz, 2001:351). These countries should be the role models and can more readily absorb the shocks that result from trade patterns that change (Stiglitz, 2001:351).

A serious problem the WTO is confronted with is the reality that promises were made to developing countries during the UR that have not been fulfilled. Specifically, developing countries were promised enhanced market access to the rich countries of the world. Even when tariffs have been reduced, NTBs have been put in their place. These unkept promises have resulted in developing countries losing trust in the WTO, most evident in the collapse of the 1999 meeting in Seattle (*The Economist*, 2001:69).

Alan Rugman argues that not only is multilateralism dead, but also that the WTO, which is the conduit for multilateralism, is a small and weak technocratic body (Rugman, 2001:2). Although portrayed as the driver of free trade, in reality the WTO has no political clout and lacks the ability to force countries to comply with its decisions (Rugman, 2001:19).

Reinforcing Rugman's claim that multilateralism is dead is Percy Mistry's assertion that multilateralism has become dysfunctional. This is the case because it is cost-inefficient, ineffective, and its institutions, including the WTO, are sclerotic and stale. Such institutions are not really neutral forums that have genuine multilateral interests and perspectives, but instead serve to reinforce the interests of the OECD and G-7 shareholder governments (Mistry, 1999:126). Therefore, Mistry currently envisages regionalism as a better alternative to multilateralism (Mistry, 1999:152).

At the other end of the continuum are those who see multilateralism as an essential part of the world economy (see Kegley & Wittkopf, 2001:261–6). While it may be too early to predict the demise of multilateralism, it does appear that it is dictated by the triad blocs, further lending credence to accusations that the voices of marginalised entities within the world economy are not taken seriously.

As a result of the fact that the WTO has not fulfilled its promises for greater market access for the developing countries, the SADC member states decided to reject the new round of WTO trade talks. Instead, they demanded that the inadequacies of the current trade regime be addressed, including the imbalances that exist within the multilateral trading system (Madakufamba, 2001e). Such a position was adopted throughout the African continent. However, on the eve of the WTO meeting in Doha, Qatar, held on 9–13 November 2000, many of the SADC member states, under the leadership of South Africa, decided to support the new trade round. It has been suggested that this decision to break away from the African consensus to reject the new trade round will have serious implications for SADC's relations with the rest of Africa (*Mail & Guardian*, 16 November 2001; *Buanews*, 19 November 2001). Since the new round will not commence for two years, this rift may have been mended by the time the talks actually begin. New areas for negotiation will include rules on investment, government procurement, competition, electronic commerce, the environment, and labour (*Mail & Guardian*, 16 November 2001).

Notwithstanding the attempt to silence the African voice in the WTO (Fleshman, 1999:1, 30–4), it is important that African governments who have the financial resources continue their active participation in this organisation. Any expectation, however, that the WTO will be a conduit for enhancing Africa's integration in the world economy should be tempered by reality. The reality is that multilateralism in practice means guaranteeing that the current trade regime supports the protectionist policies of the triad blocs. Thus, with respect to the new round of trade talks, 'EU officials said that any attempt to put the elimination of its subsidies on the agenda would be intolerable, a position that the United States has accepted' (*Washington Post*, 6 November 2001).

Again, as the world becomes more regionalised around the triad blocs, the only option that African countries might have for increased integration is through North America, via, for example, AGOA, discussed below, and the EU, discussed in the next chapter.

African Growth and Opportunity Act

On 18 May 2000, President Bill Clinton signed into the law the *Trade and Development Act of 2000*, which included the *African Growth and Opportunity Act*. At the signing ceremony, Clinton noted that the legislation would expand 'Africa's access to our markets and improve the ability of African nations to ease poverty, increase growth, and heal the problems of [its] people' (Lobe, 2000:11).

This section of the chapter is divided into three sections. The first describes the objectives and implementation of AGOA. Section two will analyse the prospective impact of AGOA on sub-Saharan Africa, and the final section will analyse AGOA in the context of the SADC textile and garment industries.

Objectives and Implementation of AGOA

Among the objectives of AGOA is the expansion of US assistance to regional integration efforts in sub-Saharan Africa. Other objectives include increasing trade between the US and sub-Saharan Africa; reducing tariff and NTBs to trade as well as other barriers; and negotiating trade agreements, including ones that might result in the establishment of FTAs (US Congress, 2000:3). In order to be eligible to benefit from AGOA, African governments must adhere to the eligibility requirements outlined in Section 104 of the Act. They include the requirement of progress toward (1) establishing a market-based economy, which includes minimal government intervention in the economy, protection of private property, and an open rules-based trading system; (2) maintaining the rule of law; (3) removing barriers to US trade and investment; (4) introducing policies to reduce poverty; (5) introducing policies to combat corruption; and (6) compliance with the rights of workers recognised internationally (US Congress, 2000:4). With respect to participation in an open rules-based trading system, such assistance will be provided to AGOA participating countries to help them legally comply with WTO standards and encourage greater future participation in the organisation (US Congress, 2000:19).

Countries that comply with the eligibility requirements under Section 104 will be rewarded, according to Section 126, with discarded air traffic control equipment. The section reads as follows:

> It is the sense of Congress that, to the extent appropriate, the United States Government should make every effort to donate to governments of sub-Saharan African countries determined to be eligible under section 104 air traffic control equipment that is no longer in use, including appropriate related reimbursable technical assistance (US Congress, 2000:21–2).

Apparently the US government desperately needs a place to dump antiquated air traffic control equipment!

In terms of enhancing US exports of goods and services, the Act stipulates that the International Trade Administration should determine the best prospects for goods and services that could be exported to sub-Saharan African countries by US companies. In addition, barriers to trade (tariff and non-tariff) should be identified that prevent or hinder the sale of goods and services to sub-Saharan Africa, as well as barriers that constrain the ability of US companies to operate. Where such barriers exist, discussions should be held with appropriate authorities in order to increase US market access for goods and services (US Congress, 2000:21).

Thirty-five countries in sub-Saharan Africa have been designated as AGOA beneficiary countries.[2] Of the 13 non-beneficiary countries,[3] three are SADC member states – Angola, the DRC, and Zimbabwe. Angola was denied status as a beneficiary country due to corruption, poor labour laws, and human rights violations. The DRC was denied beneficiary status resulting from lack of economic reforms, poor labour laws, and human rights violations, while Zimbabwe could not become a beneficiary country due to lack of economic reforms, failure to implement the rule of law, lack of political pluralism, corruption, and human rights violations (Office of the US Trade Representative, 2001:91, 95, 99).

In terms of providing greater access to the US market, 1 835 additional products were identified for duty-free entry into the US market by AGOA beneficiary countries. Such access is possible as long as the items are not import-sensitive, which means they do not compete with US domestic producers. This figure of 1 835 can be added to the existing list of 4 650 products that have duty-free entry under the Generalised Systems of Preference (GSP) Programme (US Congress, 2000:8; Office of the US Trade Representative, 2001:2, 51).

There is a special provision in the Act that gives preferential treatment to certain textiles and apparel from sub-Saharan Africa. The specifics are outlined in Section 112 of the Act. The preferential treatment of textiles and apparel can be divided into two categories: (1) items made in sub-Saharan African countries from US wholly formed yarns and fabrics; and (2) items made in sub-Saharan African countries from wholly formed yarns and fabrics made in beneficiary sub-Saharan African countries. With respect to items made in category 1, they will have duty-free access to the US market without quantitative restrictions. African countries, however, must first import yarn and fabric from the US, make the garments, and then re-export them to the US.

In terms of items made in category 2, the Act stipulates that preferential treatment will be given to such items until 2008. This provision, however, is applicable for 1.5 per cent of all apparel articles imported into the US beginning on 1 October 2000 and is not to exceed 3.5 per cent of such articles by 30 September 2008. This means that the GATT GSP Programme will be extended to these countries for eight years. The Act will also allow the lesser developed beneficiary countries of sub-Saharan Africa to export apparel articles through 30 September 2004 that are produced from fabric made in any country. A lesser developed beneficiary country is considered to be one whose per capita GNP in 1998 was less than US$1 500. This preferential treatment is allowable as long as it does not compete with goods produced in the US. If it is determined that such competition exists, duty-free access given to beneficiary countries will be withdrawn (US Congress, 2000:9–10).

Section 113 of the Act contains provisions that must be adopted by all prospective beneficiary countries in order to prevent trans-shipment. Preferential treatment will not be provided for textile and apparel articles unless the country:

(a) has adopted an effective visa system, domestic laws, and enforcement procedures applicable to covered articles to prevent unlawful transshipment of the articles and the use of counterfeit documents relating to the importation of the articles into the United States;

(b) has enacted legislation or promulgated regulations that would permit United States Customs Service verification teams to have the access necessary to investigate thoroughly allegations of transshipment through such country;

(c) agrees to report, on a timely basis, at the request of the United States Customs Service, on the total exports from and imports into that country of covered articles consistent with the manner in which the records are kept by that country;

(d) will cooperate fully with the United States to address and take action necessary to prevent circumvention as provided in Article 5 of the Agreement on Textiles and Clothing;

(e) agrees to require all producers and exporters of covered articles in that country to maintain complete records of the production and the export of covered articles, including materials used in the production, for at least 2 years after the production or export (as the case may be); and

(f) agrees to report, on a timely basis, at the request of the United States Customs Service, documentation establishing the country of origin of covered articles as used by that country in implementing an effective visa system (US Congress, 2000:14).

In addition, these countries must comply with NAFTA customs procedures (Office of the US Trade Representative, 2001:52).

In order to help facilitate the monitoring process, the US government will (1) make available technical assistance to the beneficiary sub-Saharan African countries; (2) send production verification teams to at least four beneficiary sub-Saharan African countries each year; and (3) to the extent feasible, place beneficiary sub-Saharan African countries on the Electronic Visa (ELVIS) Programme (US Congress, 2000:16).

On 16 November 2001, the US House of Representatives voted overwhelmingly to amend AGOA and double the quota African countries can export duty-free to the US. This means a possible increase from 1.5 per cent to three per cent initially, with incremental increases reaching seven per cent (instead of 3.5 per cent) by 2008. In addition, Botswana and Namibia will prospectively be reclassified as LDCs, reserving for them the same treatment accorded poor countries. This will allow them to use fabric from any source until 2004. Botswana could also benefit from a change in the original wording of AGOA, which would give it preferential access to the US market for component knitted-to-shape cloth (*Business Day*, 10 October, 19 November 2001; US House of Representatives, 2001).

The proposed amendments to AGOA are referred to as AGOA II. The US Senate passed the AGOA II bill in early August 2002. It will become law once it is signed by the president.

At the first US-sub-Saharan Africa Trade Forum, held in Washington, DC, on 29–30 October 2001, President George W. Bush announced that a US$200 million fund would be created to provide support for US companies interested in investing in sub-Saharan Africa. Through the fund, companies will have access to loans, guarantees, and political risk insurance. In addition, the president indicated that a US Trade and Development Agency office would be opening in Johannesburg to help regional governments source new investment and the Trade and African Development Enterprises Programme would be launched to assist African entrepreneurs market their products in the global market (*Addis Tribune*, 2 November 2001).

In the final analysis, the US Congress anticipates that as a result of the provisions under AGOA, eventually FTAs will be created between the US and interested sub-Saharan African countries. Although during the past year no sub-Saharan African government indicated an interest in an FTA with the US, the US plans a phased approach to the issue. This will include implementation of additional Trade and Investment Framework Agreements (TIFAs) and increased dialogue with countries via Trade and Investment Council meetings. Such meetings 'will be held under the auspices of TIFAs; conclusion of additional TIFAs with regional African organisations; bilateral meetings; the U.S.-sub-Saharan Africa Trade and Economic Cooperation Forum; and AGOA discussions' (Office of the US Trade Representative, 2001:112–13). The objectives of FTAs for the US will probably include the removal of most tariffs on farm products and industrial goods; free trade in services; and the development of commitments in the area of intellectual property rights (Office of the US Trade Representative, 2001:113).

Analysis of the Prospective Impact of AGOA on Sub-Saharan Africa

At the first US-sub-Saharan Africa Trade Forum, the representatives from the 35 AGOA beneficiary African countries applauded the US commitment to enhance development of sub-Saharan Africa with AGOA. In fact, throughout sub-Saharan Africa, great expectations have been raised regarding the tremendous benefits that will accrue to the continent as a result of AGOA. Many countries have been actively involved in reforming their economic and political structures in order to gain greater access to US markets and investment (see Office of the US Trade Representative, 2001:100–5).

Critics, however, warn that increased access to the US market might fall very short of expectations (see Tiepoh, 2001; *Public Agenda*, 22 October 2001; *Post*, 18 October 2001; Hormeku, n.d.). For Geepu Nah Tiepoh, the policies contained in AGOA to promote African trade and investment are not new. In fact, they resemble SAPs imposed on African countries over the last two decades. The market-led economic reforms presented in AGOA will, in the final analysis, benefit American and other foreign corporations the most (Tiepoh, 2001:1–2).

So what are the anticipated costs and benefits to participating African countries? The greatest benefit is expected to come from the textile and apparel provision. In 1999, sub-Saharan African apparel exports to the US totalled US$580 million, or 0.8 per cent of US apparel imports. Under AGOA I, if textile and apparel exports to the US reach 3.5 per cent by 2008, this would mean US$4.2 billion, which would represent an annual increase of approximately US$452.5 million (Lobe, 2000:11). However, under AGOA II, this figure could double by 2008.

A major problem, however, is that only a select few countries will benefit from the textile and apparel provision of AGOA. As of August 2002, only 17 of the 35 AGOA beneficiary countries were eligible for this provision. They were Botswana, Cameroon, Ethiopia, Ghana, Kenya, Lesotho, Madagascar, Malawi, Mauritius, Mozambique, Namibia, Senegal, South Africa, Swaziland, Uganda, Tanzania, and Zambia.[4] According to the US government, during 2000, US imports of knit apparel from Africa increased by 51 per cent to US$299 million, while there was an increase of 16 per cent of imports of woven apparel, totalling US$499 million. These increases, however, occurred prior to AGOA's enactment. Three countries accounted for this increase – South Africa, Madagascar, and Lesotho. Although there were significant increases, especially of knit apparel (73 per cent for South Africa, 287 per cent for Madagascar, and 43 per cent for Lesotho), total imports only represented 1.13 per cent of all knit apparel imported into the US and 1.37 per cent of woven apparel imports (Office of the US Trade Representative, 2001:106).

During the first four months of 2001, US apparel imports from sub-Saharan Africa totalled US$268 million, US$242 million of which was imported from the five countries that were eligible for the apparel provision at the time – Kenya, Lesotho, Madagascar, Mauritius, and South Africa. However, only US$11.7 million of the US$242 million represented preferences stemming from AGOA (*Business Day*, 11 July 2001).

These low figures, according to Simon Barber, indicate two realities. The first is that it is premature to conclude whether or not African exports to the US are increasing in a meaningful way as a result of AGOA. The second is that the current apparel preferences will not likely help most African countries because they are too narrow when placed within the context of African capacities (*Business Day*, 11 July 2001).

In terms of SADC, ten of the 14 member states are eligible for the apparel provision. They are Botswana, Lesotho, Malawi, Mauritius, Mozambique, Namibia, South Africa, Swaziland, Tanzania, and Zambia. As a result of AGOA, there has been an increased interest in investment in at least four of these countries, as well as two other SADC member states.

According to the US government, as a result of AGOA, 11 new factories have been proposed for Lesotho and four expansions, prospectively resulting in 10 000 new jobs. It is anticipated that these projects will inject US$122 million in new investment into Lesotho's economy, which is equivalent to four times the amount of bilateral and multilateral official development assistance Lesotho received in 1999 (Office of the US Trade Representative, 2001:108).

In Malawi, foreign direct investment has been made in two garment factories, prospectively leading to employment for between 10 000 to 20 000 textile and apparel sector workers. Estimates for new investment for Mauritius total US$50 million and for South Africa over US$500 million. With respect to Zambia, reportedly a Zambian company has received a huge contract from a US importer (Office of the US Trade Representative, 2001:108–10).

In Tanzania, reportedly a textile mill has established a partnership with a US firm to expand its operations. It is anticipated that 1 000 new jobs will be created (Office of the US Trade Representative, 2001:109).

The prospect for a significant increase in apparel provision for eligible sub-Saharan African countries is not likely. This is due to the reality that the calculation of the costs that will be incurred not only in meeting the eligibility requirements, but also in proving that the requirements have been met, are great. Another consideration will certainly have to be the level of US encroachment on the sovereignty of prospective beneficiary countries that will be tolerated.

In addition to the textile and apparel provision, as indicated above, an additional 1 835 products were identified for duty-free entry into the US market by AGOA beneficiary countries. It has been speculated that for the most part the benefits will be limited due to the fact that the majority of items eligible for duty-free access to the US market are either not currently produced in Africa or are not really competitive in the US market. Other items that are competitive are deemed threatening to domestic producers and therefore are faced with tariff and non-tariff barriers. Such items include agricultural and mining commodities (Lobe, 2000).

It appears that the only country that experienced any increase in exports to the US as a result of AGOA worth mentioning is South Africa. Even then, the figures are not very impressive. According to South Africa's Whitehouse & Associates, during the first five months of 2001, South Africa exports to the US as a result of AGOA totalled US$100 million. Of this, 60 per cent consisted of vehicles and transport equipment, 27 per cent of qualifying metal products, five per cent of textile exports, and four per cent of wines (*Freight & Trading Weekly*, 2001d).

US imports from sub-Saharan Africa for 2000 reveal that major structural changes will have to occur in trade patterns if sub-Saharan African countries are going to experience dividends from their investments in AGOA economic reforms in order to have greater access to the US market. While US imports from sub-Saharan Africa increased by 67 per cent in 2000, this was largely due to an increase in oil prices. In fact, 69 per cent of all US imports are accounted for by crude oil. An additional 6.5 per cent came from platinum group metals, and 4.1 per cent from refined petroleum products. Most of the remainder came from woven or knit apparel; iron and steel products; diamonds; ferro and non-ferrous ores; and cocoa beans and products (Office of the US Trade Representative, 2001:16–17).

More than 87 per cent of all US imports from sub-Saharan Africa come from only four countries – Nigeria, South Africa, Angola, and Gabon (Office of the US Trade Representative, 2001:6). The situation with Angola is interesting in that it is not an AGOA beneficiary country. Similarly, 72 per cent of all US exports go to four sub-Saharan African countries – South Africa, Nigeria, Kenya, and Angola (Office of the US Trade Representative, 2001:6).

Given these statistics, it is not difficult to understand why no sub-Saharan African country has indicated an interest in establishing an FTA with the US. With respect to the future creation of US FTAs with sub-Saharan African countries, the African Development Bank notes that

> [i]f the FTA is fully reciprocal and thus permits duty-free entry of US imports into African countries, it will be trade diverting. If participating African countries already have substantial preferential market access for their exports to the US (through GSP and/or least developed country preferences), the additional market access gains will be limited. In addition, African countries are likely to suffer some fiscal revenue losses for which no full compensation will be provided (ADB, 2000:191).

In addition, FTAs with the US have the potential to further divide sub-Saharan African countries and undermine regionalism (*Public Agenda*, 22 October 2001).

It is important to note that the idea of the creation of a US-SA FTA was first presented following the announcement that negotiations had begun for the creation of an EU-SA FTA. US interest in an FTA with South Africa clearly grows out of concern that the EU will have greater access to the South African market.

While the WTO does not look very promising with respect to enhancing Africa's integration into the world economy through multilateralism, it also does not appear that

AGOA will be a viable option for enhancing Africa's integration through one of the triad blocs – North America. However, if integration into the world economy through triad blocs is to become a remote possibility, it will occur through the enhanced regionalisation of production in Africa via regional blocs, an issue discussed below within the context of AGOA.

Analysis of AGOA and the SADC Textiles and Garment Industries

In a November 2001 report by SADC, the organisation called for the removal of duties on textiles throughout the region (*Business Day*, 16 November 2001). This recommendation was perhaps spearheaded as a result of the findings of major studies commissioned by SADC on the textile and garment industries in the region. The main objective of the studies was to determine how best to prepare the SADC region to benefit from the AGOA apparel provision. South Africa Textile Federation President Walter Simeoni responded to the SADC proposal by warning that it 'would lead to the death of the SA textile industry' (*Business Day*, 16 November 2001).

This section of the chapter will examine whether it is possible for the SADC member states who are signatories to the SADC FTA to move toward the regionalisation of production of the textile and garment industries in order to compete more efficiently within the world economy. The section is divided into discussion of the one country currently not eligible for the apparel provision, and the remaining countries that are eligible.

Country not Eligible for the AGOA Apparel Provision

Zimbabwe is the only country that is a signatory to the SADC FTA that is not eligible for the AGOA apparel provision. It is unfortunate that Zimbabwe is not eligible because the country could contribute greatly to the regionalisation of textile and garment production. However, unless there is a serious reversal in the current political and economic instability in the country, Zimbabwe will miss this opportunity to enhance the ability of the region to become more competitive, both regionally and internationally.

As a major producer of cotton, Zimbabwe's textile and garment industries have posed such a threat to South Africa that it has imposed serious protectionist policies against the country. First of all, as discussed in Chapter 3, under the South Africa/Zimbabwe bilateral trade agreement, a 13 per cent tariff is charged on garments imported into SACU covered by quota allocations. For exported items not covered by the quota, a 26 per cent tariff is imposed. In addition, a 22–33 per cent duty is imposed by SACU on most fabrics imported into the region, even if such fabrics are not produced in any SADC country. Then, for any garments made from these imported fabrics, SACU imposes duties of 40–60 per cent. Many Zimbabwean exporters have consequently redirected their exports to other markets (Coughlin *et al.*, 2001:17).

An addition to the above problem is the double-transformation rule imposed on Zimbabwe and Mauritius since they are not lesser developed non-SACU SADC countries. As noted in Chapter 4, this means that in order for Zimbabwean textiles and garments to have preferential access to the SACU market, they must go through two transformation processes. In essence, Zimbabwean manufacturers do not have preferential access to the SACU market for garments that have been made from fabrics not produced in the region. This therefore poses major constraints on the ability of Zimbabwe garment manufactures to expand their markets and enhance capacity (Coughlin *et al.*, 2001:28).

South Africa's insistence that its fabrics be used poses serious problems for many SADC member states in that it increases the cost of production, limits the variety of fabrics that can be used, and often reduces the quality of the final product (Coughlin *et al.*, 2001:28). Nonetheless, Zimbabwe and SACU do provide inputs for each other's industries. Zimbabwe exports cotton to South Africa and imports human-made fibre. The trade in raw and intermediate products is the largest within the SADC region, consisting of over five times the amount of finished garments. Such trade must be encouraged, according to the SADC commissioned study, if the textile and clothing industries in the region are to be successful (Coughlin *et al.*, 2001:27).

Although Zimbabwe is known for having the most efficiently produced and processed cotton in sub-Saharan Africa, questions have recently been raised about the ability of cotton producers to continue to be internationally competitive in light of the current crisis befalling the country. For example, according to a SADC commissioned report on the textile and garment industries, it has been suggested that Zimbabwe currently has cotton prices that are artificially high (due to Zimbabwe's distorted exchange rate); product defects, delays, and production inefficiencies, partially due to irregular electricity supplies; fuel shortages that cause production inefficiencies and delays; customs problems, including the clearing of imports and shipment delays; and fabrics that are poorly finished, largely as a result of lack of credit and foreign exchange to repair and upgrade equipment (Coughlin *et al.*, 2001:25–6).

Although Zimbabwe is not AGOA eligible, AGOA eligible countries are able to import Zimbabwe's excellent cotton to be converted into yarn, fabrics, and garments. The garments produced from Zimbabwe cotton can be exported to the US duty-free by AGOA apparel provision eligible countries. It would be more cost-effective, however, for the cotton to be processed in Zimbabwe into yarn and fabrics, since Zimbabwe has the capacity in yarn and fabric production. It is also cheaper to import yarn and fabric, since cotton lint weighs approximately 20 per cent more than fabric (Coughlin *et al.*, 2001:28). This further reinforces how imperative it is for Zimbabwe to become AGOA apparel provision eligible. South Africa, Mauritius, Botswana, and Namibia are required to source their yarn and fabric from AGOA eligible countries (although this should change for the latter two countries under AGOA II). Therefore, the demand for Zimbabwe yarn and fabric will be great if the country becomes AGOA eligible.

As a major producer of high-quality garments, Zimbabwe and the SADC region would benefit tremendously from Zimbabwe becoming AGOA apparel provision eligible. As the study commissioned by SADC notes, 'Zimbabwe's garment producers would find ready markets in America, without quotas and with a 16 per cent tariff advantage over producers in the Far East' (Coughlin *et al.*, 2001:30).

Countries Eligible for the AGOA Apparel Provision

As mentioned previously, ten of the SADC member countries that are signatories to the SADC FTA have been approved for the AGOA apparel provision. All of the countries, with the exception of Lesotho,[5] will be discussed in this section.

Namibia

Although Namibia has received apparel provision approval, the country has no textile factories, has few clothing manufacturers (which do not have access to modern production techniques), and the export of garments is negligible. In addition, among other things, Namibia lacks appropriate training facilities and trained staff, has high labour costs, lacks an industrial culture, and does not have access to international markets (Jeetah, 2001:1, 16).

Mozambique

In Mozambique, the textile industry has virtually collapsed (Coughlin, 2001:2), and capacity utilisation in the garment industry is low (Coughlin, 2001:14). Not surprisingly, there are serious constraints to making the industry internationally competitive. They include lack of financial resources to invest in renovating factories; lack of knowledge regarding international marketing and buying; corruption, slowness, and unreliability in the customs administration; expensive electricity; difficulties in obtaining work permits for ex-patriate workers; lack of formal training for workers in the textile and garment industries; and lack of a world-class quality control system (Coughlin, 2001:30).

In order for Mozambique to take advantage of potential regional linkages in the textile and garment industries, it would require new investments in these two sectors. However, to date the country has not been successful in attracting such investment (Coughlin, 2001:34).

Tanzania

Although some of the best quality of cotton in the world is produced in Tanzania (Coughlin & Mworia, 2001:27), the country is not well integrated into the SADC regional textile and garment industries. It buys only a small quantity of items from its SADC partners and sells even less to them. Most of Tanzania's exports are sent to Europe and North America. Although Tanzanian manufacturers have few contacts in South Africa and limited knowledge of its market, the SADC commissioned study recommends that this should be changed. Since there is a potential market in South Africa for Tanzanian textiles and garments, this potential should be explored, especially as factories are rehabilitated in Tanzania (Coughlin & Mworia, 2001:33).

Malawi

As indicated in Chapter 3, Malawi's textile and garment industries have largely collapsed as a result of South African protectionist policies. Nonetheless, Malawi produces cotton and could become an important source for yarn and fabric for countries such as South Africa and Mauritius that must source these products from AGOA-eligible African countries (Coughlin & Undenge, 2001:24). In order for this to happen, however, Malawi will need to attract significant international investments.

There are major constraints to Malawi becoming internationally competitive. They include severe underdevelopment of the textile industry; product defects, delays, and inefficiencies in production; improper finishing of fabrics; dependence on ex-patriates and the lack of proper training facilities; financial constraints, including pre-shipping financing; a highly overvalued kwacha; and customs problems, including delays in clearing imports and shipment. In addition, cotton production has been decreasing as a result of low prices paid to cotton growers (Coughlin & Undenge, 2001:22).

The prospects do not look promising for a revitalisation of Malawi's garment and textile industries. It therefore will not likely be a serious player in the regionalisation of the production of textiles and garments unless drastic changes are made immediately.

Botswana

In the introduction to the SADC commissioned study on the textile and garment industries in Botswana, the author notes three major challenges facing Botswana with respect to the country being able to take advantage of the market opportunities arising from AGOA. The first is the necessity to provide additional training in all areas of the industries and the second is Zimbabwe's failure to become AGOA-eligible. As already mentioned, Zimbabwe's status prevents Botswana garment manufacturers from using Zimbabwe's cotton yarn and fabric, although it is the most cost-effective supplier of these items in the region (Rubin, 2001a:1). With the approval of AGOA II, however, this problem should be solved.

The third challenge facing Botswana rests with the high tariff barriers South Africa imposes on imported Zimbabwean yarn and fabric under the SADC FTA. This means that Botswana garment manufacturers are not able to source fabric from the most cost-effective producer in the region for export to South Africa, which is Botswana's other major market (Rubin, 2001a:1).

Other constraints to making Botswana textile and garment industries internationally competitive include the need to attract long-term investors; the need to develop the Trans-Kalahari highway/Walvis Bay route as an alternative to exporting via Durban, which is more expensive; Zambia's low capacity utilisation in the textile industry, because it is costly for Botswana to import yarn and fabric from this AGOA-eligible country that is in close proximity; unreliable electricity supplies; and unreliable water supplies (Rubin, 2001a:20).

In terms of enhancing Botswana's capacity to make a great contribution to the regionalisation of production in the textile and garment industries, three recommendations from the SADC commissioned study stand out. The first is that it will be important to develop the country as a major corridor for the shipment of garments from Malawi, northern South Africa, Zambia, and Zimbabwe through Walvis Bay in Namibia to the US (Rubin, 2001a:20, 23–4). The second recommendation is that Botswana should concentrate on producing garments and knitted items (Rubin, 2001a:23). The third is that SACU policies regarding duties and quotas imposed on raw materials from SADC countries should be reviewed (Rubin, 2001a:24). A case in point is the reality that yarn produced in Zimbabwe costs, on average, 43 per cent of yarn produced in South Africa, and fabric 58 per cent of that produced in South Africa (Rubin, 2001a:21).

Swaziland

Although Swaziland has the potential to become a significant exporter of textile and garment products, there are numerous constraints to these two sectors becoming internationally competitive. With respect to the textile industry, constraints include low productivity; a high level of absenteeism; and poor delivery performance. In terms of the garment industry, constraints include low productivity; SACU customs rules that result in delays in Swaziland receiving raw materials; poor finishing of garments; and high rates of absenteeism (Rubin, 2001b:21).

Swaziland's strength with respect to enhancing the regionalisation of production in textiles and garments rest with its world-class production of yarn and sewing thread. It also has the potential to develop a fabric formation industry in that the work force is literate and the country has plenty of water and electricity supplies. Therefore, Swaziland has the potential to increase production in yarn and fabrics for export to AGOA apparel provision eligible countries for making garments for the US market (Rubin, 2001b:21).

The author of the SADC study on Swaziland also raises concerns about the need for SACU to revise its tariff offer under the SADC FTA to the non-MMTZ countries. Such tariffs, especially against Zimbabwe, restrict the ability of clothing manufacturers from importing yarn and fabric from Zimbabwe to be used in the production of garments to sell in South Africa. If the tariffs were lowered, the study concludes, the Swazi clothing industry could expand the exports of its clothing market to include South Africa. This could result in economies of scale and cost reductions. Currently, most Swazi garment manufacturers export out of the SADC region (Rubin, 2001b:22–3).

Zambia

Zambia's textile and garment industries have potential for contributing to the regionalisation of production. In fact, as a major producer of cotton, Zambia 'is critical for the success of the regional textile and clothing industry' (Rubin & Mudenda, 2001:1). However, such success is dependent on a large amount of investment in both industries in order to revitalise them. Unfortunately, the current investment climate in Zambia is not conducive to attracting large amounts of needed investment (Rubin & Mudenda, 2001:1). While the clothing sector is not likely to become competitive regionally or internationally (Rubin & Mudenda, 2001:4), textile production does have such potential (Rubin & Mudenda, 2001:24). There are numerous constraints, however, to the sector becoming internationally competitive. They include cotton prices that are artificially high; production inefficiencies and delays as a result of irregular electricity supplies; lack of financial resources for upgrading production equipment and investment; prohibitive transport costs; and long distances to markets (Rubin & Mudenda, 2001:29).

In terms of regional linkages, Zambia could become a major exporter of cotton yarns to Mauritius, Malawi, Mozambique, and SACU. With respect to the latter, this will be made possible under the MMTZ agreement arising from the SADC FTA discussed in Chapter 4. According to the agreement, for five years, the least developed non-SACU SADC countries will be allowed to export to SACU textiles and clothing that only undergo a one-stage transformation process. Prior to the MMTZ agreement, high duties were placed on exports to the South African market that consisted of imported human-made fibres, fabric that was made from yarn that had been imported, and garments that had been produced from such fabrics and yarns. Zambian manufacturers therefore found themselves constrained in their ability to produce for the South African market. No longer confined by the double-transformation rule, garment manufacturers in Zambian now have preferential access to the SACU market for garments made from fabric imported from outside the SADC region (Rubin & Mudenda, 2001:32).

Since Zambia's greatest advantage is in textile production and not finished garments, its contribution to regional production under AGOA will likely be as an indirect exporter to the US, since the primary US market is for finished garments. Thus, Zambia can play an important role in producing yarn and textiles for garment producing SADC member states (Rubin & Mudenda, 2001:32).

Mauritius

As a major exporter to the US market for a decade, AGOA will increase the country's access to the US market and allow Mauritius to play a more significant role in enhancing the SADC regionalisation of production in textiles and garments. Mauritius is said to have 'the most developed clothing industry in sub-Saharan Africa, and, together, the textiles and clothing industries are the country's largest single source of foreign-exchange earnings' (Jeetah & Coughlin, 2001:2).

The Mauritian textile and garment industries, like the other SADC member states, have constraints to their international competitiveness. They include both the increasing cost and scarcity of labour; lack of spinning mills for cotton fibres; the need to improve on meeting delivery schedules; the urgent need to source yarn and fabric from AGOA-eligible African countries; and the need to improve training for middle managers and technicians (Jeetah & Coughlin, 2001:22).

The main challenge for Mauritius within the region is to establish linkages with countries in order to source fibre, yarn, and fabric from AGOA-eligible African countries. Also, Mauritian textile mills need to be able to export fabric to SADC apparel provision eligible garment producing countries (Jeetah & Coughlin, 2001:23). With a view to taking advantage of the opportunities afforded by AGOA, Mauritian manufacturers have begun looking for factories to rehabilitate or prospective partners to work with (Jeetah & Coughlin, 2001:25).

The issue of SACU's tariff rates imposed on the non-MMTZ member states is brought to the forefront in the Mauritius study. The study notes that SACU has taken a protectionist stance against the country, with high tariffs being maintained against Mauritian textiles and garments. This is the case even when products, such as some synthetic yarns, are not even produced in South Africa. The study further argues that SACU's insistence on the double-transformation rule in order for Mauritian textiles and garments to enter the SACU market with preferential treatment prevents Mauritian exports that do not conform to the rule from entering the SACU market. This is reflected in the low levels of export from Mauritius to South Africa. In 2000, for example, some Mauritian manufacturers exporting to SACU paid tariffs as high as 80 per cent (Jeetah & Coughlin, 2001:25).

Again, among the recommendations of the Mauritius study is that SACU should revise the double-transformation rule and allow

> single transformation for synthetic fibres and man-made fibre under HS Chapters 61–62 whose inputs are not available in the region to qualify for preferences under SADC .... SACU's insistence on maintaining lopsided trade balances with other countries in the region is contrary to the spirit of regional integration and, in the final analysis, self-defeating since SACU's regional market can only grow if the countries therein flourish (Jeetah & Coughlin, 2001:27).

South Africa

As the discussion so far indicates, South Africa will play a major role in determining whether or not the SADC member states will be successful in regionalising the production of the textile and garment industries, thus enhancing the prospects of Southern Africa's further integration into the world economy.

In addition to maintaining protectionist policies against yarn, textiles, and garments from many of the SADC member states, South Africa also maintains protectionist policies against regional cotton producers. Although cotton producers in South Africa are only able to provide 40 per cent of local cotton fibre demand, the government requires that South African spinners must first buy the entire local cotton supply before additional supplies can be imported into the country.[6] The consequences for the local textile industry are serious for several reasons:

▶ an over-dependence on domestic cotton supplies, irrespective of the quality, is enforced;

▶ good cotton has to be used for purposes where inferior imported cotton would have sufficed;

▶ variability in local grades, classes, and general quality causes problems in blending and dyeing;

▶ inflexibility with respect to import orders is entrenched (cotton spinners are required to place their import orders so that cotton arrives in twelve equal monthly shipments); and

▶ stock keeping adds to cost (Jafta & Jeetah, 2001:37).

The constraints to making South Africa's textile and garments industries internationally competitive are significant. They include high labour costs; inland transportation costs that are too high; hindrances to the ability to attract foreign investment arising from high crime and the perception that there is a breakdown of law and order; the procedures for clearing imports are slow and complicated; duties on imported fibre, yarn, and fabric that are too high; inadequate training, especially in the garment industry; sub-standard on-time delivery performance; the requirement that locally produced cotton must be purchased; excess capacity; the fact that South African consumers have low disposable incomes; and ineffective protection against undervalued and smuggled clothing imports (Jafta & Jeetah, 2001:43). With respect to the latter, allegedly 50 per cent of textile imports are illegal (Jafta & Jeetah, 2001:7).

With a view to developing a successful SADC textile and clothing industry, the SADC commissioned study makes the following recommendations:

▶ Fibre, yarn, fabric, and garments must be sourced from the lowest cost producers in the region that can meet the buyers' requirements for quality and delivery.

▶ Interregional customs procedures must be made uniform to minimise delays in cross-border shipments.

▶ Interregional freight rates have to be studied to determine if shipping costs will compromise production-cost advantages.

▶ South Africa needs to stop its protectionist attitude towards its textile and clothing industries and adopt customs policies that permit freer movement of products.

▶ South African retailers and merchandisers, who are the most sophisticated in the region, need to take the lead in developing Quick Response alliances among suppliers in the region.

▶ Training of garment and textiles workers throughout the region has to be enhanced. South Africa will play a key role in this as it has the most advanced training resources in the region.

▶ Investment is required to revitalise potentially competitive industries throughout the region. South African investors are among the most important potential sources of this capital. The Industrial Development Corporation's role in leveraging investments for greenfields ventures and rehabilitation of existing plants will be essential in this regard (Jafta & Jeetah, 2001:46).

If used to its advantage, the AGOA apparel provision could result in the regionalisation of production in textiles and garments in the SADC region. The key to the success of such a strategy rests with South Africa taking the leadership role that transcends its previous protectionist policies against its fellow SADC member states. Such a strategy must be strategically crafted and include all the SADC member states who are signatories to the SADC FTA.

In the final analysis, the removal of barriers to trade in textiles in the region may be the only way for the region to take advantage of AGOA. Since numerous studies recommend the reversal of the SACU tariff regime against the non-MMTZ countries, it might behove South Africa to seriously consider this option. Attempts to undermine the full development potential of the SADC textile and garment industries in order to protect South Africa's industries will only create more hostility toward the country, increase regional unemployment, and further strengthen informal regional trade networks that work against formal regionalism.

It is only through the enhanced regionalisation of production in Southern Africa that the region can be further integrated into the world economy. One of the stated objectives of AGOA is to increase regional integration in Africa. Notwithstanding the fact that the US government has its own national interests in mind with the implementation of AGOA, the apparel provision of the Act does provide the SADC member states with a great incentive to consolidate their resources and enhance efficiency. The imperative to move swiftly cannot be overemphasised, given the reality that in 2005, GATT will terminate all quantitative restrictions that are imposed on highly efficient textile and garment producers in Asia (Jeetah & Coughlin, 2001:1). At this point, SADC, as well as the entire African continent, will be forced to compete with these producers on a level playing field. Without enhanced African efficiency, the continent will not be able to compete and therefore will become even further marginalised within the world economy.

Notes

1   Geneva I (1947); Annecy (1949); Torguay (1951); Geneva II (1956); Dillon (1960–61); Kennedy (1964–67); Tokyo (1973–79); and Uruguay (1986–93).

2   These countries include Benin, Botswana, Cameroon, Cape Verde, Central African Republic, Chad, Republic of Congo, Djibouti, Eritrea, Ethiopia, Gabon, Ghana, Guinea, Guinea-Bissau, Kenya, Lesotho, Madagascar, Malawi, Mali, Mauritania, Mauritius, Mozambique, Namibia, Niger, Nigeria, Rwanda, São Tomé and Príncipe, Senegal, Seychelles, Sierra Leone, South Africa, Swaziland, Tanzania, Uganda, and Zambia.

3   These countries include Angola, Burkina-Faso, Burundi, Côte d'Ivoire, the DRC, Equatorial Guinea, The Gambia, Liberia, Togo, and Zimbabwe. The remaining three countries – Comoros, Somalia, and Sudan – are apparently not interested in AGOA.

4   This information is regularly updated on the web site http://www.agoa.gov.

5   It was not possible to get a copy of the Lesotho report commissioned by SADC on the SADC textile and garment industries.

6   Most additional cotton is imported from Zimbabwe, Swaziland, Mozambique, and Zamibia.

The European Union and
Southern Africa

THE END OF the Cold War, the successful completion of the UR of GATT, and the political and economic changes taking place throughout Europe have had a significant impact on economic relations between the countries of Southern Africa and the EU. Specifically, there has been a decline in EU financial and technical support to Southern Africa, increased conditionality placed on the disbursement of economic assistance, and the implementation of EU trade policies that have been counterproductive to regionalism in Southern Africa. As a consequence, the countries of Southern Africa are forced to assess the impact the changing EU-Southern African relationship is having on the region. Of particular concern is whether the changes will leave the region further marginalised within the world economy. This is of special concern since the EU and South Africa now have in place an FTA, and it is projected that in the future, the EU will have an FTA with SADC.

The economies of the SADC member states are more integrated into the Western European bloc than into the North America or Asia blocs. Such integration, which dates back to colonial rule, has been characterised by asymmetry in that African countries have been major exporters of low value primary products and importers of capital-intensive high value products. This asymmetrical relationship leaves them marginalised within the world economy. The major argument in this chapter is that unless this structural economic relationship is altered, the SADC member states will not be able to increase the regionalisation of production, resulting in an alteration of their status within the world economy. This will pose a further challenge to regionalism in Southern Africa.

The purpose of this chapter is to assess the implications of EU-Southern African relations for regional development and integration. Data is provided on all the SADC member states except the DRC and Seychelles. The first section of the chapter places the EU's relationship with its African, Caribbean, and Pacific partners in historical perspective. In the second, EU-Southern Africa trade relations will be analysed, and in the third section, EU financial and technical assistance to the region will be examined. The fourth section will look at EU-South African relations, and the fifth section will provide an assessment of future EU-Southern African relations.

EU-ACP Relations in Historical Perspective

Although economic relations between Africa and Europe date back to the Middle Ages (Ojo, 1996:2), formal economic relationships were established in 1958, after France convinced its five European partners to agree to its African colonies being granted preferential status under the Treaty of Rome.[1] The arrangement covered trade, aid, and investments. Following the independence of the French colonies in the 1960s, the association status between the six members of the EEC and the 18 (later 19) members of the African Associated and Malagasy States (AAMS) was renegotiated (Martin, 1993:548). Between 1963 and 1974, economic relations were governed by the Yaoundé Convention (Yaoundé I, 1963–69 and Yaoundé II, 1969–74). From the late 1950s until 1974, most EEC aid went to the former French colonies of sub-Saharan Africa (European Commission (EC), 1997b:5).[2]

When Britain joined the European Community[3] in 1973, it insisted that European Community relations with the AAMS include its ACP Commonwealth partners (Martin, 1993:548–9). The new agreement, the Lomé Convention, was signed in February 1975 between the nine European Community members and 46 ACP states. Lomé I (1975–80) was followed by Lomé II (1980–85), Lomé III (1985–90), and Lomé IV (1990–2000). Lomé IV was a partnership agreement between the 15 EU[4] members and 70 ACP countries.[5] It provided the primary avenue for EU-ACP development cooperation from 1975 until February 2000, when the convention expired.

After 18 months of negotiations, a new agreement was reached between the EU and the ACP countries – the Cotonou Agreement, which replaces the Lomé Convention. The Cotonou Agreement was signed in Cotonou, Benin on 23 June 2000. It will remain in force for 20 years. The specifics of the agreement are outlined in the section on future EU-Southern African relations. For the other sections of this chapter, EU-Southern African relations will be analysed within the context of the Lomé Convention.

At the heart of EU-ACP relations is the notion of partnership. Until recently, this partnership relationship was lauded as a model for North-South cooperation.[6] According to Gordon Crawford, this was mainly because of three special features: the notion of mutual respect, equality, and interdependence; contracts negotiated between two sets of countries that were legally binding; and continuous dialogue between several joint institutions (Crawford, 1996:503). Through the Lomé Convention, EU-ACP cooperation was facilitated in economic development, regional and social cooperation, the protection of the environment, and cultural affairs (Davenport *et al.*, 1995:1). Two programmes, trade, and EU technical and financial assistance, were the major conduits for such cooperation.

At least four EU-ACP trade cooperation objectives under the Lomé Convention can be identified: (1) the development of EU-ACP trade relations; (2) decreased ACP dependence on the export of primary products through the promotion and diversification of ACP exports to the EU; (3) the promotion of regional intra-ACP cooperation; and (4) the development of agricultural sectors and support for industrialisation in ACP states (Davenport *et al.*, 1995:1).

The Lomé Convention dictated that exports to the EU by the ACP countries should enjoy the highest level of EU preferential treatment. This included preferential access to the EU market under protocols for beef and veal, sugar, bananas, and rum. Even though this was the case, to date, the ACP countries have neither increased nor maintained their market share in the EU (EC, 1997b:10). In fact, between 1990 and 1995, total EU imports from ACP countries declined by 11 per cent (EC, 1997c:8), and while in 1975 EU imports from ACP countries accounted for 7.6 per cent of all EU imports, by 1997, this figure had declined to 3.4 per cent (Panos, 1998:9). During 1998, the figure declined further to three per cent, with 60 per cent of exports concentrated in ten products (EU, 2000b). One explanation for the decline is that non-Lomé developing countries (i.e. in Asia, Latin America, and Central and Eastern Europe) have benefitted from the extension of EU preferences under its GSP.[7] Such extensions have eroded ACP preferences. They have been further eroded by the special trading agreement between the EU and Mediterranean countries. Trade liberalisation has also contributed to the decline in ACP exports to the EU, largely due to the lowering of MFN tariffs (Davenport *et al.*, 1995:2, 37). Complex EU rules of origin, the exclusion of certain agricultural products that compete with EU products, and limited opportunities for investment as a result of declining commodity prices further eroded the export of ACP goods to the EU (INZET, 1999:2).

The EU market, however, has remained important for the ACP countries. Approximately 40 per cent of ACP export earnings come from trade with the EU. Africa is the most dependent on trade with the EU at 46 per cent, as compared with the Pacific at 23 per cent and the Caribbean at 18 per cent (EC, 1997b:10). Of particular significance are the EU special protocols for ACP sugar, bananas, beef and veal, and rum. According to the EC, approximately 94 per cent of ACP exports to the EU enter duty-free. Industrial and fish products enter 100 per cent duty-free, while agricultural products enter at the rate of 80 per cent (Panos, 1998:5).[8]

With a view to providing financial compensation for export earning losses as a result of fluctuations in the price or quantity of some 49 identified products, the EU introduced STABEX, a programme for the stabilisation of export earnings. A similar programme was put in place for mining losses, SYSMIN, or stabilisation of mineral exports. When ACP countries experienced a ten per cent decline in mining production and/or export capacity, SYSMIN support was provided (Martin, 1993:549). The SYSMIN programme, however, was criticised for its slow disbursement of aid (Parfitt, 1996:53–4).

Critics of STABEX argue that it was underfinanced (see Parfitt, 1996:53–4, 59; Asante, 1996:384; Martin, 1993:549), and according to S. K. B. Asante, because of STABEX, ACP countries were not given an incentive to diversify their export markets. In the final analysis, Asante argues, the arrangement perpetuated the traditional role of the ACP countries as major exporters of primary products. Consequently, STABEX seemingly served to 'stabilize poverty' in the ACP countries (Asante, 1996:384).

Further to the point regarding the fact that ACP states continue to be suppliers of primary products, Gottfried Wellmer argues that from its inception, Lomé was a neo-colonial contract, designed to ensure that the EU continued to have access to the raw materials it needed for its industries (Wellmer, 1998:1). He further notes that through ongoing Lomé contracts, the previous colonial role of the developing countries as suppliers of raw materials for the global economy was preserved. In turn, these countries continued to be dependent on receiving capital goods (Wellmer, 1998:1; see also Panos, 1998:4). Critics of this position, however, maintain that Lomé was a generally positive, albeit flawed, example of North-South cooperation (Piening, 1997:176).

The second major component of the Lomé Convention was the EU development aid programme involving 'financial and technical cooperation'. Under this programme, grants were provided by the European Development Fund (EDF) and loans by the European Investment Bank (EIB). These resources were used for development programmes, both national and regional. The EDF was established in 1958. Between 1958 and 2000, there were eight successive funds. Until 1990, each EDF was backed up by a five-year convention. Lomé I was backed up by the fourth EDF, Lomé II by the fifth, and Lomé III by the sixth. Lomé IV, which ran a total of ten years, was backed up by EDF seven and eight (EU & EC, 1994:4). Allocation under EDF seven was known as the first financial protocol and under EDF eight, the second financial protocol. EU allocation under the second financial protocol, €13.3 billion (see Appendix 4, Currency Conversion Table), was the same as the allocation under the first protocol, adjusted for inflation. While the first protocol was divided among 12 EU members, the second was divided among 15 EU members. There were therefore no financial benefits gained from the inclusion of three new EU members under the second financial protocol. In fact, some countries decreased their contribution (Crawford, 1996:514).[9]

Approximately 70 per cent of money made available to ACP countries, called programmable funds, was used for National Indicative Programmes (NIPs). Funds were earmarked in advance for NIP projects. Twelve per cent of EDF funds under the seventh EDF were allocated for structural adjustment, through the new Structural Adjustment Facility (SAF). This facility, designed for ACP countries implementing IMF/World Bank structural adjustment programmes, consisted of Sectoral Import Programmes and General Import Programmes. Funding was in the form of grants, which were made available through a country's central bank. Such funds became 'counterpart' funds, which were used by governments for various programmes and projects, including social services (i.e. health, education), infrastructure maintenance, job creation, and financial restructuring of the parastatal sector and agricultural marketing boards. Structurally adjusting countries were also able to use a percentage of the NIP funds for structural adjustment (EC, 1996:23, 215; EU & EC, 1994:9).

Critics of the EU-ACP relationship under the Lomé Convention argue that it discontinued being a 'model' for North-South cooperation, noting that it became like any other development programme. The relatively new issue of 'conditionality' was at the core of this changed perspective on EU-ACP relations.

With Lomé I and II, limited conditions were placed on EU funds allocated to the ACP countries. Commencing with Lomé III, however, the European Commission introduced the idea of 'policy dialogue' with a view to gaining greater control and ensuring that the NIPs contained its priority sectors (Crawford, 1996:505).[10] This movement toward conditionality allegedly resulted from concerns about the misuse of EU aid. In addition, the EC had begun to feel that the failure of the ACP countries to develop and increase their exports to the EU resulted from ACP governments distorting their own markets through interventionist policies (Parfitt, 1996:55).

Under Lomé IV, the EU Council of Ministers passed a resolution making Lomé aid conditional on 'sensible economic and local policies, democratic decision-making, adequate governmental transparency and financial accountability, the creation of a market friendly environment for redevelopment, measures to combat corruption, as well as respect for the rule of law, human rights, and the freedom of the press and expression' (Parfitt, 1996:56–7). As a result of this new policy, beginning in 1992, aid was suspended to a number of ACP states (Parfitt, 1996:57). In addition, access to macroeconomic financial assistance, primarily for imports, was contingent on implementing IMF/World Bank SAPs (Crawford, 1996:505). STABEX funding was also increasingly subjected to structural adjustment conditionality (Parfitt, 1996:57). This meant that by introducing conditionalities to STABEX, it discontinued being a quick disburser of aid. This was significant, because Lomé aid in general was criticised for its slow disbursement. During Lomé IV, each STABEX recipient had to negotiate a separate contract known as the 'framework of mutual obligation' (MFO). Although designed to reduce the abuse of the system, as a result of its time-consuming procedures, in 1992, only ten MFOs were agreed, and eight in 1993. In both years there were an estimated 60 claims (Parfitt, 1996:59). In terms of macroeconomic financial assistance being made available primarily for imports from countries implementing IMF/World Bank SAPs, Trevor Parfitt criticises the programme for moving the EDF away from being an instrument for long-term development, toward becoming a facility for short-term development (Parfitt, 1996:57–8).

In defence of the severe criticism levelled at the EU and its structural adjustment initiative, Nicola Delcroix, former Economic Advisor, Delegation of the EC in Harare, Zimbabwe, feels that too much emphasis has been placed on this issue. Structural adjustment, according to Delcroix, is only a very small component of the EU-ACP programme. Since the SAF is a different allocation, it does not interfere with the larger NIP allocation unless governments specifically request that part of the NIP allocation be used for structural adjustment. He does admit, however, that the SAF allocation is subject to IMF/World Bank conditionality and, therefore, to a very limited extent, the EU is working in conjunction with the Bretton Woods institutions.[11]

With respect to import programmes being used as a mechanism to quickly disburse funding, resulting in the perception that the EU is no longer committed to long-term development, Delcroix argues that there exists a misconception about adjustment. Adjustment does not happen overnight, but at the minimum over the mid-term. While admittedly the import programmes result in fast disbursement in terms of the account mechanism, the EC still has to work with the governments to see what they have done with the money, which takes a great deal of time.[12]

Following the 1995 mid-term review of Lomé IV, a new performance criterion was introduced for programmable funds. The implementation of the new criterion grew out of concern about the effectiveness of domestic reforms arising out of the EU external aid within the ACP countries. Under the new criterion, programmable funds were to be allocated in two phases. In the first phase, 70 per cent of resources were to be allocated to member countries for the first three years of the eighth EDF. The remaining 30 per cent of the resources were only to be allocated following a review of the first phase. Four criteria were designated to determine if the second tranche would be released: (1) credibility of the country's sectoral policy; (2) performance of projects financed; (3) broader assessment of the country's development policy, and its political, social and moral credibility; and (4) degree of preparedness for the second stage of the programme (EC, 1997b:xiv; 1996:35). The purpose of the evaluation, according to the EU, was to prevent allocated resources from being blocked and to encourage countries to use their allocations more efficiently (EC, 1996:35). In addition, during the mid-term review, the European Council reaffirmed its continued commitment to support structural adjustment in the ACP countries, including regional reform programmes, especially with respect to providing customs duties harmonisation (EC, 1996:35, 37).

While the ACP countries were not pleased with the introduction of phased programming, Joao de Deus Pinheiro, former European Commissioner responsible for relations with the ACP countries and South Africa, justified the new polices within the context of 'efficiency and effectiveness', while another EC official allegedly stated 'that the objective was to encourage "good pupils" and give "bad pupils" the incentive to do better' (Crawford, 1996:510). No doubt the EU-ACP 'partnership' had changed drastically! EU policy toward the ACP countries has begun to mirror that of the IMF and World Bank. This was a drastic change from early EU and ACP relations that were based on principles of equality, mutual respect, and interdependence.

Trade Between the EU and Southern Africa

All the members of SADC were signatories to the Lomé Convention. The DRC and Mauritius were signatories to Yaoundé II and thus became members of Lomé I, along with Botswana, Lesotho, Malawi, Seychelles, Swaziland, Tanzania, and Zambia. Zimbabwe joined the group under Lomé II, Angola and Mozambique under Lomé III, and Namibia became a member under Lomé IV. South Africa became a member of the group in April 1997, with limited accession.

The SADC member states enjoy preferential access to the EU market. For the most part, these countries (excluding South Africa) export raw materials and import manufactured goods, food, and, with the exception of Angola, oil. Zimbabwe and Mauritius also export finished products. Western Europe is the main trading partner for the SADC countries, including South Africa (EU & EC, 1994:8).

Although EU-Southern African trade relations are significant, in 1995, the regional countries (excluding South Africa) experienced a decline of 34 per cent in their exports to the EU. The region as a whole exported goods totalling 11 billion ECU to the EU and imported goods worth 10.7 billion ECU. However, 7.6 billion ECU of the exports were from South Africa and 8 billion ECU worth of goods imported from the EU went to South Africa. In 1995, the region had a small trade surplus with the EU (EC, 1997c:8). In 1998, total regional exports to the EU (excluding South Africa) were €3.8 billion while imports were €2.8 billion (see Table 7.1, below). In 1999, there was a small increase in both exports to the EU and imports from the EU. During both 1998 and 1999, these countries maintained a small trade surplus with the EU.

Table 7.1: SADC Exports to and Imports from the EU 15 (excluding South Africa), 1998–99 ('000 000 euros)

	1998		1999	
	Exports	**Imports**	**Exports**	**Imports**
Angola	587.6	985.4	768.1	834.0
Botswana	145.9	90.4	308.0	91.3
Lesotho	19.9	10.1	15.0	6.6
Malawi	173.3	57.7	209.9	81.2
Mauritius	1 106.9	545.6	1 153.5	735.3
Mozambique	112.3	156.0	110.3	267.2
Namibia	384.7	153.4	505.7	151.8
Swaziland	148.7	24.8	128.8	18.8
Tanzania	255.9	315.4	230.1	308.3
Zambia	225.4	115.0	203.2	95.2
Zimbabwe	700.2	372.5	744.8	345.1
Total	**3 860.8**	**2 826.3**	**4 377.40**	**2 934.8**

Source: Eurostat

While estimates vary with respect to projected economic losses to the SADC region as a result of EU economic reforms resulting from the UR, no doubt the region will be affected adversely. According to Michael Davenport *et al.*,

> [t]he main effects of the Uruguay Round Agreement on ACP export earnings will result from: (i) changes in world prices for ACP exports and imports of temperate agricultural products, arising out of the Agreement on Agriculture, (ii) the loss of tariff preferences in the EU and other markets for tropical products, fish and industrial exports and (iii) increased competition following the phasing out of the Multifibre Arrangement (Davenport *et al.*, 1995:38).

Under the new trade regime, there will be a reduction in the protection of agricultural markets. All WTO members have to replace NTBs with tariffs, and are required, by the end of the implementation period (2000 for developed and 2004 for developing countries), to reduce their MFN tariffs (Lindland, 1997:1). These tariff reductions will likely result in the SADC countries losing their preferential market access to important developed countries. Both the agriculture and manufacturing sectors will be affected.

Agriculture

Under the Lomé Convention, nine SADC member states had preferential access to the EU market for the export of at least one of the following commodities: sugar, beef, fish, and horticultural products. Under EU trade reforms, such access will eventually change, which means that the regional countries will likely have to compete on an equal basis with other developing markets, including the fast-growing markets of Southeast Asia. John Robertson, a noted economic commentator in Zimbabwe, feels that the removal of agricultural subsidies to European farmers, and the removal of quotas on ACP countries, will be beneficial to the region. By removing such subsidies, developing countries will be able to capture some of the market left vacant by farmers in the developed world who cannot farm competitively without subsidies. The present situation of massive subsidies is a cause of dismay for those in the developing countries who are told they must eliminate all subsidies while the US and Europe continue to subsidise their farmers: '[t]hey [the US and Europe] are corrupt beyond measure ... they've dressed up a lot of these subsidies in ways that don't make them look quite like subsidies'.[13]

Unfortunately, it may take more than the 'levelling of the playing field' for the SADC member countries not to be adversely affected by the new trade regime. This is the case because of the anticipated competition from perhaps more efficient and cheaper goods from other developing countries, and the implementation of stricter sanitary requirements (Bruno, 1997).

EU-Southern Africa trade relations in the area of agriculture, as mentioned above, can be divided into four sub-sectors – sugar, beef, fish, and horticulture. Each sector will be discussed below.

Five regional countries benefit from the EU Sugar Protocol. They are Malawi, Mauritius, Swaziland, Tanzania, and Zimbabwe. With the Sugar Protocol, the EU buys a certain amount of raw sugar from these countries annually (and for an indefinite period) at a guaranteed price (see Table 7.2, opposite). Currently, the amount is fixed at 1.3 million tons, which is the quota that the EU entered at the WTO for the ACP countries (Overseas Development Institute and Zimconsult, 1999:9). The Sugar Protocol, although attached to the Lomé Convention, is actually separate and relates only to the 19 ACP countries that have a preferential EU sugar trade agreement. The Sugar Protocol has its origins in the

Commonwealth Sugar Agreement (CSA) of 1951. Under this agreement, the UK was obligated to provide the ACP countries with long-term access, totalling 1.74 million tons of raw sugar annually, to the UK market at guaranteed prices (McDonald, 1996:136). As a result of the negotiations for the UK joining the European Community, an agreement was reached that kept in place the guaranteed price and quota provisions of the CSA. The Sugar Protocol (Protocol No. 3) replaced the CSA in 1975 and for the most part the provisions under the CSA remained the same (McDonald, 1996:136–7). EU refiners in certain EU countries (UK, Portugal, France, and Finland) need raw sugar cane from the ACP countries in order to stay in business (EC, 1999a).

Under the Sugar Protocol, the ACP countries usually receive prices that are two or three times higher than the world market price. The difference between the world market price and the actual price received results in income transfers (also referred to as aid transfers) from the EU to the countries that are members of the Protocol (McDonald, 1996:139).

Table 7.2: Sugar Quotas for the SADC Member States (tons) 1996–97

	Protocol	Additional quantities	Utilisation in 1996–97	Value (ECUm)
Malawi	20 824	12 554	27 851	16
Mauritius	491 031	60 217	534 414	299
Swaziland	117 845	44 452	191 122	100
Tanzania	10 186	1 249	12 691	7
Zimbabwe	30 225	28 707	54 961	27

Source: EC (1999a:14)

Table 7.3, below, indicates the income transfers for Malawi, Mauritius, Swaziland, Tanzania, and Zimbabwe from 1975 to 1992. More than half the ACP sugar quotas are allocated to SADC countries, with Mauritius alone being allocated 37.3 per cent. In 1995, the EU introduced the Special Preferential Sugar Arrangement that allows for additional quotas of raw cane sugar to be imported into the EU from the ACP countries (see Table 7.2, above). The price paid for the sugar, however, is lower than that paid under the Sugar Protocol. This arrangement was scheduled to expire in 2001 (Overseas Development Institute and Zimconsult, 1999:9).

Table 7.3: Total Income Transfers to Southern African Countries, 1975–92

	Total transfers US$m (1987)	Avg. annual transfer per capita US$m (1987)	Transfer as % of GDP (average)	Transfers as share of merchandise exports (%)
Malawi	84.71	0.68	0.42	1.60
Mauritius	1 645.21	91.39	5.76	13.92
Swaziland	462.2	39.85	4.94	n.a.
Tanzania	38.02	0.10	0.06	0.57
Zimbabwe	147.17	1.50	0.24	1.11

Source: McDonald (1996:140)   Data for Zimbabwe is for post–1982

While it is not anticipated that EU reforms will change the guaranteed market for ACP sugar, these countries will, however, likely experience a decrease in income transfers as a result of the fact, according to Scott McDonald, 'that EU sugar prices will fluctuate with world prices, which will undermine a fundamental feature of the Sugar Protocol: consumer and produce price stability' (McDonald, 1996:144–5). Specifically, it is expected that prices will decrease by 20 per cent, while the Special Preferential Sugar Agreement might be discontinued (Overseas Development Institute and Zimconsult, 1999:13). One estimate of the loss of income transfers as a result of EU reforms is as follows: Malawi US$1.98m; Mauritius US$46.72m; Swaziland US$11.21m; Tanzania US$969 000; and Zimbabwe US$2.88m (McDonald, 1996:145).[14]

With the Beef and Veal Protocol, certain ACP countries export quantities of beef to the EU under a preferential rate. Most of the countries that benefit from the protocol are in the SADC region. They include Botswana, Namibia, Swaziland, Zimbabwe, and Namibia. The main reason the Beef and Veal Protocol was established was to compensate ACP states for the distortion that is created by the EU's Common Agricultural Policy (CAP).

CAP is embodied in the 1957 Treaty of Rome. The objectives of CAP, according to the European Parliament, are:

▶ To increase agricultural productivity by promoting technical progress and ensuring the rational development of production, and the optimum use of the factors of production, in particular labour;
▶ To ensure a fair standard of living for the agricultural Community;
▶ To stabilize markets;
▶ To assure the availability of supplies;
▶ To ensure that supplies reach consumers at reasonable prices (European Parliament, n.d.).

With a view to achieving the above objectives, the EU provides huge subsidies to its farmers. In 1998, for example, US$40 billion in such subsidies were allocated (*Financial Mail*, 23 April 1999). The consequence of this policy is that the EU fixes the prices of agricultural products at a much higher rate than the free market value. Tariffs are imposed on competitive products entering the EU market, since such products cannot be sold at lower prices than offered by the EU, making it difficult for countries in the developing world to compete. This policy is especially harmful to developing countries. CAP is a classic case of unfair competition. Although CAP has been severely criticised for its incompatibility with WTO rules, the WTO has allowed the policy to continue. Not only is CAP an obstacle to free and fair trade, but also it is designed, through subsidies, to uplift European farmers to the equivalent status of industrial workers (Bertelsmann, 1997:2). The reform of CAP is scheduled to take place by 2010 (Panos, 1998:21).

Under the Beef and Veal Protocol, participating countries are allowed to keep 92 per cent of the tax they normally pay to import certain quantities of beef into the EU. Without the protocol, beef and veal from the ACP countries would not be able to enter the EU market (Overseas Development Institute and Zimconsult, 1999:11). Table 7.4, opposite, indicates the SADC beef quotas for 1997 and the extent to which they were utilised.

It is obvious that underutilisation of quotas has been a problem in the region. In fact, because less than two-thirds of the quotas were used in 1992, the EU allocated a beef quota to Namibia (Davenport *et al.*, 1995:17).[15] While Zimbabwe was able to increase its quota from 9 100 tons to 19 742 tons in 1994 and 1995 because of the failure of other ACP countries to fill their quotas, it did not meet its quota in 1996 or 1997. One of the reasons was the declining demand for beef by European consumers (Laidler *et al.*, 1997:73).

Table 7.4: SADC Beef Quotas (tons), 1997

	Quota	Utilisation	% utilisation
Botswana	18 916	10 670	54.5
Namibia	13 000	6 026	46.4
Zimbabwe	9 100	7 825	86.0
Swaziland	3 363	225	6.7

Source: EC (1999a:13)

With respect to the inability of countries to meet their quotas, Robertson explains that drought has posed a serious problem for the industry throughout the region. When there is a drought, stock feed is expensive and the beef industry responds by increasing its slaughter rate because the animals cannot be kept alive. After you have had to slaughter cattle several times, your cattle herd has to be rebuilt. In the case of Zimbabwe, a large percentage of cattle had to be slaughtered in 1992, and then there was another drought in 1995. The years in between, 1993 and 1994, according to Robertson, were not good years for the industry. During these years and 1995–96, other problems arose, including high interest rates, which again affected the cost of food and consequently the cost of keeping animals alive.[16] For 1996–97, an estimated US$26 million was needed by commercial and small-scale farmers for cattle breeding because their breeding herd had been depleted by 50 per cent to only 450 000 as a result of the droughts. This money was necessary in order to fill the EU beef quota (*Financial Gazette*, 27 March 1997). In Botswana, lung disease resulted in the mass slaughter of 250 000 cattle in 1996 (*Weekly Mail & Guardian*, 31 January 1997).

The prospective reduction in the guaranteed price of beef under the new trade regime could result in annual financial losses to the regional countries. Such losses for three of the four countries have been calculated as follows: Botswana, US$11.3 million; Zimbabwe US$6.2 million; and Swaziland US$1.2 million (Davenport *et al.*, 1995:89–90). In the document, *Agenda 2000*, published in 1997, the EC has proposed that the intervention price of beef be cut by 30 per cent, which would result in a decrease in ACP earnings under the Beef and Veal Protocol (EC, 1999a:2).

ACP states that export fish to the EU are exempted from paying duties on 'qualifying' fish. Since the European fish market is significantly protected by the Common Fisheries Policy, ACP countries have preferential access over other countries (Davenport *et al.*, 1995:18). In terms of Southern Africa, Angola and Mozambique have a fisheries agreement with the EU. Under the agreement, the EU makes payments for fishing rights and allocates resources for training activities as well as scientific and technical programmes (EU & EC, 1994:8). It is estimated that during the 1996–97 market year, the sector earned $US13 million (*Financial Gazette*, 29 May 1997). Both Angola and Mozambique are likely to be adversely affected by their preference erosion under the new trade regime.

Within the agricultural sector in Zimbabwe, horticulture is the fastest growing sub-sector. Horticultural products include cut flowers, citrus fruits, and vegetables. Between 1990 and 1998, horticultural exports increased from US$16 million to US$63 million, representing an annual growth rate of 19.6 per cent. The growth in this sub-sector has been so phenomenal that, at the end of 1998, exports in this sector were earning more than maize and sugar (Ndlela, 2000:5). In addition, although exports in most sectors have declined as a result of the economic crisis, flower exports were expected to increase by 19 per cent in 2001 (Rushmere, 2001c). It is feared that under the new international trade regime, Zimbabwe's preferential access to the EU market will be reduced, resulting in fiercer competition and consequently trade diversion (Rushmere, 2001c:5).

Manufactures

Under the Lomé Convention, in order for manufactured products to be exempted from tariffs or levies, they had to have originated in an ACP country. Such products must have been 'wholly obtained, or sufficiently worked or processed, in an ACP state' (Davenport *et al.*, 1995:20). Until modifications were made under the Lomé mid-term review, the rules of origin stipulated that 50–60 per cent of the total value added of exported goods had to be produced within ACP countries. These restrictions were deemed too stringent to benefit most ACP countries, including fostering export diversification (Asante, 1996:383). During the mid-term review, however, the rules of origin were revised to 10–15 per cent value added in order to qualify for free access to the EU market (Parfitt, 1996:63).

In addition to the above, it is argued that EU firms who set up processing industries in ACP countries experience an advantage, since EU materials are like ACP inputs and are therefore considered to be originating products. The ACP countries are therefore placed in an unfavourable bargaining position (Asante, 1996:383).

Although Mauritius exports clocks and Swaziland and Zimbabwe export furniture, most manufactured exports to the EU are textiles and clothing. As part of Lomé, the ACP states were exempted from the Multifibre Arrangement (MFA), which meant that quantitative restrictions were not imposed on textiles and clothing entering the EU market. ACP textiles and clothing were able to enter the EU duty-free, provided that rules of origin were adhered to. Such rules stipulated that in most cases products had to begin with the yarn. Major Southern African exporters in this sector are Mauritius, Namibia, Tanzania, Zambia, and Zimbabwe (Davenport *et al.*, 1995:22–3).

ACP states, in being exempted from the MFA, have had a competitive advantage over other developing countries. However, this advantage will be eroded as a result of the fact that under the UR, it was agreed that over a ten-year period the MFA would be phased out. Not only will the ACP states lose their preferential advantage over other developing countries, but they will also find it very difficult to compete with exports from Asian countries. Significant financial losses can be anticipated for countries in Southern Africa.

Trade Between the EU and Southern Africa: Success or Failure?

As previously noted, two of the major objectives of EU-ACP trade cooperation have been to decrease ACP dependence on the export of primary products through the promotion and diversification of ACP exports to the EU, and enhance investment in new ACP export sectors. With respect to the latter, the resources for such investment, according to the EU, were to come from the financial benefits of having preferential access to the EU market (i.e. income transfers and levy rebates). In Southern Africa, only Zimbabwe and Mauritius have diversified their exports. In both cases, however, it is not believed that having preferential access to the EU market was the sole cause of diversification (Davenport *et al.*, 1995:25, 27, 36; Stevens, 1996:28–39).

At the root of the problem could be the fact that in reality the ACP countries have limited preferential access to the EU market. Specifically, according to the EC, only 36.6 per cent of ACP exports have preferential access to the EU market. The remainder, 63.4 per cent, enter the EU duty-free as a consequence of MFN or GSP, and thus do not have a preferential margin. Therefore, it appears that having preferential access to the EU market has not served as a great incentive to most countries to diversify their export sectors (Davenport *et al.*, 1995:25–6).

In terms of overall EU-Southern Africa trade, while the Southern African countries have certainly benefitted from the relationship, current EU policies, as will become evident below, have begun to result in a significant erosion of these benefits. Most importantly, however, is the reality that the long-standing trade relationship between the EU and the SADC member states has not resulted in the region being further integrated into the world economy.

EU Technical and Financial Assistance

EU technical and financial assistance to the 11 ACP countries in Southern Africa under Lomé IV (1990–2000), as previously noted, was divided into the first and second financial protocols, 1990–95 and 1996–2000. The second financial protocol commenced in 1996, following the mid-term review of Lomé IV that took place in Mauritius in 1995.

Lomé IV (1991–95)

EU financial and technical assistance to these countries in Southern Africa under the first half of Lomé IV was approximately 2.9 billion ECU (see Table 7.5, overleaf). EDF resources were available for national and sub-regional development projects, structural adjustment support, risk capital operations, food aid, emergency and refugee aid, and co-financing of NGO projects. In addition, compensation was available for the loss of earnings from exports under the STABEX programme, and assistance for mining operations facing difficulties was available under the SYSMIN programme (EC, 1996:211, 231; EU & EC, 1994:4, 9–10).

Resources for regional development in Southern Africa were allocated under the Regional Indicative Programme (RIP). Most of the money was provided for SADC and earmarked for three sectors: transport and communications; human resources development; and food security, agriculture, and natural resources. Under the first financial protocol of Lomé IV, an initial 121 million ECU was allocated under the RIP. This was later increased to a total amount of just under 129 million ECU. The Transport and Communications sector of SADC was allocated 60 million ECU, the Food Security, Agriculture and Natural Resources sector 18 million ECU, and the Human Resources Development sector 21 million ECU. The remaining allocation (22 million ECU) was for other areas (EU & EC, 1994:12; EC, n.d.a). The EU recently identified economic integration and intra-regional trade liberalisation as priority areas (EC, 1996:189; n.d.a).

Lomé IV (1996–2000)

EU allocation for the region under the second financial protocol of Lomé IV was approximately 1.5 billion ECU (see Table 7.6, page 205), a decrease of 1.4 billion ECU from the allocation under the first financial protocol. This represented a significant decline in EU commitment to financial and technical assistance.[17]

Table 7.5: EU Community Aid, Lomé IV, 1991–95 (allocation in millions of ECU)

	Angola	Botswana	Lesotho	Malawi	Mauritius	Mozambique
NIP	115	32	50	129.2	34	170.6
Other EDF and EIB	42.2	128.9	52.9	140	87.7	121.1
European budget	147.4	3.1	5.5	99.5	2.9	139.6
Total	**304.6**	**164**	**108.4**	**368.7**	**124.6**	**431.3**

EU Community Aid, Lomé IV, 1991–95 (allocation in millions of ECU)					
	Namibia	Swaziland	Tanzania	Zambia	Zimbabwe
NIP	50	28.1	185	110.7	91.5
Other EDF and EIB	102.2	17.5	226.1	202.3	240.4
European budget	16.8	4.3	22.1	44.7	30.7
Total	**169**	**49.9**	**433.2**	**357.7**	**362.6**

Source: EC (1999e)

The RIP under the second financial protocol was allocated 121 million ECU. The SADC Secretariat, for the first time, was given the authority, as the Regional Authorising Officer, to oversee the implementation of the programme. Financing for the EU/SADC regional programme was concentrated on (1) infrastructure and services; and (2) trade, investment, and finance. In addition, financial support was given to the food, agriculture, and natural resources and human resources development sectors, and for drug control, HIV/AIDS prevention, and SADC institutional capacity building (EC, n.d.b:1).

In the area of infrastructure and services, three projects dealing with the transport corridors were identified. According to the EU, they were:

▶ the Namib Corridor: sections of the road between Lubango and the Namibian border;
▶ sections of the Monze-Zimba road in Zambia which forms part of the arterial highway between Lusaka and the Zimbabwe border close to Botswana and the Caprivi strip in Namibia; and
▶ the Nacala Corridor – the rehabilitation of the railway between Cuamba and the Malawi border (EC, n.d.b:2).

Support in the area of trade, investment and finance, according to the EU, included the following studies:

▶ an EU/SADC Investment Programme which would include industrial and business forums in the SADC Region with the aim of bringing together potential investors from both Europe and Southern Africa;
▶ a guarantee fund in favour of private investment in the region, in collaboration with the *Caisse Française de Development*; and
▶ projects to improve the training of statisticians and the development of price statistics (EC, n.d.b:2).

These studies represent the EU's commitment to providing support for increased intra-regional trade and investment, the implementation of the SADC Protocol on Trade and intra-regional exchanges of information on monetary and macroeconomic issues (EC, n.d.b:2).

Other planned activities identified by the EU included:

▶ a livestock development project concentrating on combating the principal animal diseases prevalent in the region;
▶ a sustainable regional training programme for food security issues;
▶ an Intra-regional Skills Development Programme concentrating on maximising the use of regional tertiary-level educational institutions;
▶ assistance with the monitoring, control and surveillance of fishing activities in SADC coastal waters;
▶ a Regional Drug Control Programme to help combat illicit drug trafficking and reduce the effects of drug abuse; and
▶ support to the implementation of the SADC Plan of Action to combat the spread of HIV/AIDS (EC, n.d.b:3).

Table 7.6: EU Community Aid, Lomé IV, 1996–2000 (allocation in millions of ECU)

	Angola	Botswana	Lesotho	Malawi	Mauritius	Mozambique
NIP	167	38	61.5	174	39.5	214.5
Other EDF and EIB	–	–	–	8.1	–	–
European budget	78.1	0.7	0.5	27	–	78.9
Total	**245.1**	**38.7**	**62**	**209.1**	**39.5**	**293.4**

EU Community Aid, Lomé IV, 1996–2000 (allocation in millions of ECU)					
	Namibia	Swaziland	Tanzania	Zambia	Zimbabwe
NIP	52	29	240.5	138	110
Other EDF and EIB	–	–	–	–	12.1
European budget	3.4	0.9	7.0	7.7	5.8
Total	**55.4**	**29.9**	**247.5**	**145.7**	**127.9**

Source: EC (1999e)

EU Technical and Financial Assistance in Southern Africa: Toward Enhanced Self-Reliance or Greater Dependency?

During the signing ceremony for the revised Lomé IV Convention, the ACP Council President, Moi Avei, stated that 'Lomé resources provided to ACP countries amounted to just ECU 5.5 per capita over 5 years', which buys 'two pints of beer and a packet of chips in an average London pub'. He further noted that, 'while the Lomé Convention has been providing a lunchtime beer for every ACP person, declining commodity prices have been taking the food off their tables, and the debt service burden the shirts off their backs' (*The Courier*, 1996a:4).

Avei was not alone in expressing disappointment in the amount of funds allocated to the ACP countries. Among the criticisms of Carl Greenidge, acting Secretary-General of the ACP, was that sufficient funds had not been allocated for implementing human rights and democracy (*The Courier*, 1996b:22). The statements by both of these individuals display the degree to which some leaders in developing countries have still not moved beyond a 'dependency mentality'. Not only is there the expectation that the EU should assume responsibility for enhanced economic development, but also for enhanced political development.

If there has been one major failure of EU financial and technical assistance in Southern Africa, it has been the failure of African leaders to use such assistance to become more self-reliant. Unfortunately, instead of becoming more self-reliant, it appears that the impact of technical and financial assistance has had the opposite effect – increased dependency. The responsibility for this state of affairs lies with both the governments in the region and with the EU. The EU, however, has clearly indicated that financial and technical assistance is not given for altruistic purposes. Further to the point, the EU seemingly has a vested interest in maintaining the colonial framework of economic relations with Africa. As one European politician noted during the ACP-EU Joint Assembly held in September 1996 to begin discussion on future ACP-EU relations, 'the European public should know that EU development policy was not based on charity but on self-interest' (*The Courier*, 1996c:67). This statement was made after several EU countries refused to increase their financial assistance to the eighth EDF.

Obviously EU self-interest includes the contracting out of a large percentage of technical assistance work to EU consultants. Consequently, the commitment to building local capacity is more rhetoric than practice. The lack of commitment to building local capacity, along with other EU policies that do not enhance African development, are unconscionable. As the primary contributor to technical and financial assistance to Africa, the EU should be made accountable for ensuring that the stated goals and objectives of such assistance are achieved. Otherwise, the EU should reconsider its entire partnership arrangement with these countries.

Notwithstanding the reality that external factors have contributed significantly to Southern Africa's marginalisation within the world economy, African leaders have consistently squandered money that should have been allocated for economic and social development. As Robertson notes, 'aid frequently releases other money that can be stolen by corrupt officials' (Robertson, 1997:67). He further argues that some EU aid programmes have interfered with the capacity-building process in ACP countries (Robertson, 1997:66). Other consequences of aid include the fact that the ACP countries

> draw in imports from the donor countries, and often these imports undermine or ruin companies in the aid-receiving country that have invested in capacity to make the same products; tender procedures for aid-funded projects often favor foreign suppliers over domestic suppliers, and this tendency is often prompted by corrupt local officials who can extract bribes from foreign suppliers but not from locals; aid flows bolster foreign reserves and help keep domestic currencies too strong, encouraging the growth of imports and causing revenue from exports to decline; and foreign aid usually allows governments to become careless and to relax on internal disciplines ... and it adds to inflation by holding money supply too high. Aid granted is often on the condition that the funds are spent only in the country donating the money, and this leads to collusion and price-fixing by the main suppliers in the country concerned. Better prices would be obtained if the LDC was to go directly to international tender with their purchases (Robertson, 1997:67).

In the final analysis, according to Robertson, such aid flows could be more constructively utilised to enhance educational training. Investing in education would help close the knowledge gap between the EU and ACP countries, resulting in a decrease in the need for aid flows (Robertson, 1997:67). Likewise, at the second consultative conference between the SADC member states and the EU in October 1996, former SADC Executive Secretary Kaire Mbuende asked the EU to concentrate on directing foreign investment into productive regional activities in place of development assistance (Johnson, 1996).

Whatever the real benefits, EU financial and technical assistance has not contributed to greater regional self-reliance. As the EU continues to spread its resources to other priority areas, financial assistance to the SADC region is declining in real terms. With a 'dependency mentality', African leaders will find their countries even more marginalised within the world economy unless opportunities are seized upon to make EU financial and technical assistance a source for enhanced capacity-building that will result in enhanced self-reliance.

The EU's commitment to regional integration in Southern Africa is questionable, especially since it has not been inclined to enhance integration by placing greater emphasis on trade development and investment in the productive sectors (Asante, 1996:385). In fact, in the area of trade development, EU policy with respect to the dumping of beef is instructive. Specifically, in September 1993, all quantitative controls on beef imports were lifted in South Africa, resulting in an increase of oversubsidised EU beef imports into South Africa from 6 600 tons to 46 000 tons by 1995. At its peak, such beef was being sold for less than half the price charged by South African producers (Wellmer, 1998:6). This resulted in massive revenue losses by producers in South Africa, Namibia, Botswana, and Swaziland. In fact, the estimated loss to South African and Namibian producers was larger than the total EU aid package (*Weekly Mail & Guardian*, 27 March 1997). Namibia lost approximately 11 per cent of its beef export market and the EU is seen by many Zimbabwean farmers as an unfair competitor (Laidler *et al.*, 1997:73). The EU/SA FTA, which will be discussed in the next section, also raises questions about the EU's commitment to regional integration in Southern Africa.

In commenting on the EU dumping of beef, Rob Davies, a member of the South African parliament, noted that this issue highlights the reality that the EU does not always practise the trade principles it espouses. By selling a product at a price that is below the cost of local production, it is damaging to the recipient country's economy (*Weekly Mail & Guardian*, 27 March 1997).

As this example illustrates, EU policy is serving as a hindrance to regional integration in Southern Africa, and countries are experiencing an erosion of the benefits of trade preferences with the EU. Since technical and financial assistance has not resulted in significant development and some EU policies are proving to be a counter force to regional integration, the regional countries no doubt need to rethink what kind of future arrangement they want to have with the EU.

The EU and South Africa

The EU has always maintained a separate relationship with South Africa. Initially this was the case because of apartheid. During the post-apartheid era, the separate relationship has been maintained because the EU classifies South Africa as a developed country, although South Africa requested that its status be changed to that of a developing country. The EU refused this request and thus South Africa was admitted to the Lomé Convention under limited accession.

EU-South Africa relations are distinguished by: (1) the Development Cooperation Programme; (2) EU-South Africa trade relations; and (3) South Africa's limited accession to the Lomé Convention and the EU-SA Trade Development and Cooperation Agreement that includes an EU-SA FTA. This section of the chapter analyses these issues. An extensive discussion of the events that culminated in the EU-SA FTA is provided.

Development Cooperation

In response to increased repression by the apartheid regime, in 1985, the EU established the Special Programme on South Africa, which remained in existence until 1994. The programme was designed to contribute to the process of peaceful change by giving support to non-racial activities undertaken by non-violent organisations in both South Africa and Namibia. Activities under the programme included education and training, legal assistance, and social and humanitarian aid (EU & EC, 1994:48).

Following the first democratic elections in South Africa, the Special Programme was renamed the European Programme for Reconstruction and Development (EPRD). Assistance was concentrated in the areas of education and training, health, rural and urban development, good governance, and private sector development (see Table 7.7, below, for EU allocations). The EPRD is the largest development programme that exists in South Africa.

Under the first EPRD Multi-annual Indicative Programme (1997–99) for South Africa, the EU focused on providing development assistance in basic social services; private sector development; good governance, democratisation, and human rights; regional cooperation; and cooperation outside of the focal areas (e.g. science and technology). In addition, the programme provided assistance for human resources development, gender sensitivity, and environmental protection and preservation (EC, 1999c:23–4).

Table 7.7: EPRD Allocation, 1994–99 (ECU)

Year	No. of projects[1]	Commitment	Disbursement[2]
1994	97	102 147 282	58 117 581
1995	17	123 320 821	45 085 614
1996	17	129 500 000	28 514 567
1997	11	127 500 000	59 756 988
1998	16	127 500 000	71 979 677
1999	12	127 500 000	

Source: EC (1999c:26); EU (n.d.)

[1] Number of projects approved during the year   [2] Total disbursement for the year

As Table 7.7 indicates, there exists a significant gap between the commitment and disbursement of aid. Problems of disbursement largely stemmed from EC bureaucratic procedures, which were designed to maintain stringent financial controls. Such procedures have been modified and the disbursement of project funds has improved (*Business Day*, 17 December 1999).

EU-SA Trade

Between 1990 and 1995, South Africa's exports to the EU increased by 28 per cent and imports from the EU doubled (see Table 7.8, below). In 1995, the EU had a trade surplus with South Africa. The surplus continued into 1998. In 1999, however, South Africa had a small trade surplus with the EU. South Africa's exports to the EU mainly consist of primary products including diamonds, metals, minerals, and fruit. EU exports to South Africa include capital equipment and merchandise (Steward, 1996:51). Thirty to 40 per cent of all South African exports go to the EU and 40 per cent of its imports come from it. In addition, 50–70 per cent of all foreign investment is from the EU (EC, 1999c:12; Eurostep, 2000:2, 17).[18]

Table 7.8: European Union-South Africa Trade, 1990–99

1990–95					
SA Exports to the EU, 1990–95 ('000 000 of euros)					
1990	1991	1992	1993	1994	1995
5 927.4	8 378.5	9 098.4	8 618.5	6 735.5	7 575.2
SA Imports from the EU, 1990–95 ('000 000 of euros)					
1990	1991	1992	1993	1994	1995
4 090.4	5 814.9	5 420.5	5 601.5	7 091.5	8 688.9

1996–99			
SA Exports to the EU, 1996–98 ('000 000 of euros)			
1996	1997	1998	1999
8 218.0	9 089.0	9 724.1	10 793.6
SA Imports from the EU, 1996–98 ('000 000 of euros)			
1996	1997	1998	1999
8 869.2	9 741.7	10 474.8	9 851.7

Source: Eurostat.

Although the EU is a major trading partner for South Africa, South Africa is not a major trading partner for the EU. In fact, only 1.4 per cent of the EU's exports go to South Africa and 1.4 per cent of imports come from South Africa (Eurostep, 2000:3).

Limited Accession to the Lomé Convention and EU-SA Negotiations for a Trade, Development, and Cooperation Agreement[19]

In April 1997, South Africa became the 71st ACP member of the Lomé Convention under limited accession. This means that South Africa does not have access to EU aid and trade preferences. It is, however, able to compete for EU-funded tenders for development projects in ACP countries, and participate in Lomé discussions. The negotiations between the EU and South Africa that resulted in SA joining Lomé were long and arduous.

Following the first democratic elections in 1994, which marked the end of the apartheid era, the EU rejected the ANC-led government's request that it be allowed to join the Lomé Convention as a developing country. In joining Lomé, South Africa only wanted to have access to the general trade provisions, and not the special trade protocols (i.e. beef and veal and sugar) or the stabilisation mechanism. The request for access to the general trade provisions (the non-reciprocal trade regime) was for only a transitional period (1995–2000). Several reasons were given by the EU for rejecting South Africa's request, including that South Africa was a developed country; its agriculture and textile exports could damage sensitive EU sectors; and the arrangement would not be WTO compatible (Eurostep, 2000:5; Perry, 2000:5; Davies, 2000:7; Goodison, 1999:16). In addition, the EU wanted South Africa to serve as a model for its post-Lomé Convention strategy. Specifically, the EU plans to develop reciprocal FTAs with its ACP partners to replace the current non-reciprocal trade agreements.

Beth Perry argues that South Africa's classification as a 'developed' country is a mere technicality, especially since its per capita GNP is lower than that of several ACP countries. The real reason for rejecting South Africa's request for access to the general trade provisions of Lomé was fear of competitive South African products. Thus, the EU rejected the best option for really enhancing the prospects for economic growth and development in both South Africa and the SADC region (Perry, 2000:4). Both the ACP countries and the European parliament agreed that South Africa should have access to the general trade provisions for a transitional period of five years, since this was the best option for enhancing development in South Africa as well as the SADC region (Goodison, 1999:17).

In arguing that South Africa was a developed country, the EC insisted that the only way South Africa would have increased access to the EU market during the first phase of its transition was through an FTA (Goodison, 1999:18–19). The EC further argued that South Africa should join Lomé with limited accession and that financial assistance should continue, but outside the Lomé framework.

Rejecting the offer of a free trade agreement made by the EU (June 1995) and the EU Trade Mandate (March 1996), the South African government argued that the country faced too many problems, including unemployment, to consider an FTA at this early stage. In addition, concerns were raised about the impact that such an agreement might have on the members of the SACU and the overall regional integration process in Southern Africa (Davenport *et al.*, 1995:62). The South African government was especially concerned about the proposed exclusion of approximately 40 per cent of South Africa's agricultural products contained in the EU Trade Mandate (South African DTI, 1997). In the mean time, South Africa, in an ongoing attempt to get the EU to accept it as a developing country under the Lomé Convention, forged a closer alliance with the SADC region, signing the SADC Protocol on Trade in 1996 (Bertelsmann, 1997:26).

The decision to reject South Africa's request for temporary access to the general trade provisions of Lomé was the first sign indicating that the EU was not genuinely committed to South Africa's economic development. Nonetheless, during the negotiations, the EU noted that '[w]hat we propose is not just an old-fashioned Free Trade Zone. It is nothing less than a Development Free Trade Area, designed to support the South African government in the successful implementation of its economic policies' (Perry, 2000:8).

Official negotiations did not resume again on the future of EU-SA relations until January 1997. While the South Africans argued that the delay was a result of the need for them to consult widely, including with the SADC member states, many in the EU felt that the delay resulted from the attempt by white sector interests in South Africa, who control textiles, the automotive industry, etc., to put pressure on the government not to negotiate an EU-SA trade agreement. The behaviour displayed by white sector interests, EU officials argued, was an outward visible sign of the 'laager mentality' of the South Africans, stemming from many years of sanctions. EU officials also felt that it was very difficult for the government to see through the whole series of confusing issues. After the Government of National Unity was established, the EU recognised that the economy was essentially still being run by factions of the National Party (NP). These individuals were the ones who benefitted from the 'honeymoon' of the new era in SA, and the support the EU was giving to decrease the level of unemployment. The individuals (members of the NP), it was felt, were not only restrictive and protectionist in terms of their trade with the outside world, but were also actually aggressively destabilising neighbouring countries economically.[20]

During the January 1997 EU-SA negotiations, the South Africans presented a position paper on the establishment of an EU-SA trade and development agreement. According to the position paper:

- ▶ The agreement should contribute positively to placing the South African economy on a new development oriented growth path, and to achieving the broad socio-economic objectives defined in the RDP;[21]
- ▶ It should lead to the restructuring of the present unbalanced economic relationship (in terms of which South Africa exports mainly raw and semi-processed materials in exchange for highly processed capital goods) into a more balanced and mutually beneficial one. The imbalance is also reflected in the growing trade deficit that South Africa experiences with the EU;
- ▶ It should remove the discriminatory treatment which currently applies to South African exports to the EU compared to those of comparable countries;
- ▶ It should increase foreign direct investment in outward oriented South African sectors and in the region's infrastructural projects;
- ▶ It should contribute positively to the promotion of equitable and mutually beneficial cooperation and integration in the Southern African region to which both SA and the EU have repeatedly declared their commitments;
- ▶ It should ensure that meaningful economic benefits are derived from SA's qualified membership of the Lomé Convention;
- ▶ It should promote cooperation between the European Union and South Africa within the bounds of their respective powers, to their mutual interests; and
- ▶ It should provide an appropriate framework for political dialogue between South Africa and the European Union, that will allow the development of close relations in all areas of common interest (Bertelsmann, 1997:26).

In a joint press release issued after the meeting, the two parties noted that the comprehensive framework they were working toward would cover trade and development, as well as other areas. With respect to trade between the EU and South Africa, the EU agreed it would be prepared to allow South Africa access to the EU market at a quicker and more extensive pace than it would expect from South Africa in relation to their market. In addition, the South Africans indicated they would accede to the Lomé Convention under a separate protocol that would be agreed upon at a later date. As previously indicated, South Africa became a member of the Lomé Convention in April 1997. This resulted from the delinking of SA's Lomé membership from the overall talks on trade and cooperation (Bertelsmann, 1997:26-7). The agreement entered into force in June 1998.

EU-SA negotiations for an FTA continued, with South African Minister of Trade and Industry Alec Erwin noting his disappointment with the fact that while the EU wanted to exclude approximately 40 per cent of South African agricultural products from any free trade arrangement, it had not offered to do the same for highly subsidised EU agricultural products entering the South African market (*Weekly Mail & Guardian*, 18 July 1997). Following the EU-SA negotiations in November 1997, it was reported that a free trade agreement could be concluded by mid-1998. This deadline, of course, was missed. In fact, it took almost four years and 24 rounds of negotiations and a plethora of informal sessions (Lowe, 2000) for the two sides to finally reach an agreement. Negotiations for the Trade, Development and Cooperation Agreement (TDCA) were concluded in March 1999 (the agreement was officially signed in October 1999), and the agreement went into effect on 1 January 2000, albeit partly and provisionally because the national parliaments of the EU member states had not ratified the TDCA. Ratification by all EU member states was likely to take at least two years (Eurostep, 2000:2, 17). The TDCA 'provides for cooperation between the EU and South Africa in a wide range of areas such as trade, economic relations, finance and technical assistance. It also includes provisions for continued political dialogue and development assistance' (EC, 1999c:9). An agreement in the area of science and technology was reached in 1997.

Even though the TDCA negotiations had officially ended, unresolved issues remained directly related to the EU-SA FTA. One concerned the issue of wine and spirits and the other fisheries. With respect to the former, some EU members, led by France, protested against South Africa using the terms 'port' and 'sherry' for their fortified wines, arguing that these products would pose serious competition for European port and sherry. They also objected to the use of more generic terms such as 'ruby', 'vin de pays', 'grand cru', 'ouzo', and 'grappa' (Perry, 2000:9–10). A tentative agreement was reached on the use of the words 'port' and 'sherry'. It stipulated that South Africa would eventually phase out this terminology for their fortified wines. The compromise was reached after the word 'new' was inserted into the clause of the EU-SA FTA about the wines, indicating that after a 12-year transition period, a new name will be given South African port and sherry (*Financial Mail*, 2 April 1999).

The EU pledged ECU 15 million to help in the marketing of the new brand names (*Business Day*, 12 April 1999). A final agreement was reached on the issue of wines and spirits in April 2002. The agreement stipulates that 42 million litres of South African wines will be allowed to enter the EU duty-free. However, as noted above, South Africa will be required to phase out names such as port, sherry, ouzo, and grappa (*Business Day*, 16 April 2002).

The fisheries agreement became so contentious that the South African government insisted that it be delinked from TDCA negotiations. In April 2001, the South African government announced that it would be impossible to complete a fisheries agreement with the EU (*Business Day*, 4 April 2001). The problem is that the EU wants its fish operators to have access to South Africa's fishing waters and resources, although this is not in the best interest of any entities in South Africa. The South African government is under tremendous pressure from local fishing companies not to concede to the EU, because, it is argued, if the EU fishermen with their sophisticated vessels are allowed into South African waters, there will be job losses in the local fishing industry (*Business Day*, 1 September 2000). EU officials made it very clear that tariff concessions would not be given to the South African fishing industry until a fisheries agreement is finalised (EC, 1999b).

With respect to the EU-SA FTA, an estimated 300 'highly sensitive' South African agricultural products were not offered tariff liberalisation and an additional 40 other products were granted tariff reductions with quotas (EC, 1999b). With respect to the latter, the EU has stipulated that customs duties would not be imposed as long as South African exports did not exceed the allocated quotas (*Financial Mail*, 2 April 1999). It appears that many of South Africa's agricultural products will only be allowed to enter the EU market towards the end of the final phase of the agreement, which is a protectionist policy known as 'backloading'. In the mean time, the SADC region will no doubt be flooded with subsidised EU agricultural products.

The EU-SA FTA stipulates that 95 per cent of the EU's imports from South Africa will enter the market duty-free within ten years, and 86 per cent of EU imports will enter the South African market duty-free within 12 years. The liberalisation schedules are outlined in Tables 7.9–7.12, below.

As Table 7.9 indicates, 86 per cent of South African industrial goods were allowed to enter the EU market duty-free upon entry into force of the FTA in January 2000. In addition, one per cent entered at 50 per cent of the MFN tariff rate. During the first three-year linear phase-down period, an additional five per cent of industrial goods will enter duty-free; one per cent over six years; an additional seven per cent during the second three-year linear phase-down period (years three to six); and one per cent after ten years. In essence, over 99 per cent of South African industrial products will enter the EU duty-free by 2010. Less than one per cent of South Africa's industrial products were placed on the reserve list. These will not experience any tariff reductions. South African exporters will have an advantage over other competitors, although in general the tariff levels for EU industrial products is low (Mayer, 1999:4). The low tariff rates on industrial products entering the EU market is no doubt a reflection of the fact that such products do not pose a threat to EU industrial products.

Table 7.9: EU's Liberalisation Schedule: Industrial Products

Treatment	Coverage %	Cumulative coverage %
Duty-free at entry into force	86	86
3-year linear phase-down	5	91
6-year linear phase-down	1	92
3-year linear phase-down, between years 3–6	7	99
10-year linear phase-down	1	100
Reserve list	<1	100

Sources: Mayer (1999:4); Eurostep (2000:11)

In terms of sensitive products in the textiles and clothing sector, under the FTA, tariff duties will be phased out during the first three years of the agreement. In addition, when the agreement entered into force, tariffs on auto components were 'reduced to 50% of the MFN rates applied by the EU' (Mayer, 1999:4).

As Table 7.10, overleaf, indicates, 62 per cent of EU industrial goods were allowed duty-free entry into South Africa when the FTA came into force. An additional one per cent will be subjected to a three-year phase-down; eight per cent to a two-year phase-down (years three to five); two per cent to a nine-year phase-down (years three to 12); and 13 per cent to a seven-year phase-down (years five to 12). Three per cent will receive partial liberalisation (clothing and textiles), while 11 per cent will remain on the reserve list (automobiles and components). This means that by 2012, 86 per cent of the EU's industrial products will enter the South African market duty-free.

Table 7.10: South Africa's Liberalisation Schedule: Industrial Products

Treatment	Coverage %	Cumulative coverage %
Duty-free at entry into force	62	62
3-year phase-down	1	63
Phase-down in years 3–5	8	71
9-year phase-down, years 3–12	2	73
6-year phase-down, years 5–12	13	86
Partial liberalisation	3	89
Reserve list	11	100

Sources: Mayer (1999:5); Eurostep (2000:11)

The automobile and clothing and textiles sectors were deemed by South Africa to be sensitive. Consequently, automobiles and components will remain on the reserve list (see Table 7.13, page 216) and will not be subject to tariff elimination or reduction. With respect to clothing and textiles,

> South Africa was able to negotiate a slower tariff phase-down, to enable the industry to adjust to competition from EU producers. Depending on the segment of the market, South Africa will reduce tariffs on clothing and textile so that by the end of the eighth year the tariffs will vary between 5% and 20%. Between the eighth year and the end of the transition period, EU products will enjoy a preference and the MFN rate of around 40% (Mayer, 1999:4).

In terms of agricultural products, not only were 38 per cent of South African goods excluded from the FTA (see Table 7.11, opposite), but also, only 21 per cent of such products were given duty-free entry into the EU upon entry into force of the FTA. And, as Table 7.11 indicates, 62 per cent of South African agricultural products will not actually enter the EU market duty-free until 2010. As Marina Mayer, Deputy Director in the South African DTI admits, negotiations in this sector were constrained by CAP:

> Tariff phase down's [sic] are over a longer period of time, in most cases over the full ten year period and 21% of products to be liberalised have phase-downs that are back-loaded (i.e. liberalisation occurs towards the end of the period). In addition, 11.5% of agricultural products will only be partially liberalised while 28% are on the reserve list (Mayer, 1999:4).

As if to put a saving face on what clearly is to South Africa's disadvantage, Mayer notes that,

> [a]lthough South Africa did not succeed in eliminating EU export subsidies completely, there are some important breakthroughs. Firstly, the EU has committed itself not to pay export refunds on cheese exported to South Africa under the tariff quota of 5000 tonnes. Secondly, the EU is willing to eliminate export refunds on products South Africa might want to offer for

front-loading during the implementation period. Refunds will be eliminated in full once tariff liberalization starts. This is an important aspect of the agreement, as most of the EU agricultural products will not be competitive on the domestic market without refunds. Should the EU be unwilling or unable to eliminate export refunds, South Africa is likely to retract its offer of front-loading (Mayer, 1999:6).

Table 7.11: EU's Liberalisation Schedule: Agricultural Products

Treatment	Coverage %	Cumulative coverage %
Duty-free at entry into force	21	21
3-year phase-down	6	27
10-year phase-down	14	41
7-year phase-down, years 3–10	4	45
5-year phase-down, years 5–10	17	62
Partial liberalisation – processed products	11.5	73.5
Reserve list	28	99.5
Excluded	0.5	100

Sources: Mayer (1999:6); Eurostep (2000:12)

Also included in the agreement are tariff quotas for certain agricultural products. For canned fruits the quota is 60 000 tons, for fruit juices 5 000 tons, and for cut flowers 900 tons. Quotas have also been imposed on cheese, and as previously noted, wines (Mayer, 1999:6).

With respect to EU agricultural exports to South Africa, 34 per cent were able to enter the South African market duty-free upon entry into force of the FTA (see Table 7.12, below). An additional five per cent will enter duty-free during the three-year phase-down; seven per cent during the two-year phase-down (years three to five); and an additional 35 per cent during a seven-year phase-down period (years five to 12). Nineteen per cent of exports will remain on the reserve list.

The principles guiding the FTA are asymmetry and differentiation (with the EU opening its market to South Africa faster and more extensively); support for regional integration; WTO compatibility; protection for sensitive sectors; and integration of South Africa into the global economy.

Table 7.12: South Africa's Liberalisation Schedule: Agricultural Products

Treatment	Coverage %	Cumulative coverage %
Duty-free at entry into force	34	34
3-year phase-down	5	39
2-year phase-down, years 3–5	7	46
7-year phase-down, years 5–12	35	81
Reserve list	19	100

Sources: Mayer (1999:7); Eurostep (2000:12)

Although there exists a huge disparity between the EU's economy (US$8 trillion) and South Africa's economy (US$230 billion), during negotiations, the EU was extremely protectionist (Phaswana, 2000:2). In fact, the EU was not deemed to be a fair trading partner throughout the negotiations and clearly took advantage of its position as the more powerful economic partner. The EU was clearly not interested in a 'free' nor 'fair' trade regime. Instead, it was interested in managed trade (Davies, 2000:11). According to Davies, Chairperson of the Parliamentary Portfolio Committee on Trade and Industry, negotiations with the EU involved 'hard bargaining in which professed concerns to promote development and greater equity in trade relations with developing countries are often swamped by what the *Financial Times* called "commercial haggling by wealthy Europeans"' (Davies, 2000:11).

Table 7.13: Reserve List

Main products excluded on EU side (list to be periodically reviewed)	Main products excluded on SA side (list to be periodically reviewed)
Beef	Beef
Sugar	Sugar
Some dairy (incl. milk, butter, whey)	Some dairy (incl. milk, butter)
Sweet corn	Sweet corn
Maize and maize products	Maize and maize products
Rice and rice products	Barley and barley products
Starches	Wheat and wheat products
Some cut flowers	Starches
Some fresh fruits (certain citrus,	Chocolate
apples, pears, grapes, bananas)	Ice cream
Prepared tomatoes	
Some prepared fruits and fruit juices	
Vermouth	
Ethyl alcohol	
Some fish	
Unwrought aluminium	Petroleum and petroleum products
	Some chemical products
	Some textiles
	Automotive
Total of 304 tariff positions, representing 3.4% of total imports from SA	Total of 120 tariff positions, representing 10.9% of total imports from EU

Source: EC (1999d)

Throughout the four years of negotiations for an EU-SA FTA, concern was raised about the possible impact such an agreement would have on Botswana, Lesotho, Namibia, and Swaziland (the BLNS countries who, along with South Africa, make up SACU), and non-SACU SADC members (members of SADC excluding SACU).

The Debate: The EU-SA FTA Will Have Positive Consequences for the SADC Region

For the South African government, the TDCA, especially the EU-SA FTA, is deemed to be extremely important for spearheading South Africa's further integration into the world economy. It is anticipated that the EU-SA FTA will support the process of economic restructuring in South Africa as a result of increased trade, investment, and use of technology. In addition, as a result of further market openness, productivity will be enhanced and exports will be stimulated, resulting in economic growth. Finally, it is expected that intra-regional trade among the member states of SADC will increase (Mayer, 1999:2; Erwin, 2000:vii).

For the EU, the TDCA represents an opportunity to forge a closer political relationship with its most important African partner; further solidify its dominant political, trade and investment position in South Africa over that of the US and Japan; display the EU's commitment to provide stability to emerging markets; expedite the creation of a SADC free trade zone; and provide a positive model for a post-Lomé arrangement (EC, 1999b).

Numerous studies have been undertaken to determine the impact the EU-SA FTA will have on South Africa and the SADC region. Using a multicountry computable general equilibrium (GME) model, Jeffrey D. Lewis, Sherman Robinson, and Karen Thierfelder conclude that South Africa stands to benefit more from the agreement than the EU. While only negligible changes are identified for the EU, it is anticipated that real GDP in South Africa will increase by 0.44 per cent. Trade creation, not trade diversion, will occur, with South Africa increasing its exports to the EU by 5.3 per cent. The sectors that will experience the largest gains are those that had been protected, including fruits and vegetables and food processing. EU exports to South Africa, according to the study, will increase by 4.3 per cent, with the greatest gains experienced in the export of grains, food processing, and apparel.[22] Lewis, in another study, does caution that the benefits to the South African economy will emerge slowly (Lewis, 2001:22).

With respect to the impact of the EU-SA FTA on the region, Lewis *et al.* conclude that the gains will be slight, resulting in a real GDP increase of 0.1 per cent. Exports to the EU and South Africa will similarly only increase by 0.1 per cent (Lewis, 2001:38). Other benefits to the SADC region are said to include the ability of some local businesses to import inputs at a cheaper rate, resulting in increased profits and corporate tax revenues; increased competition that might result in some local businesses becoming more competitive; and the ability to import some consumer goods into the region cheaper (Irving, 1999:2).

Carolyn Jenkins and Lynne Thomas argue that 'it is in the interests of SADC as a whole for the dominant partner to accelerate its growth through expanding trade with the rest of the world'. Thus, not only should the EU-SA FTA be encouraged, but South Africa should also consider FTAs with NAFTA, East Asia, and possibly Australasia (Jenkins & Thomas, forthcoming). Since it is the case that South Africa will experience limited benefits as a result of the SADC FTA, further economic growth dictates that South Africa must look beyond the region in order to enhance its economic growth. Economic growth in South Africa will in turn have a spin-off effect, resulting in greater regional economic growth. At the heart of this reasoning are studies that indicate a strong positive correlation between trade openness and economic development. Jenkins and Thomas do note that a liberal trade regime alone does not explain economic growth. Other important explanatory factors include, for example, human capital, type of investment, market distortions, political stability, and export diversification (Jenkins & Thomas, forthcoming).

Davies anticipates that the agreement will significantly improve South Africa's access to the EU market, albeit limited to only a number of sectors, such as agriculture, where South Africa is competitive. Manufacturing industries that should benefit from the agreement include steel and steel products, furniture and automotive products, and ferro aluminum products (Davies, 2000:10).

The Debate: The EU-SA FTA Will Have Negative Consequences for the SADC Region

During the negotiations for the EU-SA FTA, workers in South Africa were protesting against the negative impact EU exports were already having on South Africa's economy. For example, in November 1998, trade unions marched to parliament and to European embassies to protest 'the EU's attempts to "re-colonise our country" through unfair trade practices'. They were protesting against the EU-SA negotiations for an FTA on the grounds that the EU maintained high duties on South African imports while the South African market was being flooded with heavily subsidised European products. The result was job losses and threats of further retrenchments (*Electronic Mail & Guardian*, 17 November 1998).

Throughout the EU-SA FTA negotiations, the South African government was taking action to prevent the EU from engaging in unfair trade practices. For example, in order to curtail the devastating impact European canned tomatoes were having on the South African canned tomato industry, in January 1998, the South African government increased the import duty on canned tomatoes from Europe from 23 to 30 per cent. This policy had no effect in the end because the EU sector is so highly subsidised that the prices for canned tomatoes were still lower than the production cost in South Africa. As a result, South Africa's largest food processing company, Langeberg Foods, was forced to close its major canning plant, Paarl factory, located in the Western Cape. This resulted in 2 500 people losing their jobs (*Electronic Mail & Guardian*, 17 November 1998).

With a view to stopping heavily-subsidised EU flour from being imported into the country, the National Chamber of Milling asked the South African government to impose countervailing duties on imported EU flour, because the local industry is under threat. According to chamber executive director Jannie de Villiers,

> [w]hile we support trade liberalisation, it is naïve to assume that we can win a trade war when the EU, for example, still pays its wheat farmers a US$103/t production subsidy, while SA farmers do not receive a cent. Similarly, the EU applies a wheat import tariff of 73%, against zero protection in SA (*Financial Mail*, 2 April 1999).

The extent of EU beef dumping in South Africa is so massive that highly-subsidised beef accounts for 70 to 80 per cent of meat that is involved in canned meat production. This beef is sold at one-fourth its market value in the EU. Local beef producers are consequently not able to compete in this market (Panos, 1998:9).

In March 1999, the same month that the EU-SA FTA was finalised, the South African government became involved with a group of countries that are campaigning to get the EU and other countries to reduce their trade-distorting policies, including agricultural subsidies and high duties, which have a negative impact on South African exports (*Business Day*, 5 March 1999). One would have thought that the South African government would have rectified this problem before finalising an FTA with the EU. After Turkey concluded an FTA with the EU, the country was flooded with subsidised agricultural products, leaving the agricultural sector in a very precarious position. Did not South African trade officials study the case of Turkey before finalising the agreement (Panos, 1998:33)?

With respect to the non-competitive clothing and textiles industry, Marina Mayer acknowledges the devastating impact the FTA will have on workers in South Africa, mostly women, and the breadwinners in their households. She noted that, '[i]t is unfortunate that some of these women are going to be losing as a result of this agreement. But we are very clear about the fact that you can't protect industries just because there's competition from the other countries, because the point is to encourage trade and to provide to the South African markets.'[23]

In the final analysis, according to a study by Eurostep, the EU will benefit more from the EU-SA FTA than South Africa. For example, according to the study:

> [t]he final result of the agreement means that the EU will increase duty-free access to its market by 14% for South African industrial exports and by 41% for South African agricultural products. For its part South Africa will expand duty-free access to its market by 24% for EU industrial exports and by 47% for EU agricultural exports. By the end of the transitional period the EU will concede greater duty-free access in absolute terms to South African total exports (95%) than South Africa will to EU total exports (86%). However South Africa will open up its market to a significantly greater extent (26%) than the EU (20%) in relative terms (Eurostep, 2000:13).

This is the case because prior to the implementation of the EU-SA FTA, 75 per cent of South African exports had duty-free access to the EU market while the level for the EU was only 60 per cent (Eurostep, 2000:4).

In addition to the above, the Eurostep study argues that while the EU economy will not be threatened by the full opening of its market to South African exports, this is not the case with South Africa opening its market to the EU. It is anticipated that it will result in a current account deficit for South Africa. According to Eurostep,

> [t]he overall conclusion of the present comparative static analysis on the EU-South Africa trade liberalization is, therefore, that the EU-South Africa FTA will very likely have a greater positive economic impact in the EU than in South Africa. An improvement in South Africa's favour, however, could be reached if during the implementation of the TDCA the EU agrees to increase duty-free access to its market for South African agricultural products. Trade between the EU and South Africa will be certainly be [sic] enhanced by the FTA, but benefiting to a much greater extent the EU than South Africa (Eurostep, 2000:16).

In terms of dynamic effects, Eurostep warns that although the agreement may result in increased efficiency as a result of increased competitiveness, the end result might mean the closure of firms and increased unemployment. In addition, the anticipated new European foreign investment might not result in the creation of new production capacity, but instead might just be the acquisition of existing domestically owned capacity (Eurostep, 2000:17).

Although very few in South Africa are aware of the specifics regarding the EU-SA FTA, the public became alarmed in January 2000, when it appeared that the agreement would not enter into force. The problem began when Portugal and Greece protested against South Africa using the terms 'grappa' and 'ouzo' in the wine and spirit part of the agreement. Ouzo is not even produced in South Africa. In response to this, Britain's minister for Africa noted that his 'European partners were effectively reneging on the trade deal' (Ryan, 2000:17). In order to resolve the dispute, South Africa agreed to phase out these terms. There exists a perception among many in South Africa that while some EU countries have expressed a desire to promote stronger ties with South Africa, this does not include making trade concessions (Ryan, 2000:17).

Although SACU's treaty stipulates that all member states must approve any trade agreements with parties external to the treaty, South Africa did not consult its SACU partners – Botswana, Lesotho, Namibia, and Swaziland – about the EU-SA FTA. Nonetheless, as a result of the customs union (see Chapter 3) between the five countries, the EU-SA FTA is a *de facto* EU-SACU FTA. The BLNS countries will be the most adversely affected by the EU-SA FTA. Given this reality, the negotiators put clauses in the trade agreement that allegedly would help protect these countries against the implications of the agreement. For example, they will continue to have preferential access to the EU under the beef and sugar protocols and, according to the agreement,

> [t]here may be sectors of the economy, both in South Africa and in other SACU countries, that might suffer adjustment costs from the gradual opening up to competition with EU producers. Some of them may actually require continued protection. In order to minimise any possible adverse effects from the BLNS countries, most sensitive products, i.e. beef and sugar, are excluded from the FTA. Furthermore, the Agreement provides for a safeguard clause that can also be invoked for protection of infant industries in both South Africa and BLNS states (EC, 1999c:18).

While this is commendable in theory, it will be interesting if pre-emptive measures will be implemented in practice.

The greatest loss for BLNS will result from a decrease in income from SACU's common revenue pool. As a customs union, there exists a common external tariff (CET) on goods imported into the area, and the revenue from the CET is distributed among the member countries. Such revenue represents a significant part of annual government revenue. For Swaziland it represents approximately 50 per cent, for Lesotho 50–60 per cent, for Namibia, 28 per cent, and for Botswana 17 per cent. Prior to the implementation of the EU-SA FTA, 40 per cent of goods imported into the region were sourced from the EU, and the level of tariff protection was high (Sidiropoulos, 2000:12). In terms of revenue losses to the BLNS countries, one estimate is between US\$400 and 800 million annually (Panos, 1998:20). These losses, according to Mpho Malie, Lesotho's Minister of Trade and Industry, could result in funding cuts for health care and schools. In addition, public sector workers could be retrenched, farming incomes could be reduced, factories closed, and road infrastructure neglected. In the final analysis, the potential adverse economic consequences could result in challenges to nascent democracies (Goodison, 1999:90).

According to a study done in conjunction with the SACU Parliamentary Liaison Group, numerous sectors have been identified that could experience problems as a result of competition from EU duty-free products.[24] Such competition could result in a reduction in profits for BLNS producers and the loss of the South African market, resulting in the closure of enterprises (Goodison, 1999:49–50).

An estimated 12 000 full-time jobs could be lost as a result of the EU-SA FTA. This does not include the down-stream linkages with other sectors, nor the effect on employment in the public sector (Goodison, 1999:50). Total losses for BLNS may be the equivalent of eight to ten times the amount of EU aid granted (Sidiropoulos, 2000:12; European Research Office, 1996). According to Elizabeth Sidiropoulos of the South African Institute of International Affairs,

> [i]nvariably, there will be some trade diversion by South African importers, from manufacturers in the BLNS to ones in Europe, which, with the reduction/elimination of tariffs, are now more cost-effective. The difficulty of policing rules of origin may negatively affect BLNS firms' own domestic market competitiveness. BLNS producers will also have to compete in Europe with SA products which will now be entering duty free (Sidiropoulos, 2000:14).

In a study undertaken by Imani Development International on the economic impact of an EU-SA FTA on the BLNS countries, it is recommended that these countries request compensation costs for border controls, the loss of revenue and access, and for industrial restructuring arising from investment diversion away from them to South Africa (quoted in SADC, 1998a). In what appeared to be an insult to and mockery of the estimated millions Swaziland will lose as a result of the EU-SA FTA, on 19 May 1999 the EU gave Swaziland an estimated US$1.3 million to help the country deal with the negative impact the agreement would have on its economy. Money for Botswana, Lesotho, and Namibia, the EU noted, would possibly be forthcoming (UNIRIN, 19 May 1999). Two issues are of primary concern. The first is the notion that a small monetary hand-out from the EU can begin to rectify the projected economic destabilisation arising from the FTA. Will the EU pump into the economies of the BLNS countries annually and indefinitely US$400–800 million to prevent them from collapsing? Or will they invest in productive sectors that will allow them to develop and compete fairly with the EU and South Africa? A great possibility exists that these countries will be further underdeveloped as a result of this agreement. Although Trade and Industry Minister Alec Erwin said that SA and the EU would share the cost of the losses (*Business Day*, 22 April 1999), no details have been forthcoming. In any event, South Africa does not have the resources to compensate these countries, and if the EU compensates them adequately, it would perhaps defeat the entire economic purpose of creating an FTA.

What are the alternatives for the BLNS countries? Mayer is very clear about what must happen: the SACU countries (as well as the non-SACU SADC countries) must move away from tariffs as a form of revenue to domestically generated taxes.[25] William Bosman, Director of Regional Economic Organisations within the Ministry of Foreign Affairs is more blunt about the SACU nations:

> there is perhaps a shock treatment that is necessary to tell them, now you are on your own, South Africa cannot any longer provide for you 50% of your budget .... Now you have to tax your own people; you have to work according to the structures of a free independent country.[26]

Such a statement reeks of the arrogance with which the South African government negotiated with the EU to the exclusion of both the SACU and non-SACU SADC countries. For the BLNS countries, this must be a wake-up call to realise that after years of being exploited by South Africa economically, they are now dispensable in the name of trade liberalisation. While no doubt the SA-BLNS economic relationship needs to be reformed, it is only fair that restructuring occur over a reasonable and agreed period of time. What is most interesting about South Africa's response to the SACU countries is that they, as well as the non-SACU SADC countries, are a captive market for South Africa's non-competitive industrial products.

Hopefully the South African government realises that they are similarly pawns in the hands of the EU and consequently will also become dispensable once the relationship is no longer in its interest. Unlike the EU, however, the South African government will find the problem of the economic destabilisation caused by this agreement at its borders, with BLNS nationals seeking employment in South Africa.

With respect to increased domestic taxes as an alternative to SACU revenue, Swaziland's Finance Minister John Carmichael noted that while tax reform is key, in order to attract direct foreign investment, the government was planning to decrease Swaziland's corporate rate from 37 per cent to 30 per cent (*Business Day*, 7 May 1999). Further to the point, however, it has been suggested that the only country that really has the capacity to increase personal and corporate taxes is Botswana (Sidiropoulos, 2000:14).

The non-SACU SADC countries are extremely concerned about the impact the FTA will have on the region. There will likely be de-industrialisation, and because South Africa's economy is the strongest in the region, coupled with the FTA, it will be in a position to 'steal' foreign investment from the other SADC member states. In addition, because of the porous regional borders, the flooding of regional markets by heavily subsidised EU products is likely. This will occur because of the huge regional informal trade regime. For example, as discussed in Chapter 3, more informal trade exists between Malawi and her neighbours (Zambia, Mozambique, and Tanzania) than formal trade. Justin Malewezi, Vice President of Malawi, speculates that as much as 70 per cent of trade in the SADC region takes place in the informal sector (Madakufamba, 2001d).

South Africa will probably begin to purchase subsidised agricultural products from the EU that it normally buys from non-SACU SADC member states. This will therefore decrease their access to the South African market. The end result will be a widening of the trade gap between South Africa and the non-SACU member states. Concerns have been raised that the SADC agricultural sector, as well as the SADC regional agenda, will be severely undermined by the EU-SA FTA (*Business Day*, 16 April 1999).

In the final analysis, Bosman admitted that South Africa was putting itself on the line and making a bold move in going along with the FTA.[27] If, in fact, the economic stakes are so high for South Africa as well as the region, why did South Africa follow through on negotiating the agreement? It appears that the answer lies in the belief that such an arrangement will give South Africa the opportunity to become a serious player within the world economy. Consequently, it believes that if the neo-liberal orthodoxy is adopted, South Africa will become better incorporated within the world economy. As Mayer notes, '[t]he logic within the EU agreement is that it falls within the broader policy and strategy of global repositioning. The EU is our largest export partner and in a context in which we're liberalising vis-à-vis the rest of the world, it makes sense to enter into an agreement where you get something back'.[28] Notwithstanding this logic, the reality is that South Africa's economic power was built on the backs of its regional neighbours, and South Africa remains dependent on them to maintain its economic strength. A de-industrialised region with higher levels of unemployment than currently exist will not bode well for South Africa's future. To forsake the working class and poor of South Africa and the region in the name of neo-liberal orthodoxy could send South Africa into an economic and political crisis. If this occurs, there will be no winners.

Implementation of the EU-SA FTA

In January 2001, on the first anniversary of the agreement, Tshediso Matona, Director for Trade in the South African DTI, noted that South Africa was unhappy 'with the implementation of the agreement' (*Business Day*, 16 January 2001). For example, while there were clear gains for the canned fruit sector, this was not the case for the dairy and cheese industries. With respect to the latter, the benefits collapsed because the EU introduced 'a licensing system for importers of the products' (*Business Day*, 12 January 2001). With respect to the introduction of new regulations, the EU-SA TDCA has been criticised as being rigged by the EU 'so that it can regularly apply leverage to win fresh concessions from Pretoria' (*Business Day*, 21 June 2001). As a result of red tape, the cut flower industry in the Western Cape was not able to meet its quota allocation under the

EU-SA FTA during the first year of the agreement (*Business Day*, 12 February 2001). The failure to finalise the Wine and Spirits Agreement until April 2002 meant that South Africa was not able to benefit from its 32 million litre duty-free export quota (*Business Day*, 21 June 2001).

On 26 June 2001, in Brussels, Belgium, the South Africa-European Union Co-operation Council held its second meeting to assess progress in the provisional implementation of the TDCA and the Wine and Spirits and Fisheries Agreements. Both the EU and South Africa decided they were satisfied with the implementation of the TDCA.

In a 5 June 2001 press release, the trade figures for the first year of the TDCA were announced. South Africa increased exports to the EU in 2000 by 35 per cent while the EU increased exports to South Africa by 20 per cent. South Africa has a trade surplus with the EU of R17 billion, which represents a significant increase over the 1999 surplus of R6 billion (EU, 2001). These are indeed commendable figures and indicate that South Africa's objective of having greater access to the EU market has been realised.

Increased agriculture exports included grapes and citrus fruits. Exports of local wines have increased as well as fruit juices and bottled water. Although a Fisheries Agreement has not been reached, the export of fresh, chilled, and frozen fish increased during the first year of the EU-SA FTA. Other sectors that have benefitted include iron and steel, ferro alloy, flat-rolled products of stainless steel, tyres, paper products, and purifying and filtering equipment (EU, 2001). Unfortunately, the press release does not indicate the sectors in which the EU has successfully increased its penetration of the SA/SACU market.

While all the projected positive and/or negative consequences of the EU-SA FTA will likely not be realised until the free trade area is officially created in 2012, several factors are worth highlighting. The first is that while increased access to the EU market is significant, trade liberalisation alone will not result in sustained economic growth. Consequently, a development strategy that spearheads a new socio-economic dispensation for the impoverished masses must become a priority for the ANC-led government if openness is to result in sustained economic growth.

To date South Africa's strategy for economic growth relies heavily on attempts to further integrate the country into the world economy. In fact, the government seemingly has focused on international integration to the neglect of implementing a viable development strategy. With respect to the latter, after seven years, the ANC-led government finally realised the need to put in place a human resources development strategy to address 'endemic poverty, chronic unemployment, dire skills shortage and shockingly poor education levels' (*Mail & Guardian Online*, 9 May 2001). It is estimated that it will take at least 20 years for the strategy to bear fruit. The announcement of the strategy followed on the heels of the acceptance that while macroeconomic stability had been realised under GEAR, economic growth and poverty alleviation remained elusive (*Mail & Guardian Online*, 23 February 2001).

The second factor that needs to be highlighted is that FDI to South Africa is decreasing, not increasing. One of the problems, according to BusinessMap, is that the government has not put in place a clear strategy for attracting FDI (BusinessMap, 2000a:7). The unresolved land redistribution issue has the potential to create massive political instability in the country, which will serve as a further deterrent to both domestic and foreign investors. In this regard, the response of the South African government to the land invasions on Elandsfontein Farm 12 in Johannesburg during July 2001 was to forcibly remove the invaders with a view to restoring law and order, in order to reassure existing and potential investors that South Africa is safe for investments. In addition, a public relations campaign was initiated to make certain it was understood that South Africa was not like Zimbabwe, where the rule of law is non-existent and land invasions are supported by the government.

It is true that in many respects South Africa is not like Zimbabwe. However, in one very important respect it is. In both countries, the masses of people live in poverty and were dispossessed of their land under white-settler rule. In the post-independence period, neither government has fulfilled its promise to enhance the socio-economic status of the impoverished masses. From 1980 to 1997, the Zimbabwe government maintained the rule of law and forced land invaders off both private and government owned land. However, in 1997, it was no longer politically expedient for the ruling ZANU-PF party to continue this practice. As has been evident throughout the African continent, unresolved social and economic problems lead to economic decay. That South Africa is inextricably linked to the member states of SADC is most evident by the negative economic impact the political and economic instability in Zimbabwe is having on the country. The SADC region has been warned that foreign investors are hesitant about investing in the region because it is not perceived to be politically stable. Anticipated EU investments to help facilitate economic restructuring will likely follow only in the wake of major social and economic development in South Africa.

The third point to be highlighted is that although macroeconomic stability is in place in South Africa, the level of unemployment is rising (the official estimate is 36 per cent) and poverty is increasing. Amidst all these problems, economic growth is sluggish (an estimated three per cent for 2001). Any expectation that the EU financial assistance component of the TDCA will enhance economic growth in South Africa must be tempered by the realisation that the EU has a poor record of disbursement in this area as a result of rigid bureaucratic procedures.

With a viable development strategy in place designed to enhance economic growth and development, it is likely that South Africa's strategy of openness would result in sustained economic growth. At this juncture it is reasonable to conclude that perhaps resources that should have been used for such a strategy were instead used to enhance South Africa's position within the international community. Davies does admit that '[f]orging a new relationship with the EU ... has commanded considerable resources and negotiating effort – some would say too much' (Davies, 2000:6). In the final analysis, one can only wonder if postponing the negotiations for an EU-SA FTA until South Africa had implemented a viable development strategy that had resulted in significant economic growth would have strengthened its bargaining power with not just the EU, but the international community at large. Openness has clearly not produced the results the South African government expected.

The EU-SA FTA therefore appears to be in the best interest of the EU. The EU will have direct access to the SACU market for its cheap and/or subsidised products, and indirect access to the non-SACU SADC market as a result of the porous regional borders. This access will secure its position as the dominant external actor in the SADC region, thus holding at bay any serious economic competition from the US or Japan. Furthermore, in negotiating from a position of strength, the EU has ensured that South African exports will not result in enhanced EU unemployment or de-industrialisation.

Future EU-Southern Africa Relations: The Cotonou Agreement

During his welcoming address at the ACP-EU Joint Assembly meeting held during the latter part of 1996 to discuss future ACP-EU relations, Luxembourg's Prime Minister Jean-Claude

Junker told participants that '[t]here is no question of the European Union getting out of the relationship which took decades to build' (*The Courier*, 1996c:5). The impending post-Lomé world for the EU and the ACP countries forced both sides to begin discussions on the type of partnership that would evolve between the two groups after February 2000. The outcome of 18 long and arduous months of negotiations was the Cotonou Agreement. Negotiations ended in February 2000, and on 23 June, the agreement was signed in Cotonou, Benin. This section of the chapter will discuss future EU-Southern African relations. The first part will place them in the historical context of the negotiations for a post-Lomé EU-ACP relationship. The second part will describe and analyse the Cotonou Agreement and the third will examine future EU-SADC trade relations under the Cotonou Agreement.

Eighteen Months of Negotiations

In preparation for the negotiations, during September 1996, the EC issued a *Green Paper*[29] on relations between the European Union and the ACP countries on the eve of the twenty-first century. In the paper, four possible options for future EU-ACP cooperation were identified:

▶ the status quo, with a few adjustments;
▶ an overall agreement supplemented by bilateral agreements;
▶ splitting up the Lomé Convention into regional agreements; and
▶ a specific agreement for the least developed of the ACP countries (EC, 1997b:ix).

The paper was to serve as an impetus to begin the discussion by all parties on a future EU-ACP relationship. It was developed following major changes in the international trade regime. Under the new international trade regime that came into existence following the UR and the creation of the WTO, tariff discrimination is forbidden against exporting countries. Consequently, according to the EC, it was determined that the Lomé Convention was illegal because:

▶ It discriminates between member countries of the WTO, as not everyone is granted the same, non-reciprocal access to the European market; and
▶ It discriminates between developing countries ... and least developed countries in the world; also not all under-developed states form part of the Lomé Convention (Bertelsmann, 1997:18).

As a result of the above, the EU requested a waiver of this WTO rule for five years (1995–2000), which meant until February 2000, when Lomé IV expired.

In October 1997, the EC produced the 'Guidelines for the negotiation of new cooperation agreements with the African, Caribbean and Pacific countries,' which was followed by the 'Draft Negotiating Mandate' in January 1998 (House of Commons, 1998:vii). Of the four options outlined in the *Green Paper* for future EU-ACP relations, the EU identified as its major objective number three, 'splitting up the Lomé Convention into regional agreements'. To this end, the EU envisaged the gradual creation of regional economic partnership agreements (REPAs) that would eventually become reciprocal FTAs. The FTAs were to be between the EU and the three ACP regions. The foundation for the FTAs was to be established between 2000 and 2005, which was to be the transitional period during which Lomé IV would remain in place. This would mean that the EU would have to request another five-year waiver from the WTO. During this period, the EU was planning to create EU-ACP economic areas that were highly integrated. In the process of creating the FTA, the EU planned to negotiate with regional sub-groups that were pursuing regional integration strategies. The final agreements would be compatible with WTO rules (House of Commons, 1998:vii).

The LDCs who are not members of a regional sub-group would not have been requested to participate in reciprocal trade agreements. Instead, these countries would continue to enjoy the same preferential access to the EU as existed under Lomé IV. Such access would have been expanded to LDCs who are currently non-Lomé Convention members. This access would continue after 2005. Any non-LDC countries that had not negotiated a REPA with the EU by 2005 would be placed under the EU's GSP arrangements (House of Commons, 1998:vii).

The ACP countries were opposed to the creation of REPAs, largely because they did not feel their economies could withstand FTAs with the EU. This strategy, they argued, would result in their further marginalisation within the world economy. The proposed strategy was severely criticised by other entities as well. For example, the International Development Committee of the House of Commons, in response to the EU proposal for the creation of the FTAs, said it was immoral.

> It is immoral for the EU to misuse its economic strength to dictate clearly unfavourable terms to the ACP. Regional integration and subsequent liberalizing agreements with the EU should take place on a genuinely voluntary and consensual basis, not out of fear at the prospect of migration to an un-enhanced GSP (House of Commons, 1998:xxxvii).

The committee further argued,

- ▶ That the economies of the ACP were not sufficiently developed to withstand the arrival of duty-free imports from the EU;
- ▶ That the EU would not be willing to open up its market to ACP products, in particular those 'sensitive' products currently protected by the Common Agricultural Policy (CAP);
- ▶ That the timetable for the agreement of regional economic partnership agreements (five years from 2000 to 2005) was impossible to achieve and that the ACP countries lacked the capacity to enter into such negotiations;
- ▶ That there was at present inadequate regional integration amongst ACP countries and thus no basis for the proposed regional economic partnership agreements (particular mention was made of the problem of the presence in a sub-region of countries at different stages of development);
- ▶ That there was danger of trade diversion resulting from the establishment of such FTAs which would hinder the process of global trade liberalisation;
- ▶ That those non-Least developed ACP countries which failed to join an economic partnership agreement would be faced with the alternative of the inferior preferences of the GSP (House of Commons, 1998:xxxvii).

The ACP states, in their critique of the EU proposal, concurred with the above analysis. They requested a ten-year instead of a five-year waiver and therefore wanted a new EU-ACP agreement to be reached by September 2006 instead of February 2000. In addition, they wanted as much of the current arrangement to remain in place as possible, including the protocols (*The Courier*, 1999:73). They also rejected being divided as a group and the GSP as an option for future EU-ACP relations. The House of Commons International Development Committee, in quoting from a study by Jane Kennan and Chris Stevens, warned that if the non-LDC ACP countries were transferred to the GSP, their tariffs would be the equivalent of over 40 per cent of EDF funding disbursed to all ACP countries in 1994.

In addition, they would forgo an estimated ECU 767 million annually in foreign exchange (House of Commons, 1998:xxxi).

The SADC region was identified as a regional sub-group that would be targeted for a REPA and eventually an EU-SADC FTA. Although it would seem to be a huge task to get the SADC member states to unanimously agree to an EU-SADC FTA, the consequences for the region could be significant. First and foremost, the conditions in the region do not currently exist for an EU-SADC FTA. Perhaps more importantly, following the implementation of the EU-SA FTA, the region could be even farther away from being prepared to agree to an EU-SADC FTA. The former, as already indicated, could result in the destabilising of both the regional agricultural and industrial sectors. If this occurs, what would be left for the SADC member states to bargain with?

With respect to the LDCs, Wellmer notes that they would no longer have non-reciprocal EU privileges once their region entered into an FTA with the EU. In the case of Mozambique, for example, if an EU-SADC FTA was successfully negotiated, the government would have to decide whether to remain in SADC and lose its differential and favourable EU privileges, or abandon SADC and maintain the privileges. The idea of EU-FTAs with ACP countries consequently has the capacity to split up regional economic organisations (Wellmer, 1998:13–14). In the case of SADC, half the member states are LDCs.

Why did the EU propose a strategy that is clearly counterproductive to trade and development in the ACP countries? Mayer argues that in terms of Africa, there has been a 'shift in the EU from Africa as a source of resources to Africa as a market. Because they do think if they get this market they can bring down their 10 per cent unemployment'.[30] In a similar vein, Wellmer thinks the EU has determined that as a result of the end of the Cold War and developing country debt, it no longer has to pay for raw materials it needs with Lomé contracts. Consequently, the notion of non-reciprocity is now being replaced with that of reciprocity (Wellmer, 1998:1).

Needless to say, after 18 months of negotiations, the EU and ACP countries agreed not to extend Lomé IV. Instead, the Lomé Convention was replaced by the Cotonou Agreement, which is to guide EU-ACP relations for 20 years.

The Cotonou Agreement

The major objective of the Cotonou Agreement, according to the EC, is poverty reduction, which is 'to be achieved through political dialogue, development aid and closer economic and trade cooperation' (EU, 2000b). Emphasis will also be placed on democratic principles and the rule of law, respect for human rights, and good governance (EU, 2000b). With respect to the latter, many ACP countries objected to good governance being included in the new provision because, they argued, 'the concept is too vague and subjective to allow for a clear definition, let alone a balanced and equitable application' (*Lomé 2000*, 1999:1). Others feel it compromises the sovereignty of ACP countries. An integral part of the agreement contains provisions for imposing sanctions on countries that violate human rights and maintain corrupt regimes. Part of the reason for this is to send a message to European taxpayers and investors that economic aid will not be given to countries that do not maintain stable and transparent governments. This is with a view, no doubt, to satisfying critics from EU member states that are not in favour of continued EC economic support for the ACP partners. Under the new agreement, six new countries have been added, bringing the total ACP countries to 77.

The Cotonou Agreement also supports greater participation by non-state actors (civil society, trade unions, and the private sector). This is to enhance the democratic process and the more efficient implementation of project cooperation. In addition, efforts will be made to enhance peace-building and conflict prevention and resolution (EU, 2000b).

At the heart of the Cotonou Agreement remains EC support for regional integration. It is through such integration, according to the EC, that ACP countries' integration into the world economy can be facilitated. To this end, the EC still envisages the creation of REPAs, through economic partnership agreements (EPAs). The EPAs are to be negotiated between September 2002 and 31 December 2007 (the preparatory period), and are to be implemented at the latest by 1 January 2008. During a period of 12 years commencing in 2008, it is anticipated that under the EPAs, the ACPs will liberalise their trade regimes.

Although the Cotonou Agreement was signed in June 2000, it was anticipated that it would take 15 to 18 months for all the partner countries to ratify it. The EC anticipated that by September 2002 at the latest, negotiations will commence for the EPAs, which will be compliant with WTO rules and regulations, resulting in the progressive removal of barriers to trade between ACP members and the EU. During the two-year period before the beginning of negotiations, it is projected that the regional integration process will be strengthened among ACP countries as well as their capacity to be active participants in trade negotiations. A six-year period is scheduled for the negotiations for EPAs (see EU, 2000b; 2000a, part 3, title 2, chap. 2, art. 37, p. 57).

During the transition period for the creation of EPAs (September 2002 to 31 December 2007), the non-reciprocal trade preferences between the EU and the ACP countries under Lomé IV will remain in place. In 2006, a review of the arrangement for all countries will be undertaken in order to determine if negotiations are on schedule. This year was selected because the ACP countries mandated that alternative trade arrangements should be considered 'from 2006 when there will be more clarity on the revision of the EU's Generalised System of Preferences (GSP), the reform of the Common Agricultural Policy (CAP), the new millennium round in the World Trade Organisation (WTO) and EU enlargement' (*Lomé 2000*, 1999:1).

It appears that the EU, with respect to the impending negotiations for new trade agreements, is more flexible than it was when negotiations first started for a post-Lomé agreement in September 1998. For example, instead of threatening non-LDC countries with GSP rates if they did not successfully negotiate a regional FTA with the EU, EPAs will be established with ACP countries that feel they are capable of doing so (EU, 2000a, part 3, title 2, chap. 2, p. 56). If in 2004, when the EU makes an assessment as to whether non-LDCs feel they are in a position to establish EPAs, and it is determined that they are not, other alternative trade agreements will be examined 'in order to provide these countries with a new framework for trade which is equivalent to their existing situation and in conformity with WTO rules' (EU, 2000a, part 3, title 2, chap. 2, p. 56). There is no indication, however, as to what other arrangements could be made that would be compatible with WTO rules and regulations.

With fully compatible WTO regimes in place, the EC anticipates that domestic and foreign investment will flow into the ACP countries, technology transfer will occur, and there will be enhanced economic relations between ACP and EU partners. In the final analysis, the ACP countries will become more competitive and will be gradually integrated into the world economy (EU, 2000b). In addition, with the EU acting as an anchor, under the new approach, economic reforms (national and regional) will be locked in and 'open trade policies combined with social development policies will lead to economic growth with poverty reduction' (EU, 2000b). With respect to ACP and non-ACP LDCs, during early 2001, the EU agreed to give them duty-free access to the EU market for most products. Products excluded include sugar, rice, and bananas. They are to be liberalised between 2006 and 2009 (*Business Day*, 1 March 2001).

The Cotonou Agreement will be in place for 20 years. Every five years, revisions can be made to the agreement, and there will be a financial protocol every five years. Although the first financial protocol should be from 2000 to 2005 under the 9th EDF, as indicated below, it appears that this will be expanded until 2007. Allocation for the first financial protocol, which began in March 2000, is €13.5 billion for the EDF and €1.7 billion for the EIB. With respect to the EDF, €10 billion is allocated for grants, €1.3 billion for regional cooperation and integration programmes, and €2.2 billion for financing the new Industrial Facility (see below). In addition, the EIB will provide €1.7 billion in the form of loans. Added to this will be €9.9 billion of previous EDF funds that are uncommitted (EU, 2000b). Total available funds under the first financial protocol, which is scheduled to run from 2000 to 2007, will therefore be €25.1 billion.

Significant changes have been made in the Cotonou Agreement in the area of ACP-EU financial cooperation. They relate to the instruments of cooperation and programming reform. With respect to the former, the EDF instruments have been rationalised into two instead of several. EDF funding will now be channeled either through an envelope that provides grants or one that provides risk capital and loans to the private sector (EU, 2000b).

In terms of EDF grants, which are for long-term development, each ACP country will receive a lump sum that can be used for all the various programmes and projects outlined under Lomé IV. The major difference between Lomé IV and the Cotonou Agreement rests with the fact that under the new arrangement, funds are not locked into specific projects or programmes. Resources can therefore be reallocated, if necessary, where they are needed (EU, 2000b).

With respect to the envelope for risk capital and loans to the private sector, under the Cotonou Agreement, as previously mentioned, an Investment Facility (IF) has been created that will replace the risk capital and interest-rate subsidy facilities that were in existence under Lomé IV. The EIB will manage the IF, which will have €2.2 billion in allocated funds. The facility will be used to finance certain private business as well as public enterprises. It will also be involved in providing resources for privatisation and private sector development. Other funds will be made available through the EIB (EU, 2000b).

The second major change in the area of financial cooperation has to do with programming reform. Under the new arrangement, grants will be allocated following an assessment of the needs of a country and its performance. Therefore, grant allocations will no longer be an entitlement, which means that funds can be increased or decreased following the mid-term or end-of-term review of a Country Support Strategy (CSS), which each ACP country has to prepare in conjunction with the EC. Previously, the CSS was unilaterally prepared by the EC. The criteria for needs 'include per capita income, population size, economic and social development indicator (Human Development Index), level of indebtedness and dependence on export earnings' (EU, 2000b). Performance assessments will be based on the following, according to the agreement:

▶ *Progress in implementing institutional reforms*. Relates to efforts of the country concerned in reforming its institutions to ensure respect for human rights and create a climate of democracy and rule of law/fight against corruption. Link to essential elements without creating a double conditionality.

▶ *Country performance in the use of resources.* Transparency and accountability in the management of resources and quality of budget management.

▶ *Effective implementation of current operations.* Efficiency in the implementation of Community assistance, quality of dialogue with the Community in programming and implementation, respect of timetables for implementation and reviews.

▶ *Poverty alleviation or reduction.* Public expenditure in social sectors and quality of anti-poverty strategies, in particular in the social sectors. Commitment to programmes for raising the status of women and enforcing labour and social standards.

▶ *Sustainable development measures.* Commitment to principles for environmentally sustainable management of the environment and natural resources.

▶ *Macroeconomic and sectoral policy performance.* Policies and institutional framework for fiscal balance, debt sustainability and external economic and trade balance. Policy and institutional framework for encouraging competition and private sector development (EU, 2000b).

In keeping with performance assessment, the notion of rolling programming has been introduced, which stipulates that the release of financial resources will be based on needs and performance (*Lomé 2000*, 1999:2). Needless to say, not all ACP countries are pleased with the implementation of rolling programming. Both NIPs and RIPs will be subjected to rolling programming. Under the new arrangement the EC has decided that administrative and financial control will be decentralised to the Head of Delegation. The Head of Delegation will therefore have economic discretion over projects that have a certain threshold and responsibility for the review of the CSS and NIP (EU, 2000b). Although resources will be provided for fluctuations in export earnings, STABEX and SYSMIN will be discontinued.

Questions have been raised about the ability of the EU to actually implement the new approach under the Cotonou Agreement in light of the earlier problems with the EU aid programmes that include serious delays in delivery, projects that have been abandoned, shortages of staff, chronic problems with disbursement of funding, and infighting between Commission departments (IPS, 23 June 2000). It is hoped that the internal review that was undertaken by the EU in May 2000 will begin to correct these problems. How else, for example, will the EU get countries with governance capacity constraints to implement participatory development principles that involve non-state actors? Or how will the EU manage to put other new proposed policies in place, including poverty reduction, conflict prevention and resolution, anti-corruption, the integration of the ACP countries into the world economy, reform of trade cooperation and development aid, as well as reform of financial cooperation? In the final analysis, will the outcome of the Cotonou Agreement be better than that of the Lomé Convention, which S. K. B. Asante concludes became an 'empty shell' since it has not resulted in enhanced development but instead greater inequalities (Asante, 1996:385).

EU-SADC Trade Relations: The Cotonou Agreement

While it is difficult to project EU-SADC trade relations past the transitional period (September 2002 to 31 December 2007) of the Cotonou Agreement, it has been suggested that the EU would like the EU-SA FTA to serve as a model for establishing FTAs with the other ACP countries (e.g. see Eurostep, 2000; Keet, n.d.b; Morrissey, 2000b). Ideally, this is to be in the form of REPAs, that would eventually result in FTAs. In the Cotonou Agreement, however, as previously noted, there exists flexibility in the types of future trade relations between the EU and the ACP countries. The non-LDCs would seemingly have a choice between creating reciprocal REPAs, individual reciprocal EPAs, or some other undefined arrangement that would be WTO compatible. The LDCs, on the other hand, would have the option of maintaining the status quo, joining in a REPA, establishing an EPA, or some other undefined arrangement. The development of EU-SADC trade relations after 31 December 2007 will indeed be interesting.

Without the added dimension of a new EU-SADC relationship, regional trade relations will already be extremely complex, as discussed in Chapter 4. The EU-SA FTA would have been in existence for eight years and consequently would have likely re-shaped regional trade relations and industrial policy. EU competition would have resulted in regional de-industrialisation and enhanced unemployment, with more efficiently produced and cheaper EU goods having flooded the regional market. Neither regional macroeconomic stability nor economic convergence will be in place as a result of the economic destabilisation caused by both the EU-SA FTA and the SADC FTA. The bilateral trade agreements that exist among the SADC member states are likely to still be in place, thus causing conflict with the implementation of the SADC FTA. In addition, the SADC members of COMESA will likely still be involved in struggling with the inherent contradictions that are associated with being active members of two regional economic organisations involved in pursuing market integration. This will add to the complexity involving the members of SACU reconciling conflicts with the SADC-FTA. Under the best of circumstances, none of the other SADC member states would have joined the list of ACP LDCs, which currently include Angola, the DRC, Lesotho, Malawi, Mozambique, Tanzania, and Zambia. Unless efforts are made to arrest the decline of Zimbabwe's economy, it could join the ranks of this group of countries.

Under these circumstances, is it realistic to imagine the development of an EU-SADC FTA? Ideally, of course, the EU-SADC FTA would be a spin-off from the SADC FTA, assuming, of course, that the SADC FTA is functioning as a free trade area by 31 December 2007. Since the EU will have in place a *de facto* FTA with SACU, this would mean merely an extension of the agreement to the remaining nine SADC member states. The only problem, however, is that six of the nine countries would be LDCs. So would these six countries, as active members of SADC, have to be included in such an arrangement, or would the SADC FTA be established just between the EU and Mauritius, Seychelles, and Zimbabwe (provided it has not joined the ranks of the LDCs)? Or, alternatively, would individual EPAs be established between these three countries, while the current non-reciprocal arrangements remain in place between the EU and the LDCs? After all, it would be unconscionable for the EU to establish reciprocal EPAs with the LDCs.

G. K. Helleiner raises a very interesting point regarding the question of the removal of trade preferences for developing countries. He notes that

> [n]o one seems to begrudge the lowest-income countries their special terms within the IMF or the World Bank group (concessional interest rates and longer terms to maturity). Nor do many challenge their continuing need for external grants or technical assistance from bilateral donors, NGOs and the UN system. (There is no debate about the appropriate size of the need.) The only contentious question in respect of the desirability of preferential treatment therefore seems to relate to preferential *trading* arrangements (Helleiner, 1999:107).

At the foundation of the attempt to decrease or remove preferential trading arrangements is the ideology of neo-liberalism/globalisation; namely, free trade and the ability of TNCs and developed countries to have unlimited access to the markets in the developing world. This reality, however, begs the question of who ultimately will buy the products produced by the developed world if the economies of the developing world are further destroyed? With unemployment levels in some SADC member states as high as 50 per cent (70 per cent in Zimbabwe), how can the EU be preoccupied with developing reciprocal trading arrangements that will increase these statistics? Given the economic realities of the SADC region, it is not likely that REPAs or EPAs will be established between the non-SACU SADC member states in the near or distant future. However, if they are established, they will be catastrophic to regionalism in Southern Africa (Gibb, 2000:473–8).

Although the EU has indicated that the WTO rules mandate that preferential trade agreements are illegal and must be eliminated, Dot Keet argues that this is not in fact the case. The reality, according to Keet, is that the Enabling Clause allows the EU to make concessions to developing countries and LDCs that are non-reciprocal under the 'Special Differential Treatment Terms' (Keet, n.d.b:15–16). In the final analysis, Richard Gibb argues that the EU has the power to change WTO rules to allow ACP members to continue to have preferential access to the EU market. The problem, however, is that the 'EU is ... unlikely to pursue this option precisely because it supports the regulatory framework enforced by WTO rules and regulations' (Gibb, 2000:478).

REPAs with the EU under the Cotonou Agreement are obviously not a viable option for the SADC member states to pursue. It will clearly be counterproductive to regionalism and serve to split the organisation into various segments. This would be a serious contradiction in the EU's professed commitment to supporting regional integration among the ACP countries.

It will therefore be up to the SADC member states to determine the future direction of EU-SADC trade relations. Such relations must be negotiated from the perspective of not only enhancing the current preferences that the member states enjoy with the EU, but also altering the current colonial economic structures. In order to enhance SADC's integration into the world economy, greater access to the EU market must be based on the regionalisation of production in Southern Africa. In order for this to be possible, the SADC member states need to concentrate less on enhanced openness and more on national and regional development. The latter will do more to alter the region's peripheral status within the world economy than will negotiating with the triad blocs for greater access to their markets from a position of weakness. It is therefore imperative that a strategy of market integration be replaced with one that takes into consideration the realities of the SADC region and prepares Southern Africa to play a more significant role in the world economy. Otherwise, the processes of globalisation and regionalisation will leave one of the wealthiest regions in the world further marginalised.

Notes

1   The EEC was created by the Treaty of Rome on 27 March 1957.

2   For a more detailed overview of EU-ACP relations see Piening (1997, chap. 8, pp. 169–91).

3   By the end of the 1960s, the European Coal and Steel Community (ECSC), the European Atomic Energy Community (Euratom) and the EEC were fused together as the European Community.

4   The European Community became the EU in November 1993, following the coming into force of the Maastricht Treaty of 1992.

5   The EU partners include 48 African countries, 15 Caribbean countries, and eight Pacific countries. South Africa, however, joined as the 71st member in 1997 with limited accession and therefore does not enjoy the major privileges accorded to the other Lomé partners.

6   For a description and critique of the partnership, see Crawford (1996); Asante (1996); Parfitt (1996); Brigaldino (1997).

7   The GSP was approved by GATT in 1971. With the GSP, developed countries give preferential tariff treatment to developing countries.

8   These figures vary slightly from study to study. For example, a joint ACP-EC study notes that, '[t]oday, 92% of the products originating in the ACP countries enter the Community duty free (abolition of duties without quantitative limits). If we include agricultural products subject to tariff quota with zero duty, this percentage rises to over 99%. Four-fifths of the agricultural products covered by Chapters 1 to 24 of the Combined Nomenclature (CN) are completely liberalised. All industrial products falling within Chapters 25 to 97 have a tariff exemption under Lomé' (EC, 1999a:6).

9   The three new EU members were Austria, Finland, and Sweden.

10 On the question of 'policy dialogue', see also Parfitt (1996:58).

11 Interview with Nicola Delcroix, former Economic Adviser, Delegation of the European Commission in Harare, Zimbabwe, 7 July 1997.

12 *Ibid.*

13 Interview with John Robertson, Managing Director, Robertson Information Service, 13 January 1997, Harare, Zimbabwe.

14 Since it is difficult to forecast prices, McDonald provides figures from the World Bank that estimate the losses to the ACP countries in terms of the 'upper and lower bound prices of a 70% probability distribution. These estimates are used to provide an indication of the range of income transfer losses for ACP countries' (McDonald, 1996:144). The figures for the Southern African countries are as follows: Malawi – lower bound US$3 700 000, upper bound US$255 000; Mauritius – lower bound, US$88 893 000, upper bound US$6 004 000; Swaziland – lower bound US$21 334 000, upper bound US$1 441 000; Tanzania – lower bound US$1 844 000, upper bound US$125 000; and Zimbabwe – lower bound US$5 472 000, upper bound US$370 000 (McDonald, 1996:144–5).

15 Namibia was not able to participate in the Beef Protocol until the early 1990s.

16 Interview with John Robertson (see en. 13).

17 Although I was informed by Brian Kelly (DG Development) at the EC that this data was not correct, repeated efforts to get updated information were of no avail. Kelly instructed me to contact Michel Meulewaeter (Unit DEV/4), who in turn requested the information from several of his colleagues. Again, I did not receive the updated information. I can therefore only assume that the figures in Table 7.6 are correct.

18 According to the EC, 40 per cent of all South African exports go to the EU, while according to Eurostep, this figure is 30 per cent. Similarly, according to the EC, 70 per cent of all South African foreign investment is from the EU, while Eurostep indicates this figure to be 50 per cent.

19 Most of this section was published as 'The European Union-South Africa Free Trade Agreement: In whose interest?' *Journal of Contemporary African Studies*, Vol. 20, No. 1, 2002, pp. 81–106.

20 Interview with EU official, Delegation of the EC in Harare, Zimbabwe, 16 January 1997.

21 RDP stands for Reconstruction and Development Programme. This was the programme implemented by the ANC-led government to begin redressing the injustices committed during the apartheid era.

22 These findings are in Lewis (2001:38). The original study is Lewis *et al.* (1999).

23 Interview with Marina Meyer, Deputy Director, DTI, Pretoria, South Africa, 3 June 1998.

24 The sectors are as follows: meat products (Namibia, Botswana, Swaziland); dairy products (Namibia); flour-based products (Namibia); confectionery (Swaziland); sugar-based pre-mixes (Swaziland); canned fruit and jam (Swaziland); asparagus (Lesotho); glacé cherries (Swaziland); polyester material (Botswana); bath towels (Botswana); umbrellas (Lesotho); glass fibre pipes (Botswana); cars (Botswana) (Goodison, 1999:49).

25 Interview with Marina Meyer (see en. 24)

26 Interview with Willem Bosman, Director of Regional Economic Organisations, 2 June 1998, Pretoria, South Africa.

27 *Ibid.*

28 Interview with Marina Meyer (see en. 24).

29 The paper was actually published in 1997: EC, 1997b.

30 Interview with Marina Mayer (see en. 24).

E I G H T

The Way Forward

THIS BOOK HAS discussed the major challenges to regionalism in Southern Africa during the first decade of the twenty-first century. It has focused on the attempt by the SADC member states to integrate the region economically and enhance its integration into a world economy that is characterised by the processes of globalisation and regionalisation. In Chapter 1, the theoretical foundation for the book was laid by examining regionalism in Africa within the larger context of the literature on the political economy of regionalism. The second chapter provided an historical overview of the history of SADC and then described and analysed the economic and political dynamics of the region. It was determined that economic and political instability in the region poses major challenges to the implementation of a successful strategy of regionalism.

In order to understand the prospective problems associated with implementing market integration in Southern Africa, which is a major goal of SADC, the complexities of trade relations in the region were discussed in Chapter 3. Challenges to market integration identified include the lack of political commitment to regionalism by African leaders, most evident in the overlapping of membership in regional economic organisations that have similar goals and objectives. Such overlapping prevents the successful implementation of market integration specifically, and regionalism in general. Other challenges include a plethora of bilateral trade agreements, the fact that South Africa maintains a huge trade surplus with the majority of the member states, informal trade that undermines regionalism, and significant non-tariff barriers to trade.

The negotiations resulting in the creation of the SADC FTA were described and analysed in Chapter 4. It is in this chapter that the real constraints to implementing market integration are brought to the fore. The fierce competition that took place among the SADC member states during the negotiations raises concerns about the possible impact that greater openness among the member states will have on national economic development. Although increased intra-regional trade is a laudable objective, such trade should perhaps, for the present time, be concentrated in areas where countries have products that are internationally competitive and available for export to South Africa and the other SACU countries. Questions about the viability of a SADC FTA are further raised by the fact that the overlapping of membership in more than one regional economic organisation means that there exists different rules of origin and tariff regimes that make the implementation of any one trade regime very problematic. For example, while SADC has one trade regime, COMESA has another, which means that the SADC/COMESA countries can decide which trade regime is most advantageous to them. Similarly, since the bilateral trade agreements are still in place, countries can chose to trade under these arrangements instead of those agreed to under the SADC FTA. The viability of market integration is further challenged by

South Africa's plans to expand free trade agreements with other countries. Already in place is an FTA with the EU. By the beginning of the second decade of the twenty-first century, in addition to SADC and the EU, South Africa could possibly have FTAs with the US, India, Brazil (or MERCOSUR), and EFTA. Added to these challenges is the fact that the government of Zimbabwe has already begun to renege on its SADC FTA tariff commitments as a result of the economic and political instability in that country. In the end, it appears that the SADC FTA could become obsolete.

Chapter 5 examines the issue of investment in the SADC region. With the declining level of FDI, the region is challenged to put in place the necessary conditions that will result in greater private and government investment from within the region. Such investment is needed at both the national and regional levels to spearhead economic development. The Maputo Development Corridor is discussed at length, since it is an example of the successful attempt by the governments of South Africa and Mozambique to harness domestic, regional, and international investment to work toward sustained development in the region. Although lauded as a great success, it has resulted in the displacement of communities and the undermining of the economic foundation of others. In the final analysis, the chapter demonstrates that the SADC member states cannot wait on FDI to flow into the region to spearhead development.

The question of how best to integrate the SADC region into the world economy is the subject of Chapters 6 and 7. Should such integration take place through multilateralism/globalisation (e.g. the WTO) or through regionalisation via the triad blocs (US, Western Europe, Asia)? Based on the discussion in Chapter 6, it appears that increased integration through the triad blocs is a more realistic strategy for the member states to pursue. Although it is recommended that African countries, to the extent that their financial resources permit, should continue to be actively involved in the WTO, for the most part the African voice is not heard in the organisation. Integration via triad blocs is envisaged as an alternative to multilateralism, but only if such integration takes place through regional economic organisations and is facilitated by the regionalisation of production. The prospect for such integration is examined within the context of AGOA. If in fact the best option is integration through the regionalisation of production, member states are cautioned that the establishment of special trade agreements with individual member states will be counterproductive to enhanced regionalism in Southern Africa.

The triad bloc that the SADC member states are most integrated into is the EU. Economic links date back to colonial rule and are based on the SADC member states exporting low value, primary products to the EU and importing from them high value, capital-intensive products. This asymmetrical relationship has resulted in the SADC member states being further marginalised. As the EU alters its trade relationship with the SADC region, the member states will be challenged to resist attempts by the organisation to divide the region through the creation of an EU-SADC FTA. Such an FTA would be modelled after the EU-SA FTA, which is deemed to be counterproductive to the viability of regionalism in Southern Africa. With respect to openness at both the regional and international levels, the SADC member states are challenged with the reality that sustained economic development will only be realised with the implementation of viable national development strategies. Without such strategies in place, openness will result in increased economic decline for countries that are economically vulnerable.

The major findings of this book point to the reality that there are serious national, regional, and international challenges to regionalism in Southern Africa. These challenges can only be overcome if the leaders of Southern Africa are willing to rethink how they approach regionalism. This is especially the case when it comes to the issue of market integration and the degree of importance trade integration plays in the SADC regional agenda. As discussed in Chapter 2, the SADC regional agenda consists of more than the implementation of market integration via the creation of a SADC FTA. Regional cooperation through the development of sectors continues to play a prominent role in SADC's goals and objectives.

The remainder of the present chapter will focus on the prospective way forward for the SADC region. In proposing the way forward, the ideas presented originate from myself, other scholars, and SADC. The recommendations are placed within the context of the four premises that have guided the study. They are as follows:

▶ Market integration is not a viable strategy for the SADC member states to pursue. Instead, they must adopt a regional strategy that deals with the economic and political realities of the SADC region.
▶ Although market integration is not a viable strategy, many of the prerequisites for market integration must be in place for regionalism to be successful in Southern Africa.
▶ The growing regionalisation of the world economy means that Southern Africa's further integration will likely occur via the triad blocs (North America, Western Europe, Asia).
▶ Enhanced openness at the regional and international levels will not result in sustained economic development unless national development strategies are in place.

Regionalism within the Context of SADC Realities

Previously a devoted advocate of trade-focused market integration schemes, the African Development Bank, in its 2000 publication on regional integration in Africa, acknowledges that such endeavours have failed in Africa. The bank notes that '[e]ven if increased intra-regional trade is viewed as a significant means of promoting overall African economic growth and development, it would appear reasonable to embark on a road other than the narrow trade-focused approach that has been experimented with in Africa over the past four decades or so' (ADB, 2000:165–6). Both the ADB and the World Bank are advocating that a strategy be adopted by African countries that goes beyond trade-focused market integration schemes (see ADB, 2000, chap. 6; World Bank, 2000, chap. 7).

A regional strategy that deals with the economic and political realities of the SADC region should begin by unequivocally rejecting market integration at this juncture. Without the requirements imposed by market integration as discussed in Chapter 1 and operationalised in Chapter 4, instead of forcing governments to liberalise trade regimes that are not competitive, governments would be given the flexibility to determine the best strategy for enhancing trade without adversely affecting the weaker member states. For example, they would be able to consider if a strategy of planned regional comparative advantage should be developed and implemented before further trade liberalisation is pursued. In addition, consideration can be taken of the prospects for increased intra-regional trade without creating a free trade area or common market. Such increased trade would be a natural response to economic growth spearheaded from policies that enhance macroeconomic stability. This could result in the creation of a complementary trade regime. How can the production structures of regional countries be transformed without planning for such transformation? An integral part of this transformation requires governmental investment in both human capital and advanced technology for development. A strategy of regionalism that rejects market integration would allow for such planning, along with the creation of formal economic arrangements, to enhance economic interaction among member countries. The competition that arises when states at different levels of development attempt to integrate their economies by adopting a strategy of market integration can be so fierce that trade wars are created. There are indeed more productive ways to increase intra-regional trade if it remains a major priority of regional governments.

A regional strategy that transcends market integration also allows for a broader assessment of the integration process. If half of Malawi's trade with its neighbours takes place in the informal trade sector, it can be concluded that a high degree of integration exists. While such unrecorded trade would not be considered in an assessment of the degrees of integration under market integration, such integration is nonetheless significant. Huge sums of government revenue are lost annually as a result of the volume of informal trade that takes place.

Instead of being preoccupied with whether or not a country is implementing the agreed tariff regime under the SADC FTA, governments can begin to refocus their attention on providing support to informal traders in the hope of reincorporating this important sector into the formal trade sector. The need to reattach the informal sector with the formal is very apparent in Southern Africa. After all, as Belmiro Malate, former SADC Focal Point for Mozambique, argues, 'the informal traders are probably the closest thing the region has to successful entrepreneurs'. What these traders need is support from SADC governments.[1] By keeping the informal traders marginalised from the formal economy, the SADC governments lose out. For example, informal traders should be given incentives to put their money in banks. For some time the banks have been trying to tap into the financial resources of this sector. According to Malate, 'it may be that the informal ultimately become formal traders as they grow more wealthy – if the governments and banks are flexible enough to allow them to move from one sector to another easily'.[2] In addition, it has been suggested that if tariffs in the region are lowered, then informal traders will have less reason to operate illegally.[3] In the final analysis, SADC governments need to begin to provide support to this important sector.

By acknowledging the importance of the informal trade sector, a better assessment can be made of the level of regional integration that actually exists in the SADC region. After all, how can regionalism in Southern Africa be successful if people in the informal sector are not considered as an integral part of the region? Reattaching the informal sector to the formal economy would lend itself to more potential for enhancing economic development and regionalism than a policy in which member states argue over having access to each other's markets for goods they all produce.

The above approach to regionalism should be underpinned by the existing SADC regional cooperation strategy, albeit with the recommended changes outlined in Chapter 2. SADC has experienced its greatest success in implementing regional projects designed to help facilitate economic growth and development. The success of the Southern African Power Pool in integrating the electrical power grids of all the member states will not only serve to guarantee the availability of electricity when states experience shortages, but it will also make available reliable and affordable electricity to the larger population. This is simultaneously both development and integration. The development of, or improvement in, existing regional infrastructure enhances the ability of countries to have access to each other's markets, and it allows those historically marginalised because of poor infrastructure to become active participants in either their national or regional economy. Again, this is simultaneously both development and integration.

The Prerequisites for Regionalism

Although market integration as a strategy should be rejected, many of the prerequisites of market integration are required for the successful implementation of regionalism in Southern Africa. These include economic and political stability; increased intra-regional trade; enhanced investment; and a political commitment to regionalism.

Economic Stability

Macroeconomic stability is essential not only for regionalism to be successful, but also for economic growth and employment creation. All the SADC member states that are the subject of this study have at one time attempted to stabilise their macroeconomic indicators,[4] the majority through SAPs. It is the case, however, that most of these countries have experienced economic reform policy reversals. Numerous studies have been undertaken regarding the need for macroeconomic stability to be realised in order for market integration to be successful in the SADC region (e.g. SADC, 1998a; Jenkins & Thomas, 2000; Harvey, 2000a). Again, even though market integration as a strategy should be rejected, macroeconomic stability is essential if regionalism is going to be successful.

For Charles Harvey, solving the issue of macroeconomic stability among the SADC member states can only be accomplished from within the region. This could possibly be accomplished through the creation of a SADC Regional Agency of Restraint that would be designed to constrain macroeconomic extravagance. Such an agency, Harvey argues, would need to be created, 'not necessarily in order to establish a free trade area, but in order for it to have a chance of being sustained'. The agency would have to be created 'by voluntary negotiated agreement, with credible sanctions against breaking its rules' (Harvey, 2000a:17).

Harvey's idea of creating a SADC Regional Agency of Restraint should be considered as a mechanism to prevent the reversal of macroeconomic stability. At this juncture, however, creating such a mechanism might be premature, according to a comprehensive SADC study on macroeconomic convergence and adjustment discussed below.

In the above-mentioned study (SADC, 1998a) undertaken by the SADC Finance and Investment Sector Coordinating Unit, it was determined that for some time to come, SADC member states will remain committed to achieving national goals and objectives. Therefore, none of the member states are currently prepared to 'cede sovereignty and transfer even minimal macroeconomic policy-making from the national to the sub-regional level' (SADC, 1998a:7-5). A major problem the region is confronted with is the reality that the SADC economies have different: (1) structures and sizes; (2) adjustment problems; and (3) capabilities in addressing the problems. Consequently, the foundation must be laid for developing a region-wide approach to macroeconomic policy-making. This can be achieved, according to the FISCU study, through a twin-track programme designed to create institutional structures to handle macroeconomic policy-making at both the national and sub-regional levels. The overall objective of the strategy is to enhance the ability of the SADC member states to realise their regional integration objectives.

The key to laying the foundation for macroeconomic policy-making at the national level is for the SADC member states to begin to share information among themselves about their macroeconomic policy environments (including how policies are made), constraints to macroeconomic stability, and successful efforts to create macroeconomic stability. One of the major objectives of this exercise is for member states to gain an understanding of how their respective macroeconomic policies impact on other member states. The sharing of information would be designed to rid the region of the problem of 'institutional dissonance' with respect to macroeconomic policy debates and discussions. The SADC agenda can be advanced, according to the FISCU study, if each member state undertakes a national institutional macroeconomic audit in order to 'enhance the efficiency, effectiveness and transparency with which policies and outcomes that have impacts and implications for other SADC members are understood' (SADC, 1998a:7-8). The ultimate objective of the exercise would be to create a nationally based framework 'to integrate national and extra-national macroeconomic policies better and to enhance information exchange and research between member states on macroeconomic issues' (SADC, 1998a:7-8).

The national programme is to be underpinned by a sub-regional component. The success of the latter, however, is dependent on the successful implementation of the former. The immediate objective of the sub-regional approach to macroeconomic policy-making would be the exchange of information and the monitoring of national macroeconomic performance. Eventually, the FISCU study envisages that the objective of the sub-regional approach would be the coordination and harmonisation of regional macroeconomic policy-making. These objectives are to be achieved through the creation of a SADC-wide Macroeconomic Analysis and Monitoring Unit (MAMU). The only way for the MAMU to gain legitimacy is for it to be fully supported by all the SADC member states (SADC, 1998a:7-10, 7-12).

This study undertaken by FISCU and the recommendations made should be seriously considered as a way to begin to facilitate macroeconomic stability in the SADC region. As an internal regional study that included researchers from 12 SADC countries, the study is very methodical in identifying the economic problems of the region. It is also realistic in its reasoning that the first step to creating a region-wide approach to macroeconomic policy-making is for the SADC member states to undertake an assessment of their policy environment. If the member states are serious about implementing the SADC regional agenda, a collective approach to macroeconomic stability is imperative. The FISCU study therefore should be taken off the shelves in the offices of the SADC Ministries of Finance and its policy recommendations implemented.

Political Stability

At the 2001 SADC Summit held in Blantyre, Malawi, on 12–14 August the Chair of SADC, Bakili Muluzi, President of Malawi, noted that 'SADC's economic goals will be irrelevant unless the region achieves peace and security'. He expressed grave concern at the conflicts in Angola and DRC, and stressed that peace and stability were a 'prerequisite for economic growth and development' (SADC, 2001b). As mentioned in Chapter 2, the conflicts in the DRC and Angola have had a negative impact on efforts to integrate the economies of the SADC region, most evident by the fact that neither country was able to participate in the SADC FTA negotiations. Political stability is also needed in Zimbabwe in order for regionalism to be successful.

Although South Africa is deemed to be politically stable, the level of criminal violence in the country is a deterrent to foreign and domestic investors. Similarly, the fledgling democracies in Malawi and Zambia and the monarchy in Swaziland add to a growing perception that democracy has not been institutionalised in the region. As a result of ongoing challenges to the democratic process, many government leaders are using vital financial resources for patronage, instead of for development.

It is imperative that the SADC Organ on Politics, Defence and Security is utilised in such a manner that the Heads of State and Government take it upon themselves to end the various conflicts in the region and help institutionalise a culture of democracy. Otherwise, as President Muluzi notes, SADC's effort to integrate the region and foster development will be a waste of time.

Increased Intra-Regional Trade

In a study undertaken by the International Trade Centre (ITC) of UNCTAD, it was determined that significant potential for increased trade exists between SACU and the non-SACU SADC countries. In the study, the latter are referred to as the SADC 7. The DRC and Seychelles are excluded. In order to determine the increased trade potential, the ITC identified products that the SADC 7 successfully export to the world that SACU sources from the world. The study concluded that if SACU were to import these products from its regional neighbours instead of the world, intra-regional trade would be enhanced. The total potential value of this increased trade would be an estimated US$3.6 billion (see Appendix 5). A large percentage of this, US$2.6 billion, would result from SACU importing crude petroleum from Angola. Table 8.1, below, gives an indication by exporting country for this increased SACU/SADC 7 trade potential. Although the study was published in 1998, the information is based on 1995 trade statistics. This means that some of the trade potential could have already been realised. In addition to importing crude petroleum from Angola, other sectors that have tremendous potential for increased trade potential (exports to SACU) include minerals, food, beverages, tobacco, and textiles.

Table 8.1: SADC 7 Export Products with the Highest Potential for Exports to SACU by Exporting Country

Country	Products
Angola	crude petroleum; shrimps and prawns; coffee; copper waste and scrap; diamonds
Malawi	sugar; coffee; tea; tobacco; cotton; bed linen; shirts; T-shirts
Mauritius	live animals; fish; sugar; tea; dog and cat food; woven fabrics; diamonds; trousers; shirts; dresses; skirts; blouses; babies' garments; jerseys; women's apparel; tracksuits; shawls, scarves, etc.; spectacles; wrist watches; toys; articles of jewelry
Mozambique	shrimps and prawns; sugar; cotton; copra

⇨

Tanzania	live animals; shrimps and prawns; fish; beans; sugar; coffee; tea; tobacco; hides and skins; cotton; twine; refined copper; cobalt; parts for turbojets or turbopropellers; motor vehicles; shirts; T-shirts
Zambia	sugar; coffee; tobacco; copper waste and scrap; cotton and copper yarn; refined copper; cobalt mattes; electronic conductors; motor vehicles; aeroplanes and other mechanically-propelled vehicles
Zimbabwe	live animals; meat of bovine animals; wheat; maize seed; malt; sugar; coffee; tea; fruits; oilcake; tobacco; cigarettes; wood; cotton and cotton yarn; other woven fabrics; asbestos; waste and scrap of alloy steel; nickel oxide; leather products; portland cement; laminated safety glass; diamonds; refined copper; nickel (not alloyed); cloth; household articles; parts of turbojets or turbo-propellers; furniture; luggage; trousers; shirts; blouses; jerseys; T-shirts; pantihose; instruments and apparatus for physical or chemical analysis; articles of jewelry; gold; footwear

Source: Von Kirchbach and Roelofsen (1998:11)

protection
keeps from
growth

Why has this potential for increased intra-regional trade not been realised? Part of the reason, according to the ITC, is because from the perspective of South African importers, their 'import requirements are too sophisticated to be met by African countries with a generally low level of economic development' (Von Kirchbach & Roelofsen, 1998:8). Regional exporters, according to a similar study, assert that the problem stems from the fact 'that South Africa unfairly protects its industries by maintaining high levels of import duties and other barriers to products from the region' (ITC, UNCTAD/WTO, 1999:2).

Clearly, under a strategy of regionalism that is more conducive to the region, the SADC member states would seemingly be able to determine a way to foster this trade potential between SACU and the SADC 7. This could occur without fierce negotiations transpiring over having access to each other's market. All the SACU countries would have to do is make a decision to source these competitive products from their neighbours instead of from mainly Europe and the US.

Enhanced Investment

Notwithstanding the potential for increased intra-regional trade as outlined above, the real challenge for the SADC member states with respect to increased intra-regional trade is how to diversify the regional export regime in order to decrease the trade imbalance that exists between the SACU and non-SADC SACU countries. This will require a level of investment in the region that presently does not exist. Similarly, enhanced regional investment is also required to increase regional industrial development that could result in economic growth and employment creation. Also, investment is particularly needed in the development of the regional infrastructure in order to enhance the overall investment environment.

Trade Diversification

In terms of export diversification, the World Bank posits that it should be accompanied by 'a strategy for structural economic transformation', the management of which should be the responsibility of the state (World Bank, 2000:232). This will require the state to invest in new technology and provide support to domestic firms that have the potential for producing non-traditional exports. The development of non-traditional exports will be necessary if the untenable trade imbalance between SACU and the non-SACU SADC countries is to be narrowed. This should be part of a regional strategy to develop comparative advantages.

Regional Industrial Development

In the regional study conducted by FISCU on investment in the SADC region, the researchers concluded that aggressive government efforts that focus heavily on attracting foreign investment are misplaced and misdirected. Therefore, the study recommends that SADC governments begin to confront the real constraints to development in their countries instead of 'indulging in counterproductive competition ... through investment promotion missions abroad and intra-regionally competitive investment incentives to attract more foreign investment' (SADC, 1998b:7-1). Alternatively, the focus should be on increased domestic investment. According to the study,

> the key problem in SADC is not a shortage of foreign investments per se but a paucity of overall investment reflecting the absence of a strong foundation of domestic investment on which foreign investment can build. In other words, SADC's governments do not appear to have fully recognised as yet that foreign investment can only be the icing on the cake; it cannot be the cake itself (SADC, 1998b:7-1).

This emphasis on foreign investment, according to the FISCU study, appears to be two dimensional: (1) that with the diminishing levels of foreign aid, governments feel the need to focus on attracting foreign investment; and (2) public officials find it more appealing to travel abroad in search of foreign investment than remaining at home and persuading domestic entrepreneurs that they should put more of their resources into investing at home (SADC, 1998b:7-1). The researchers concluded that in order for the SADC region to attract the type of investment that is needed, primarily in the manufacturing sector, domestic investment has to be significant. Otherwise, foreign investors will be deterred from investing in a region where domestic investors are hesitant to invest (SADC, 1998b:7-4).

The FISCU report on investment outlines recommendations to SADC governments on the way forward with respect to regional investment strategies. They include major policy reforms at both the national and regional levels. In the final analysis, the FISCU report concludes that if SADC governments are going to deliver on their promises of economic and political change, they must radically revise their approaches to attracting foreign investment (SADC, 1998b:7-15).

Infrastructure Development

The importance of investing in infrastructure development as a catalyst for attracting investment as well as for enhanced regionalism was outlined in Chapter 5. Infrastructure development includes, in addition to transport systems, water systems, telecommunication services, and electricity networks. Although SADC through its sectoral development strategy continues to make tremendous progress in the area of infrastructure development, such development must continue to be a major priority for the organisation.

Political Commitment to Regionalism

It goes without saying that the SADC member states have to make a political commitment to regionalism in order for it to be successful. This means developing the ability to sacrifice short-term national interests for long-term regional interests. Can such a commitment be made, however, given the present level of tension among the leaders of the region? There is no doubt that the issues that are the greatest constraints to regional harmony must be resolved and political stability must be in place before the full benefits of the SADC regional agenda can be realised.

The ability to cede some level of sovereignty is also important if regionalism is going to work. In addition, there must be some rationalisation of the membership in regional economic organisations. Until the latter is done, how can the international community believe that the SADC member states are really serious about regionalism? As long as this is the case, the region will remain vulnerable to being exploited by external forces (governments and TNCs) that want to have access to the SADC market for their own interests.

Although all SADC member states must assume responsibility for creating a more harmonious regional environment, South Africa, as the regional giant, should take the lead. What a powerful statement South Africa would be making to the world if it announced that it would discontinue taking any actions that would be counterproductive to the SADC regional agenda. Instead of taking a protectionist stance against the other SADC member states and spreading its wings to take advantage of every opportunity that avails itself, more energy needs to be expended on enhancing regional economic development. This could help reverse the current economic decline and resultant political turmoil that is befalling all the regional countries. This seemingly would send a powerful message to both domestic and foreign investors that serious measures are being taken to correct some of the structural problems of the region. With respect to Zimbabwe, admittedly, until the crisis is resolved, the government will not likely be responsive to such a gesture.

Further Integration into the World Economy

It is imperative that the SADC region's further marginalisation within the world economy be arrested. This is going to be a daunting task as the forces of globalisation and regionalisation continue to transform the world economy. It appears that the most viable means for integration will be via the triad blocs. As discussed in this book, the only way that this integration can transpire is through the regionalisation of production in the SADC region. The attempt to comply with the apparel provision of AGOA is an example of how this can be accomplished. Beyond the textile and garment industries, however, the member states must pool their resources together to determine other areas were the regional productive capacity can be enhanced. The prospects of this occurring will depend on the SADC member states making a decision to create a complementary as opposed to a competitive trade regime.

It will also require that the South African government discontinue its effort to enhance the country's integration into the world economy unilaterally. The more FTAs South Africa signs, the greater the probability that its neighbours will be faced with more competition as a result of the porous regional borders. Such competition will result in increased de-industrialisation and further economic decline. As the regional giant, South Africa should make the prosperity of its own region its number one priority. It is precisely because the members of the triad blocs made the development of their respective regions a priority that the blocs are such powerful economic forces.

The only way that the SADC region is going to alter its status within the world is to increase the regionalisation of production. This will require all member states to make regional growth and development a priority. As noted in Chapter 1, only strong regional markets can strengthen Africa's bargaining leverage in the global economy.

Implementation of Viable National Development Strategies

As trade liberalisation under SAPs has revealed, openness to the world economy does not result in sustained economic growth or development. South Africa is a case in point to be studied by the other SADC member states. It took the government seven years to realise that without a viable development strategy in place, increased openness to the world economy would not result in sustained economic growth. Openness via the SADC FTA, participation in the WTO, AGOA, or the EU will only result in sustained economic development with the implementation of viable development strategies. In turn, only sustained economic development will result in the further integration of the SADC member states into the world economy.

The challenges to regionalism in Southern Africa are daunting. That SADC needs to reconsider its strategy of market integration is made poignant by an assessment that many politicians in the region have become disheartened because they feel that increased trade within the region may never be realised.[6] It is hoped that the alternative strategy to regionalism among the SADC member states as outlined in this chapter will be considered as SADC reassesses its goals and objectives for both integrating the region and arresting its further marginalisation within the world economy.

Notes

1   Statement made by Belmiro Malate at a conference on SADC sponsored by the Harry Frank Guggenheim Foundation, Cape Town, South Africa, 8–10 January 2001.

2   *Ibid.*

3   Discussion at the Guggenheim conference (see en. 1). Notwithstanding, NTBs to trade are more problematic than tariff barriers to trade.

4   Macroeconomic indicators include current account balance, budget deficits, foreign exchange reserves, inflation, and employment.

5   This does not ignore the fact that AGOA and the Cotonou Agreement are suppose to be WTO compatible. Some would therefore argue that all the triad bloc agreements are leading to multilateralism.

6   Discussion at the Guggenheim conference (see en. 1).

Bibliography

Ackello-Ogutu, C. and P. Echessah. *Unrecorded Cross-Border Trade Between Tanzania and Her Neighbors: Implications for Food Security.* Technical Paper No. 89, USAID, 1998.

Adedeji, Adebayo. 'Within or apart?' in Adebayo Adedeji (ed.), *South Africa and Africa: Within or Apart?* London: Zed Books, 1996.

African Business. 'Sugar warriors call cease-fire', July/August 1998, p. 38.

African Development Bank (ADB). *Economic Cooperation in Southern Africa,* Executive Summary. Great Britain: Biddles, 1993.

African Development Bank (ADB). *African Development Report 2000: Regional Integration in Africa.* London: Oxford University Press, 2000.

Alexander, Peter. 'Zimbabwean workers, the MDC & 2000 election', *Review of African Political Economy,* No. 85, 2000, pp. 385–406.

Alexander's Gas & Oil Connections, 1997. http://www.gasandoil.com/goc/news/nta72301.htm.

Aly, A. H. M. *Economic Cooperation in Africa: In Search of Direction.* Boulder: Lynne Rienner, 1994.

Amin, Samir. 'Regionalization in response to polarizing globalization', in Björn Hettne, András Inotai and Osvaldo Sunkel, (eds), *Globalism and the New Regionalism, Volume 1.* London: Macmillan, 1999.

Amin, Samir, Derrick Chitala, and Ibbo Mandaza (eds). *SADCC: Prospects for Disengagement and Development in Southern Africa.* London: Zed Books, 1987.

Arkwright, Dave and Geoff de Beer. 'The role of the private sector in regional infrastructure development', Paper presented to the ADB Regional Seminar on the Study of Economic Integration in Southern African, Johannesburg, 20–21 April 1998.

Aryeetey, Ernest and Abena D. Oduro. 'Regional integration efforts in Africa: An overview', in Jan Joost Teunissen (ed.), *Regionalism and the Global Economy: The Case of Africa.* The Hague: FONDAD, 1996.

Asante, S. K. B. 'The European Union-Africa-Caribbean-Pacific (ACP), Lomé Convention: Expectations, reality and the challenges of the 21st century', *Africa Insight,* Vol. 26, No. 4, 1996, pp. 381–91.

Asante, S. K. B. *Regionalism and Africa's Development: Expectations, Reality and Challenges.* London: Macmillan, 1997.

A. T. Kearney. *FDI Confidence Audit: South Africa,* March 2000.

Atkins, Steve and Alan Terry. 'The changing role of sugar as a vehicle for economic development within Southern Africa', in David Simon (ed.), *South Africa in Southern Africa: Reconfiguring the Region.* Oxford: James Currey, 1998; Athens: Ohio University Press; Cape Town: David Philip.

Axline, Andrew. 'Underdevelopment, dependence, and integration: The politics of regionalism in the Third World', *International Organization,* Vol. 31, No. 1, 1977, pp. 83–105.

Bach, Daniel C. 'Regionalism versus regional integration: The emergence of a new paradigm in Africa', in Jean Grugel and Wil Hout (eds), *Regionalism Across the North-South Divide.* Routledge: London, 1999a.

Bach, Daniel C. 'Revisiting a paradigm', in Daniel C. Bach (ed.), *Regionalisation in Africa: Integration and Disintegration.* Oxford: James Currey and Bloomington: Indiana University Press, 1999b.

Bach, Daniel C. 'ECOWAS: Trade, security and regionalization in West Africa. Supranationalism, hegemony and multilateralism', Paper presented at the ECOWAS/International Peace Academy seminar entitled Towards a Pax West Africana: Building Peace in a Troubled Sub-Region, ECOWAS Secretariat, Abuja, Nigeria, 27–29 September 2001.

Balaam, David N. and Michael Veseth. *Introduction to International Political Economy.* Upper Saddle River: Prentice-Hall, 1996.

Balassa, Bela A. *The Theory of Economic Integration.* Homewood: Irvin, 1961.

Bell, Paul. 'Truth or consequences', *Leadership,* Vol. 17, No. 2, 1998, pp. 27–32.

Bertelsmann, Talitha. *The European Union and South Africa: Reaching Agreement?* SAIIA Reports, No. 6, 1997.

Bertelsmann-Scott, Talitha and Claudia Mutschler. *MERCOSUR & SADC: Regional Integration in the South,* SAIIA Reports, No. 15, 1999.

Bertelsmann-Scott, Talitha, Greg Mills, and Elizabeth Sidiropoulos (eds), *The EU-SA Agreement: South Africa, Southern Africa and the European Union.* Johannesburg: SAIIA, 2000.

Bhinda, Nils, Jonathan Leape, Matthew Martin, and Stephany Griffith-Jones. *Private Capital Flows in Africa: Perception and Reality.* The Hague: FONDAD, 1999.

Bischoff, Paul-Henri and Roger Southall. 'The early foreign policy of the democratic South Africa', in Stephen Wright (ed.), *African Foreign Policies.* Boulder: Westview Press, 1999.

Black, Anthony. 'The impact of trade liberalisation on the South African automobile industry', Paper presented at the TIPS Forum, Gauteng, South Africa, September 1998.

Black, Anthony and Samson Muradzikwa. 'Prospects for the automotive industry in the SADC free trade area', *Trade and Industry Monitor,* Vol. 14, June 2000, pp. 7–14.

Bøås, Morten. 'Regions and regionalisation: A heretic's view', in *Regionalism and Regional Integration in Africa: A Debate of Current Aspect and Issues,* Discussion Paper 11, Nordic Africa Institute, 2001, pp. 27–39.

Bøås, Morten, Marianne H. Marchand and Timothy Shaw. 'The weave-world: Regionalism in the south in the new millennium', *Third World Quarterly,* Vol. 20, No. 5, 1999, pp. 1061–70.

Bourenane, Naceur. 'Theoretical and strategic approaches', in Réal Lavergne (ed.), *Regional Integration and Cooperation in West Africa: A Multidimensional Perspective.* Trenton: Africa World Press, 1997.

Bresser-Pereira, Luiz Carlos. 'The New Left viewed from the South', in Anthony Giddens (ed.), *The Global Third Way.* Cambridge: Polity Press, 2001.

Bridges Weekly Trade News Digest. ''News from the regions: Africa – COMESA launches FTA', 31 October 2000.

Bridges Weekly Trade News Digest. 'FDI flows to Africa decline', 17 July 2001.

Brigaldino, Glenn. 'African-European relations at the turning point', *Africa Today,* Vol. 44, No. 1, 1997, pp. 51–9.

Brown, William. 'Restructuring North-South relations: ACP-EU development co-operation in a liberal international order', *Review of African Political Economy,* No. 85, 2000, pp. 367–83.

Bruno, Annamaria. 'GATT agreements: Sanitary and phytosanitary measures and technical barriers to trade', Paper presented at a workshop organised by the Food and Agriculture Organisation and SADC entitled Uruguay Round Agreements – Implications for Agriculture in the SADC Region, Harare, Zimbabwe, 21–23 January 1997.

Buhera, Grace. 'Direct foreign investment trickles into SADC', SARDC, 3 April 2000.

Buhera, Grace. 'As poverty soars, how reliable is the World Bank, IMF development policy?' SARDC, 1 June 2000.

Business Day. 'More European states moot free trade with SA', 8 November 2000.

BusinessMap. *SA Insider: South African Investment Report 1997.* Johannesburg: BusinessMap, 1997.

BusinessMap. *SA Insider: South African Investment Report 1998.* Johannesburg: BusinessMap, 1998a.

BusinessMap. 'SADC Investment: Building home away from home', 27 October, 1998b.

BusinessMap. *SA Investment 1999: The Millennium Challenge.* Johannesburg: BusinessMap, 1999a.

BusinessMap. 'Maputo Corridor hits ground', 7 January 1999b.

BusinessMap. 'Investment nudge for regional transport', 7 July 1999c.

BusinessMap. *SADC Infrastructure Investment Review*, 26 August 1999d.

BusinessMap. *SA Country Risk Rating, December 2000*. Johannesburg: BusinessMap, 2000a.

BusinessMap. 'The South Africans are coming', 28 June 2000b.

BusinessMap. 'Mozal – Propelling Mozambican industrialisation', 22 September 2000c.

BusinessMap. 'The numbers game – FDI hinging on make and break deals', 17 October 2000d.

BusinessMap. 'Question mark over world FDI flows', 18 September 2001a.

BusinessMap. 'Rand devaluation – consolidating a silver lining of export growth?', 28 November 2001b.

BusinessMap. 'FDI in 2001 picks up slightly', 15 May 2002.

Bussolo, Maurizio and Henri-Bernard Solignac Lecomte. 'Trade liberalisation and poverty,' ODI Poverty Briefing, 6 December 1999.

Cassim, Rashad and Marina Mayer. 'Regional industrial development', in Lolette Kritzinger-van Niekerk (ed.), *Towards Strengthening Multisectoral Linkages in SADC*, Development Paper No. 33, Development Bank of Southern Africa, March 1997.

Cawthra, Gavin. *Brutal Force: The Apartheid War Machine*. London: International Defence and Aid Fund for Southern Africa, 1986.

Chenje, Munyaradzi. 'Internal security impacts SADC regional defence', SARDC, 21 May 1998.

Chigwedere, John. 'Zimbabwe/South Africa trade brief', Zimbabwe Ministry of Industry and Commerce, Harare, Zimbabwe, 20 July 1999.

Chimowa, Fred. 'Opportunities for private power generating companies in Southern Africa', Paper prepared for Southern African Electricity Summit Conference and Exhibition, International Conference Centre, Harare, Zimbabwe, 15–17 June 1998.

Cheru, Fantu. *The Not So Brave New World! Problems and Prospects of Regional Integration in Post-Apartheid Southern Africa*, Bradlow Series No. 6, SAIIA, May 1992.

Cilliers, Jakkie. *The SADC Organ for Defence, Politics and Security,* IDS Papers, 10 October 1996.

Cilliers, Jakkie and Mark Malan. 'South Africa and regional peacekeeping', *CSIS Africa Notes,* No. 187, August 1996.

Clapham, Christopher. 'Regional integration in Africa: Lessons and experiences', in Antoinette Handley and Greg Mills (eds), *South Africa and Southern Africa: Regional Integration and Emerging Markets.* Johannesburg: SAIIA, 1998.

Collier, Paul and Jan Willem Gunning. 'Restraint, co-operation and conditionality in African trade policy', in Ademola Oyejide, Benno Ndulu, and David Greenway (eds), *Regional Integration and Trade Liberation in SubSaharan Africa: Volume 4: Synthesis and Review.* London: Macmillan, 1999.

COMESA Trade & Customs. 'Free trade area: Concerns and options', 1 September 2000. http://www.comesa.int/trade/tradflao.htm.

Congress of South Africa Trade Unions (COSATU). Press Release, 7 June 2001.

Cornwell, Richard. 'Zimbabwe: 90 Days after the elections', Paper 46, Institute for Security Studies (ISS), October 2000.

Coughlin, Peter, Samuel Undenge, Musa Rubin, Rajesh Jeetah, and Elizabeth Mundenda. *Zimbabwe: SADC Study of the Textile Garment Industries*. SADC, March 2001.

Coughlin, Peter and Samuel Undenge. *Malawi: SADC Study of the Textile and Garment Industries*. Draft Report, SADC, March 2001.

Coughlin, Peter and Tobias Mworia. *Tanzania: SADC Study of the Textile and Garment Industries*. SADC, April 2001.

Coughlin, Peter. *Mozambique: SADC Study of the Textile and Garment Industries*. SADC, May 2001.

Courier, The. 'The signing ceremony: Relief and expectancy', No. 155, January–February 1996a, pp. 3–7.

Courier, The. 'Seeking to make the Convention more effective: An interview with Carl Greenridge, acting Secretary-General of the ACP group', No. 155, January–February 1996b, pp. 22–3.

Courier, The. 'Joint assembly begins discussion on future ACP-EU relations', No. 160, November–December 1996c, pp. 5–7.

Courier, The. 'Joint assembly in Brussels: Mulling over the Green Paper', No. 163, May–June 1997, pp. 5–10.

Courier, The. 'Comparing the ACP and EU negotiating mandate', No. 173, January–February 1999, pp. 72–4.

Crawford, Gordon. 'Whither Lomé? The mid-term review and the decline of partnership', *The Journal of Modern African Studies,* Vol. 34, No. 3, 1996, pp. 503–18.

Daily Mail and Guardian, The. 'Direct foreign investment needed to fuel economy', 23 October 2000a.

Daily Mail and Guardian, The. 'SA's economy geared for growth', 23 October 2000b.

Dalziel, Paul. 'A Third Way for New Zealand', in Anthony Giddens (ed.), *The Global Third Way.* Cambridge: Polity Press, 2001.

Dasgupta, Biplab. *Structural Adjustment, Global Trade and the New Political Economy of Development.* London and New York: Zed Books, 1998.

Davenport, Michael, Adrian Hewitt, and Antonique Koning. *Europe's Preferred Partners? The Lomé Countries in World Trade.* London: Overseas Development Institute, 1995.

Davies, Rob. 'Approaches to regional integration in the Southern African context', *Africa Insight,* Vol. 24, No. 1, 1994, pp. 11–17.

Davies, Rob. 'Promoting regional integration in Southern Africa: An analysis of prospects and problems from a South African perspective', in Larry A. Swatuk and David R. Black (eds), *Bridging the Rift: The New South Africa in Africa.* Boulder: Westview Press, 1997.

Davies, Rob. 'Forging a new relationship with the EU', in Talitha Bertelsmann-Scott, Greg Mills, and Elizabeth Sidiropoulos (eds), *The EU-SA Agreement: South Africa, Southern Africa and the European Union.* Johannesburg: SAIIA, 2000.

De Melo, Jaime and Arvind Panagriya. *The New Regionalism in Trade Policy.* Washington, DC: World Bank and London: Centre for Economic Policy Research, 1992.

De Melo, Jaime and Arvind Panagriya. 'Introduction', in Jaim de Melo and Arvind Panagriya (eds), *New Dimensions in Regional Integration.* New York: Cambridge University Press, 1993.

Dhliwayo, Dominic. 'SA-Zim trade relations nose dive', *African Business,* July/August 1997.

Dieter, Heribert, Guy Lamb and Henning Melber. 'Prospects for regional co-operation in Southern Africa', in *Regionalism and Regional Integration in Africa: A Debate of Current Aspect and Issues,* Discussion Paper 11, Nordic Africa Institute, 2001.

Driver, Amanda. 'Infrastructure, corridors, and regional integration in Southern Africa', *Trade and Industry Monitor,* Vol. 4, March 1999, pp. 16–18.

Driver, Amanda and João Gabriel de Barros. 'The impact of the Maputo Development Corridor on freight flows: An initial investigation', Working Paper 00/38, Development Policy Unit, March 2000.

Economist, The. 'Special report: Agricultural trade', 9 June 2001.

Economist Intelligence Unit, *The. EIU Country Report, Botswana, 1st Quarter 1999* (1999a).

Economist Intelligence Unit, *The. EIU Country Report, Mozambique, 1st Quarter 1999* (1999b).

El-Agraa, Ali M. (ed.). *Economic Integration Worldwide.* New York: St. Martin's Press, 1997.

Erwin, Alec. 'Preface', in Talitha Bertelsmann-Scott, Greg Mills, and Elizabeth Sidiropoulos (eds), *The EU-SA Agreement: South Africa, Southern Africa and the European Union.* Johannesburg: SAIIA, 2000.

Esterhuyen, Pieter (ed.). *Africa A–Z: Continental and Country Profiles*. Pretoria: Africa Institute of South Africa, 1998.

European Commission (EC). 'Regional cooperation in Southern Africa' [1], n.d.a.

European Commission (EC). 'Regional cooperation in Southern Africa' [2], n.d.b.

European Commission (EC). *EU-ACP Cooperation in 1995: What Form of Structural Adjustment?* Belgium: Philippe Soubestre, 1996.

European Commission (EC). *EU-ACP Cooperation in 1996: The Fight Against Poverty*. Belgium: Philippe Soubestre, 1997a.

European Commission (EC). *Green Paper on Relations between the European Union and the ACP Countries on the Eve of the 21st Century: Challenges and Options for a New Partnership*. Luxembourg: Office of Official Publications of the European Communities, 1997b.

European Commission (EC). 'Preferential trade and its perspective for Southern Africa', Paper presented at a workshop organised by the Food and Agriculture Organisation and SADC entitled Uruguay Round Agreements – Implications for Agriculture in the SADC Region, Harare, Zimbabwe, 21–23 January 1997c.

European Commission (EC). 'Analysis of trends in the Lomé Trade Regime and the consequences of retaining it', February 1999a.

European Commission (EC). 'Conclusion of EU/SA Trade, Development and Co-operation Agreement', Memo, 25 March 1999b.

European Commission (EC). 'The European Union and South Africa: An overview of the relationship in light of the conclusion of the Trade, Development and Cooperation Agreement', April 1999c.

European Commission (EC). *Partners in Progress: The EU/South Africa Trade, Development and Cooperation Agreement for the 21st Century*. Luxembourg: Office for Official Publications of the European Communities, October 1999d.

European Commission (EC). *EU-ACP Cooperation in 1998: Towards a New Long-Term Partnership Agreement*. Belgium: Philip Lowe, 1999e.

European Parliament. 'European Parliament's fact sheets – The Treaty of Rome and Green Europe', n.d. http://www.europarl.eu.int/dg4/factsheets/en/4_1_.htm.

European Research Office. 'Case studies: Analysis of the impact of an FTA on the SACU', in *Trading and Development*, Appendix IV, Brussels, 1996, pp. 183–202.

European Union (EU). *History of EU/SA Cooperation*, n.d. http://www.eusa.org./Content/ Development/ Cooperation.htm.

European Union (EU). *Partnership Agreement Between the Members of the African, Caribbean and Pacific Group of States on the One Part, and the European Community and Its Member States on the Other Part*, June 2000a.

European Union (EU). 'The European Community and its member states sign a new Partnership Agreement with the African, Caribbean and Pacific states in Cotonou, Benin', Press Release, Brussels, 21 June 2000b.

European Union (EU). 'The TDCA begins to prove its worth', Press Release, 5 June 2001. http://www. eusa.org.za/Content/TradeandEconomic/fta.html.

European Union and European Commission (EU & EC). *Development – Southern Africa and the European Union*, No. 78, July 1994.

Eurostep. 'The EU-South Africa Trade, Development and Co-operation Agreement: An analysis of the negotiating process, the agreement and the economic impact', Eurostep Briefing Paper, March 2000.

Fajgenbaum, José, Robert Sharer, Kamau Thugge, and Hema DeZoysa. 'The Cross-border initiative in Eastern and Southern Africa', IMF, 14 July 1999.

Fawcett, Louise. 'Regionalism in historical perspective', in Louise Fawcett and Andrew Hurrell (eds), *Regionalism in World Politics: Regional Organization and International Order*. Oxford: Oxford University Press, 2000.

Fawcett, Louise and Andrew Hurrell (eds), *Regionalism in World Politics: Regional Organization and International Order*. Oxford: Oxford University Press, 2000.

Financial Mail. 'When Southern Africa is nothing but a drag', 24 March 2000, pp. 1–2.

Fine, Jeffery and Stephen Yeo. 'Regional integration in sub-Saharan Africa: Dead end or a fresh start?', in Ademola Oyejide, Ibrahim Elbdawi, and Paul Collier (eds), *Regional Integration and Trade Liberalization in SubSaharan Africa, Volume 1: Framework, Issues and Methodological Perspectives*. London: Macmillan, 1997.

Fleshman, Michael. 'WTO Impasse in Seattle spotlights inequalities of global trading system', *Africa Recovery*, Vol. 13, No. 4, December 1999, pp. 1 and 30–4.

Frankel, J. and D. Romer. 'Does trade cause growth?', *American Economic Review*, Vol. 89, No. 3, 1999, pp. 379–99.

Freight & Trading Weekly. 'SADC free trade agreement makes "insignificant impact"', 2 October 2000a.

Freight & Trading Weekly. 'Maputo managers positioned to bring port up to speed', 6 October 2000b.

Freight & Trading Weekly. 'Zimbabwe now demands a carbon paper tax', 11 May 2001a.

Freight & Trading Weekly. 'Harare block trains maintain 7–10 day frequency', 22 June 2001b.

Freight & Trading Weekly. 'Zimbabwe now demands hard currency from foreigners for fuel', 17 August 2001c.

Freight & Trading Weekly. 'Vehicles account for bulk of US trade pact winners', 7 September 2001d.

George, Susan. 'TNCs: Employment is not the point', February 1999. http://www.tni.org/george/articles/point.htm.

Gerber, James. *International Economics*. Reading, Mass.: Addison-Wesley, 1999.

Gibb, Richard. 'Regional integration in post-apartheid Southern Africa: The case of renegotiating the Southern African Customs Union', *Journal of Southern African Studies*, Vol. 23, No. 1, March 1997, pp. 67–86.

Gibb, Richard. 'Post Lomé: the European Union and the South', *Third World Quarterly*, Vol. 21, No. 3, 2000, pp. 457–81.

Giddens, Anthony. 'Introduction', in Anthony Giddens (ed.), *The Global Third Way Debate*. Cambridge: Polity Press, 2001.

Gill, Stephen. 'Knowledge, politics, and neo-liberal political economy', in Richard Stubbs and Geoffrey R. D. Underhill (eds), *Political Economy and the Changing Global Order*. New York: St. Martin's Press, 1994.

Gilpin, Robert. *The Political Economy of International Relations*. Princeton: Princeton University Press, 1987.

Gilpin, Robert. *The Challenge of Global Capitalism: The World Economy in the 21st Century*. Princeton: Princeton University Press, 2000.

Global Witness. *A Crude Awakening: The Role of Oil and Banking Industries in Angola's Civil War and the Plunder of State Assets*. London: Global Witness, 1999.

Global Witness. *Conflict Diamonds: The Possibilities for the Identification, Certification and Control of Diamonds*. London: Global Witness, 2000.

Gonçalves, Fernando. 'Is SADC ready?' *Southern African Economist*, February 1998, pp. 6–7.

Goodison, Paul. 'Marginalisation or integration: Implications for South Africa's customs union partners of the South Africa-European Union trade deal', Occasional Paper, No. 22, Institute for Global Dialogue, October 1999.

Gordon, Chris. 'Zimbabwe army seeks payback in Congo', *The Daily Mail and Guardian*, 1 October 1999.

Gorjestani, Nicolas. 'Cross-border initiative in Eastern and Southern Africa: Regional integration by emergence', Africa Region FINDINGS, No. 166, World Bank Group, September 2000a.

Gorjestani, Nicolas. 'Africa cross-border initiative: Trade and investment facilitation', Africa Region INFOBRIEFS, No. 58, World Bank Group, November 2000b.

Graumans, Anne. 'The European Union-South Africa negotiations: The sting in the tail', Occasional Paper, No. 1, The Netherlands Institute for Southern Africa, Amsterdam, July 1998.

Gray, John. *False Dawn: The Delusions of Global Capitalism*. New York: New Press, 1998.

Gruhn, Isebill V. *Regionalism Reconsidered: The Economic Commission for Africa*. Boulder: Westview Press, 1979.

Haarlov, Jens. *Regional Cooperation and Integration within Industry and Trade in Southern Africa: General Approaches, SADCC and the World Bank*. Aldershot: Averbury, 1997.

Haggard, Stephen. 'Regionalism in Asia and the Americas', in Edward D. Mansfield and Helen V. Milner (eds), *The Political Economy of Regionalism: New Directions in World Politics*. New York: Columbia University Press, 1997.

Hanekom, Hermann. 'Is Zimbabwe on the brink of a dangerous precipice? A test for SADC security', *Africa Insight*, May 2000, pp. 25–8.

Hanlon, Joseph. *Beggar Your Neighbours: Apartheid Power in Southern Africa*. London: Catholic Institute for International Relations, London: James Currey, and Bloomington: Indiana University Press, 1986.

Harvey, Charles. 'Macroeconomic policy and trade integration in Southern Africa', Working Paper 00/39, Development Policy Research Unit, April 2000a.

Harvey, Charles. 'The climate for Foreign Direct Investment (FDI)', *Traders*, No. 2, April–July 2000b, pp. 28–30.

Harvey, Charles. 'The impact of the agreement on Botswana, Lesotho, Namibia and Swaziland', in Talitha Bertelsmann-Scott, Greg Mills, and Elizabeth Sidiropoulos (eds.), *The EU-SA Agreement: South Africa, Southern Africa and the European Union*. Johannesburg: SAIIA, 2000c.

Hazlewood, Arthur. 'Economic integration in East Africa', in Arthur Hazlewood (ed), *African Integration and Disintegration: Case Studies in Economic and Political Union*. London: Oxford University Press, 1967.

Hazlewood, Arthur. 'The end of the East African Community: What are the lessons for regional integration schemes?' in Ralph I. Onwuka and Amadu Sesay (eds), *The Future of Regionalism in Africa*. New York: St. Martin's Press, 1985.

Heese, Karen. 'Assessing the (slow) process of SDIs and IDZs', in *SA Investment 1999: The Millennium Challenge*. Johannesburg: BusinessMap, 1999a.

Heese, Karen. 'The investment test – policy and practice', in *SA Investment 1999: The Millennium Challenge*. Johannesburg: BusinessMap, 1999b.

Heese, Karen. 'Foreign direct investment in South Africa (1994–9) – confronting globalisation', *Development Southern Africa*, Vol. 17, No. 3, September 2000, pp. 389–400.

Helleiner, G. K. 'Linking Africa with the world: A survey of options', in Ademola Oyejide, Benno Ndulu, and David Greenway (eds), *Regional Integration and Trade Liberation in SubSaharan Africa, Volume 4: Synthesis and Review*. London: Macmillan, 1999.

Herbst, Jeffery. 'Developing nations, regional integration and globalisation', in Antoinette Handley and Greg Mills (eds), *South Africa and Southern Africa: Regional Integration and Emerging Markets*. Johannesburg: SAIIA, 1998.

Heri, S. T. 'Success stories in the export market of agricultural commodities', Paper prepared for a workshop organised by the Food and Agriculture Organisation and SADC entitled Uruguay Round

Agreements – Implications for Agriculture in the SADC Region, Harare, Zimbabwe, 21–23 January 1997.

Hess, Richard. 'Constraints on foreign direct investment', in Carolyn Jenkins, Jonathan Leape, and Lynne Thomas (eds), *Gaining from Trade in Southern Africa: Complementary Policies to Underpin the SADC Free Trade Area*. London: Macmillan, 2000.

Hettne, Björn. 'The new regionalism: Implications for development and peace', in Björn Hettne and András Inotai (eds), *The New Regionalism: Implications for Global Development and International Security*. Helsinki: United Nations University World Institute for Development Economics Research, 1994.

Hettne, Björn, 'Globalization and the new regionalism: The second great transformation', in Björn Hettne, András Inotai, and Osvaldo Sunkel (eds), *Globalism and the New Regionalism, Volume 1*. London: Macmillan, 1999a.

Hettne, Björn. 'The new regionalism: A prologue', in Björn Hettne, András Inotai, and Osvaldo Sunkel (eds), *Globalism and the New Regionalism, Volume 1*. London: Macmillan, 1999b.

Hettne, Björn, András Inotai, and Osvaldo Sunkel (eds). *Globalism and the New Regionalism, Volume 1*. London: Macmillan, 1999.

Hettne, Björn, András Inotai, and Osvaldo Sunkel (eds). *National Perspectives on the New Regionalism in the North, Volume 2*. London: Macmillan, 2000a.

Hettne, Björn, András Inotai, and Osvaldo Sunkel (eds). *National Perspectives on the New Regionalism in the South, Volume 3*. London: Macmillan, 2000b.

Hettne, Björn, András Inotai, and Osvaldo Sunkel (eds). *The New Regionalism and the Future of Security and Development, Volume 4*. London: Macmillan, 2000c.

Hettne, Björn, András Inotai, and Osvaldo Sunkel (eds). *Comparing Regionalisms: Implications for Global Development, Volume 5*. London: Macmillan, 2000d.

Hill, Nora. 'Appendix A3 – export and investment incentives by country', in Carolyn Jenkins, Jonathan Leape, and Lynne Thomas (eds), *Gaining from Trade in Southern Africa: Complementary Policies to Underpin the SADC Free Trade Area*. London: Macmillan, 2000.

Holden, Merle. *Economic Integration and Trade Liberalization in Southern Africa: Is there a Role for South Africa?* Washington, DC: World Bank, 1996.

Holland, Martin. 'South Africa, SADC, and the European Union: Matching bilateral with regional policies', *The Journal of Modern African Studies*, Vol. 35, No. 2, 1995, pp. 263–83.

Hormeku, Tetteh. 'US-Africa trade policy: In whose interest?' n.d. http://www.corpwatch.org/trac/globalization/treaties/trade8.html.

House of Commons (International Development Committee). *The Renegotiation of the Lomé Convention, Volume 1: Report and Proceedings of the Committee*. London: The Stationery Office, 21 May 1998.

Humphrey, Mike, Eline van der Linden, and Mark Gibbins. *A Study on Zimbabwe's Sensitive Products and the Non-Tariff Barriers It Faces in Its Trade with SADC*. Harare: Gemini Consulting, 1998.

Hurrell, Andrew. 'Regionalism in theoretical perspective', in Louise Fawcett and Andrew Hurrell (eds), *Regionalism in World Politics: Regional Organization and International Order*. Oxford: Oxford University Press, 2000.

Hveem, Helge. 'Political regionalism: Master or servant of economic internationalization?' in Björn Hettne, András Inotai, and Osvaldo Sunkel (eds), *Globalism and the New Regionalism, Volume 1*. London: Macmillan, 1999.

IBRD. *The New Regionalism and Its Consequences*. Washington, DC: World Bank, 1994.

Imani Development International. *Study to Determine Tariff Schedules for the Implementation of the SADC Protocol on Trade, Parts I and II*. July 1997.

International Financial Institution Advisory Commission (IFIAC). *The Meltzer Commission Report*. Washington, DC, March 2000.

International Monetary Fund (IMF). *South Africa: Selected Issues*. IMF Staff Country Report No. 98/96, September 1998.

International Monetary Fund (IMF). *Report of the Managing Director to the International Monetary and Financial Committee on the IMF in the Process of Change*. Washington, DC, 25 April 2001.

International Trade Centre (ITC), UNCTAD/WTO. *Exporting to South Africa: Statistical Indicators for Subregional Trade Potential*. Geneva, March 1999.

Intra-COMESA Imports and Intra-COMESA Exports. n.d. http://www.comesa.int/statistic/statntr.htm.

INZET, '*Prix fixe or a la carate*? Trade between the European Union and the ACP in the post-Lomé era', August 1999.

Irving, Jacqueline. 'South Africa and European Union conclude sweeping trade agreement', *Africa Recovery*, Vol. 13, No. 1, June 1999.

Jachia, Lorenza and Ethél Teljeur. 'Free trade between South Africa and the European Union: A quantitative analysis', UNCTAD Discussion Papers, No. 141, May 1999.

Jafta, Rachel and Rajesh Jeetah. *South Africa: SADC Study of the Textile and Garment Industries*. SADC, April 2001.

Jebuni, Charles D. 'Trade liberalization and regional integration in Africa', in Ademola Oyejide, Ibrahim Elbadawi, and Paul Collier (eds), *Regional Integration and Trade Liberalization in SubSaharan Africa, Volume 1: Framework, Issues and Methodological Perspectives*. London: Macmillan, 1997.

Jebuni, Charles, D., Olawale Ogunkola, and Charles C. Soludo. 'A case-study of the Economic Community of West African States (ECOWAS)', in Ademola Oyejide, Ibrahim Elbadawi, and Stephen Yeo (eds), *Regional Integration and Trade Liberation in SubSaharan Africa, Volume 3: Regional Case Studies*. London: Macmillan, 1999.

Jenkins, Carolyn and Lynne Thomas. *Is Southern Africa Ready for Regional Monetary Integration?: Convergence, Divergence and Macroeconomic Policy in SADC*, Research Report No. 10, Centre for Research into Economics and Finance in Southern Africa, June 1997.

Jenkins, Carolyn and Lynne Thomas. 'What drives growth in Southern Africa?' *Quarterly Review*, No. 1, 1999, pp. 2–11.

Jenkins, Carolyn and Lynne Thomas. 'The macroeconomic policy framework', in Carolyn Jenkins, Jonathan Leape, and Lynne Thomas (eds), *Gaining from Trade in Southern Africa: Complementary Policies to Underpin the SADC Free Trade Area*. London: Macmillan, 2000.

Jenkins, Carolyn and Lynne Thomas. 'Creating a sustainable regional framework for development: The Southern African Development Community', in Deryke Belshaw and Ian Livingston (eds), *Renewing Development in Sub-Saharan Africa: Policy, Performance and Prospects*. London and New York: Routledge, forthcoming.

Jenkins, Carolyn, Jonathan Leape, and Lynne Thomas (eds). *Gaining from Trade in Southern Africa: Complementary Policies to Underpin the SADC Free Trade Area*. London: Macmillan, 2000.

Jeetah, Rajesh and Peter Coughlin. *Mauritius: SADC Study of the Textile and Garment Industries*. SADC, April 2001.

Jeetah, Rajesh. *Namibia: SADC Study of the Textile and Garment Industries*. SADC, June 2001.

Johnson, Phyllis. 'SADC and EU minister reconfirm cooperation', SARDC, 18 October 1996.

Johnson, Phyllis and David Martin (eds). *Destructive Engagement: Southern Africa at War*. Harare: Zimbabwe Publishing House, 1986.

Jourdan, Paul. 'Spatial Development Initiatives (SDIs) – the official view', *Development Southern Africa*, Vol. 15, No. 5, Summer 1998, pp. 717–25.

Jovanovic, Miroslav. *International Economic Integration*. London and New York: Routledge, 1992.

Kaplan, David and Raphael Kaplinsky. 'Trade and industrial policy on an uneven playing field: The case of the deciduous fruit canning industry in South Africa', *World Development*, Vol. 27, No. 10, 1999, pp. 1787–801.

Kasekende, Louis A. and Nehemiah Ng'eno. 'Regional integration and economic liberalization in Eastern and Southern Africa', in Ademola Oyejide, Ibrahim Elbadawi, and Stephen Yeo (eds), *Regional Integration and Trade Liberalization in SubSaharan Africa, Volume 3: Regional Case Studies*. London: Macmillan, 1999.

Keet, Dot. 'The implications of the EU's proposed "Regional Partnership Agreements" with respect to regional integration and development in Southern Africa', n.d.a. http://www.aidc.org.za/archives/dkeet_regional_economic_partnership.html.

Keet, Dot. 'Globalisation and regionalisation: Contradictory tendencies? Counteractive tactics? Or strategic possibilities?', n.d.b. http://www.aidc.org.za/archives/dot-Keet_2.html.

Keet, Dot. 'Free-trade agreements fatal for Southern Africa', *The Weekly Mail and Guardian*, 11 August 2000.

Kegley, Charles W., Jr. and Eugene R. Wittkopf. *World Politics: Trend and Transformation* (8th edition). Boston and New York: Bedford St. Martin's Press, 2001.

Khosa, Meshack M. 'Towards a sustainable transport and communications sector in Southern Africa', *Africa Insight*, Vol. 27, No. 2, 1997, pp. 131–45.

Keohane, Robert O. and Joseph S. Nye, Jr. 'Globalization: What's new? What's not? (And so what?)', *Foreign Policy*, No. 118, Spring 2000, pp. 104–19.

Konrad Adenauer Foundation, SADC, and Advisory Service for Private Business (GTZ). *Non Tariff Trade Barriers and Regional Trade Promotion*, Conference Report, 1997.

Kornegay, Francis. 'Recasting South Africa's role in the regional and global context', unpublished submission to the forthcoming UNDP 1999/2000 *Human Development Report for South Africa*, n.d.

Krieger, Norma. 'Zimbabwe today: Hope against grim realities', *Review of African Political Economy*, No. 85, 2000, pp. 443–68.

Kritzinger-van Niekerk, Lolette (ed.). 'Towards strengthening multisectoral linkages in SADC', African Development Paper No. 33, African Development Bank, March 1997.

Krugman, Paul. *The Return of Depression Economics*. New York and London: Norton, 1999.

Kumar, Umesh. *Southern African Customs Union: Lessons for the Southern African Region*. Southern African Perspective, Working Paper Series, No. 16, Centre for Southern African Studies, Bellville, South Africa, 1992.

Kwitny, Jonathan. *Endless Enemies: The Making of an Unfriendly World*. New York: Penguin, 1986.

Lähteenmäki, Kaisa and Jyrki Käkönen. 'Regionalization and its impact on the theory of international relations', in Björn Hettne, András Inotai, and Osvaldo Sunkel (eds), *Globalism and the New Regionalism, Volume 1*. London: Macmillan, 1999.

Laidler, Michael, Claude Maeteen, and Artur Runge-Metzer. 'EU support for Zimbabwe's livestock sector: The present picture and some thoughts for the future', *The Courier*, No. 163, May–June 1997, pp. 72–3.

Landsberg, Christopher. 'The impossible neutrality? South Africa's policy towards the conflict in the DRC', unpublished paper, 2000.

Lavergne, Réal (ed.). *Regional Integration and Cooperation in West Africa: A Multidimensional Perspective*. Trenton: Africa World Press, 1997.

Leape, Jonathan. 'Taxation and fiscal adjustment', in Carolyn Jenkins, Jonathan Leape, and Lynne Thomas (eds), *Gaining from Trade in Southern Africa: Complementary Policies to Uunderpin the SADC Free Trade Area*. London: Macmillan, 2000.

Lee, Margaret C. 'Political and economic implications of sanctions against South Africa: The case of Zimbabwe', *Journal of African Studies*, Vol. 15, Nos. 3 and 4, Fall/Winter 1988, pp. 52–60.

Lee, Margaret C. *SADCC: The Political Economy of Development in Southern Africa*. Nashville: Winston-Derek, 1989.

Lee, Margaret C. 'Republic of South Africa', in Constantine P. Danopoulos and Cynthia Watson (eds), *The Political Role of the Military: An International Handbook*. Westport: Greenwood Press, 1996.

Lee, Margaret C. 'South Africa: The long and arduous road to a new dispensation', in George Akeya Agbango (ed.), *Issues and Trends in Contemporary African Politics: Stability, Development, and Democratization*. New York: Peter Lang, 1997a.

Lee, Margaret C. 'The long way to transformation in South Africa', *AAPS Newsletter,* May–August 1997b, pp. 2–6.

Lee, Margaret C. 'Development, cooperation and integration in the SADC region', in Dani Nabudere (ed.), *Globalization and the Post-Colonial African State*. Harare: AAPS Books, 2000.

Lee, Yoon. *Draft #5 Analysis of Trade and Investment Constraints in SADC for USAID's Regional Center for Southern Africa*, unpublished report, USAID, Johannesburg, 14 August 1996.

Leistner, Erich. 'Regional cooperation in sub-Saharan Africa', *Africa Insight,* Vol. 27, No. 2, 1997, pp. 112–23.

Leonard, Richard. *South Africa at War: White Power and the Crisis in Southern Africa*. Westport: Lawrence Hill, 1983.

Lewis, Jeffrey D. 'Reform and opportunity: The changing role and patterns of trade in South Africa and SADC: A synthesis of World Bank research,' Africa Region Working Paper Series, No. 14, World Bank, Washington, DC, March 2001.

Lewis, Jeffrey D., Sherman Robinson, and Karen Thierfelder. 'After the negotiations: Assessing the impact of Free Trade Agreements in Southern Africa', Trade Macroeconomic Division Working Paper No. 46, IFPRI, World Bank, September 1999.

Lindland, Jostein. 'Market opportunities for Southern Africa arising from the Uruguay Round in non-preferential agricultural commodities', Paper presented at the workshop organised by the Food and Agriculture Organization and SADC entitled Uruguay Round Agreement – Implications for Agriculture in the SADC Region, Harare, Zimbabwe, 21–23 January 1997.

Lipman, Vivienne. 'Transport: The engine of regional cooperation', in Lolette Kritzinger-van Niekerk (ed.), *Towards Strengthening Multisectoral Linkages in SADC*, Development Paper No. 33, Development Bank of Southern Africa, March 1997.

Lobe, Jim. 'New law to boost US-Africa trade: But impact on African exports will be limited', *Africa Recovery,* Vol. 14, No. 2, July 2000, pp. 11 and 26.

Lomé 2000. 'ACP-EU actors meet in Dakar', No. 10, European Centre for Development Policy Management, March 1999.

Lowe, P. 'Main parameters of the EU-SA Partnership', in Talitha Bertelsmann-Scott, Greg Mills, and Elizabeth Sidiropoulos (eds), *The EU-SA Agreement: South Africa, Southern Africa and the European Union*. Johannesburg: SAIIA, 2000.

Lowvelder, The. 'Protest against tolls continues', Supplement, 30 July 1999, p. 37.

Lyakurwa, William, Andrew McKay, Nehemiah Ng'eno, and Walter Kennes. 'Regional integration in sub-Saharan Africa: A review of experiences and issues', in Ademola Oyejide, Ibrahim Elbadawi, and Paul Collier (eds), *Regional Integration and Trade Liberalization in SubSaharan Africa, Volume 1: Framework, Issue and Methodological Perspective*. London: Macmillan, 1997.

Maasdorp, Gavin. 'A century of customs unions in Southern Africa 1889–1989', *The South African Journal of Economic History,* Vol. 5, No. 1, March 1990, pp. 10–30.

Maasdorp, Gavin. *Economic Co-operation in Southern Africa: Prospects for Regional Integration,* Conflict Studies 253, Research Institute for the Study of Conflict and Terrorism, July/August, 1992.

Maasdorp, Gavin. 'The advantages and disadvantages of current regional institutions for integration', in Pauline H. Baker, Alex Boraine, and Warren Krafchik (eds), *South Africa and the World Economy in the 1990s*. Cape Town and Johannesburg: David Philip, 1993.

Maasdorp, Gavin (ed.). *Can South and Southern Africa Become Globally Competitive Economies?* New York: St. Martin's Press, 1996.

Maasdorp, Gavin. 'Progress and issues in regional cooperation in energy utilisation, transport and communications', ADB-SEOSA Seminar, 20–21 April 1998.

Macamo, José Luis. *Estimates of Unrecorded Cross-Border Trade Between Mozambique and Her Neighbors*, Technical Paper No. 88, USAID, June 1998.

Machipisa, Lewis. 'Politics – Zimbabwe warns aid workers', *TERRAVIVA*, Vol. 4, No. 142, 25 July 2002.

MacEwan, Arthur. *Neo-Liberalism or Democracy? Economic Strategy, Markets, and Alternatives for the 21st Century*. London: Zed Books, 1999.

Madakufamba, Munetsi. 'SADC on restructuring mission', SARDC, 16 February 2001a.

Madakufamba, Munetsi. 'Major changes as SADC reforms its management structure', SARDC, 7 March 2001b.

Madakufamba, Munetsi. 'SADC trade ministers reach consensus on textiles', SARDC, 12 August 2001c.

Madakufamba, Munetsi. 'SADC integration agenda gradually comes to fruition', SARDC, 7 September 2001d.

Madakufamba, Munetsi. 'SADC joins in rejecting new round as WTO faces self-inflicted demise', SARDC, 20 September 2001e.

Madava, Tinashe. 'Land reform basis for economic development in SADC', SARDC, 5 October 2001.

Makumbe, John Mv. 'The stolen presidential election', in Margaret C. Lee and Karen Colvard (eds), *Unfinished Business: The Land Crisis in Southern Africa*. Johannesburg: Institute for Global Dialogue and New York: Harry Frank Guggenheim Foundation, forthcoming.

Malan, Mark and Jakkie Cilliers. 'SADC organ on politics, defence and security: Future development', *ISS Papers*, No. 19, March 1997.

Mandaza, Ibbo. 'Perspectives on economic cooperation and autonomous development in Southern Africa', in Samir Amin, Derrick Chitala, and Ibbo Mandaza (eds), *SADCC: Prospects for Disengagement and Development in Southern Africa*. London: Zed Books, 1987.

Mandaza, Ibbo and Arne Tostensen. *Southern Africa: In Search of a Common Future*. Gaborone: Printing & Publishing Company of Botswana, 1994.

Mansfield, Edward D. and Helen V. Milner. *The Political Economy of Regionalism: New Directions in World Politics*. New York: Columbia University Press, 1997.

Maphanyane, Emang Motlhabane. 'SADCC – future challenges', in Bertil Odén (ed.), *Southern Africa after Apartheid: Regional Integration and External Resources*. Uppsala: Nordic Africa Institute, 1993.

Marais, Hein. *South Africa: Limits to Change*. London: Zed Books, 1998.

Marchand, Marianne H., Morten Bøas, and Timothy M. Shaw. 'The political economy of new regionalisms', *Third World Quarterly*, Vol. 20, No. 5, 1999, pp. 897–910.

Martin, Guy. 'Lomé Convention', in *The Oxford Companion to Politics of the World*. New York and Oxford: Oxford University Press, 1993.

Marx, Michael T. and Christian Peters-Berries (eds). *Business Climate in Southern Africa*, Occasional Papers, Konrad Adenauer Foundation, Harare, November 1997.

Maputo Corridor Company (MCC). *Maputo Development Corridor: Summary Report*, May 1998.

Maputo Corridor Company (MCC). *Maputo Development Corridor: Summary Report*, April 1999.

Matlosa, Khabele. 'Dilemmas of security in Southern Africa: Problems and prospects for regional security co-operation', Paper prepared for the conference entitled A United States of Africa, Africa Institute of South Africa, Pretoria, 30 May–2 June 2000.

Matsebula, Michael Sisa. 'SACU and SADC: Strategic options for the future', in Chinyamata Chipeta (ed.), *Trade and Investment in Southern Africa: Towards Regional Economic Co-operation & Integration.* Harare: SAPES Books, 1998.

Matshe, Thoko. 'Just say no: Zimbabwe's National Constitutional Assembly and the constitutional referendum', *Africa Insight,* May 2000, pp. 20–4.

Mayall, James. 'National identity and the revival of regionalism', in Louise Facwett and Andrew Hurrell (eds), *Regionalism in World Politics: Regional Organization and International Order.* Oxford: Oxford University Press, 2000.

Mayer, Marina. 'The implications of the South Africa-European Union trade, development and co-operation agreement for the proposed Southern African Development Community's Free Trade Agreement', South African Department of Trade and Industry, 1999.

Mayer, Marina and Rosalind Thomas. 'Trade integration in the Southern African Development Community: Prospects and problems', in Lolette Kritzinger-van Niekerk (ed.), *Towards Strengthening Multisectoral Linkages in SADC,* African Development Paper No. 33, Development Bank of Southern Africa, March 1997.

Mazur, Jay. 'Labor's new internationalism', *Foreign Affairs,* Vol. 79, No. 1, January/February 2000, pp. 79–93.

Mbekeani, Kennedy K. 'Foreign direct investment and economic growth', NIEP Occasional Paper, September 1997. http://www.niep.org.za/resort23.htm.

Mbekeani, Kennedy. 'Obstacles to foreign investment in Southern Africa', Botswana Institute for Development Policy Analysis, September 1999.

McCarthy, Colin. 'Regional integration: Part of the solution or part of the problem?' in Stephen Ellis (ed.), *Africa Now: People, Policies, Institutions.* London: James Currey, 1996.

McCarthy, Colin. 'Regional integration in SubSaharan Africa: Past, present and future', in Ademola Oyejide, Benno Ndulu, and David Greenway (eds), *Regional Integration and Trade Liberalization in SubSaharan Africa, Volume 4: Synthesis and Review.* London: Macmillan, 1999.

McDonald, Scott. 'Reform of the EU's sugar policies and the ACP countries', *Development Policy Review,* Vol. 14, 1996, pp. 131–49.

McGowan, Patrick J. 'South Africa in SADC', Paper presented at a conference entitled New Directions in the Southern African Development Community, sponsored by the Bureau of Intelligence and Research, United States Department of State, Meridian International Center, Washington, DC, 10 December 1999.

McGowan, Patrick J. and Fred Ahwireng-Obeng. 'Partner or hegemon? South Africa in Africa, Part Two', *Journal of Contemporary African Studies,* Vol. 16, No. 2, 1998, pp. 165–95.

McQueen, Matthew. 'ACP-EU trade cooperation after 2000: An assessment of reciprocal trade preferences', *Journal of Modern African Studies,* Vol. 36, No. 4, 1998, pp. 669–92.

Meagher, Kate. 'Throwing out the baby to keep the bathwater: Informal cross-border trade and regional integration in West Africa', in *Regionalism and Regional Integration in Africa: A Debate of Current Aspects and Issues,* Discussion Paper 11, Nordic Africa Institute, 2001.

Melber, Henning. 'Regional integration in Africa: The case of SADC', *News from the Nordic Africa Institute,* No. 2, May 2001, pp. 2–4.

Mills, Greg and Claudia Mutschler (eds). *Exploring South-South Dialogue: MERCOSUR in Latin America & SADC in Southern Africa.* Johannesburg: SAIIA, 1999.

Minde, I. J. and T. O. Nakhumwa. 'Unrecorded cross-border trade between Malawi and neighboring countries', Technical Paper No. 90, USAID, September 1998.

Mistry, Percy S. 'Regional dimensions of structural adjustment in Southern Africa', in Jan Joost Tenuissen (ed.), *Regionalism and the Global Economy: The Case of Africa*. The Hague: FONDAD, 1996.

Mistry, Percy S. 'The new regionalism: Impediment or spur to future multilateralism?' in Björn Hettne, András Inotai, and Osvaldo Sunkel (eds), *Globalism and the New Regionalism, Volume 1*. London: Macmillan, 1999.

Mistry, Percy S. 'Africa's record of regional co-operation and integration', *African Affairs*, No. 99, 2000, pp. 553–73.

Mitchell, Jonathan. 'The Maputo Development Corridor: A case study of the SDI process in Mpumalanga', *Development Southern Africa*, Vol. 15, No. 5, Summer 1998, pp. 757–69.

Mittelman, James H. 'Rethinking the "New Regionalism" in the context of globlization', in Björn Hettne, András Inotai, and Osvaldo Sunkel (eds), *Globalism and the New Regionalism, Volume 1*. London: Macmillan, 1999.

Mkandawire, Thandika and Charles C. Soludo. *Our Continent, Our Future: African Perspectives on Structural Adjustment*. Dakar: CODESRIA, 1999.

Morrissey, Dorothy. 'Post-Lomé – new partnership agreed', *The Courier*, No. 179, February–March 2000a, pp. 5–7.

Morrissey, Dorothy. 'The devil is in the detail', *The Courier*, No. 180, April–May 2000b.

Mowatt, Rosalind and Themba Zulu. 'Intra-regional private capital flows in Eastern and Southern Africa: A study of South African investment', SADC Finance and Investment Sector Coordinating Unit, Department of Finance, South Africa, n.d.

Mozambique News Agency. 'Agreement on site for steel slabs factory', AIM Reports, No. 177, 1 March 2000.

Mpumalanga Report, The. Second Quarter, 1999a.

Mpumalanga Report, The. 'In deep water: Private sector bidders are losing interest in naming Maputo port the Maputo Development's Corridor's lifeline', Second Quarter, 1999b, pp. 14–15.

Mushauri, Joshua G. *Opportunities and Problems of Regional Road Freight Transport*, Occasional Papers, Konrad Adenauer Foundation, Harare, November 1997.

Mwase, Ngila and Gavin Maasdorp. 'The Southern African Customs Union', in Ademola Oyejide, Ibrahim Elbadawi, and Stephen Yeo (eds), *Regional Integration and Trade Liberation in Southern Africa, Volume 3: Regional Case Studies*. London: Macmillan, 1999.

Mytelka, Lynne Kreiger. 'Regional integration in the Third World: Some internal factors', in *International Dimensions of Regional Integration in the Third World*, Proceedings of the 5th International Conference of the ICI. Ottawa: University of Ottawa Press, 1975.

Nadal, Alejandro. '*World Investment Report 1999* flawed on many fronts', Third World Network, 2000. http://www.twnside.org.sg/title/nadal-cm.htm.

Naím, Moisés. 'Washington Consensus or Washington Confusion? *Foreign Policy*, No. 118, Spring 2000, pp. 87–103.

Ndlela, Daniel. 'Tariffs and non-tariff barriers: The case of SACU', in Chinyamata Chipeta (ed.), *Trade and Investment in Southern Africa: Towards Economic Co-operation and Integration*. Harare: SAPES Books, 1998.

Ndlela, Daniel. 'Zimbabwe's price responsiveness of exports: An analysis of export response to changes in exchange rates', Zimconsult, November 2000.

Ndlela, Daniel. Memo, 5 March 2001.

Ndlela, Daniel. 'Zimbabwe's economy since 1990', in Margaret C. Lee and Karen Colvard (eds), *Unfinished Business: The Land Crisis in Southern Africa*. Johannesburg: Institute for Global Dialogue and New York: Harry Frank Guggenheim Foundation, forthcoming.

Ndzinge, Shabani. 'Trade: Botswana in the post-apartheid era', in W. A. Edge and M. H. Lekowe (eds), *Botswana: Politics and Society*. Pretoria: J. L. van Schaik, 1998.

New York Times, The. 'Insider view: South Africa', Special Advertising Supplement, 18 September 2000.

Nkiwane, Solomon M. (ed.). *Zimbabwe's International Borders: A Study in National and Regional Development in Southern Africa*. Harare: University of Zimbabwe Publications, 1997.

Nkrumah, Kwame. *Neo-Colonialism: The Last Stage of Imperialism*. New York: International Publishers, 1965.

Odén, Bertil. 'New regionalism in Southern Africa: Part of or alternative to the globalization of the world economy?', in Björn Hettne, András Inotai, and Osvaldo Sunkel (eds), *Globalism and the New Regionalism, Volume 1*. London: Macmillan, 1999.

Office of the United States (US) Trade Representative. *U.S. Trade and Investment Policy Toward Sub-Saharan Africa and Implementation of the* African Growth and Opportunity Act. Washington, DC, May 2001.

Ojo, Oladeji, O. (ed.). *Africa and Europe: The Changing Economic Relationship*. London and New Jersey: Zed Books, 1996.

Ojo, Otatunde B. J. 'Integration in ECOWAS: Success and difficulties', in Daniel C. Bach (ed.), *Regionalism in Africa: Integration and Disintegration*. Oxford: James Currey, 1999.

Oluksohi, Adebayo O. *The Elusive Prince of Denmark: Structural Adjustment and the Crisis of Governance in Africa*, Research Report No. 104, Nordic Africa Institute, 1998.

Oman, Charles. *Globalisation and Regionalisation: The Challenge for Developing Countries*. Paris: OECD, 1994.

Onitiri, H. M. A. 'Changing political and economic conditions for regional integration in Africa', in Ademola Oyejide, Ibrahim Elbadawi, and Paul Collier (eds), *Regional Integration and Trade Liberalization in SubSaharan Africa, Volume 1: Framework, Issues and Methodological Perspectives*. London: Macmillan, 1997.

Østergaard, Tom. 'Classical models of regional integration – what relevance for Southern Africa?', in Bertil Odén (ed.), *Southern Africa After Apartheid: Regional Integration and External Resources*. Uppsala: Nordic Africa Institute, 1993.

Overseas Development Institute and Zimconsult. *SADC-EU Trade Relations in a Post-Lomé World*. London: ODI and Zimconsult, 10 April 1999.

Oxfam. *Rigged Rules and Double Standards: Trade, Globalization and the Fight against Poverty, Summary*, 2002. http://www.markettradefair.com.

Oyejide, Ademola. 'Options for future trade liberalization in SubSaharan Africa', in Ademola Oyejide, Benno Ndulu, and David Greenway (eds), *Regional Integration and Trade Liberation in SubSaharan Africa, Volume 4: Synthesis and Review*. London: Macmillan, 1999.

Oyejide, Ademola, Ibrahim Elbadawi, and Paul Collier (eds). *Regional Integration and Trade Liberalization in SubSaharan Africa, Volume 1: Framework, Issues and Methodological Perspectives*. London: Macmillan, 1997.

Oyejide, Ademola, Benno Ndulu, and Jan Willen Gunning (eds). *Regional Integration and Trade Liberation in SubSaharan Africa, Volume 2: Country Case Studies*. London: Macmillan, 1999a.

Oyejide, Ademola, Ibrahim Elbadawi, and Stephen Yeo (eds). *Regional Integration and Trade Liberation in SubSaharan Africa, Volume 3: Regional Case Studies*. London: Macmillan, 1999b.

Oyejide, Ademola, Benno Ndulu, and David Greenway (eds). *Regional Integration and Trade Liberation in SubSaharan Africa, Volume 4: Synthesis and Review*. London: Macmillan, 1999c.

Page, Sheila. 'The SADC trade protocol: Progress and constraints affecting the expansion of regional trade', EU SADC Liberalisation Seminar, Dar es Salaam, Tanzania, 5–7 May 1998.

Page, Sheila. *Regionalism among Developing Countries*. London: ODI and Macmillan, 2000.

Panos. 'Trading in futures – EU-ACP relations: Putting commerce before cooperation?', Panos Briefing No. 31, November 1998.

Panos. 'Globalisation and employment: New opportunities, real threats', Panos Briefing No. 33, May 1999.

Parfitt, Trevor. 'The decline of Eurafrica: Lomé's mid-term review', *Review of African Political Economy*, No. 67, 1996, pp. 53–66.

Partnership Agreement between the Members of the African, Caribbean and Pacific Group of States on the One Part, and the European Community and Its Member States, on the Other Part, June 2000 (the Cotonou Agreement). Brussels. More information available at http://www.europa.eu.int/comm/index_en.htm.

Peat, Alan. 'Stats bear out gloomy Zimbabwe trade picture', *Freight and Trading Weekly*, 22 June 2001.

Perry, Beth. 'Rhetoric or reality?: EU policy towards South Africa 1997–2000', Discussion Paper No. 19, Development Studies Association, European Development Policy Group, 2000.

Phaswana, F. 'Foreword: Assessing the EU-SA Agreement', in Talitha Bertelsmann-Scott, Greg Mills, and Elizabeth Sidiropoulos (eds), *The EU-SA Agreement: South Africa, Southern Africa and the European Union*. Johannesburg: SAIIA, 2000.

Piening, Christopher. *Global Europe: The European Union in World Affairs*. Boulder: Lynne Rienner, 1997.

Ralinala, Moses and Christopher Saunders. 'South Africa's regional approach, 1994–1999', Paper prepared for the conference entitled A United States of Africa, Africa Institute of South Africa, Pretoria, 30 May–2 June 2000.

Ramsamy, Prega. 'Challenges and opportunities for regional trade integration in SADC', *SADC Today*, April 1998.

Ravenhill, John. 'The future of regionalism in Africa', in Ralph I. Onwuka and Amadu Sesay (eds), *The Future of Regionalism in Africa*. New York: St. Martin's Press, 1985.

Ravenhill, John. 'Collective self-reliance or collective self delusions: Is the Lagos Plan a viable alternative?', in John Ravenhill (ed.), *Africa in Economic Crisis*. London: Macmillan, 1986.

Ravenhill, John. 'Overcoming constraints to regional cooperation in Southern Africa: Coordination rather than integration?', in *The Long-Term Perspectives Study of Sub-Saharan Africa, Volume 4: Proceedings of a Workshop on Regional Integration and Cooperation*. Washington, DC: World Bank, 1990.

Reno, William. *Warlord Politics and African States*. Boulder: Lynne Rienner, 1998.

Republic of Botswana. 'Botswana position paper: Establishment of the SACU Secretariat', Gaberone, 5 March 1999.

Republic of South Africa (RSA), 'Trade agreement between the Government of the Republic of South Africa and the Government of the Republic of Malawi', in *Government Gazette*, No. 4509, Pretoria, 20 June 1990.

Robertson, John. 'Property rights are key to successful development', *The Courier*, No. 163, May–June 1997, pp. 65–7.

Robson, Peter. *The Economics of International Integration* (2nd edition). London: George Allen and Unwin, 1980.

Rodríguez, F. and Dani Rodrik. 'Trade policy and economic growth: A skeptic's guide to the cross-national evidence', Working Paper Series 7081, National Bureau of Economic Research, 1999.

Rodrik, Dani. *The New Global Economy and Developing Countries: Making Openness Work*. Washington, DC: Overseas Development Council, 1999.

Rodrik, Dani. 'Trading in illusions', *Foreign Policy*, March/April 2001, pp. 55–62.

Rodney, Walter. *How Europe Underdeveloped Africa*. Washington, DC: Howard University Press, 1974.

Röhm, Thomas and Axel J. Halbach. 'South Africa's future economic role in Southern Africa', *Africa Insight,* Vol. 29, Nos. 1–2, 1999, pp. 56–63.

Rubin, Musa. *Botswana: SADC Study of the Textile and Garment Industries.* SADC, March 2001a.

Rubin, Musa. *Swaziland: SADC Study of the Textile and Garment Industries.* SADC, May 2001b.

Rubin, Musa and Elizabeth Mudenda. *Zambia: SADC Study of the Textile and Garment Industries.* SADC, March 2001.

Rugman, Alan. *The End of Globalization: Why Global Strategy is a Myth and How to Profit from the Realities of Regional Markets.* New York: AMACOM, 2001.

Rushmere, Martin. 'New Zimbabwe tariffs draw fire', *Freight and Trading Weekly,* 18 May 2001a.

Rushmere, Martin, 'Embattled Zimbabwe hikes import tariffs', *Freight and Trading Weekly,* 15 June 2001b.

Rushmere, Martin. 'Blooms lift Zimbabwe gloom', *Freight and Trading Weekly,* 26 July 2001c.

Ryan, Ciaran. 'Trade agreements hang in the balance', *South Africa: The Journal of Trade, Industry and Investment,* First Quarter 2000, pp. 16–19.

Sachs, J. and A. Warner. 'Economic reform and the process of global integration', *Brookings Papers on Economic Activity,* No. 1, 1995.

SADCC. 'Southern Africa: Toward economic liberation – A declaration by the governments of independent states of Southern Africa made at Lusaka on the 1st of April, 1980.'

SADC Today. 'Five member states begin implementing trade protocol', Vol. 4, No. 3, February 2001, p. 1.

Santoro, Lara. 'Carving up Congo as world stands by', *The Christian Science Monitor,* 7 August 1998.

Saunders, Richard. 'Regional focus – an investment in the making', in *SA Investment 1999: The Millennium Challenge.* Johannesburg: BusinessMap, 1999.

Sidaway, James D. and Richard Gibb. 'SADC, COMESA, SACU: Contradictory formats for regional "integration" in Southern Africa', in David Simon (ed.), *South Africa in Southern Africa: Reconfiguring the Region.* Oxford: James Currey, 1998; Athens: Ohio University Press; Cape Town: David Philip.

Sidiropoulos, Elizabeth. 'Is the EU-SA FTA a good idea for SADC?', *Traders,* No. 1, January 2000, pp. 12–14.

Sikhakhane, Jabulani. 'It's not easy being Africa's big new coloniser', *Financial Mail,* 11 December 1998.

Simon, David (ed.). *South Africa in Southern Africa: Reconfiguring the Region.* Oxford: James Currey, 1998; Athens: Ohio University Press; Cape Town: David Philip.

Söderbaum, Fredrik. *The New Regionalism and the Quest for Development Cooperation and Integration in Southern Africa,* Minor Field Study Series, No. 73, Department of Economics, University of the Lund, 1996.

Solomon, Robert. *The Transformation of the World Economy* (2nd edition). London: Macmillan, 1999.

South Africa, the Journal of Trade, Industry and Investment. 'Spoilt for choice', Fourth Quarter 1999, pp. 19–31.

South Africa, the Journal of Trade, Industry and Investment. 'Regional ports and transport corridors', First Quarter 2000, pp. 30–4.

South African Customs and Excise. *Trade Statistics for the Continent of Africa, 1998.* Pretoria, 1999.

South African Department of Trade and Industry (DTI). 'Renegotiation of the Southern African Customs Union (SACU) agreement', Mimeo, Pretoria, n.d.

South African Department of Trade and Industry (DTI). 'Granting of tariff concessions by the Republic of South Africa to the People's Republic of Mozambique', Notice 749 of 1989, Pretoria.

South African Department of Trade and Industry (DTI). 'Briefing document released to the media by the Department of Trade and Industry on 21 January, 1997', Pretoria.

South African Department of Trade and Industry (DTI). 'Briefing on SADC', Pretoria, June 1999.

Southern African Political and Economic Monthly (SAPEM). 'Interview with Kaire Mbuende', August 1996.

South African Reserve Bank (SARB). *Quarterly Bulletin*, No. 214, December 1999.

South African Reserve Bank (SARB). Research Department memo, January 2000.

Southern African Research and Documentation Centre (SARDC). 'Region upgrades transport network to boost integration', 21 May 1998a.

Southern African Research and Documentation Centre (SARDC). 'SADC aims for higher intra-regional trade', 1 October 1998b.

Southern African Research and Documentation Centre (SARDC). 'SADC drums up support for its action programme', 4 April 2000.

Southern African Research and Documentation Centre (SARDC). 'SADC puts on a new face', 30 March 2001a.

Southern African Research and Documentation Centre (SARDC). '2001 SADC summit final communiqué', 7 September 2001b.

Southern African Transport and Trade Commission (SATCC). 'Agenda Item No. 4, Transport and communications integration study for Southern Africa', Maputo, May 1998.

'Spatial Development Initiatives in Southern Africa', n.d. http://www.sdi.org.za.

Stahl, Heinz-Michael. '"Hard core" tariffs on intra-SADC trade, and their elimination in the context of the implementation of the SADC Trade Protocol', Briefing Paper, Trade and Industrial Policy Secretariat, December 1997.

Stern, Matthew and Christopher Stevens. 'FTAs with India and Brazil: An initial analysis', TIPS Working Paper No. 10, Johannesburg, TIPS, 2000.

Stevens, Christopher. 'The single European market: Opportunities and challenges in trade', in Oladeji O. Ojo (ed.), *Africa and Europe: The Changing Economic Relationship.* London and New Jersey: Zed Books, 1996.

Steward, John. 'When trade is not free', *Enterprise,* Vol. 104, November 1996, pp. 51–3.

Stiglitz, Joseph. 'More instruments and broader goals: Moving toward the post-Washington Consensus', the 1998 WIDER Annual Lecture, Helsinki, 7 January 1998.

Stiglitz, Joseph. 'What I learned at the world economic crisis', *The New Republic Online,* 7 April 2000. http://www.thenewrepublic.com/041700/stiglitz041700.html.

Stiglitz, Joseph. 'An agenda for development for the twenty-first century', in Anthony Giddens (ed.), *The Global Third Way Debate.* Cambridge: Polity Press, 2001.

Swatuk, Larry A. and David R. Black (eds). *Bridging the Rift: The New South Africa in Africa.* Boulder: Westview Press, 1997.

Tandon, Yash. 'The role of foreign direct investment in Africa's human development', Paper commissioned under a project funded by UNCTAD, 2000. http://www.attac.org/fra/list/doc/tandon.htm.

Tenuissen, Jan Joost (ed.). *Regionalism and the Global Economy: The Case of Africa.* The Hague: FONDAD, 1996.

Theobald, Stuart. 'Watch out for the law of unintended consequences', *Financial Mail*, 15 September 2000.

Thomas, Rosalind H. *A SADC Sugar Agreement in the Context of the WTO and Global Sugar Trade.* Johannesburg: Institute for Global Dialogue, 2001.

Tiepoh, Geepu Nah. 'The AGOA: Another dictated trade regime?', *The Perspective*, 30 May 2001.

Trans African Concessions (TRAC), 'Frequently asked questions,' n.d. http://www.tracn4.co.za/FAQcat.htm.

Traders. 'Cross border business linkages in the Maputo Development Corridor', No. 1, January 2000, pp. 42–4.

Tsie, Balefi. 'States and markets in the Southern African Development Community (SADC): Beyond the neo-liberal paradigm', *Journal of Southern African Studies*, Vol. 22, No. 1, March 1996, pp. 75–98.

Tsikata, Yvonne M. 'Southern Africa: Trade, liberalization and implications for a Free Trade Area', TIPS 1999 Annual Forum, Muldersdrift, 19–22 September, 1999.

United Nations (UN). *The ECA and Africa: Accelerating a Continent's Development*. New York and Geneva: UN, 1999.

United Nations (UN). *Expert Panel Report on Sanctions Against Unita*. New York: UN, March 2000.

United Nations (UN). *World Economic and Social Survey 2001: Trends and Policies in the World Economy*. New York: UN, 2001.

United Nations Conference on Trade and Development (UNCTAD). *Foreign Direct Investment in Africa: Performance and Potential*. New York and Geneva: UN, 1999.

United Nations Conference on Trade and Development (UNCTAD). *World Investment Report 2000: Cross-Border Mergers and Acquisitions and Development*. New York and Geneva: UN, 2000.

United Nations Development Programme (UNDP). *Human Development Report 1999*. New York and Oxford: Oxford University Press, 1999.

United Nations Development Programme (UNDP). *Human Development Report 2000*. New York and Oxford: Oxford University Press, 2000.

United Nations Development Programme (UNDP). *Human Development Report 2001*. New York and Oxford: Oxford University Press, 2001.

United Nations Development Programme (UNDP). *Human Development Report 2002*. New York and Oxford: Oxford University Press, 2002.

United Nations Security Council. *Addendum to the Report of the Panel of Experts on the Illegal Exploitation of Natural Resources and Other Forms of Wealth of the Democratic Republic of the Congo, November 13, 2001*. New York: UN.

United States Congress. *Trade and Development Act of 2000*, 24 January 2000.

United States House of Representatives. 'Royce lauds progress on Africa trade bill enhancement', Press Release, 17 October 2001.

Van Nieuwkerk, Anthoni. 'Regionalism into globalism? War into peace? SADC and ECOWAS compared', *African Security Review*, Vol. 10, No. 2, 2001, pp. 8–18.

Van Rooyen, Carina. 'Regional integration as a development strategy: The case of the SADC', *Africa Insight*, Vol. 28, Nos. 3–4, 1998, pp. 125–32.

Viner, Jacob. *The Customs Union Issue*. New York: Carnegie Endowment for International Peace, 1950.

Von Kirchbach, Friedrich and Hendrik Roelofsen. *African Development in a Comparative Perspective*. Geneva: UNCTAD/WTO, 1998a.

Von Kirchbach, Friedrich and Hendrik Roelofsen. *Trade in the Southern Africa Development Community: What is the Potential for Increasing Exports to the Republic of South Africa?* Study No. 11, International Trade Centre, UNCTAD/WTO, Geneva, September 1998b.

Watts, Patrick. 'Losing Lomé: The potential impact of the commission guidelines on the ACP non-least developed countries', *Review of African Political Economy*, No. 75, 1998, pp. 47–71.

Weekly Mail and Guardian, The. 'New scramble for Africa', 13 November 1998.

Weeks, John. 'Regional cooperation and Southern African development', *Journal of Southern African Studies*, Vol. 22, No. 1, March 1996, pp. 99–117.

Wellmer, Gottfried. 'SADC agricultural trade with the EU in the post Lomé future', Paper prepared for Action for Southern Africa, June 1998.

Williamson, John. 'What Washington means by policy reform', in John Williamson (ed.), *Latin American Adjustment: How Much Has Happened?* Washington, DC: Institute for International Economics, 1990.

World Bank. *Cross-Border Initiative: Eastern and Southern Africa and Indian Ocean, Volume 2.* Washington, DC, 1995.

World Bank. *Cross-Border Initiative: Eastern and Southern Africa and Indian Ocean, Volume 3.* Washington, DC: 1998.

World Bank. *Can Africa Claim the 21st Century?* Washington, DC, 2000.

World Bank. 'World Bank calls on rich countries to open their market for the poor and their children', News Release No. 2001/243/S, 26 February 2001.

World Trade Organisation (WTO). *Trade Policy Review: Republic of South Africa,* Report by the Secretariat, April 1998.

Wyatt-Walter, Andrew. 'Regionalism, globalization, and world economic order', in Louise Fawcett and Andrew Hurrell (eds), *Regionalism in World Politics: Regional Organization and International Order.* Oxford: Oxford University Press, 2000.

Yergin, Daniel. *The Commanding Heights: The Battle Between Government and the Marketplace that is Remaking the Modern World.* New York: Simon & Schuster, 1998.

ZANU-PF. http://www.zanupfpub.co.za/resettlement.html.

Zehender, Wolfgang. *Cooperation Versus Integration: The Prospects of the Southern African Development Coordination Conference (SADCC).* Berlin: German Development Institute, 1983.

Zimbabwe Human Rights Non-Governmental Organisations Forum. 'Who is responsible? A preliminary analysis of pre-election violence in Zimbabwe', 20 June 2000. http://www.hrforumzim.com/evmpreports/whoisresp/whois000620.htm.

Zimbabwe Ministry of Industry and Commerce. 'Trade brief on Zimbabwean/Namibia trade agreement', Harare, 1997.

Zimbabwe Ministry of Industry and Commerce. 'SADC Trade Protocol negotiation and the wayforward [*sic*] in the year 2000', Presentation by the Secretary for Industry and Commerce to the 1999 ZNCC Congress, Victoria Falls, Zimbabwe, 24–26 June 1999a.

Zimbabwe Ministry of Industry and Commerce. 'Zimbabwe/South Africa trade negotiations held on 15th July 1999', Harare, 20 July 1999b.

Zimbabwe Ministry of Industry and Commerce. *Report of the First SADC High-Level Committee Meeting on Rules of Origin.* Harare, 18 February 2000a.

Zimbabwe Ministry of Industry and Commerce. *Report on the 18th SADC Trade Negotiating Forum Meeting (TNF) and the 10th Special Industry and Trade Ministers Committee (CMT) Meeting, 28th August – 1 September 2000.* Harare, 15 September 2000b.

SADC Documents

SADC. n.d. http://www.eia.doe.gov/emeu/cabs/sadc.html.

SADC. *Declaration Treaty and Protocol of Southern African Development Community.* Gaborone: Printing & Publishing Company Botswana, 1993.

SADC. SADC Protocol on Trade, 24 August 1996.

SADC. *Review and Rationalisation of the SADC Programme of Action, Volume1: Executive Report.* April 1997a.

SADC. *Review and Rationalisation of the SADC Programme of Action, Volume 2: Main Report.* April 1997b.

SADC. *Transport and Communications.* Windhoek, 9–10 February 1997c.

SADC. *Finance and Investment Sector Co-ordinating Unit Research Project on: Macroeconomic Convergence and Adjustment.* March 1998a.

SADC. *Finance and Investment Sector Co-ordinating Unit Research Project on: Investment.* March 1998b.

SADC. *Finance and Investment Sector Co-ordinating Unit Research Project on: Development Finance and the Need for a Sub-Regional Development Financing Institution in SADC.* March 1998c.

SADC. *The Official SADC Trade, Industry and Investment Review 1998.* Gaborone, Botswana: Southern African Marketing and SADC, 1998d.

SADC, 1999a and 1999b: see under the heading **Trade Negotiation Documents**, below.

SADC. *SADC Garment and Textile Industry Roundtable: Consultants' Report,* 9 October 1999c.

SADC. *The Official SADC Trade, Industry and Investment Review 2000: The Millennium Issue.* 2000a. http://www.sadcreview.com

SADC. *Report of the SADC Council of Ministers on the Review of the Operations of SADC Institutions.* 28 November 2000b.

SADC. *SADC Annual Report 2000.* 2000c.

SADC. '2001 SADC summit final communiqué', 7 September 2001.

SADCC. *Southern Africa: Toward Economic Liberalization – A Declaration by the Governments of Independent States of Southern Africa Made at Lusaka on the 1st of April, 1980.*

SADCC. *Towards Economic Integration: The Proceedings of the 1992 Annual Consultative Conference Held in Maputo, Republic of Mozambique, 29th–31st January 1992.* Gaborone: Printing & Publishing Company Botswana, 1992.

Trade Negotiation Documents

'Consolidated Text on Rules of Administration of MMTZ/SACU Quota System for Textile and Clothing Products', Working Paper, Mauritius, 28 August 2000.

'Record of the 6th Meeting of the SADC Trade Negotiating Forum (TNF)', Windhoek, 2–4 November 1998.

'Record of the 7th Meeting of the SADC Trade Negotiating Forum (TNF)', Harare, 25–29 January 1999.

'Record of the 8th meeting of the SADC Trade Negotiating Forum (TNF)', Pretoria, 22–26 February 1999.

'Record of the 9th Meeting of the SADC Trade Negotiating Forum (TNF)', Maputo, 22–26 March 1999.

'Record of the 10th Meeting of the SADC Trade Negotiating Forum (TNF)', Blantyre, 19–23 April 1999.

'Record of the 11th Meeting of the SADC Trade Negotiating Forum (TNF)', Lusaka, 7–11 June 1999.

'Record of the 12th Meeting of the SADC Trade Negotiating Forum (TNF)', Gaborone, 7–9 July 1999.

'Record of the 13th Meeting of the SADC Trade Negotiating Forum (TNF)', Cape Town, 6–8 September 1999.

'Record of the 14th Meeting of the SADC Trade Negotiating Forum (TNF)', Dar es Salaam, 3–5 November 1999.

'Record of the 15th Meeting of the SADC Trade Negotiating Forum (TNF)', Pretoria, 14–15 December 1999.

'Record of the 18th Meeting of the SADC Trade Negotiating Forum (TNF)', Pointe Aux Piments, Mauritius, 29–30 August 2000.

Report on the SADC-USAID Textiles and Garments Roundtable. Johannesburg, 9 October 1999.

Report of the Third Meeting of the Technical Committee on Sugar, Pretoria, 14 December 1999.

'Record of the 1st Meeting of the SADC High Level Committee (HLC) on Rules of Origin', Pointe Aux Piment, Mauritius, 31 January–4 February 2000.

'Record of the 2nd Joint Meeting of the SADC Sub-Committee on Customs Cooperation and Trade Facilitation', Dar es Salaam, 1–2 November 1999.

'Record of the 4th Joint Meeting of the SADC Sub-Committee on Customs Cooperation and Trade Facilitation', 31 January–1 February 2000.

'Record of the 6th Joint Meeting of the SADC Sub-Committee on Customs Cooperation and Trade Facilitation', Pointe Aux Piments, Mauritius, 28–29 August 2000.

'Record of the 6th Special Meeting of the SADC Industry and Trade Committee of Ministers', Dar es Salaam, 8 November 1999.

'Record of the 7th Special Meeting of the SADC Industry and Trade Committee of Ministers', Pretoria, 17 December 1999.

'Record of the 8th Special Meeting of the SADC Industry and Trade Committee of Ministers', Sandton, South Africa, 31 March 2000.

'Record of the 9th Special Meeting of the SADC Industry and Trade Committee of Ministers', Windhoek, 4 August 2000.

'Record of the 10th Special Meeting of the SADC Industry and Trade Committee of Ministers', Pointe Aux Piments, Mauritius, 1 September 2000.

'Record of the 14th Meeting of the SADC Industry and Trade Committee of Ministers', Maseru, 16 June 2000.

'Record of the 1st Meeting of the Committee on Wheat Flour', Pointe Aux Piment, Mauritius, 28 August 2000.

SADC. 'Consideration for product specific rules of origin in the context of the SADC Trade Protocol', Dar es Salaam, 27 May 1999a.

SADC. 'SADC rules of origin', Gaborone, 13 July 1999b.

Electronic Resources

http://www.comesa.int/background/backhist.htm.

http://www.eusa.org./Content/Development/Cooperation.htm.

http://www.mozal.com/news/press/pr58.htm.

http://www.ft.com/ftsurvey/country/sc86ea.htm.

http://www.eia.doe.gov/emeu/cabs/sadc.html.

Newspapers, Magazines, etc.

Addis Tribune (Addis Ababa)

African Eyes News Service

BBC News

Bridges Weekly Trade News Digest (Geneva)

Buanews (Pretoria)

Business Day (Johannesburg)

Freight & Trading Weekly (South Africa)

Inter Press Service (IPS)

Mozambique News Agency

New Vision (Kampala)

Panafrican News Agency (Dakar)

Public Agenda (Accra)

Reuters

SADC Today

Southern African Political and Economic Monthly (SAPEM)

Slate

The Christian Science Monitor

The Courier (Brussels)

The Daily Mail and Guardian (Johannesburg)

The Daily News (Zimbabwe)

The Economist

The Economist Intelligence Unit

The Electronic Telegraph

The Financial Mail (Johannesburg)

The Financial Gazette

The Financial Gazette (Zimbabwe)

The Guardian (Lagos)

The Insider (Harare)

The Namibian (Windhoek)

The New York Times

The Perspective (Smyma, Georgia, USA)

The Post (Lusaka)

The Times (London)

The Times of Zambia (Lusaka)

The Washington Post

The Weekly Mail and Guardian (Johannesburg)

The Zimbabwe Independent (Harare)

The Zimbabwe Standard (Harare)

THISDAY (Lagos)

Trade and Industry Monitor

UN Integrated Regional Information Network (UNIRIN)

WildNet Africa News Archive

Appendix 1: Direction of Trade Tables

Trade by Exporting Country, 1990–98

Total – all commodities (US$ '000)	Value								
Exporter **Angola**	1990	1991	1992	1993	1994	1995	1996	1997	1998
Importer DRC	0	890	0	0	0	0	0	0	0
Importer Malawi	0	0	0	0	0	0	0	0	0
Importer Mauritius	0	0	0	0	0	0	0	0	0
Importer Mozambique	0	0	0	0	0	0	0	0	0
Importer Seychelles	0	0	0	0	0	0	0	0	0
Importer South Africa	298	0	239	342	4 747	978	779	4 420	2 738
Importer Tanzania	0	9 364	0	0	0	0	0	5	0
Importer Zambia	0	0	0	0	0	0	0	0	0
Importer Zimbabwe	0	0	0	0	232	0	7	0	0

Total – all commodities (US$ '000)	Value								
Exporter **DRC**	1990	1991	1992	1993	1994	1995	1996	1997	1998
Importer Angola	0	0	0	0	0	0	0	0	0
Importer Malawi	0	0	0	0	0	10	0	0	0
Importer Mauritius	556	248	492	939	659	188	1 138	72	309
Importer Mozambique	0	0	0	0	0	0	0	0	0
Importer Seychelles	0	0	0	0	0	16	7	0	0
Importer South Africa	0	0	3 924	80 305	99 453	100 701	111 880	89 133	3 863
Importer Tanzania	0	0	0	0	0	0	0	144	0
Importer Zambia	0	0	0	0	0	0	0	0	0
Importer Zimbabwe	1 098	414	374	227	24	391	222	241	0

Total – all commodities (US$ '000)		Value								
Exporter	**Malawi**	1990	1991	1992	1993	1994	1995	1996	1997	1998
Importer	Angola	0	284	0	0	79	0	0	0	0
Importer	DRC	0	965	0	0	766	498	0	0	0
Importer	Mauritius	418	485	310	93	58	368	449	74	72
Importer	Mozambique	0	1 494	0	0	4 339	8 722	10 735	0	0
Importer	Seychelles	45	0	0	38	38	81	50	0	0
Importer	South Africa	0	44 400	46 821	48 809	50 233	45 794	68 942	85 123	71 525
Importer	Tanzania	0	2 162	0	0	2 222	6 453	0	2 773	0
Importer	Zambia	0	3 271	0	0	4 033	5 096	0	0	0
Importer	Zimbabwe	4 844	3 293	2 641	2 107	6 169	7 000	23 685	15 937	0

Total – all commodities (US$ '000)		Value								
Exporter	**Mauritius**	1990	1991	1992	1993	1994	1995	1996	1997	1998
Importer	Angola	0	0	0	0	14	0	0	0	0
Importer	DRC	69	0	473	79	21	43	0	40	0
Importer	Malawi	117	5	133	595	1 647	669	3 877	3 352	1 717
Importer	Mozambique	0	33	1 142	4 935	678	217	22	41	362
Importer	Seychelles	3 771	11 071	2 650	3 849	3 582	3 521	2 390	3 455	4 685
Importer	South Africa	6 917	5 192	12 230	7 152	5 720	6 348	12 198	9 084	7 664
Importer	Tanzania	71	183	636	2 108	140	948	4 701	637	3 164
Importer	Zambia	269	1 356	1 090	1 191	593	247	41	791	171
Importer	Zimbabwe	4 170	4 776	4 213	5 746	6 265	9 068	10 475	14 745	6 677

Total – all commodities (US$ '000)		Value								
Exporter	**Mozambique**	1990	1991	1992	1993	1994	1995	1996	1997	1998
Importer	Angola	0	0	0	0	727	138	479	0	0
Importer	DRC	0	0	0	0	288	5	129	0	0
Importer	Malawi	0	1 647	0	0	1 075	2 556	1 423	0	0
Importer	Mauritius	47	1 337	143	0	0	121	0	962	5 316
Importer	Seychelles	0	656	0	0	0	0	0	0	0
Importer	South Africa	0	0	17 810	18 440	28 606	41 277	43 323	37 059	36 151
Importer	Tanzania	0	0	0	0	1 080	114	4 060	5 067	0
Importer	Zambia	0	0	0	0	102	47	106	0	0
Importer	Zimbabwe	671	4 971	5 012	701	7 057	7 847	10 923	22 819	0

Total – all commodities (US$ '000)	Value								
Exporter	**Seychelles** 1990	1991	1992	1993	1994	1995	1996	1997	1998
Importer	Angola	0	0	0	0	0	0	0	0
		0							
Importer	DRC	0	0	0	0	0	0	0	0
		0							
Importer	Malawi	0	31	0	0	0	0	0	0
		0							
Importer	Mauritius	135	1 057	1 186	1 809	246	256	407	250	1 340
Importer	Mozambique	0	39	0	0	0	0	0	0
		0							
Importer	South Africa	124	59	279	255	375	425	999	1 330	1 543
Importer	Tanzania	0	0	0	0	0	22	0	0
		0							
Importer	Zambia	0	0	0	0	0	0	0	0
		0							
Importer	Zimbabwe	0	0	124	0	0	0	0	0
		0							

Total – all commodities (US$ '000)	Value								
Exporter	**South Africa** 1990	1991	1992	1993	1994	1995	1996	1997	1998
Importer	Angola	0	0	131 046	82 419	87 050	113 290	362 458	183 796	198 393
Importer	DRC	0	0	103 998	98 086	104 157	191 237	143 959	181 921	182 520
Importer	Malawi	0	229 299	250 455	185 474	175 270	172 427	224 432	236 015	222 253
Importer	Mauritius	148 732	200 815	145 236	161 987	169 574	219 050	201 565	202 458	179 248
Importer	Mozambique	0	0	244 742	302 734	322 599	444 589	414 933	427 334	403 270
Importer	Seychelles	25 233	22 196	22 175	29 662	27 662	35 572	40 185	40 291	33 519
Importer	Tanzania	0	0	9 836	18 264	50 930	156 781	99 948	103 044	135 988
Importer	Zambia	0	0	400 680	409 432	317 902	360 214	421 734	452 671	378 834
Importer	Zimbabwe	445 758	578 570	573 745	762 428	727 391	1 228 940	1 188 735	1 080 531	899 366

Total – all commodities (US$ '000)	Value								
Exporter	**Tanzania** 1990	1991	1992	1993	1994	1995	1996	1997	1998
Importer	Angola	0	0	0	0	0	0	0	108	0
Importer	DRC	0	0	0	0	0	0	0	8 842	0
Importer	Malawi	0	488	0	0	1 366	2 086	0	5 473	0
Importer	Mauritius	420	6 861	1 633	2 360	900	1 630	225	832	22
Importer	Mozambique	0	0	0	0	0	0	0	273	0
Importer	Seychelles	70	0	0	0	0	46	0	0	0
Importer	South Africa	0	0	3 562	6 488	4 415	4 552	5 176	8 318	3 903
Importer	Zambia	0	0	0	0	0	0	0	1 602	0
Importer	Zimbabwe	1 764	2 751	6 030	1 381	699	1 806	2 288	17 023	0

Total – all commodities (US$ '000)		Value								
Exporter	**Zambia**	1990	1991	1992	1993	1994	1995	1996	1997	1998
Importer	Angola	0	0	0	0	0	0	0	0	0
Importer	DRC	0	0	0	0	0	0	0	0	0
Importer	Malawi	0	5 373	0	0	13 342	6 064	0	0	0
Importer	Mauritius	14	20	0	0	0	12	0	1 475	74
Importer	Mozambique	0	0	0	0	103	352	206	0	0
Importer	Seychelles	0	0	0	0	0	0	8	0	0
Importer	South Africa	0	0	15 525	23 206	28 869	26 200	22 449	37 082	41 767
Importer	Tanzania	0	0	0	0	0	0	0	4 073	0
Importer	Zimbabwe	10 815	11 165	14 016	13 999	6 507	15 695	14 808	26 942	0

Total – all commodities (US$ '000)		Value								
Exporter	**Zimbabwe**	1990	1991	1992	1993	1994	1995	1996	1997	1998
Importer	Angola	11 881	7 231	4 522	3 283	10 628	11 982	7 198	7 473	0
Importer	DRC	14 685	7 977	3 449	3 967	18 263	8 675	6 416	9 912	0
Importer	Malawi	73 013	37 779	41 274	43 784	80 856	50 252	62 389	80 808	0
Importer	Mauritius	789	996	3 777	5 547	7 097	8 434	3 485	4 667	5 770
Importer	Mozambique	55 598	34 961	43 246	55 311	55 260	54 526	74 776	72 343	0
Importer	Seychelles	166	477	1 018	365	431	1 381	4 865	2 547	0
Importer	South Africa	229 525	218 396	246 105	261 197	354 279	348 954	318 305	356 872	177 487
Importer	Tanzania	12 212	3 666	3 024	5 013	25 168	9 942	5 180	13 678	0
Importer	Zambia	52 958	45 508	49 180	68 607	65 608	95 719	93 531	119 193	0

Trade by Importing Country, 1990–98

Total – all commodities (US$ '000)	Value								
Importer **Angola**	1990	1991	1992	1993	1994	1995	1996	1997	1998
Exporter DRC	0	0	0	0	0	0	0	0	0
Exporter Malawi	0	284	0	0	79	0	0	0	0
Exporter Mauritius	0	0	0	0	14	0	0	0	0
Exporter Mozambique	0	0	0	0	727	138	479	0	0
Exporter Seychelles	0	0	0	0	0	0	0	0	0
Exporter South Africa	0	0	131 046	82 419	87 050	113 290	362 458	183 796	198 393
Exporter Tanzania	0	0	0	0	0	0	0	108	0
Exporter Zambia	0	0	0	0	0	0	0	0	0
Exporter Zimbabwe	11 881	7 231	4 522	3 283	10 628	11 982	7 198	7 473	0

Total – all commodities (US$ '000)	Value								
Importer **DRC**	1990	1991	1992	1993	1994	1995	1996	1997	1998
Exporter Angola	0	890	0	0	0	0	0	0	0
Exporter Malawi	0	965	0	0	766	498	0	0	0
Exporter Mauritius	69	0	473	79	21	43	0	40	0
Exporter Mozambique	0	0	0	0	288	5	129	0	0
Exporter Seychelles	0	0	0	0	0	0	0	0	0
Exporter South Africa	0	0	103 998	98 086	104 157	191 237	143 959	181 921	182 520
Exporter Tanzania	0	0	0	0	0	0	0	8 842	0
Exporter Zambia	0	0	0	0	0	0	0	0	0
Exporter Zimbabwe	14 685	7 977	3 449	3 967	18 263	8 675	6 416	9 912	0

Total – all commodities (US$ '000)	Value								
Importer **Malawi**	1990	1991	1992	1993	1994	1995	1996	1997	1998
Exporter Angola	0	0	0	0	0	0	0	0	0
Exporter DRC	0	0	0	0	0	10	0	0	0
Exporter Mauritius	117	5	133	595	1 647	669	3 877	3 352	1 717
Exporter Mozambique	0	1 647	0	0	1 075	2 556	1 423	0	0
Exporter Seychelles	0	31	0	0	0	0	0	0	0
Exporter South Africa	0	229 299	250 455	185 474	175 270	172 427	224 432	236 015	222 253
Exporter Tanzania	0	488	0	0	1 366	2 086	0	5 473	0
Exporter Zambia	0	5 373	0	0	13 342	6 064	0	0	0
Exporter Zimbabwe	73 013	37 779	41 274	43 784	80 856	50 252	62 389	80 808	0

Total – all commodities (US$ '000)	Value								
Importer	**Mauritius**	1990	1991	1992	1993	1994	1995	1996	1997	1998
Exporter	Angola	0	0	0	0	0	0	0	0	0
Exporter	DRC	556	248	492	939	659	188	1 138	72	309
Exporter	Malawi	418	485	310	93	58	368	449	74	72
Exporter	Mozambique	47	1 337	143	0	0	121	0	962	5 316
Exporter	Seychelles	135	1 057	1 186	1 809	246	256	407	250	1 340
Exporter	South Africa	148 732	200 815	145 236	161 987	169 574	219 050	201 565	202 458	179 248
Exporter	Tanzania	420	6 861	1 633	2 360	900	1 630	225	832	22
Exporter	Zambia	14	20	0	0	0	12	0	1 475	74
Exporter	Zimbabwe	789	996	3 777	5 547	7 097	8 434	3 485	4 667	5 770

Total – all commodities (US$ '000)	Value								
Importer	**Mozambique**	1990	1991	1992	1993	1994	1995	1996	1997	1998
Exporter	Angola	0	0	0	0	0	0	0	0	0
Exporter	DRC	0	0	0	0	0	0	0	0	0
Exporter	Malawi	0	1 494	0	0	4 339	8 722	10 735	0	0
Exporter	Mauritius	0	33	1 142	4 935	678	217	22	41	362
Exporter	Seychelles	0	39	0	0	0	0	0	0	0
Exporter	South Africa	0	0	244 742	302 734	322 599	444 589	414 933	427 334	403 270
Exporter	Tanzania	0	0	0	0	0	0	0	273	0
Exporter	Zambia	0	0	0	0	103	352	206	0	0
Exporter	Zimbabwe	55 598	34 961	43 246	55 311	55 260	54 526	74 776	72 343	0

Total – all commodities (US$ '000)	Value								
Importer	**Seychelles**	1990	1991	1992	1993	1994	1995	1996	1997	1998
Exporter	Angola	0	0	0	0	0	0	0	0	0
Exporter	DRC	0	0	0	0	0	16	7	0	0
Exporter	Malawi	45	0	0	38	38	81	50	0	0
Exporter	Mauritius	3 771	11 071	2 650	3 849	3 582	3 521	2 390	3 455	4 685
Exporter	Mozambique	0	656	0	0	0	0	0	0	0
Exporter	South Africa	25 233	22 196	22 175	29 662	27 662	35 572	40 185	40 291	33 519
Exporter	Tanzania	70	0	0	0	0	46	0	0	0
Exporter	Zambia	0	0	0	0	0	0	8	0	0
Exporter	Zimbabwe	166	477	1 018	365	431	1 381	4 865	2 547	0

Total – all commodities (US$ '000)	Value								
Importer **South Africa**	1990	1991	1992	1993	1994	1995	1996	1997	1998
Exporter Angola	298	0	239	342	4 747	978	779	4 420	2 738
Exporter DRC	0	0	3 924	80 305	99 453	100 701	111 880	89 133	3 863
Exporter Malawi	0	44 400	46 821	48 809	50 233	45 794	68 942	85 123	71 525
Exporter Mauritius	6 917	5 192	12 230	7 152	5 720	6 348	12 198	9 084	7 664
Exporter Mozambique	0	0	17 810	18 440	28 606	41 277	43 323	37 059	36 151
Exporter Seychelles	124	59	279	255	375	425	999	1 330	1 543
Exporter Tanzania	0	0	3 562	6 488	4 415	4 552	5 176	8 318	3 903
Exporter Zambia	0	0	15 525	23 206	28 869	26 200	22 449	37 082	41 767
Exporter Zimbabwe	229 525	218 396	246 105	261 197	354 279	348 954	318 305	356 872	177 487

Total – all commodities (US$ '000)	Value								
Importer **Tanzania**	1990	1991	1992	1993	1994	1995	1996	1997	1998
Exporter Angola	0	9 364	0	0	0	0	0	5	0
Exporter DRC	0	0	0	0	0	0	0	144	0
Exporter Malawi	0	2 162	0	0	2 222	6 453	0	2 773	0
Exporter Mauritius	71	183	636	2 108	140	948	4 701	637	3 164
Exporter Mozambique	0	0	0	0	1 080	114	4 060	5 067	0
Exporter Seychelles	0	0	0	0	0	22	0	0	0
Exporter South Africa	0	0	9 836	18 264	50 930	156 781	99 948	103 044	135 988
Exporter Zambia	0	0	0	0	0	0	0	4 073	0
Exporter Zimbabwe	12 212	3 666	3 024	5 013	25 168	9 942	5 180	13 678	0

Total – all commodities (US$ '000)	Value								
Importer **Zambia**	1990	1991	1992	1993	1994	1995	1996	1997	1998
Exporter Angola	0	0	0	0	0	0	0	0	0
Exporter DRC	0	0	0	0	0	0	0	0	0
Exporter Malawi	0	3 271	0	0	4 033	5 096	0	0	0
Exporter Mauritius	269	1 356	1 090	1 191	593	247	41	791	171
Exporter Mozambique	0	0	0	0	102	47	106	0	0
Exporter Seychelles	0	0	0	0	0	0	0	0	0
Exporter South Africa	0	0	400 680	409 432	317 902	360 214	421 734	452 671	378 834
Exporter Tanzania	0	0	0	0	0	0	0	1 602	0
Exporter Zimbabwe	52 958	45 508	49 180	68 607	65 608	95 719	93 531	119 193	0

Total – all commodities (US$ '000)		Value								
Importer	**Zimbabwe**	1990	1991	1992	1993	1994	1995	1996	1997	1998
Exporter	Angola	0	0	0	0	232	0	7	0	0
Exporter	DRC	1 098	414	374	227	24	391	222	241	0
Exporter	Malawi	0	3 271	0	0	4 033	5 096	0	0	0
Exporter	Mauritius	4 170	4 776	4 213	5 746	6 265	9 068	10 475	14 745	6 677
Exporter	Mozambique	671	4 971	5 012	701	7 057	7 847	10 923	22 819	0
Exporter	Seychelles	0	0	0	0	0	0	0	0	0
Exporter	South Africa	445 758	578 570	573 745	762 428	727 391	1 228 940	1 188 735	1 080 531	899 366
Exporter	Tanzania	1 764	2 751	6 030	1 381	699	1 806	2 288	17 023	0
Exporter	Zambia	10 815	11 165	14 016	13 999	6 507	15 695	14 808	26 942	0

Notes: 1) Source of data used by TIPS: *World Trade Analyzer 1980–98* (Statistics Canada)
2) All figures in current US dollars
3) South African data refers to the Southern African Customs Union (SACU) and hence includes data for Botswana Lesotho, Namibia, and Swaziland

Tables prepared by Arjen van Zwieten, Data Unit Manager, TIPS.

Appendix 2: Informal Trade Tables

Table 1: Malawi and Neighbouring Countries: Informal Trade Balance Sheet (US$ '000)

Trade with	Exports			Imports			Balance		Trade balance
	Agricul-tural	Non-agricultural	Total	Agricul-tural	Non-agricultural	Total	Agricul-tural	Non-agricultural	Total
Zambia	732	2 592	3 324	7 884	9 303	17 187	–7 152	–6 711	–13 863
Mozambique	945	2 933	3 878	6 501	255	6 756	–5 556	2 678	–2 878
Tanzania	762	5 738	6 500	660	5 749	6 409	102	–11	91
Total	2 439	11 263	13 702	15 045	15 307	30 352	–12 606	–4 044	–16 650

Source: Minde and Nakhumwa (1998:32)

Table 2: Malawi Export and Import Trade: A Comparison of Formal and Informal Trade (US$ '000)

Trading with	Exports			Imports		
	Formal	Informal	% of formal to informal	Formal	Informal	% of formal to informal
Zambia	2.5	3.3	75.8	13.2	17.2	76.7
Mozambique	5.2	3.9	133	4.4	6.8	64.7
Tanzania	1.8	6.5	27.7	1.3	6.4	20.3
Total	9.5	13.7	69.3	18.9	30.4	62.2

Source: Minde and Nakhumwa (1998:39)

Table 3: Estimated Annual Value of Mozambique's Informal Trade with Neighbours and Overall Trade Balance (US$ '000)

Neighbours	Mozambique's exports	Mozambique's imports	Total informal trade	Informal trade balance
Swaziland	30 599	50 689	81 288	–20 090
South Africa	1 303	32 092	33 395	–30 789
Zimbabwe	406	7 295	7 701	–6 889
Malawi	1 367	2 812	4 179	–1 445
Zambia	217	417	634	–200
Tanzania	2 950	4 643	7 593	–1 693

Source: Macamo (1998:4)

Table 4: Comparison of Formal and Informal Trade with Mozambique and Her Neighbours (US$ '000)

Mozambique and Swaziland				
Type of activity	Formal trade	Informal trade	Total trade	Share of informal trade %
	1996	1995–96		
Exports to Swaziland	103	30 599	30 702	99.66
Imports from Swaziland	10 000	50 689	60 689	83.52
Total	**10 103**	**81 288**	**91 391**	**88.95**

Mozambique and South Africa				
Type of activity	Formal trade	Informal trade	Total trade	Share of informal trade %
	1996	1995–96		
Exports to SA	43 800	1 303	45 103	2.89
Imports from SA	255 000	32 092	287 092	11.18
Total	**298 800**	**33 395**	**332 195**	**10.05**

Mozambique and Zimbabwe				
Type of activity	Formal trade	Informal trade	Total trade	Share of informal trade %
	1996	1995–96		
Exports to Zimbabwe	9 800	406	10 206	3.98
Imports from Zimbabwe	29 700	7 295	36 995	19.72
Total	**39 500**	**7 701**	**47 201**	**16.32**

Mozambique and Malawi				
Type of activity	Formal trade	Informal trade	Total trade	Share of informal trade %
	1996	1995–96		
Exports to Malawi	1 400	1 367	2 767	49.40
Imports from Malawi	10 700	2 812	13 512	20.81
Total	**12 100**	**4 179**	**16 279**	**25.67**

Mozambique and Zambia				
Type of activity	Formal trade	Informal trade	Total trade	Share of informal trade %
	1996	1995–96		
Exports to Zambia	106	217	323	67.18
Imports from Zambia	207	417	624	66.83
Total	**313**	**634**	**947**	**66.95**

Mozambique and Tanzania				
Type of activity	Formal trade	Informal trade	Total trade	Share of informal trade %
	1996	1995–96		
Exports to Tanzania	3 956	2 950	6 906	42.72
Imports from Tanzania	54	4 643	4 697	98.85
Total	**4 010**	**7 593**	**11 603**	**65.44**

Source: Macamo (1998:32–42)

Table 5: Tanzania and Neighbouring Countries: Informal Balance Sheet (US$ '000)

	Exports	Imports	Total	Trade balance
Malawi				
Agricultural	272	3 471	3 743	–3 199
Other	1 081	767	1 848	314
Total	**1 353**	**4 238**	**5 591**	**–2 885**
Zambia				
Agricultural	3 374	5 670	9 044	–2 296
Other	358	157	515	201
Total	**3 372**	**5 827**	**9 559**	**–2 095**
Mozambique				
Agricultural	287.3	2 246	2 533.3	–1 958.7
Other	4 229	929	5 158	3 300
Total	**4 516.3**	**3 175**	**7 691.3**	**1 341.3**
Overall total	**9 241.3**	**13 240**	**22 841.3**	**–3 638.7**

Source: Ackello-Ogutu and Echessah (1998)

Table 6: Comparison of Formal and Informal Trade Statistics (US$ million)

Country	Formal 1995	Informal 1995–96	Total	Informal trade as % of total trade
Zambia	14	9.7	23.7	40.9
Malawi	3	5.7	8.7	65.5
Mozambique	12	7.7	19.7	39.1
Total	**29**	**23.1**	**52.1**	**48.5**

Source: Ackello-Ogutu and Echessah (1998:23)

Appendix 3: SADC Trade Offers

Table 1: Mozambique's Trade Offers

Offer to South Africa				
Category	Tariff lines	%	Trade (US$ '000)	%
A	1 223	23.42	59 719	17.12
B	3 551	68.02	198 733	56.97
B1	1 526	29.23	44 101	12.64
B2	2 025	38.79	154 632	44.33
C	447	8.56	90 386	25.91
C1	259	4.46	29 344	8.41
C2	85	1.63	60 998	17.49

Differentiated Trade Offer							
Share of imports by categories				Liberalisation schedule			
	US$ '000	SADC %				US$ '000	SADC %
A	54 523	15.63	Immediate	(to zero on year 1)	A	54 523	15.63
B	166 465	47.72	Frontloaded	(started on year 0)		74 163	21.26
B1 (from year 0)	21 263	6.10		(linear till year 8)	B1	21 263	
B2 (from year 6)	145 202	41.62		(linear till year 15)	C1	52 900	
C	114 994	32.96	Backloaded	(satisfying asymmetry criterium)		207 296	59.42
C1 (from year 0)	52 900	15.16	Strict gradual	(from year 6 to 8)	B2	145 202	41.62
C2 (from year 10)	62 094	17.80	Strict sensitive	(from year 11 to 15)	C2	62 094	17.80
E	12 858	3.69	Excluded	(not liberalising)	E	12 858	3.69
Total imports from SADC	348 840	100.00				348 840	

Note: Trade figures based on 1997 imports

Source: 'Record of the 14th Meeting of the SADC Industry and Trade Committee of Ministers', Maseru, Lesotho, 16 June 2000, p. 10.

Table 2: Zambia's Trade Offers

Offer to South Africa						
	Tariff lines	%	1997 SADC imports (US$)	%	Non-RSA imports (US$)	%
Category A	3 229	53.7	208 337 629	48.9	37 945 734	45.4
Category B	2 550	42.4	166 491 063	39.1	36 650 564	43.9
Category C	233	3.9	51 377 473	12.0	8 900 610	10.7
Total	6 012		426 206 165		83 496 907	

Differentiated Trade Offer						
	Tariff lines	%	1997 SADC imports (US$)	%	RSA imports	%
Category A	1 947	32.4	99 386 918	23.3		
Category B1	3 664	60.9	218 026 155	51.2		
Category B2	166	2.8	56 902 049	13.4		
Category C	235	3.9	51 891 044	12.2		
Total	6 012		426 206 165			

Source: 'Record of the 14th Meeting of the SADC Industry and Trade Committee of Ministers', Maseru, Lesotho, 16 June 2000, pp. 18–19.

Tanzania's Trade Offers

Table 3A: Tanzania's Offer to the Republic of South Africa (US$ '000)

Category	Tariff lines	Tariff lines (%)	RSA trade	RSA trade (%)
Category A	965	15.5	8 668	9.2
Category B	4 127	66.4	50 687	53.7
Category B2	178	2.9	23 476	24.9
Category C	903	14.5	11 486	12.2
Category E	43	0.7	10	0.0
Total	6 216	100.0	94 327	100.0

Table 3B: Tanzania's Offer to the Rest of SADC (US$ '000)

Category	Tariff lines	Tariff lines (%)	Non-RSA trade	Trade (%)
Category A	1 077	17.3	4 064	14.2
Category B	4 268	68.7	19 608	68.7
Category B2	39	0.6	1 181	4.1
Category C	789	12.7	3 707	13.0
Category E	43	0.7	0.7	0.0
Total	6 216	100.0	28 560.7	100.0

Note:

Category A: 0 duty from year 2000

Category B: Less sensitive products: 0 duty will commence from year 2006 ⇨

Category B: More sensitive products: 0 duty will commence from year 2008
Category B2:   More sensitive products: 0 duty will commence from year 2008 in the context of minimisation of trade creation or diversion
Category C: 0 duty will be achieved in year 2012 subject to positive results of a review to be carried out in year 2010
Category E: Exclusion

Source: 'Record of the 14th Meeting of the SADC Industry and Trade Committee of Ministers', Maseru, Lesotho, 16 June 2000, pp. 12–13.

Table 4: Mauritius' Trade Offer

	Improved offer		
	No. of tariff lines	% on total tariff lines	% on total value of SADC imports
Immediate liberalisation list	3 247	60	37
Gradual liberalisation list	1 661	30	48
Sensitive list	571	10	15
Total no. of tariff lines	**5 479**	**100**	**100**

Source: 'Record of the 8th Special Meeting of the SADC Industry and Trade Committee of Ministers', Sandton, South Africa, 31 March 2000, p. 18.

Table 5: Malawi's Trade Offers

Offer to South Africa		
Category	Offer to RSA	
	Trade %	Tariff lines %
A	37.2	33
B	46.2	52
C	16.6	15
Total	**100**	**100**

Malawi's Differentiated Trade Offer		
	Differentiated offer to the rest of SADC	
Category	Trade %	Tariff lines %
A	50	33.5
B	38.2	51.9
C	11.7	14.6
Total	**100**	**100**

Source: 'Record of the 14th Meeting of the SADC Industry and Trade Committee of Ministers', Maseru, Lesotho, 16 June 2000, p. 17.

Appendix 4

Currency Conversion Table

For the following tables the convertibility rate is US$1.

US$1 = _____

European EUR
1996 – .79
1997 – .88
1998 – .89
1999 – .94

South African rand
1994 – 3.54
1995 – 3.64
1996 – 4.68
1997 – 4.86
1998 – 5.86
1999 – 6.15

Malawi kwacha
1994 – 15.29
1995 – 15.30
1996 – 15.32
1997 – 21.22
1998 – 43.88
1999 – 46.43

Botswana pula
1994 – 2.71
1995 – 2.82
1996 – 3.64
1997 – 3.80
1998 – 4.45
1999 – 4.63

Zimbabwe dollar
1993 – 6.5
1994 – 8.2
1995 – 8.7
1996 – 9.9
1997 – 11.9
1998 – 23.7

Appendix 5

Potential for Increased Trade between SACU and the SADC 7

Rank	Product	Potential for increased trade (US$m)
1	Crude petroleum	2 635
2	Diamonds, sorted (other than industrial diamonds), unworked, or simply saw	197
3	Nickel, not alloyed	100
4	Cotton (other than linters), not carded or combed	178
5	Coffee, not roasted, not decaffeinated	49
6	Tobacco, not stemmed/stripped	27
7	Tobacco, wholly or partly stemmed/stripped	25
8	Other bovine and equine leather, without hair on, tanned	21
9	Meat of bovine animals, frozen, boneless	18
10	Tunas, skipjack, and Atlantic bonito (Sarda spp), whole or in pieces	17
11	Other black tea (fermented) and other partly fermented tea	15
12	Articles of jewelry and parts thereof of precious metal	14
13	T-shirts, singlets and other vests, knitted or crocheted	12
14	Refined copper	12
15	Footwear, n.e.s., with uppers of leather or composition leather	11
16	Wood of coniferous species, sawn or chipped lengthwise, sliced or peeled	11
17	Oilcakes and other solid residues of oil from cotton seeds	10
18	Wood of coniferous species, sawn of chipped lengthwise, sliced or peeled	9
19	Shrimps and prawns, frozen	9
20	Wire, of refined copper	9

Rank	Product	Potential for increased trade (US$m)
21	Other fish, frozen (including livers and roes)	9
22	Cotton yarn (other than sewing thread), containing 85% or more by weight	8
23	Waste and scrap of alloy steel other than slnts steel	8
24	Other woven fabric, >85% cotton, weight more than 200 g/m^2, denim	8
25	Shirts, men's or boys', not knitted or crocheted	7
26	Beans, other than broad beans and horse beans, dried, shelled	6
27	Toilet and kitchen linen of cotton	6
28	Blouses, shirts, and shirt-blouses, women's or girls', of textile material	6
29	Diamonds, rough, unsorted	6
30	Hides and skins (excluding those of heading 211.2) of bovine animals	6
31	Cane sugar, raw, in solid form, not containing added flavouring or colour 456	6
32	Bed-linen, not knitted or crocheted, of cotton	6
33	Trousers, bib and braces overalls, breeches and shorts, men's or boys'	6
34	Portland cement	6
35	Parts for turbojets or turbopropellers	5
36	Spectacles, goggles and the like, corrective, protective	5
37	Asbestos	5
38	Preparations of the kind used for animal food, n.e.s.	5
39	Jerseys, pullovers, cardigans, waistcoats, and similar articles, knitted	5
40	Other beet or cane sugar in solid form, other than flavoured or coloured	5
41	Babies' garments and clothing accessories, knitted or crocheted	5
42	Dresses, women's or girls', of textile materials, not knitted or crocheted	5
43	Motor vehicles for the transport of persons, n.e.s.	4
44	Maize seed	4
45	Cobalt mattes and other intermediate products of cobalt metallurgy	4
46	Furniture, n.e.s., of wood of a kind used in the bedroom	4
47	Cuttlefish, octopus, and squid, frozen, dried, salted, or in brine; flours	4

Rank	Product	Potential for increased trade (US$m)
48	Cloth (including endless bands), grill, netting and fencing, of iron	4
49	Nickel oxide sinters and other intermediate products of nickel metallurgy	4
50	Veneered panels and similar laminated wood, n.e.s.	4
51	Toys representing animals or non-human creatures	4
52	Parts and accessories for the machines of group 752	4
53	Skirts and divided skirts, women's or girls', of textile materials	4
54	Gold (including gold plated with platinum), non-monetary	4
55	Dog or cat food put up for retail sale	4
56	Other woven fabrics, >85% cotton, weight more than 200 g/m^2, dyed	4
57	Cocoa beans, whole or broken, raw or roasted	4
58	Aeroplanes and other mechanically-propelled, of an unladen weight >15 000	4
59	Trunks, suitcases, vanity cases, executive cases, briefcases	3
60	Other electric conductors, for a voltage exceeding 80 V	3
61	Shirts, men's or boys', knitted or crocheted of textile materials	3
62	Malt, whether or not roasted (including malt flour)	3
63	Other woven fabrics >85% cotton, weight more than 200 g/m^2, dyed	3
64	Twine, cordage, ropes, and cables, whether or not plaited or braided	3
65	Other wheat (including spelt) and meslin, unmilled	3
66	Other outer garments, n.e.s., men's or boys'	3
67	Other maize, unmilled	3
68	Copper waste and scrap	3
69	Seats, n.e.s., with wooden frames	3
70	Cotton seeds	3
71	Particle board and similar board of wood, whether or not agglomerated	3
72	Tracksuits, knitted or crocheted	3
73	Copra	3
74	Other woven fabric, >85% cotton, weight more than 200 g/m^2, printed	3

Rank	Product	Potential for increased trade (US$m)
75	Cotton, carded or combed	6
76	Shawls, scarves, mufflers, veils, and the like	3
77	Frames and mountings for spectacles, goggles or the like	3
78	Other travel goods, handbags, and similar containers	3
79	Articles of iron or steel, n.e.s.	3
80	Instruments and apparatus for physical or chemical analysis, n.e.s.	3
81	Wrist-watches, battery or accumulator powered	3
82	Other parts of aeroplanes or helicopters	3
83	Fabrics, woven, of a weight not exceeding 170 g/m, of polyester staple	3
84	Shirts, other textile material	3
85	Household articles and parts thereof, n.e.s., of aluminium	3
86	Furniture, n.e.s., of wood	3
87	Shirts, men's or boys', knitted or crocheted of cotton	3
88	Groundnuts (peanuts), not roasted or otherwise cooked, shelled	3
89	Ferrous waste and scrap, n.e.s.	2
90	Blouses, shirts, and shirt-blouses, women's or girls', knitted or crocheted	2
91	Bran, sharps and other residues, of wheat	2
92	Pantihose and tights, knitted or crocheted	2
93	Articles of a kind normally carried in the pocket or handbag	2
94	Fruits of the genus Capsicum or the genus Pimenta, dried or crushed	2
95	Other beet or cane sugar in solid form, containing added flavouring	2
96	Live animals, n.e.s.	2
97	Laminated safety glass	2
98	Other bovine and equine leather, without hair on, parchment dressed	2
99	Cigarettes containing tobacco	2
100	Articles of apparel, women's or girls', n.e.s., not knitted or crocheted	2
Total		3 585

Source: Von Kirchbach and Roelofsen (1998, Annex 1, pp. 34–6).

Appendix 6

Individuals Interviewed for the Study*

Botswana
Willem Goeiemann
Senior Economist
SADC Secretariat
Gaborone, Botswana

Mandla M. Z. Madonsela
Senior Economist
SADC Secretariat
Gaborone, Botswana

E. S. S. Nebwe
Special Advisor
SADC Secretariat
Gaborone, Botswana

Fudzai Pamacheche
Principal Economist
SADC Secretariat
Gaborone, Botswana

Prega Ramsamy
SADC Acting Executive Secretary
SADC Secretariat
Gaborone, Botswana

Malawi
Newby Kumwembe
Consul (Trade)
Malawi Consulate-General
Johannesburg, South Africa

Mauritius
V. S. Chuckun
Secondary Secretary
Mauritius High Commission
Pretoria, South Africa

Mozambique
Smak Kaombwe
Planning Co-ordinator
Southern African Transport and Communications
Commission
Maputo, Mozambique

Belmiro Malate
SADC Focal Point
Ministry of Foreign Affairs and Cooperation
Maputo, Mozambique

Celeste Mapasse
Head of Documentation Department
SADC Culture & Information Sector
Co-ordinating Unit
Maputo, Mozambique

Alfredo F. S. Namitete
Chairman, Coordinating Committee
Southern African Transport and Communications
Commission
Maputo, Mozambique

Leonardo Santos Sim
Minister of Foreign Affairs and Cooperation
Maputo, Mozambique

Nicolau L. Sululo
National Directorate of External Trade
Maputo, Mozambique

Namibia
Neville Gertze
Commercial Counsellor
Republic of Namibia
Pretoria, South Africa

South Africa
Dave Arkwright
CEO, Mozambique Corridor Company
Nelspruit, South Africa

Jayanthi T. Basdew
FISCU
Pretoria, South Africa

Coen Bezuidenhoudt
SADC National Contact Point
Department of Foreign Affairs
Pretoria, South Africa

Eli Bitzer
Regional Economic Organisations
Pretoria, South Africa

Willem Bosman
Director, Regional Economic Organisations
Department of Foreign Affairs
Pretoria, South Africa

Horst Brammer
SADC National Contact Point
Department of Foreign Affairs
Pretoria, South Africa

W. Brummerhoff
Advisor
South African Reserve Bank
Pretoria, South Africa

Liezel Castleman
SADC National Contact Point
Department of Foreign Affairs
Pretoria, South Africa

Xolisile Duda
SADC National Contact Point
Department of Foreign Affairs
Pretoria, South Africa

Henning Herbst
Desk Officer for Zimbabwe
Department of Foreign Affairs
Pretoria, South Africa

Ben Joubert
SADC National Contact Point
Department of Foreign Affairs
Pretoria, South Africa

Leslie Kekana
Department of Foreign Affairs
Pretoria, South Africa

Erich Leistner
Former Director
Africa Institute
Pretoria, South Africa

Mpho B. J. Maloka
FISCU
Pretoria, South Africa

Bhadala M. T. Mamba
Deputy Director
FISCU
South African Department of Finance
Pretoria, South Africa

Phemelo Marishane
Deputy Director
FISCU
Pretoria, South Africa

Marina Mayer
Deputy Director: Africa Trade Relations
Department of Trade and Industry
Pretoria, South Africa

Booi Mbelengwa
Department of Foreign Affairs
Pretoria, South Africa

Tandi Mgxwati
Department of Foreign Affairs
Pretoria, South Africa

Lolette Kritzinger-van Niekerk
Policy Analyst/Economist
Development Bank of Southern Africa
Midrand, South Africa

Peter H. van Niekerk
Chief Director: Planning
Department of Water Affairs and Forestry
Pretoria, South Africa

Mfundo Nkuhlu
Chief Director: Africa Trade Relations
Department of Trade and Industry
Pretoria, South Africa

Adrian du Pisanie
Department of Foreign Affairs
Pretoria, South Africa

Yolande Poley
Statistics Economist
South African Reserve Bank
Pretoria, South Africa

Brian Thabang Thoka
Assistant Economist
South African Reserve Bank
Pretoria, South Africa

Nelson Salmani
Department of Foreign Affairs
Pretoria, South Africa

Sandile Tyatya
Director: International Coordinator
Department of Minerals and Energy
Pretoria, South Africa

Hestie Jansen van Vuuren
Junior Economist
South African Reserve Bank
Pretoria, South Africa

N. J. van Wyk
Chief Engineer: Project Planning
Department of Water Affairs and Forestry
Pretoria, South Africa

Themba Zulu
Economist
FISCU
South African Department of Finance
Pretoria, South Africa

Zambia
Renee Nglazi
Trade Commissioner
High Commission of the Republic of Zambia
Harare, Zimbabwe

Zimbabwe
John Chigwedere
External Trade
Ministry of Industry and Commerce
Harare, Zimbabwe

Fred E. Chimowa
System Planning Manager
Zimbabwe Electricity Supply Authority
Harare, Zimbabwe

Rongai Chizema
Marketing and Research – Executive
Zimbabwe Investment Centre
Harare, Zimbabwe

Z. R. Churu
Chief Economist, Macroeconomic Policy Analysts
Ministry of Finance
Harare, Zimbabwe

D. S. Durham
Deputy Director Planning and Hydrology
Department of Water Resources
Harare, Zimbabwe

R. Claudious Madembo
SADC Programme Officer
Konrad Adenauer Foundation
Harare, Zimbabwe

Itayi Matiyenga
Principal Administration Officer and SADC
Contract Point
Ministry of Foreign Affairs
Harare, Zimbabwe

G. Mawere
Chief Hydrologist/Hydro Engineer
Ministry of Rural Resources and Water
Development
Harare, Zimbabwe

Victor Murambiwa
Ministry of Industry and Commerce
Harare, Zimbabwe

Stella Mushiri
Trade Policy and Research Specialist
ZimTrade
Harare, Zimbabwe

Sam Mutanhaurwa
Principal Administrative Officer
Ministry of Industry and Commerce
Harare, Zimbabwe

Daniel B. Ndlela
Zimconsult
Harare, Zimbabwe

Vusumuzi Ntonga
Principal Administrator Officer and SADC Contact
Point
Ministry of Foreign Affairs
Harare, Zimbabwe

John Robertson
Managing Director
Robertson Economic Information Services
Harare, Zimbabwe

Edward K. Tsikirayi
Principal Generation Planner
Zimbabwe Electricity Supply Authority
Harare, Zimbabwe

European Commission
Nicola Delcroix
Economic Advisor
Delegation of the European Commission
Harare, Zimbabwe

Michael D. Laidler
Ambassador
Head of Delegation of the European Commission
Harare, Zimbabwe

United States
Scott Allen
Trade and Agricultural Policy Advisor
USDA Regional Center for Southern Africa
USAID
Gaborone, Botswana

*The interviews were conducted between November 1996 and March 2000. Numerous individuals have changed their affiliations and/or titles since the interviews. These changes are not reflected here.

Index

Notes: names of countries are alphabetised unabbreviated in headings: they are abbreviated in subentries and where they are included in names and acronyms of organisations and regional communities. A list of abreviations and acronyms appears on p. xiii. Page numbers in italics refer to figures and tables.)